DPIC's Contract Guide

By Richard D. Crowell and Sheila A. Dixon

A RISK MANAGEMENT
HANDBOOK FOR
ARCHITECTURAL, ENGINEERING
AND ENVIRONMENTAL
PROFESSIONALS

DPIC Companies, Inc.
2959 Monterey-Salinas Highway
Monterey, California 93940-6439
800.227.4284

© 1987, 1993, 1999 DPIC Companies
Revised edition.
Formerly titled *The Contract Guide: DPIC's Risk Management Handbook for Architects and Engineers*
Formerly titled *DPIC Companies Guide to Better Contracts*

ISBN 0-932056-12-1
Library of Congress Catalog Card Number 98-071916

All rights reserved. This book may not be duplicated without the written consent of DPIC Companies, Inc. except in the form of excerpts or quotations for the purposes of review.

Printed on recycled paper with soy ink.

TABLE OF CONTENTS

ACKNOWLEDGMENTS

ABOUT THE AUTHORS

FOREWORD xiii

INTRODUCTION xv

HOW TO USE THIS BOOK xvii

I. PROFESSIONAL SERVICES AGREEMENTS: A PRIMER

    Why Have a Written Agreement? 3

    Dealing with Risk 5

    Contract Basics 7

    Qualifications-Based Selection 13

    Types of Agreements You'll Encounter 15

    Professional Association Standard Agreements 19

    How to Review Client-Generated Agreements 23

    Resources for Contract Review 29

    Negotiating a Contract 33

    Deal Makers and Deal Breakers 35

II. PRE-CONSTRUCTION SERVICES

    Design Without Construction Administration 3

    Excluded Services 7

    Opinions (Estimates) of Probable Construction Costs 11

    Prototype Designs 15

    Quality Control Standards 19

    Retaining Subconsultants 23

    Right of Entry 27

    Scope of Services 29

    Substitutions 33

Table of Contents

III. CONSTRUCTION ADMINISTRATION

- Claims Arbiter Service 3
- Construction Observation 7
- Inspection 13
- Jobsite Safety 19
- Record Documents 23
- Requests for Information 27
- Shop Drawing Review 33
- Stop Work Authority 39

IV. SCHEDULE, PAYMENT AND TERMINATION

- Billing and Payment 3
- Changed Conditions 9
- Pay-When-Paid 13
- Retainage 17
- Retainers 19
- Suspension of Services 23
- Termination 27
- Timeliness of Performance 31

V. ALLOCATION OF RISK

- Certifications, Guarantees and Warranties 3
- Consequential Damages 9
- Contingency Fund 13
- Defects in Service 17
- Delays 21
- Extension of Protection 25
- Indemnities 27
- Information Provided by Others 37
- Insurance 39
- Interpretation 49
- Limitation of Liability 53
- Liquidated Damages 61
- Non-Negligent Services 65
- Performance Bonds 67

	Standard of Care 69
	Third-Party Beneficiaries 73
	Unauthorized Changes to Plans 75

VI. DISPUTE AVOIDANCE AND RESOLUTION

Attorneys' Fees 3
Betterment 7
Corporate Protection 11
Dispute Avoidance and Resolution 15
    Partnering 17
    Jobsite Dispute Resolution 22
    Mediation 25
    Arbitration 28
    Other Dispute Resolution Methods 31
    Resolving International Disputes 34
Frivolous Lawuits 37

VII. STATUTES, CODES AND REGULATIONS

Americans with Disabilities Act 3
Code Compliance 9
Copyrights 13
Hazardous Materials 17
Permits and Approvals 23
Public Responsibility 27
Specification of Materials 31
Statutes of Repose and Limitation 35

VIII. GENERAL TERMS AND CONDITIONS

Assignment 3
Authorized Representatives 7
Confidential Communications 11
Confidentiality 15
Contractual Reference to the Consultant 19
Definitions 23
Entire Agreement 27
Governing Law and Jurisdiction 29
Incorporation by Reference 33

Table of Contents

	Lenders' Requirements 37
	Notices 41
	Ownership of Instruments of Service 45
	Severability and Survival 49
	Titles 53

IX. SPECIFIC SERVICES

CADD/Electronic Files 3
Condominiums 13
Emergency Services 23
International Projects 29
Renovation/Remodeling 39
Subconsultants 43
Supplanting Another Consultant 47
Testing Laboratories 51
Underground Improvements 55
Value Engineering 59
Year 2000 (Y2K) 65

X. PROJECT DELIVERY

Construction Management 3
Design-Build 9
Fast Track Projects 15
Multiple Prime Contracts 19

XI. APPENDICES

Agreement for Emergency Professional Services 1
Terms and Conditions 2
The Teamwork Ethic 3

XII. FURTHER READING

XIII. ADDITIONAL RESOURCES

INDEX

Table of Contents

EXHIBITS

1. Sample Contract Review Checklist I-25
2. Deal-Maker Provisions I-37
3. Deal-Breaker Provisions I-38
4. Substitution Approval Request Form II-36
5. Loss Prevention Points for Construction Observation III-12
6. Shop Drawing Stamps III-37
7. Schedule of Insurance V-46
8. Professional Liability Insurance Limitations V-47
9. CADD/Electronic File Transfer to Contractor IX-10
10. Condominium Loss Prevention Checklist IX-20
11. Deal-Maker Clauses for Condominium Projects IX-21
12. Design-Build Relationships X-10

NOTICE TO READERS

This publication and each of the clauses herein are designed to provide useful information in regard to the subject matter covered. It is not to be regarded as providing opinion or legal advice for or about any individual case. This publication is produced and distributed with the understanding that the publisher is not engaged in rendering legal or other professional services. If legal advice or other expert assistance is or may be required, the services of a competent professional should be sought.

ACKNOWLEDGMENTS

In writing this edition of *DPIC's Contract Guide*, we called upon the expertise of many individuals — all of whom deserve our thanks.

Most particularly, we are grateful for the counsel of broker Jeff Cavignac of Cavignac & Associates, Dale Ellickson, FAIA, Counsel for AIA Contract Documents Department, Donald Kline, P.E., of Kimley-Horn and Associates, James Pierce, PEPP Director of NSPE, Bernard Sacks, Esq., P.E., from Gogick & Seiden, consultants Larry Segrue, FAIA, and Bruce Sellery, FAIA-E, and Howard Schirmer, Jr., P.E. of Transnational Associates.

In addition, members of the Geotechnical and Environmental Consultants Advisory Board (GECAB) provided invaluable geotechnical and environmental consulting perspective, especially Mary Moran, C.P.G., P.G., of Gallet & Associates, John Payne, P.E., of The Payne Firm, Joseph Petraus, P.E., of EDP Consultants, Ralph Russell, P.E., of Howard R. Green Company and Sara Smith, Esq., of Scott R. Smith Environmental Management Consultants.

Our thanks especially to David Hatem, Esq., of Burns and Levinson, who conducted a painstaking independent legal review and who gave us very welcome guidance. Sam Muir, Esq., of Collins, Collins, Muir & Traver also willingly stepped forward with assistance.

At DPIC Companies, General Counsel William Beers' thoughtful in-house legal review, answers to our endless questions and overall support were of enormous help. Chief Claims Officer William Meisen and E/E Product Manager Gary Prather had the daunting task of critiquing the manuscript. Resource Center Librarian Susan Gilroy lent her considerable talents to the Further Reading and Additional Resources sections, while Project Manager Diane Mika undertook the coordination of the book's final production.

Ruth Menmuir once again wielded her deft red pen to copyedit the enormous manuscript. Consultant d'Aulan Gentry kept track of countless drafts, revisions and details. We are grateful to both.

Finally, our appreciation goes to the DPIC Marketing/Communications Department for undertaking the monumental task of the final production of this book.

DPIC COMPANIES

About the Authors

Richard D. Crowell is a senior vice president for DPIC Companies, headquartered in Monterey, California. He is in charge of DPIC's Architects, Engineers and Environmental Consultants Programs. His duties include marketing large A/E/E accounts, working in client relations and state and national legislative affairs, and serving as liaison with national professional associations. Previously, he was president and founder of the Crowell Insurance Agency, one of the largest specialist retail brokerage firms in the nation serving architects and engineers. Prior to his insurance career, Mr. Crowell was vice president of finance for a large nationwide civil engineering, surveying and planning firm. Nationally, he serves as an insurance advisor to the AIA Contract Documents Committee, the EJCDC and ACEC's Risk Management and Professional Procurement Committees. He is also a member of the FIDIC Risk Management Committee, the AIA California Council Legislative Committee and the California State Board of Architectural Examiners' Regulatory and Enforcement Committee. Mr. Crowell is a trustee of the California Architectural Foundation and of the AIACC ARCPAC and was honored in 1990 by being named an honorary AIACC member. A frequent speaker on professional practice and insurance issues, Mr. Crowell has appeared at Harvard, Yale, Penn State, UCLA, the national conventions of AIA, ACEC, AGC, CSI, DBIA, the FIDIC international convention and numerous CEC, AIA and NSPE state and local meetings. Mr. Crowell holds a bachelor's degree in psychology from UCLA, and his graduate work is in business administration. Although he flies more than 200,000 business miles a year, Mr. Crowell makes his home on the Monterey Peninsula in California.

Sheila A. Dixon has more than 25 years' experience in research, communications and public affairs for government, political organizations and major corporations. Since 1985, as an independent consultant, she has provided communications services and corporate and political research services for a variety of business and private clients. Previously, Ms. Dixon was a senior member of the White House Press Office. Her responsibilities included briefing the White House press corps on domestic and foreign policy issues, providing news analyses for the President and administration officials and directing specific news-related research projects. She was editor of the *White House News Summary*, the daily review of major news media reports, relied upon by the administration. Ms. Dixon later served as a senior policy analyst for a national presidential campaign. Ms. Dixon's political work as a consultant includes in-depth research and analysis for state candidate and initiative campaigns. Most recently, she has served on the Board of Trustees of the AIA California Council and Fed Up, working to defeat an onerous initiative in a California election. In addition to her work on *DPIC's Contract Guide*, Ms. Dixon has written and edited a number of major publications for DPIC, including *Lessons in Professional Liability for Environmental Consultants* (1996), *Professional Liability in the Construction Process: A Guide for Risk Managers* (1997), and *Lessons in Professional Liability for Architects and Engineers* (1998), and numerous articles, white papers and educational materials. Born into a diplomatic family, Ms. Dixon spent most of her childhood and teen years in Asia and the Middle East. She is a graduate of the University of Maryland and lives in Carmel, California.

DPIC COMPANIES

FOREWORD

David J. Hatem, Esq.
Burns & Levinson LLP
Boston, Massachusetts

The 1998 edition of *DPIC's Contract Guide* is a must for any professional — architect, engineer, surveyor, environmental consultant, construction manager, program manager, management consultant, risk manager, attorney, insurance advisor — involved in the design and construction process. Although there are several publications available to those professionals that address contractual and associated risk management issues, the *Guide* is distinctive in its combined in-depth and substantive treatment of these issues and its user-friendly style and presentation.

Unlike other publications addressing these subjects, *DPIC's Contract Guide* takes a realistic and pragmatic approach to contract formation by promoting the principles of fairness and balance in that process. In that respect, the *Guide* fosters and enables client development and maintenance of good relations with existing clients. Contract negotiations governed by purely one-sided motivations and incentives — advanced with equal zeal and vigor by both parties — typically result in an unproductive and protracted expenditure of time and effort; and, even if one party is "successful," the success typically is short-lived and more often than not plants the seed of a pathological relationship between the client and the professional down the road.

Given the balance of the *Guide's* approach, you should have no reservations about sharing a copy with your clients; education about the realities of professional practice often serves to increase the client's understanding of the professional's contractual "issues" and practice constraints and, at a minimum, enhances the respect and trust that are essential ingredients of any successful professional-client relationship.

DPIC's Contract Guide provides a "blueprint" for the negotiation and preparation of good contracts. As an attorney representing design and construction management professionals, I have encouraged my clients to reference *DPIC's Contract Guide* during contract negotiations. In addition, I have used selective portions of the *Guide* for educational purposes — both in my course at Tufts University School of Engineering on Professional Liability and in

Foreword

risk management/loss prevention seminars that I present for design and construction management professionals. Although the *Guide* is neither intended nor should be used as a substitute for legal advice, it will, in many instances, be the first and final source for many design and construction management professionals with respect to a number of standard and frequently encountered contractual issues and, for that reason alone, will be an enormously valuable resource to those professionals. Of course, more complex or otherwise "difficult" issues or client negotiations will require legal counsel.

Good contracts — i.e., contracts that reflect a fair and balanced allocation of risk and reward between the parties — are essential predicates of a sound risk management program for design and construction management professionals. Contract negotiations may serve as a vehicle for "testing" the client's sense of fairness and reasonableness and may also serve as a mechanism to "weed out" those clients who hold unrealistic, unreasonable or one-sided views of that process. Similarly, a good contract reduces the potential for disputes, conflict and claims by clearly and realistically defining the respective expectations and responsibilities of each party. This increases the stakes for a party contemplating avoidance or repudiation of its end of the bargain and thereby enhances the prospects of a more expeditious and cost-efficient resolution of disputes by a neutral third party, such as a mediator or judge. Finally, provisions of a "good" contract often serve as a frontline defense to many professional liability claims against the professional. Conversely, an ambiguously or otherwise inadequately drafted contract may lead to problems — often insurmountable — in the defense of professional liability claims or, at a minimum, will complicate and protract that resolution, thereby making more expensive and unpredictable the defense effort.

In addition to enhancing the discussion of basic risk management and contractual topics (such as indemnification, standard of care and limitation of liability), this new edition of the *Guide* includes a number of new topics — such as "substitutions," "requests for information," "Year 2000," "construction management," and "design-build." The addition of these and other topics not only expands the scope and depth of the *Guide* but, as importantly, demonstrates and evidences DPIC's commitment to responsibly listening to the evolving concerns and interests of design professionals and seeing the trends in the design and construction industry.

DPIC has made a diligent, comprehensive and conscientious effort to solicit review of and comments on its *Guide* from a variety of respected sources on contract negotiation subjects and strategy. The best of the collective wisdom of these sources is contained herein. DPIC is to be commended for its extraordinary efforts in this regard and for the enormous benefits that will be derived by all professionals from publication of *DPIC's Contract Guide*.

INTRODUCTION

Thomas M. Okarma, CPCU
President and Chief Executive Officer
DPIC Companies, Inc.

This edition of *DPIC's Contract Guide* reflects five years of experience, research and investment. As always, we've listened to and learned from our family of DPIC insureds. We've sought the best available legal advice and worked to make it understandable and usable. We've monitored our claims files to keep abreast of lawsuit and dispute trends in the construction industry. We've also worked with professional associations to help update their standard form agreements, revisions that are reflected in this publication.

Readers of previous editions of the *Guide* will note several significant changes. Nearly every subject has been substantially rewritten to reflect changes in the construction industry and new things we've learned. We've addressed a number of "hot topics" our readers have been asking about, such as design-build and Year 2000. We've reorganized the book so that the subjects appear in a more logical sequence. We've added a wealth of information on contract basics and provided step-by-step suggestions for reviewing a client-drafted agreement. The result, we believe, is a timely, practical tool to help you understand how to develop professional services agreements.

Negotiating a good contract is essential to reducing your liability. Your goal is to develop professional services agreements that, while equitable, assume only the risk that is rightfully yours. One of the best loss prevention steps is to avoid litigious clients. The contract formation and negotiation process offers you an excellent opportunity to size up your clients' potential for litigiousness and their attitudes on risk allocation.

There are other measures you can take to avoid unnecessary litigation. Include alternative dispute resolution provisions in your agreements. Since its founding, DPIC has been committed to early intervention when claim problems arise. We've found that many disputes can be resolved fairly, quickly and inexpensively if consultants and their clients attempt formal mediation and other ADR techniques before resorting to litigation.

Introduction

You can strive for a Limitation of Liability (LoL) clause in your contracts that caps the amount of liability you assume if there is a problem on the project. Admittedly, this isn't easy. While our hope is that you can obtain such a clause in every contract, there is still resistance to the concept from some owners, contractors and even consultants. But the tide has turned. More and more architects and engineers are successfully asking for and getting LoL clauses.

You can teach your employees the effect of everyday business practices on your exposure to litigation. Engineering and architectural schools don't teach much about the real-world problems of low-bidding contractors, failed expectations and lawsuits. So it falls to you to undertake your own education program in loss prevention practices. That's where DPIC comes in. This *Guide*, along with DPIC's *Lessons in Professional Liability* (see **Further Reading**), alerts you to professional practices that cause the most disputes.

Unfortunately, the best, most protective contract in the world can only go so far to protect you from third-party and frivolous lawsuits. Although we've recently seen the rates of construction lawsuits decline somewhat, the "litigation crisis" is not over, not by a long shot. Americans continue to file millions of lawsuits annually at a cost of more than $150 billion per year.

Our system seems to encourage the filing of frivolous lawsuits. Some people sue anyone in sight, no matter how minimally connected they are to the injury or loss. They claim the defendants should have protected them against any injury regardless of circumstances. And they attempt to establish any conceivable level of negligence against the party with "deep pockets," so it can be forced to pay all of the damages. In most cases, it is cheaper to settle an unfounded lawsuit than to fight and win. Sadly, that is often exactly what happens. But even if you prevail against a nonmeritorious suit, you still lose — time, money and your peace of mind. Here is an example of this all too common phenomenon: a night watchman on a construction site became terrified when he saw a skunk. He leapt into a clearly marked hole and injured himself. Predictably, he sued everyone involved on the project, including the design professionals, who endured years of filings, motions, discovery, interrogatories — and legal expenses — before they could extricate themselves from the claim.[1]

Is there a solution? State and national professional associations are working to promote legislation that would ease the "litigation crisis." Their aim is to replace joint and several liability laws with proportionate liability, and to enact certificate of merit laws and more equitable statutes of limitation. You can help. These organizations need your time, your expertise and your support. The responsibility lies with each of us to help improve the legal climate for the professions and our society.

---

[1] *(American Consulting Engineers Council Member Survey, 1995.)*

HOW TO USE THIS BOOK

In this *Guide*, we discuss a number of contract provisions you may encounter when working with your clients. These are the provisions that can prove most troublesome and that surface most frequently when we examine the causes of disputes and claims.

You'll find this *Guide* a useful reference in a number of common, but contrasting, approaches to contract formation. You may have developed your own standard contract language. But no matter how confident you may be about it, we recommend that you sit down with your attorney and compare the provisions in your current contract with the ones in this *Guide*. (You might want to look at the sample Contract Review Checklist in *Exhibit 1*. Also, pay particular attention to provisions we've flagged as **Deal Makers** or **Deal Breakers**. See *Exhibits 2* and *3*.) In addition, each section also notes relevant AIA and EJCDC standard form agreement provisions, to which you also can refer. Then, using the suggestions in this book as a starting point, strengthen the wording of your contract as appropriate.

Some clients prefer to use their own contract forms. Often these client-developed agreements attempt to shift a great deal of the client's risk onto your shoulders. Again, you should carefully review these documents (using your lawyer's help as needed), compare the provisions with those offered here and make any modifications necessary to protect yourself. With the help of this *Guide*, and the related standard form agreement provisions, you'll learn to recognize onerous language and unacceptable provisions often hidden in client-written contracts and be able to suggest a more equitable allocation of risk.

Perhaps you prefer to rely on the standard contract forms developed by professional societies. These standard contracts also may need to be adapted to your particular situation. Talk to your attorney and look carefully at each potential project. You can also work with your attorney to supplement standard contract forms with some of the ideas embraced in this *Guide*, perhaps by strengthening some protective provisions and adding clauses such as Limitation of Liability and Dispute Resolution to every contract you sign. You may want to develop your own checklist of additional clauses.

How to Use This Book

Not all the clauses in this *Guide* are meant to be included in one agreement. Nor would all the clauses comprise a complete contract. In many instances, you could combine two or more clauses into one. We present them for your reference and guidance only; they need to be tailored to fit your practice, the circumstances of your projects and the rest of your contract.

We have tried to keep the clause language as precise and unambiguous as possible. Sometimes this makes the provisions longer than usual, but that is infinitely preferable to leaving a clause open to interpretation. You'll also want to keep this in mind when reviewing client-developed provisions. If the language isn't clear and unequivocal to you, it won't be clear to a jury. If your client says, "What that means is thus-and-so," ask your client to rewrite the provision to say just that.

The discussions that accompany each clause are explanatory and may provide you with effective "ammunition" to help educate your clients. It is important to note that when your clients are other design professionals, they should seek similar indemnifications or other protections or concessions from the owner. Encourage them to become more familiar with their own liability exposures perhaps by obtaining a *Guide* such as this.

Any and all statements presented in this *Guide*, including those pertaining to fees and client dealings, are based on generally accepted concepts of risk management and prudent business behavior. In all cases, your fees, client selection measures and related practices are your business and your business only. Recognize, also, that this publication is a general guide and should be used in conjunction with specific guidance from competent legal counsel experienced in the design and construction industry and familiar with the laws in your state or the state whose laws will govern your contract.

PART I

PROFESSIONAL SERVICES AGREEMENTS: A PRIMER

Why Have a Written Agreement?

Dealing with Risk

Contract Basics

Qualifications-Based Selection

Types of Agreements You'll Encounter

Professional Association Standard Agreements

How to Review Client-Generated Agreements

Resources for Contract Review

Negotiating a Contract

Deal Makers and Deal Breakers

I-2

WHY HAVE A WRITTEN AGREEMENT?

The construction process involves a complex series of relationships. Owners, contractors, subcontractors, material suppliers, fabricators, environmental consultants, architects, engineers, subconsultants, construction managers, program managers — all may be involved in today's construction project. With so many parties, each under intense pressure to provide more service for less money, it is essential that everyone understands his or her role and responsibilities. That is the primary function of a contract — to memorialize these understandings.

A written contract may be required for design services in some jurisdictions. In California, for instance, there is a statute requiring a written contract before an architect may provide services. Other states are considering similar laws, which are intended to protect both consumer and consultant by requiring them to reduce their agreements to writing.

Even if the law does not require a written agreement, it is still important to have one. The most significant benefits are: 1) you and your client reach a mutual understanding; 2) you have the opportunity to establish your own rules; 3) you can size up your client, and vice versa; and 4) you can identify and allocate the risks. Let's review these in more detail:

1. *Mutual understanding.* The process of developing the scope of services, compensation, schedule and terms by which you will operate requires both of you to communicate your own views on each of these issues. As a result, you both will derive a better understanding of the other's needs and concerns. And better understanding promotes better relationships. After all, if you can't agree on basic terms of a contract, how could you hope to work together under the pressures encountered during a project?

2. *Establishing your own rules.* When a contract is silent on certain issues, the law may impose its own default condition to address those issues. For example, when a contract does not specify how a dispute will be resolved, the default is generally to the civil court system, and either party can institute litigation. But you and your client can agree by contract to use some other dispute resolution mechanism, such as mediation or arbitration, instead (or at least as a condition precedent) of the courts. Similarly, parties to a

Why Have a Written Agreement?

contract can agree that neither will sue the other for *consequential damages* or that the period during which either can initiate a claim is shorter than may otherwise be allowed by the applicable statutes of repose or limitation. (See **Consequential Damages** and **Statutes of Repose and Limitation**.) Bear in mind that the ability to establish your own rules does not permit you to specify measures that are against public policy or are illegal (such as resolving your disputes by pistols at dawn). Nevertheless, setting your own rules can eliminate or at least lessen problems that might otherwise arise.

3. *Sizing up your client.* It is important to understand your client's attitudes and motivations. The process of contract formation and negotiation allows you to assess the people with whom you are dealing and to decide whether you want to work with them. Beware of clients who have little compunction about sacrificing quality or unfairly shifting their own liabilities to you. Does the client have a realistic budget and schedule? What is the client's experience with this type of project? Is the client sophisticated or will you have to spend a lot of time educating and hand-holding? Why did the client select you? How will the contractor be chosen? Does the client have a reputation for slow payment (or nonpayment) of fees? Does the client have a history of claims and litigation? What does your "gut" tell you about the client? Exercise great care in selecting your clients; it is one of the best loss prevention tools at your disposal.

4. *Identifying and allocating risk.* The process of contract formation should always include a candid discussion of the project risks. It's also easier to evaluate a client's attitudes and motivations when the subject of risk is brought up at the beginning of the relationship. This helps assure that risk reduction and risk handling mechanisms are incorporated into the workscope as well as the business terms and conditions of the contract. For instance, who should bear the risk of redesign if construction bids exceed the budget? Who should bear the risk of changes to your design by others and without your knowledge? Who bears the risk if your documents are reused to build another iteration of the structure you designed? Does your prospective client intend to use its economic power to force you to accept an unreasonable share of the project risk? Or is the client willing to consider the risks and rewards from your perspective as well, and to seek a fair position in which you both can succeed?

An open discussion of risk is essential, and the process of contract formation and negotiation provides a ready opportunity. Informed clients are more apt to accept a scope of services that will reduce needless liability problems and other exposures. They also are more likely to agree to the allocation of risks to the party best able to control them.

DEALING WITH RISK

Whenever you accept a project, you also accept some risks. There are many forms of risk. Business or economic risks, for example, include not being able to complete the services for the fee quoted or within the agreed-upon schedule.

One of the most common risks is having to defend yourself from a claim for an allegedly negligent act. The impact of such a claim can be severe, particularly because you owe a duty of care to more parties than just your client. If your negligence damages others who reasonably foreseeably could have been damaged, you may be liable to them, too. In most jurisdictions, they would not need a contract with you in order to file a claim and win. (See *Third-Party Beneficiaries*.)

You can manage your risks in a number of ways:

1. You can minimize or reduce risk by offering more comprehensive services. Quality-oriented clients will want such services; many have learned the hard way that it is less expensive in the long term. To promote better quality, assess client attitudes and reduce risk, many consultants always offer a full scope of design and construction phase services in their initial proposals. (See *Construction Observation* and *Scope of Services*.)

2. You can transfer some of your risk by purchasing professional liability insurance. Do not expect this to protect you from your risk, however. Much of the initial cost of claims and legal defense is still likely to be paid directly by you under your deductible. Since all professional liability policies have limits (maximum amounts of coverage), it is also conceivable that large claims might exceed the amount of coverage you purchased. All insurance policies have exclusions — certain kinds of claims they don't cover. Keep in mind, too, that insurance will not necessarily compensate for your lost staff time and loss of productivity in defending a claim. (See *Insurance*.)

3. You can educate your clients about their responsibilities regarding risks that are within their control (such as the potential for claims arising from the unauthorized reuse of your plans). You can then use your contract terms to require your clients to indemnify

you for any costs that you should not but might otherwise have to bear. Fair and reasonable clients will accept such risk allocation. (See *Indemnities*.)

4. You should identify potential problems that both you and your client are powerless to prevent. Inform the client about these risks and the options available for dealing with them. Assuming the risks are not major, you may be willing to accept some of them. If you decide to do this, however, it may be appropriate to charge an additional fee to compensate for your increased liability. Alternatively, your client can retain the risk (typically through a clause accepting the risk or by an indemnification), or perhaps your client can transfer it (via insurance) to someone else. A combination of these approaches is possible by inserting a properly worded Limitation of Liability clause into your agreement. (See *Limitation of Liability*.)

5. You should identify those risks that are so significant that you cannot or will not accept them under any circumstances, such as risks stemming from the discovery of unanticipated toxic materials or asbestos on the site. Let clients know that they must retain such risks and protect you (through indemnities) from potential third-party claims if you are to provide services on the project. (See *Hazardous Materials*.)

6. You can use your contract to close certain loopholes that could otherwise become traps. For example, you could list services you have explained and offered to the client, but which the client has declined. This could prevent future attempts to hold you liable for failing to perform an optional service the client decided to forgo. (See *Excluded Services*.)

7. You can establish conditions in the contract reducing certain risks that otherwise would exist by virtue of law. For example, you and your client can specify a dispute resolution mechanism that is more effective and less costly than litigation, reduce the length of a Statutes of limitation or restrict either party's ability to sue the other for consequential damages. (See *Consequential Damages, Dispute Avoidance and Resolution* and *Statutes of Repose and Limitation*.)

8. You can reduce overall risk by developing comprehensive contracts that precisely state the intent and expectations of both parties. Such agreements help prevent misunderstandings and enable a judge or jury to easily understand your rights and duties. This alone may discourage the pursuit of a marginal claim.

Reducing your exposure to risk largely depends on your contract formation and negotiation efforts. Clients should be made aware of the risks and the techniques for dealing with them. If they insist on "dumping" all the risks on you, refuse to compensate you adequately for the risks you are assigned, or are unwilling to accept reasonable risks themselves, then the ultimate risk-reduction method must be considered: declining the project. There are other clients and other projects where you can better spend your time — projects that are more profitable, less stressful and more rewarding. If you can't achieve a fair and reasonable agreement with a client before you undertake a project, the relationship can only go downhill from there.

CONTRACT BASICS

TERMINOLOGY

When negotiating contracts, you will most likely encounter some of the following commonly used legal terms:

The words *agreement* and *contract* are often used synonymously in the construction industry. Professional associations tend to call their documents *agreements*, to distinguish them from the construction contract documents. It makes little difference which word you choose to use in your documents, but it is a good idea to pick one and use it consistently. For the purposes of this *Guide*, however, we shall use the words interchangeably to mean a mutual agreement between two or more parties to do — or not to do — something.

A contract can take many forms. It may be *implied* by law or by the conduct of the parties. Let us say, for example, that an engineer and her client exchange drafts of an agreement but neither of them signs a final copy. If the engineer begins to perform and submits invoices, which the client pays, the law implies a contract even though all the final terms may not have been agreed upon.

An *express* agreement may be some form of written agreement ranging from a simple letter or one-page form to a heavily lawyered document consisting of dozens or even hundreds of pages. Or an express contract may be *oral*: "I'll pay you $1,000 to survey my property." "Okay, I'll do it." Not a great contract, perhaps, but a contract nonetheless.

An *oral contract* is one that is based on the spoken word. A *written contract* is, obviously, one that is in writing. Both may be binding and enforceable but it is more difficult to prove the precise terms of an oral agreement.

An *enforceable contract* is one that has all the elements necessary to bind the parties — that is, to create a legal obligation for both to perform their contractual duties. Someone who reneges on his or her contractual duties, without any legal excuse, *breaches the contract*. The party injured by that breach might find it necessary to seek *judicial relief*. In granting relief, the *trier of fact* (a judge or a jury) may assess monetary damages against the one who breached or, rarely, may require that party to perform his or her part of the contract as originally agreed. The cost of obtaining judicial relief usually must be borne by the party seeking it, unless the contract specifies otherwise. (See **Attorneys' Fees**.)

A contract may be either *void* or *voidable*, depending on the circumstances. A contract is *void* when one of the elements required to bind it is missing and the defect cannot be cured. A contract that is void cannot be ratified or made effective, because it never had any legal force. When a contract is *voidable*, one party has the legal right to call it void. That party may exercise this right because the other party used fraud, duress, disparate bargaining power or some other improper means to gain acceptance of the contract, thus making its enforcement contrary to public policy. For example, if a client threatened that if you didn't agree to the terms of its contract, the client would "spread the word that you are almost bankrupt" and you reluctantly signed, you could later claim this duress makes the contract voidable. It would, however, be enforceable by you if you so chose.

An *unenforceable* contract is similar to a voidable one, in that something about it makes it legally impossible to enforce. For instance, suppose you perform $10,000 worth of engineering for a city client. You then learn that the project was not in the city's budget and the city was prohibited by law from exceeding its budget. Sadly for you, that contract is probably unenforceable.

ELEMENTS OF A CONTRACT

For a contract to be considered *binding* and enforceable, it must comprise several elements. There must be an *agreement* between the parties and *consideration*. It must be in a *legal form*, between *competent parties* and for a *legal purpose*.

1. *Agreement* exists when one party makes an offer and the other party accepts. An *offer* is just that: one party's tender or proposal to perform a service or provide goods in return for some form of consideration. The offer will be considered valid until its acceptance or rejection by the "offeree" or withdrawal by the offeror. Withdrawal is automatic if it was stated that the offer would expire if not accepted within a certain period of time. *Acceptance* means the unequivocal assent or approval of the offer by the party to whom the offer is made and then communicated to the offeror.

2. *Consideration* is the inducement or motive to enter into a contract — the bargained-for exchange of something of value to bind the contract. The amount of the consideration doesn't have to be substantial, so long as it is negotiated and agreed to by the parties. In most circumstances, it is valid consideration to exchange a promise for another promise. For instance, if an architect promises to prepare plans and the client promises to pay the fee, there is mutual consideration.

3. *Legal form* means the contract terms are enforceable because they are neither illegal nor against public policy. It is not uncommon for certain terms of an agreement to violate law or interpretations of law (a payment clause containing a usurious rate of interest, for example). In some jurisdictions, only the offending clause is struck; in others, the entire contract may be considered void or unenforceable. To help prevent this, contracts

should include a *severability* provision, which sets forth your intent to delete any provision found to be illegal or improper while keeping the rest of the agreement intact. (See **Severability and Survival**.)

4. A contract must be executed by *competent parties*, individuals who are of legal age, mentally competent and who have the authority to bind or make commitments for the entities they represent. Many contracts include a provision that states that the individuals signing the contract are legally authorized to do so. They may also require a board of director's resolution or other appropriate documentation as proof of authorization.

5. A contract must be for a *legal purpose*. A contract to undertake illegal activity is not enforceable in courts of law. "Illegal activity" may be more subtle than it appears. Clearly, a contract for murder is neither legal nor enforceable (at least, not in a court of law). But also illegal and unenforceable, is a contract to design a building that contains known and intentional violations of building codes or ADA requirements. (See **Americans with Disabilities Act** and **Code Compliance**.)

BASIC RULES OF CONTRACTS

In the event of a dispute over the wording or meaning of a contract, courts generally will apply certain "rules" when interpreting an agreement.

When there is an ambiguity, courts will normally interpret it against the party who drafted the agreement. For instance, if you wrote a contract with an ambiguous provision regarding your right to terminate the agreement, the court would likely interpret that provision in the most favorable way for your client.

To interpret the meaning of words and terms of a contract, courts will generally assign the ordinary or *plain meaning*. They will also look to *specific terms* in favor of general terms.

The *patent ambiguity* rule says that if you see a mistake or a problem, you can't go blindly ahead; you've got to make inquiry. In other words, you cannot take advantage of an obvious mistake (such as trying to profit from a client's misplaced decimal point in stating your fee).

When looking at a contract, a court will likely favor handwritten modifications over typewritten ones and will generally prefer either of these to the printed form.

Conflicts among various contract documents are not unheard of. For instance, the drawings may say one thing while the specifications say another. Or your agreement with your client may not agree with the contractor's General Conditions. The courts have anticipated this by establishing a sort of "legal hierarchy." In this hierarchy, the Basic Agreement generally controls all other documents. General Conditions are favored over Supplemental Conditions. The courts generally hold that drawings and specifications complement and supplement each other and must be taken as a whole. It is possible to peremptorily settle such potential conflicts in your agreement with your client. You can add a clause that states, "Anything mentioned in the specifications and not shown on the drawings, or shown in the drawings but not in the specifications will be interpreted as being in both." Or you might add, "If there is a question as to which material to use, the Contractor must choose the material of higher quality." You can even include a clause that establishes your own precedence of documents. For example, you and your client could agree that 1) the Basic Agreement takes precedence over the General Conditions, 2) the Supplemental Conditions take precedence over the General Conditions, or 3) specifications take precedence over drawings.

There are some other rules of contract interpretation. For instance, you may have seen the term *"including but not limited to . . ."* in reference to lists of items or events in agreements. For example, "services to be provided by Owner, *including but not limited to*, telephone systems, computer wiring, sound systems, security systems and alarms" would be broadly interpreted to mean the listed items and any other similar items. Courts generally consider this enlarging language to mean "in addition to." If a list is meant to be specific and includes all intended items, be sure it reads that way by adding words such as "only" or "shall be limited to."

On the other hand, you may have named several items and say "and other similar items/events." For example, when listing causes for additional compensation and time to complete a contract, such as "fire, windstorm, flood, earthquake and *other similar events*," this would not be interpreted to include dissimilar causes for delay, such as labor strikes, civil riot, power or transportation shortages and the like.

Courts generally interpret all the parts of a contract as a whole. They speak of the "four corners rule," which means the intentions of the parties are to be gathered from the entire document — not from its isolated parts. They will also interpret the parts of a contract consistently with one another. The interpretation given to a term in one part of the agreement will be the same as that given to the same term elsewhere in the agreement.

Finally, be aware that you can amend a contract simply by virtue of your conduct or actions after the contract is signed. You should caution your field personnel that what they say and do during the project may change the terms of the contract. To counter this, add a clause that requires any amendments to the agreement be in writing and signed by appropriate authorized parties.

STEPS TO AN AGREEMENT

When a client wishes to procure professional services, the process generally begins with a Request for Proposal (RFP) or a solicitation by the client to one or several consultants to submit proposals for the needed services. A draft agreement is usually submitted by one of the parties, either in the solicitation or with the proposal. When a proposal is accepted, the parties then negotiate the terms and an agreement is reached.

This contract formation and negotiation process should encompass all of the basic parts of a professional services agreement: the *scope of services, schedule, compensation* and *general terms and conditions*.

1. The *scope of services* is a detailed description of everything you intend to do for the client. It should be as precise and complete as possible. It should leave no ambiguity or question as to whether or not some duty or deliverable item is included within your basic fee.

    It is very risky to generalize when writing a workscope. For instance, if you agree to a workscope that says you will provide "*complete* services necessary for the project," or that you'll "assist in obtaining *all approvals needed* for starting the Work," you could be promising something you do not intend to deliver. (See **Excluded Services**, **Permits and Approvals** and **Scope of Services**.)

    The scope is normally developed by consultation between you and your client, but sometimes is written unilaterally by one of you. It is particularly important to review a unilateral client-developed scope with a fine-tooth comb to be sure you can meet all the requirements and expectations. It should describe your duties in language that is clear and not subject to misinterpretation. A safer approach is to use your proposal as the basis for the scope, modified as necessary by you and the client.

2. In proposing and negotiating the *schedule* for your services, take into account the client's needs, your staff availability, time for review, approval or decision-making by your client and various public agencies, and the myriad other factors affecting the time needed for completion of your part of the agreement. Remember, there are many elements you cannot control: the weather, contractor performance, delays in decision-making by others, and availability of labor and building materials. In fact, after you prepare the construction documents, almost everything is beyond your control. Your contract should reflect these factors and allow you sufficient time to perform your services in an orderly and professional manner; overly restrictive schedule and penalty clauses usually spell trouble. (See **Liquidated Damages** and **Timeliness of Performance**.)

3. The *compensation* portion of an agreement can take on many forms. There are at least ten commonly used methods to determine your fee, based on the type of project, the risks and uncertainties involved and the needs of the parties. It is not unusual to "mix and match" compensation modes for different parts of the scope of services. The EJCDC and AIA standard forms provide substantial guidance regarding the various methods of compensation for professional services.

    Some clients (and even some consultants) believe that negotiation of a professional services contract mostly involves "hammering down" the consultant's fee. In fact, the scope, fee, schedule and terms all interact. There is an appropriate fee for a particular scope item to be performed on a particular schedule under a particular set of business terms. Changing any one of these factors affects all the others. When negotiating your contract, keep all these elements in balance and try to find an acceptable compromise.

4. *Terms and conditions* describe the business understandings relating to the services to be rendered, the mutual responsibilities of the parties, payment terms, allocation of various risks and ownership of the documents — in other words, the ground rules

under which you will operate. Many architectural and engineering firms have developed their own standard terms and conditions that they submit as part of their proposals. Most of the topics discussed in this *Guide* relate to business terms and conditions that frequently become problematic and show up in professional liability claims.

QUALIFICATIONS-BASED SELECTION

Qualifications-based selection (QBS) is the best method for procuring professional services. It is also required for most federal and state agencies and is normally used by most private-sector clients. In QBS, the client selects the best-qualified consultant based on competency, skill and experience. Together, the client and consultant develop a scope of services and the selected firm submits a fee proposal for that scope. There may follow some negotiation over terms, scope items and fee until an agreement is reached. If agreement cannot be reached, the client goes to the next best-qualified firm, and so on. Price is not — and should not be — the sole determining factor in selecting qualified firms.

Selecting a design and environmental professional based on the lowest fee is no more appropriate than choosing the cheapest surgeon, CPA or babysitter. Clients who use bidding and the lowest fee to hire consultants, and consultants who allow themselves to be treated as price-based commodities, may deserve each other. The results will inevitably be poor service, inferior design, inadequate construction, unmet expectations and increased exposure for everyone.

Clients who want to buy your services on a competitive-bid basis — no matter what they call it: two envelopes, two steps or just an outright call for bids — are not following normal industry practice and are obviously more concerned with price than quality. Proceed with such clients at your own peril.

TYPES OF AGREEMENTS YOU'LL ENCOUNTER

PROFESSIONAL ASSOCIATION STANDARD AGREEMENTS

Many architects, engineers and environmental consultants rely on standard professional services agreements and construction contract forms developed by the American Institute of Architects (AIA), the Engineers Joint Contract Documents Committee (EJCDC), the Council of American Structural Engineers (CASE) or other professional organizations. Carefully researched and compiled, these forms are good starting points for negotiating an agreement. Because they are written as general-purpose contracts and represent a consensus of the groups who developed them (with input from owners' and contractors' organizations), you will need to adapt and modify the terms to suit your own practice and the specific project. In addition, there are some terms that the sponsoring organizations have not included in their documents in order to achieve consensus. You may decide some of these missing provisions are critical. For instance, this *Guide* recommends several additions, such as an Attorneys' Fees provision, a statement of the standard of care and a Limitation of Liability clause. (See *Attorneys' Fees*, *Limitation of Liability* and *Standard of Care*.)

Because standard forms are carefully integrated, cross-referenced and coordinated with other agreements that will be used on a project, any change — minor or otherwise — may need to be reflected in other clauses and documents. To ensure the integrity and completeness of the final documents when modifying standard association forms, it is important to obtain competent legal advice.

CLIENT-GENERATED AGREEMENTS

The need for legal review and advice is even more important when dealing with clients — such as government entities, developers and large corporations — who insist on using their own contracts. Such contracts are often derived from construction or supplier contracts and usually contain terminology inappropriate for procuring services from professionals, words such as *work*, *warrant*, *guarantee* and *supervise* to describe what you will do. Typically, you will find language referring to you as "contractor" or clauses that require liquidated damages, a performance bond and retainage from your fees. (See *Contractual Reference to*

Types of Agreements You'll Encounter

the Consultant, Liquidated Damages, Performance Bonds and *Retainage*.) In addition, certain provisions are often one-sided and seek to transfer the client's liability to you.

If you can't persuade the client to use a professional services form, then you must drastically modify the contract to reflect your professional status, describe your scope of services in proper terms and eliminate the unfair shifting of risk to you.

Have you ever agreed to onerous terms, fearing that attempting to modify client-drafted contracts would cause an important client to seek a more amenable consultant? You should be much more concerned about the exposure to serious liability for circumstances you would be powerless to control. As difficult as it may be to change the attitude of major clients, it is even more difficult to defend yourself after you have signed an onerous contract that eliminates or limits your protections. Also bear in mind that some client-drafted terms may undermine your insurance carrier's ability to defend you, may be excluded by your insurance policy or may affect the cost of (or even your ability to obtain) insurance in the future.

When you are presented with a preprinted form, and the client tells you it cannot be changed and you must "take it or leave it," carefully review exactly what you are being asked to sign. Be willing to take a strong stand on unacceptable provisions and the modifications needed to reach acceptable terms.

PURCHASE ORDERS

Some clients will want to use a purchase-order form for your services. Purchase orders are intended to be used to procure materiel — "sticks and bricks" — and general services needed by an owner. They usually have some language on the front side, with a number of fill-in-the-blanks intended to satisfy the client's accounting department. The back of the form is often crammed with fine print, most of which is totally inappropriate for the procurement of the professional services. These forms generally call for warranties and certifications (see *Certifications, Guarantees and Warranties*) and would have you assume responsibility for product defects, which is rarely provided for under professional liability insurance policies.

If you do a thorough job of reviewing the fine print and striking out the offending or uninsurable language, you will probably end up with a document with more words deleted than retained. The result would doubtless be ambiguous and contradictory. Even more serious, important provisions will be missing. Clearly, this is not a good starting place for a professional services agreement.

CONSULTANT-DRAFTED AGREEMENTS

Many consulting firms have developed their own contract forms over the years. Often, these documents have evolved from many different sources, sometimes in response to problems encountered in the past. It is a simple matter to customize these contracts for each individual project. If you have (or decide to develop) such an agreement, be especially careful. Your agreement could be missing important protections or be ambiguously or inconsistently worded. Do-it-yourself contract writers must review these documents periodically with a skilled attorney (in conjunction with, perhaps, this *Guide*) to modify and strengthen their custom agreements.

ORAL AGREEMENTS

You've probably heard about the "good old days" when all that was required was a person's word, an understanding and a handshake. Maybe you still do an occasional project on the basis of a phone call. Oral agreements can be just as binding as written ones, but it's poor business practice to rely on one when providing professional services. The world we live in and the civil justice system that governs our business dealings have become highly complex. Architects and engineers are personally responsible for their professional acts, not only to their clients but, in most jurisdictions, to any other party who reasonably and foreseeably could be damaged or injured as a result of their services. Should a claim arise, each of the parties involved will be required to prove what was promised and what was agreed to months or even years earlier. Even the best-intentioned people have trouble remembering details and, especially when it comes to monetary or liability issues, some may have "difficulty" remembering what the deal was.

Despite these risks, some consultants commence work on projects based on a verbal go-ahead from the client. Nevertheless, within a day or two, they will present a written proposal for client acceptance. This approach is not for everyone. It is used only as an accommodation to long-time clients for whom the consultant has frequently worked and who have accepted their standard agreements before. It would be foolhardy to do this on a large, complex or risk-prone project, or when there is not a sufficient track record or pre-existing relationship with the client. There is danger in complacency. It is easy to let one's guard down and forgo a written agreement, especially with a long-term client. But these are just the sort of situations that spell "claim" if something goes wrong. Sadly, when large sums of money are involved or there is a change of ownership, a good relationship may be forgotten. Oral agreements with public owners may not even be enforceable. When you're tempted to rely on a handshake and a good memory, remember the old adage: *oral contracts aren't worth the paper they're written on.*

LETTER AGREEMENTS

Letter agreements are another form of contractual shortcut often used for small projects, such as property inspections, lot surveys or studies. They may be as simple as a surveyor writing to a prospective client, "I will locate and stake the corners of your property for

"$750." The client agrees, signs a copy and the survey is done. There is a pretty good understanding of what the lot survey and staking job entail, and the fee is clear. But the schedule, business terms and allocation of risks are missing.

You may think it is a waste of time to execute a 15- to 20-page agreement for low-value projects. Perhaps you don't want to frighten away a client with too much legal "gobbledygook." But compare a letter agreement to even the most pared-down list of **Deal Makers** — or must-have items (see the related discussion later in Part I) — and notice that many important provisions are missing, such as clauses dealing with payment terms, limitation of liability or unanticipated hazardous conditions. DPIC's files are replete with claims — sometimes very expensive claims — that have grown out of disputes over a survey, inspection or small study performed under a letter agreement with no protective language. (See ***Billing and Payment***, ***Hazardous Materials*** and ***Limitation of Liability***.)

To address this problem, some consultants and their professional associations have developed their own set of terms and conditions that are intended to be appended to letter agreements.[1] This is certainly an improvement over a bare letter agreement with no business terms, but it still falls short of a properly written and negotiated contract between the parties.

If a simple agreement is needed, it is a better idea to use one of the short-form agreements available from AIA, EJCDC or CASE — making sure they are appropriate to the services you intend to offer. These short forms have been carefully prepared and usually contain most of the protections you should have. As with any standard forms, though, they must be tailored to the specifics of your project.

CONTINUING SERVICES AGREEMENTS

Consultants who provide services to a single client on a number of individual projects over a period of time may wish to use a *continuing service* or *master agreement*. Such an agreement will set forth the business terms and conditions and sometimes the fee schedule agreed to for a period of time, perhaps a year or two. This establishes a framework within which you can provide services on short notice without having to go through detailed contract negotiations each time. The scope, schedule and perhaps fee can then be easily established with a short-form "task order" for each specific project.[2]

Such ongoing arrangements may offer greater convenience and, assuming the basic terms are properly worded, may provide better details of the relationship between the parties than a letter agreement. There are some drawbacks. A continuing services agreement should be updated periodically to account for changes in law and current compensation schedules. It may also raise questions about when a statute of limitation begins to run on a project. This can be specifically addressed in the task order and in the basic agreement forms.

---

[1] *The Consulting Engineers and Land Surveyors of California (CELSOC) has long had such a document, now titled CELSOC Form B. These terms and conditions are similar to those contained on the reverse side of CELSOC's short-form agreement Form A. (Refer to **Additional Resources** for details on how to contact CELSOC.)*

[2] *EJCDC will publish a Master Services Agreement and Task Order Forms in 1999.*

PROFESSIONAL ASSOCIATION STANDARD AGREEMENTS

AIA AND EJCDC STANDARD FORMS

The best and most widely used forms of professional services agreements for consultants are those published by the American Institute of Architects (AIA) and the Engineers Joint Contract Documents Committee (EJCDC). They are carefully drafted to describe the services, rights and responsibilities of both parties. The sponsoring organizations periodically update their documents to reflect changes in the construction industry and developments in the law.

Both sets of documents are developed by the consensus method, with input from contractor organizations, owner groups, legal and insurance counsel and others involved in the construction process. (A DPIC representative provides insurance and risk management advice to both the AIA Documents Committee and the EJCDC.) Equally important, the courts have tested the agreements over time, so users may confidently rely on the meaning and interpretation of their terms.

The AIA has published standard form agreements for over a hundred years. Many of the current documents can be purchased individually, in electronic form or in bulk from most local AIA component offices and bookstores or directly from the AIA Document Distribution Center (800.365.2724). The AIA also offers a newsletter service and a supplement service that provide information and copies of new and revised documents. (See *Additional Resources* for information on contacting the AIA.)

The EJCDC is an effort sponsored by the American Consulting Engineers Council, the American Society of Civil Engineers and the National Society of Professional Engineers. The EJCDC and its predecessor organization have been publishing documents for 30 years and now has over 50 different documents available. Documents are listed in a catalog on the websites of all three sponsoring organizations. Hard copies are available individually, in bulk or in complete sets in a binder. The documents may be ordered from the offices of the sponsoring organizations or by calling 800.417.0348. The major EJCDC documents are available in electronic format for an annual license fee. In the future, EJCDC documents will be delivered directly from the sponsors' websites. (See *Additional Resources* for information on contacting the ACEC and other member organizations.)

Both the AIA and EJCDC publish many of their standard forms in electronic format. When you purchase the electronic format version, you are buying a license to use a disk containing the documents for a year. During this license period, you may print out as many copies of the documents as you wish, so firms using many copies will find it economical to have the electronic version.

Both organizations' forms have a number of blanks to be filled in and, while they attempt to place the blanks at the beginning and end of the forms, you still have to take the hard copy apart, page by page, and insert it into a typewriter. This may pose a problem: it is common today to find design offices with no typewriters! The same may be true for many clients. The use of electronic forms facilitates filling in the blanks. The electronic forms method makes editing easier, clearly shows the changes made and produces a professional-looking final document.

Although both the AIA and EJCDC documents are intended to be used mainly in their original form, all standard forms of agreement can and should be modified to fit the circumstances of a particular project and the needs of your firm and your client.

MODIFYING STANDARD DOCUMENTS

When modifying a standard hard-copy form agreement, you should maintain certain conventions. People are familiar with and rely on what a standard form contains. Thus, when making changes on hard-copy standard forms, it is important to show any deleted language as lined out and any added language as shaded or highlighted, to make it clear what changes were made. (Both EJCDC and AIA electronic documents will automatically display all changes this way.) This serves two purposes. First, it saves a great deal of time and effort. Parties don't have to search and compare line by line, word by word for edits and they can focus instead on the changes. Second, it won't appear as though one party is trying to deceive the other by making a change look like standard language.

THE AIA APPROACH

In late 1997, AIA republished its flagship design and construction standard forms of agreement. The new owner-architect agreement represents a substantial departure in both form and substance from the 1987 documents. It is conceived as a modular, or building-block, document that the consultant and client can use to assemble an agreement that is tailor-made for each project. This modular approach is in response to a call by AIA members for agreements that support and facilitate an expanded range of services that architects may offer.

The Standard Form of Agreement Between Owner and Architect, B141-1997, consists of at least two parts. The first part contains the understandings on which the agreement is based plus the basic business terms and conditions of the agreement as well as methods of compensation. The second part, Standard Form of Architect's Services: Design and Contract Administration, describes the detailed scope of services for design and construction-related services for designing a building. Additional Standard Forms of Architect's Services are being developed by the AIA to describe other types of services, such as project programming and other expanded services during construction, building operation and maintenance. Also envisioned is a third part, which will consist of reference documents that expand and define the services to be performed, such as the Duties, Responsibilities and Limitations of Authority of the Architect's Project Representative (AIA Document B352). Thus, a complete AIA agreement for services might comprise the three parts described above plus appropriate attachments, exhibits and addenda.

THE EJCDC APPROACH

The 1996 edition of the EJCDC 1910-1, Standard Form of Agreement Between Owner and Engineer for Professional Services, consists of a basic agreement, which sets forth the business terms and conditions and incorporates by reference ten exhibits (A-J). These exhibits are used, as appropriate, to describe in detail the engineer's scope of services, owner's responsibilities, method of compensation, construction administration services, insurance requirements, allocation of risk and a number of other key issues.

OTHER PROFESSIONAL STANDARD FORM AGREEMENTS

ASFE: Professional Firms Practicing in the Geosciences, the Coalition of American Structural Engineers (CASE), the Design-Build Institute of America (DBIA) and the Federation Internationale des Ingeniures Counseils (FIDIC) all publish a limited number of contract documents for specific kinds of projects. (Refer to *Additional Resources* for information on how to contact these and other professional organizations.)

How to Review Client-Generated Agreements

If you are unable to convince your client to use your agreement or the AIA, EJCDC or other standard form, and you are forced to use a client-generated form, be prepared for a lot of detail work. Clients' attorneys are not paid to worry about consensus, balance, equity or even insurability. Instead, the client and its attorney have doubtless developed a form that attempts to transfer an inordinate amount of the project risk to your shoulders.

If the client says its contract is "non-negotiable" or that you should "take it or leave it," you are faced with some tough business decisions. First, you must decide whether or not you are willing to work with such a client. In successful business relationships, as in most things, virtually everything is negotiable. If you decide to press forward, you must then carefully examine every aspect of the form presented to you.

You will need the help of your attorney, your risk manager, your insurance broker, perhaps your insurance carrier — and this *Guide* — to try to untangle the contractual web woven by your client's attorney. Client-generated agreements are often written by individuals who have little or no understanding of the construction process, the normal relationships therein, standard terminology or even the problems that may arise.

Thus, one of your biggest tasks is educating the client. In addition to this *Guide*, you may find that another DPIC publication, *Professional Liability in the Construction Process: A Guide for Risk Managers* (1997), will be helpful in explaining real-world construction issues to your client.

In reviewing client-generated agreements, you may find it helpful to have a methodology in mind and some checklists and resources at hand. **Exhibit 1** is a sample Contract Review Checklist. Such a form, tailored to your firm's policies and procedures, may be helpful in reviewing nonstandard agreements.

Assuming the scope, schedule and fee provisions are either as you have proposed or are generally acceptable to you, proceed with caution. First, quickly read the entire document to get a general sense of what it contains and the client's overall approach. Is the language

How to Review Client-Generated Agreements

specific and unambiguous? Does it properly allocate the risks? Can you meet the requirements and expectations as they are expressed in the document?

Next, look for certain specific (and often vexatious) clauses that may or may not be there. Are there indemnity provisions? Are they one-way — against you? Are they insurable? (See *Indemnities*.) Are the insurance requirements attainable? (See *Insurance*. You will want to ask your insurance broker's advice on this and on the insurability of other aspects of the agreement.) Are you asked to give any certifications or warranties? (See *Certifications, Guarantees and Warranties*.) Are you protected from liability for environmental or health hazards? (See *Hazardous Materials*.) Who will be responsible for jobsite safety or construction means and methods? (See *Jobsite Safety*.) Who will own the documents? (See *Ownership of Instruments of Service*.) Are you being asked to assume risks not normally those of the consultant, such as those for delays or cost estimates? (See *Delays* and *Opinions (Estimates) of Probable Construction Cost*.) Are there provisions that will enable you to collect your fees in a timely manner? (See *Billing and Payment*.) Are the suspension and termination provisions two-way? (See *Suspension of Services* and *Termination*.) How are any special risks associated with the project handled? Is there a dispute resolution procedure, or does it default to the civil courts? (See *Dispute Avoidance and Resolution*.)

Then, go back and carefully reread the entire document, line by line, applying the worst case interpretation to the wording. For example, suppose you were presented with language such as "all services to be performed for Client hereunder shall be rendered by architects licensed and fully qualified to perform such services in this state." A worst case interpretation of this provision might be that only licensed personnel could be employed on the job — no designers or draftspersons allowed. That was probably not your intention.

Finally, compare the client's language with the model language we provide in this *Guide*. In addition, ask yourself how the document compares to the standard professional association agreements. How do the associations treat a particular issue? How does your client's language differ? Does it change the nature of risk or the standard of care in such a way that is unacceptable to you?

Having done all of this, you'll probably need to obtain some help from outside resources before you sit down with your client to actually negotiate the agreement. Attorneys, insurance brokers and insurance companies are available to help you.

Exhibit 1

Sample Contract Review Checklist

Project _____ Client _____

Client contact _____ Telephone _____

Fax _____ Date of draft _____ Draft # _____

Customer Provision	Topic/Solution	Comments
	Billing and Payment ❑ Provide specific payment terms ❑ Provide for interest, attorneys' fees and collection costs ❑ Provide for suspension and termination ❑ *Contract Guide* pages IV-3–IV-7	
	Certifications, Guarantees and Warranties ❑ Delete all warranties and guarantees ❑ Properly define as *opinions* ❑ *Contract Guide* pages V-3–V-7	
	Code Compliance ❑ Delete certifications of compliance ❑ Delete *all*; insert *applicable* ❑ *Contract Guide* pages VII-9–VII-12	
	Construction Phase Services ❑ Observation included in scope? ❑ For *general compliance* only ❑ *Contract Guide* pages III-7–III-12	
	Delays ❑ Allow for delays due to force majeure ❑ Delete *liquidated damages* ❑ *Contract Guide* pages V-21–V-23	
	Dispute Resolution ❑ Mediation as primary ADR method ❑ Avoid mandatory arbitration ❑ *Contract Guide* pages VI-1–VI-40	
	Indemnities ❑ Avoid the word *defend* ❑ Limited to your *negligence* ❑ *Contract Guide* pages V-27–V-36	

How to Review Client-Generated Agreements

Customer Provision	Topic/Solution	Comments
	Inspection ❏ Delete word *inspection* or ❏ Define the word ❏ *Contract Guide* pages III-13–III-17	
	Insurance Requirements ❏ Consistent with current coverage? ❏ Special requirements attainable? ❏ Reviewed with broker/risk manager ❏ *Contract Guide* pages V-39–V-47	
	Jobsite Safety ❏ Delete responsibility for safety ❏ No responsibility for construction means and methods ❏ Define safety as contractor duty ❏ *Contract Guide* pages III-19–III-22	
	Lenders' Requirements ❏ Avoid mandatory cooperation clauses ❏ Require sufficient time to review lenders' forms ❏ *Contract Guide* pages VIII-37–VIII-39	
	Liquidated Damages ❏ Delete provision entirely (See *Timeliness of Performance*) ❏ *Contract Guide* pages V-61–V-64	
	Opinion of Probable Construction Costs ❏ Define responsibility for costs/redesign ❏ Delete word *estimate* ❏ *Contract Guide* pages II-11–II-14	
	Ownership of Instruments of Service ❏ Retain ownership of documents ❏ Limit/prohibit reuse ❏ Get indemnity if documents reused ❏ *Contract Guide* pages VIII-45–VIII-48	
	Permits and Approvals ❏ *Assist* client in obtaining permits ❏ List specific permits/approvals ❏ *Contract Guide* pages VII-23–VII-25	

How to Review Client-Generated Agreements

I-27

Customer Provision	Topic/Solution	Comments
	Record Documents ❏ Avoid term *as-built* ❏ Define basis of record documents ❏ *Contract Guide* pages III-23–III-25	
	Scope of Services ❏ Sufficient detail in scope ❏ Exclude services not intended ❏ *Contract Guide* pages II-29–II-31	
	Shop Drawing Review ❏ Define contractor's responsibility ❏ Define your responsibility ❏ *Contract Guide* pages III-33–III-37	
	Standard of Care ❏ Limit to *ordinary skill, care, judgment* ❏ Avoid superlatives (*highest, best*) ❏ *Contract Guide* pages V-69–V-72	
	Stop Work Authority ❏ Owner is solely responsible ❏ *Advise* owner of need to stop ❏ *Contract Guide* pages III-39–III-40	
	Termination ❏ Not one-way for client ❏ Expenses if terminated for convenience ❏ Right to suspend if client is in default ❏ *Contract Guide* pages IV-23–IV-26	
	Timeliness of Performance ❏ Delete *time is of the essence* ❏ Reasonable time to perform ❏ *Contract Guide* pages IV-31–IV-33	

Date reviewed with legal counsel _____

Date reviewed with insurance broker _____

How to Review Client-Generated Agreements

This Sample Contract Review Checklist is designed to assist you in reviewing and negotiating proposed contractual provisions. It is *not* to be regarded as opinion or advice for any specific contracts. If legal advice or expert assistance is required, the services of a competent professional should be sought. You should develop your own form based on your firm's procedures and experience in reviewing and approving contracts written by other parties. You may also wish to seek the advice of your professional liability insurance broker.

RESOURCES FOR CONTRACT REVIEW

YOUR LEGAL COUNSEL

To assist you in your contract needs, you should have an experienced and knowledgeable attorney. You may need help preparing a standard agreement tailored to your firm's services, reviewing an onerous client-generated contract, preparing for or during a complex negotiation, or with a variety of other contract-related services. An attorney who is already knowledgeable about the standard agreements, the services of your firm and the practices of architects, engineers or consultants in the construction industry will be invaluable to you.

Where do you find such counsel? Start with the recommendations of your peers, DPIC's regional claims manager and your professional liability insurance specialist. Your local or state professional association's executive director may also have some suggestions.

Your clients select you based (we hope) on your experience, skill and knowledge. You should use the same criteria for your professional advisors — including your attorney. Interview several whose names have been recommended to you. Make sure they understand the nuances of your business and that they share your business and ethical standards. There are a number of excellent attorneys who have chosen to specialize in serving designers and consultants. (See also *Lessons in Professional Liability: DPIC's Loss Prevention Handbook for Design Professionals* (1998) or *Lessons in Professional Liability: DPIC's Loss Prevention Handbook for Environmental Consultants* (1996) for more on the selection of legal counsel.)

YOUR INSURANCE BROKER

Selecting your insurance broker is another critical business decision. Brokers used to be chosen largely on the basis of personal relationships: neighbors, Rotary or Kiwanis associates, fellow country-club members or classmates. But insurance has become so complex and specialized that it requires much more than a pleasing personality and good salesmanship. General lines insurance brokers may lack the specialized knowledge and experience you need.

Choose your insurance broker based on his or her knowledge, skill, creativity and experience, in addition to high ethical standards. A specialized professional liability insurance broker should be very familiar with your discipline and the construction process. The broker should be able to provide an extensive reference list of professional firms he or she serves and should be highly involved on a state and local level with your associations, working on legislation, public agency contracts and other critical issues affecting your profession. The broker should also be engaged in ongoing education and training in his or her specialty field.

A specialist broker will provide you with a number of services. He or she will review your contracts and advise you regarding exposure and coverage. Your broker should conduct risk management seminars for your firm and provide you with loss prevention advice and consultation. Specialist brokers can offer these extra services becuase they are knowledgeable about your profession's liability issues. In fact, it's what sets them apart. You should consider the value of these services to your firm when selecting your broker.

One resource for broker referrals is the Professional Liability Agents Network (PLAN), the association of the nationwide network of DPIC's independent agents. These individuals do all of the above and more. They provide loss prevention newsletters, seminars, contract review and advice, appear as speakers for your state and local professional associations and hold themselves to an exceptionally high standard of service. (See *Additional Resources* for information on how to contact PLAN.)

Other good resources for referrals are your peers, your local and state professional association executive directors and attorneys specializing in serving design professionals and consultants. If several people refer the same broker, you can assume he or she is a specialist serving your profession. Interview and make your selection based on the qualifications of the broker and his or her firm. As with any of your trusted professional advisors, once you have found a knowledgeable and well-qualified broker, you will be well served by developing a long-term professional relationship.

YOUR INSURANCE COMPANY

You might expect advice on how to select an insurance carrier in a book published by an insurance company to be somewhat biased . . . and you won't be disappointed. But the criteria we suggest here are used by a large number of experienced design and environmental consultants and are, we feel, worthy of consideration.

Your professional liability insurance company should provide a high level of service and advice to help you develop your professional services agreements. Producing reference materials such as this *Guide* is a major investment and a good indication of your carrier's commitment to your profession. Other contract-related services your insurance company should provide include: personal or on-line advice and consultation on contract issues; educational programs and seminars on contract review and negotiation topics; newsletters and articles in industry media on related subjects; active involvement in the AIA and

EJCDC document-writing process; assistance to local, state and national professional associations in reviewing and rewriting onerous owner and public agency agreement language; and participation at all levels of government in legislative efforts on behalf of the professions to achieve equitable laws involving contract and liability matters.

There are many insurance companies competing for the business of architects, engineers and environmental consultants, but few are truly involved in all of the above activities. Carriers who do not willingly help the professions are taking a "free ride" and aren't delivering full services to their policyholders.

There are other criteria to consider when you select your insurance company. Although cost is certainly important, selecting your professional liability insurance company solely on the basis of premium is unwise. Up-front expense is only one factor you need to consider when making your insurance-buying decision. You should choose a carrier that actively pursues prevention of losses by early intervention, and assists you with pre-claim counseling at no cost to help resolve disputes and project upsets before they become claims. You should choose a carrier that is innovative in seeking alternative means of dispute resolution — a leader in applying mediation and other methods to keep claims out of the mire of litigation. And if you do have a claim, you'll want a carrier with a highly knowledgeable and well-trained claims staff, people who will guide you through the nightmare of a claim to a prompt and reasonable conclusion. You want a claims department that will step forward if the claim is justified but that will not roll over and pay unnecessarily just to settle a case. You want claims people who understand your profession thoroughly and who specialize in your type of claims, who don't handle auto and homeowners claims one day and professional negligence the next. And you want claims people who help control legal expenses and who communicate with you (and require the attorneys to communicate with you) promptly and frequently.

You should choose an insurer who believes in educating its clients to prevent or mitigate losses and claims. And you should choose an insurer who stands up and fights for you and for your profession, whether the fight is against a frivolous lawsuit, for meaningful tort reform or against unfair competition.

Does all this sound biased? Please indulge us. We — and many professional engineers, architects and environmental consultants in private practice — think these are reasonable criteria to use in choosing your professional liability insurance carrier.

I-32

NEGOTIATING A CONTRACT

Although many believe contract negotiation is an adversarial procedure, it doesn't have to be. In fact, it shouldn't be. Even if you've received little or no training in negotiating, that doesn't mean you can't be a good negotiator. Fortunately, the skills of effective negotiation are learnable; no one is born with a "negotiating gene." If you stop and think about it, negotiation is little more than finding a solution to a problem. And who is better suited to problem solving than an architect, engineer or an environmental consultant? You analyze problems, come up with options and design creative solutions that must satisfy multiple and often diverse parties at interest.

Failed negotiations usually can be traced to one of a few causes. One or both of the parties:

- have no plan or clear objectives
- have unrealistic objectives
- are not adequately prepared.

Successful negotiation has to do with *interests* — knowing your own (which is what this *Guide* is all about) and learning about and appreciating your client's. People's interests — their needs, fears, concerns, desires and hopes — are what motivate them. And good negotiators negotiate about *interests*, not about *positions*. (A *position* is something that is already decided.) The essence of successful negotiation is finding those areas where your interests and the interests of your client overlap — a common ground. If you find that, you should be able to reach agreement on the issue.

It is also important to understand the extent of *power* on your side and on that of your client. By knowing more about the balance of power, you can make the most of your relative situations and, it is hoped, reach an agreement that will satisfy you both. Both sides usually have some power, something the other person needs. The key is to know and appreciate the power you have and to use it to reach a mutually satisfying agreement. If you believe you are totally without any power, you are doomed; you might as well give up and go play golf!

Negotiating a Contract

During the life of the project, you are expected to serve as the client's trusted professional advisor, and the contract negotiation phase of your relationship gives you an opportunity to demonstrate your professionalism. One way to do this is to articulate your concerns and your needs regarding project risks. You must also understand your client's concerns and the risks he or she faces. What you are seeking is a "win-win" solution, in which both your client's concerns and your own are appropriately addressed.

Do your homework. You need to think about the important interplay between your fee, your scope of services and the business terms of the contract, so you are in a position to give and take. Before you enter into negotiation, you need to understand the issues and arguments and know your bottom-line position on each critical provision.

There are many alternatives and trade-offs available to you to manage these risks. If the client's budget is so restrictive that you have to reduce the scope of your services, your risk is increased. You may be able to counteract this increased risk with certain provisions in your terms and conditions, assuming the scope is not reduced to such an extent that it creates a public safety concern. If the client is unwilling to accept certain provisions in your business terms, discuss an appropriate fee to account for the heightened risk. Can you expand the services you offer, and reduce the unknowns and the risks arising from them and eliminate your need for protective provisions?

Be candid and objective in discussing these issues with your client. Good clients who are aware of your concerns and who want you to solve their problems will work with you to develop fair and equitable agreements. Candor and objectivity between you and your client very often establish the foundation on which lasting relationships are built.

Much research has been done on negotiation skills and principles in recent years. Courses, books and seminars on the subject are readily available. If you or members of your staff will do most of your negotiating, some instruction is highly recommended. (See *Further Reading* for some resources.)

DEAL MAKERS AND DEAL BREAKERS

Some contract clauses are so important that if, despite your best negotiating attempts, your client will not agree to include them, you must consider walking away from the project. In this *Guide*, we call these provisions **Deal Makers**. Conversely, some clients will try to impose on you certain clauses that are so onerous or unfair that you must never agree to them. We call these provisions **Deal Breakers**.

There are several important provisions that, depending on how they are written, can be either Deal Makers or Deal Breakers. For example, a clause that asks your client to indemnify you for claims arising from hazardous materials discovered on his or her own property is a Deal Maker. On the other hand, a clause that asks you to warrant the quality of the contractor's work is a Deal Breaker. We use this rather severe terminology to identify crucial terms and to underscore their serious implications.

In an otherwise acceptable agreement, rarely will a single provision cause you to turn down a project. Contract negotiation is usually not that black and white. Instead, you may be faced with a number of less-than-fully desirable provisions that, individually or collectively, you might be willing to accept. In addition to these, however, there may lurk a truly onerous provision, say one that asks you to indemnify and defend the client for the client's own negligence, or one that calls for liquidated damages from you. This provision becomes the Deal Breaker, the one that causes you to put your foot down.

We sometimes have to draw the line when making agreements. The point is to know in advance where that line is, so you won't unwittingly agree to a deal you would otherwise find unacceptable. Having the courage of your convictions and knowing when to say "no" will keep you from stepping into too many bear-trap agreements.

This *Guide* identifies some of the clauses we consider Deal Makers or Deal Breakers. However, because no two firms have the same appetite or tolerance for risk, and because each project is different with varying degrees of risk and reward, you must carefully consider and develop your own list of Deal-Maker and Deal-Breaker provisions — your

Deal Makers and Deal Breakers

own bottom line on risk — and then use it in your negotiations. (For a suggested list of Deal-Maker and Deal-Breaker provisions, see *Exhibits 2* and *3*.)

Recognize that even if you terminate negotiations, you may not necessarily lose the job. Often, clients with whom you are unable to come to terms will be sufficiently impressed by your professionalism and rethink their own position. On the other hand, you may never hear from that client again. And that may be the best loss prevention measure of all.

Exhibit 2

DEAL MAKERS

Certain contract clauses are so important to the protection of your firm that you want them included in each agreement you sign. We call these clauses **Deal Makers**. If your client won't agree to these vital provisions, you may want to seriously consider whether to accept or decline the project. Your practice and your clients are different from those of other firms, and you may find that what constitutes your level of acceptable risk varies from project to project. As a starting point, here's our list of suggested Deal Makers. (Please refer to each chapter for more discussion on each subject.)

- **Attorneys' Fees**
- **Dispute Avoidance and Resolution**
- **Hazardous Materials**
- **Jobsite Safety**
- **Limitation of Liability**
- **Ownership of Instruments of Service**
- **Termination**

Of course, not every clause will apply to every project. What's more, depending on the particular project, other important clauses in this *Guide* may become Deal Makers. Here are some suggested Deal Makers to consider if your project includes these risks or elements:

- **Condominiums**
- **Fast Track Projects**
- **Multiple-Prime Contracts**
- **Prototype Designs**
- **Renovation/Remodeling**

Bear in mind, this is our suggested list. It is important to think about and determine your firm's philosophy and standards regarding risks — what you feel is the appropriate level of risk to take and what risks you should not take — and then develop your own list of must-have Deal Makers. Review the Table of Contents of this *Guide*. It may suggest additional clauses to add to your list, either for certain types of projects or for all your agreements.

EXHIBIT 3

DEAL BREAKERS

A **Deal Breaker** is a client-written clause that is so burdensome and onerous that you must insist it be deleted from any agreement. If your client refuses to delete or substantially modify such a clause, you'll need to seriously consider refusing the project.

Here is our list of Deal Breakers. You may want to modify this list or add others clauses, based on your experience and your firm's standard contract procedures.

Assignment (without your consent)

Certifications, Guarantees and Warranties (by you of virtually anything)

Indemnities (not limited to your negligence, or requiring defense of the client)

Insurance (containing unattainable requirements)

Jobsite Safety (assuming responsibility for construction means, methods, techniques, sequence or procedures, or safety precautions and programs)

Liquidated Damages (in excess of actual damages)

Stop Work Authority (not merely the right to reject portions of the Work)

PART II

PRE-CONSTRUCTION SERVICES

Design Without Construction Administration

Excluded Services

Opinions (Estimates) of Probable Construction Costs

Prototype Designs

Quality Control Standards

Retaining Subconsultants

Right of Entry

Scope of Services

Substitutions

II-2

DESIGN WITHOUT CONSTRUCTION ADMINISTRATION

Design and technical consultants sometimes are prevented from providing full construction phase services for a number of reasons. An architect, for instance, may design a "spec" warehouse. Although her agreement offers construction phase services as an on-call Change in Service (Additional Service), that call from the client never comes. Or an engineer might provide for construction administration and observation in his contract, only to have his contract terminated as soon as the client has the building permits in hand. In a military housing project, the government agency may refuse construction phase services from the designer because it has in-house engineers who will perform them. More often than not, the geotechnical engineer is excluded during the construction phase and cannot observe conditions as exposed by excavation to determine if changes are required. In still another fairly common scenario, the architect for a large residential project may be contracted to provide construction observation of only five model homes, but the finished development will comprise 300 units.

Clients who eliminate construction phase services do so simply to cut costs. Perhaps they do not understand that the role of the architect or engineer during construction is to minimize expensive problems. Maybe they do not appreciate the importance of project observation, field interpretation of plans and specifications, and submittal review. Or maybe they are simply unconcerned about quality and want only minimal services at minimum cost. Whatever the client's reason, if a consultant cannot provide construction phase services, he or she is denied perhaps the single most important loss prevention technique available.

THE PROBLEM

Your involvement during construction is in everyone's best interest: the owner, the builder and you. In any project, issues arise during construction that require the designer's input. No set of plans is perfect; every set requires some interpretation. There are always inconsistencies, discrepancies and questions that are best addressed by the consultant. The impact of errors can be mitigated substantially if you are on the scene (or at least available) to resolve problems or to create a field change to minimize the consequences of a mistake.

Design Without Construction Administration

If your contract does not require construction observation and submittal review, you have no way of assuring that a contractor's interpretation of your design is correct. You cannot determine if construction is proceeding according to your plans and specifications. You cannot call for critical shop drawings. You cannot determine if unauthorized changes have been made to your plans. (See *Unauthorized Changes to Plans*.) But your name is on the design, construction phase services or not. If damages can in any way be attributed to your services, it is quite likely you will be named in a suit, either by the owner or a third party.

THE SOLUTION

Your best course by far is to provide for full services in your agreement. (Please refer to *Construction Observation* for discussion and a sample provision.) We strongly recommend that you do everything in your power to provide construction phase services on each and every project you undertake. Certainly, in any complex or especially risky project such as renovation work or condominium design, we believe a contractual provision that provides for full construction phase services should be considered a **Deal Maker**. In other words, if construction phase services are not provided for in your contract, strongly consider turning down the project.

In the real world, however, providing construction phase services is not always possible. If that is the case, tread very carefully. If you cannot provide full services, negotiate for the best indemnity protection possible. Show in your workscope's Excluded Services section that the owner has declined your construction phase services, and then get contractual protection for not being allowed to provide those services. Don't let your client promise to decide later or on an if-called-for basis. Chances are he or she will decide against it (or had no intention of asking for it in the first place). Make certain, up front, that your client either agrees to full construction phase services or gives you protection for the additional risk you assume.

Although a foolproof hold harmless agreement for consultants who do not provide construction phase services does not exist, you will want to obtain as strongly worded a waiver and indemnity as you and your attorney can negotiate. Consider the following example:

DESIGN WITHOUT CONSTRUCTION ADMINISTRATION

It is understood and agreed that the Consultant's Basic Services under this Agreement do not include project observation or review of the Contractor's performance or any other construction phase services, and that such services will be provided for by the Client. The Client assumes all responsibility for interpretation

> of the Contract Documents and for construction observation, and the Client waives any claims against the Consultant that may be in any way connected thereto.
>
> In addition, the Client agrees, to the fullest extent permitted by law, to indemnify and hold harmless the Consultant, its officers, directors, employees and subconsultants (collectively, Consultant) against all damages, liabilities or costs, including reasonable attorneys' fees and defense costs, arising out of or in any way connected with the performance of such services by other persons or entities and from any and all claims arising from modifications, clarifications, interpretations, adjustments or changes made to the Contract Documents to reflect changed field or other conditions, except for claims arising from the sole negligence or willful misconduct of the Consultant.
>
> If the Client requests in writing that the Consultant provide any specific construction phase services and if the Consultant agrees in writing to provide such services, then they shall be compensated for as Additional Services as provided in Section ____ .

If you are going to provide the design services without the protection of performing construction phase services, you will want to include some other very important provisions in your contract. Your attorney may suggest you add clauses such as Unauthorized Changes to Plans, Supplanting Another Consultant and Ownership of Instruments of Service. (See those titles for additional information and suggested contract clauses.) Because of the high degree of risk involved if you are not providing full services, you should also consider it a **Deal Maker** to negotiate a reasonable Limitation of Liability provision as well as an acceptable means for dispute resolution. (See *Limitation of Liability* and *Dispute Avoidance and Resolution*.)

If your client later wants you to provide limited construction phase services — for instance, to observe only a small or very specific portion of the work — get the request in writing. Then document and get your client's acknowledgment of the exact purpose of the visit and the restrictions on your construction phase services.

It is crucial to look at the General Conditions of the construction contract to make sure they also reflect your duties and responsibilities accurately. If you don't have responsibility for construction phase services, make certain the General Conditions clearly state that fact in order to avoid confusion by the contractor and inadvertent assignment of liability to you.

Design Without Construction Administration

Many seasoned consultants believe that construction phase services are so important to their overall risk management that they choose to perform those services whether or not their contract provides for them. Anyone who has been involved in a protracted lawsuit probably agrees that the cost of providing construction phase services is modest when compared to the expense of a legal dispute. Just bear in mind that if you decide to perform this service, even if unpaid, you have the duty to do it properly and in accordance with the applicable professional standard of care.

SEE ALSO:

Construction Observation
Dispute Avoidance and Resolution
Excluded Services
Indemnities
Limitation of Liability
Prototype Designs
Scope of Services
Standard of Care
Unauthorized Changes to Plans

RELEVANT STANDARD FORM AGREEMENT PROVISIONS:

AIA B141-1997: No applicable provisions.
(See also: AIA B511-1996.)
EJCDC 1910-1 (1996 edition): Article 6.03

EXCLUDED SERVICES

To help avoid misunderstandings over what is and is not included in the Scope of Basic Services, design and environmental professionals should consider including in their agreements a list of *excluded services*. These are either services that are not available from the consultant or services that the consultant feels may be necessary but the client has refused or opted to obtain from another source.

THE PROBLEM

Clients who are inexperienced in procuring design or environmental consulting services may not know what to expect in a scope of services. If a service the client expected is not included in the scope, misunderstandings may arise and eventually lead to a dispute or a claim involving fees for additional services.

A related problem may arise when agreements use statements such as the consultant "will perform *all necessary* services" or "will provide a *complete* service" or even "will provide *normal* design services." All of these phrases are too broad and can lead to unrealistic client expectations. Your client may have different ideas of what constitutes *necessary, complete* or *normal* services. Such language could obligate you to working ad infinitum to try to satisfy the client's idea of your workscope.

You may increase your liability if you do not inform your client about services necessary to the project that you will not be providing. Since the client relies on your professional expertise, it could be alleged that you were negligent in not informing your client that certain services might be needed for the project and were either available from you or should have been obtained from another source, such as a specialist consultant.

THE SOLUTION

Work closely with your client to develop your scope of services. It is important that you review together a comprehensive workscope (or checklist) of all the services you might render. (You might want to refer to AIA Document B141-1997, Instructions, pp. 5, 6 and 7 for an example of a detailed checklist to help identify those services needed for a project.) Go over all your recommended services and discuss any of those rejected by your client

Excluded Services

that you believe will be needed, are advisable and should be obtained from another source. By doing so, you not only allow the client to make an informed decision, but you also protect yourself if your client later claims ignorance of the necessity for obtaining such services. (Refer to *Scope of Services*.)

There may be services you recommend as desirable but the client chooses either to contract for directly or to do without. Unless a public safety issue is involved, you may be willing to leave these decisions in the hands of the client, but your agreement should at least explicitly state that the client is aware of and has decided not to obtain certain services from you. (See *Public Responsibility*.) Consider the following:

EXCLUDED SERVICES

In addition to the Basic Services to be provided under this Agreement, the Consultant has offered and recommended to the Client certain other services, which the Consultant deems necessary or advisable for the Project. The Client has declined to include such services in this Agreement and has decided to obtain those services from another source or to forgo those services. The following recommended services are therefore excluded from this Agreement:

{Listing or annotated listing of Excluded Services}

In consideration of the risks to the Consultant as a result of the Client's decision to exclude these recommended services from this Agreement, the Client hereby agrees, to the fullest extent permitted by law, to indemnify and hold harmless the Consultant, its officers, directors, employees and subconsultants (collectively, Consultant) from any damages, liabilities or costs, including reasonable attorneys' fees and defense costs, arising out of or in any way connected with the Consultant's not providing these Excluded Services.

It may be difficult to obtain the suggested indemnity protection. If the client objects strenuously, and if you have a comprehensive scope of services or a good checklist attached, you may be willing to forgo it. Check with your attorney.

As discussed in the Scope of Services section, if you choose to append a checklist of services, you can reference this fact by modifying the above paragraph to read:

> **... These Excluded Services are listed in the appended Scope of Services checklist, Exhibit ___, and are shown in the column headed "Not Included"** *{or in "Responsibility" as the Client's Responsibility}.* **The Client hereby agrees to indemnify ...**

Caution: if such a checklist is used to delineate both included and excluded services, be thorough in identifying who is responsible for each and every item on the checklist.

If your client chooses to exclude a service that you consider critical to the success of the project or to public safety, you should call special attention to this. Write a letter reminding the client of the necessity of obtaining these services from other sources and asking the client to provide you with the results of these services. This step may help avert a serious problem and will certainly reduce your liability.

SEE ALSO:

Indemnities
Public Responsibility
Scope of Services

RELEVANT STANDARD FORM AGREEMENT PROVISIONS:

AIA B141-1997:	Articles 1.2.2.4; 2.2.1; 2.8.3
EJCDC 1910-1 (1996 edition):	Exhibit A 1.01A.2
	Exhibit B 2.01

II-10

OPINIONS (ESTIMATES) OF PROBABLE CONSTRUCTION COSTS

Quite often, the workscope of a design or environmental professional services agreement includes the preparation of construction-cost estimates at various stages of the project. Cost estimates are certainly critical planning tools for project owners; without them, projects could not be budgeted, funded or managed. But some clients have unrealistic expectations about the accuracy or reliability of cost estimates provided by consultants. These clients believe consultants can provide them with definitive pricing information on which precise budgets can be based and may seek to hold consultants responsible if the construction costs exceed the latest estimates.

THE PROBLEM

Many clients (and certainly the public) do not understand that a cost estimate is only that — an *estimate* — and not a guaranteed maximum price. You don't have a crystal ball at your disposal when you prepare your preliminary design or prepare the construction documents. Future availability and costs of labor, equipment and materials, market conditions, the actual construction techniques and processes to be bid by a contractor — all are beyond your knowledge or control and defy precise estimating. Other than rendering a reasonable professional opinion based on your firm's recent experience, you cannot be expected to provide infallible construction-cost figures.

Preparing estimates can be like shooting blindfolded. A client generally has a limited budget and wants to maximize what the project will contain within this budget. Your first job is to determine if the client's requirements are reasonably attainable within that budget. Once you have identified most of the client's requirements, you prepare a preliminary estimate and refine this estimate as the project progresses. Ideally, the client works with you to modify the project scope and quality to keep your estimates within his or her budget or to modify the budget. Just how your estimate stands up won't become apparent, though, until the bids come in or the client negotiates a price for construction. You may have based your estimate on perfectly sound judgment and experience. But perhaps that was before area contractors suddenly had plenty of work or lumber prices went up. If your estimates are far off the mark and your client doesn't understand the limitations of those estimates, a dispute could ensue, with your client claiming that he or she had made critical decisions relying on your estimates.

Without a contract clause that clearly explains the limitations of your estimates, your client (and a jury) might not accept the fact that the figures you gave were mere opinions. If your agreement doesn't explain the ground rules, a court may allow the argument that your client had a right to rely on your estimates as being more precise than you intended.

Unfortunately, no matter how explicit your contract language seems, some courts may remain unsympathetic. Depending on the jurisdiction and the project size, scope and complexity, a court may decide that if the actual construction cost comes within approximately five to ten percent of your figures, you have made a reasonable estimate. But if your estimate varies from the actual construction cost by more than a small percentage, you are on much shakier ground, and the court may decide you had a duty to do a better job of estimating.

Finally, you should be aware that although DPIC Companies does provide coverage in its professional liability policies for claims arising from cost estimates based on your designs, many professional liability insurers do not; you may find coverage for such services is excluded under some, more limited, insurance policies.

THE SOLUTION

One solution is not to provide construction cost estimates. Discuss the matter candidly with your client and explain that there are many firms who choose not to perform this service simply because of the potential for error and the liability issues involved. Instead, suggest that your client hire a professional cost estimator.

You could offer to hire the cost estimator as your subconsultant, although that would mean taking on some increased risk — the vicarious liability for the acts of the estimator. If you follow this approach, you will need, at the very least, to make certain the estimator has adequate insurance coverage, something not always available to cost estimators. (See *Subconsultants*.)

Another alternative — the one followed by most professional firms — is to provide the service and attempt to protect yourself in your agreement as best you can. Don't rely on even the most tightly worded contract clause for total protection, however. If you are going to provide estimates or opinions of cost, you must, of course, do a reasonable, professional job. Avoid the mistake of trying to please your client with an estimate that is in line with the client's budget. If anything, the estimate should be on the conservative side with adequate contingencies. It is far less costly to modify a design early in the design process than to do so after the construction documents are complete. If the contractor is to be selected on a negotiated basis rather than low bid, suggest he or she be brought into the cost estimating process early. In this way, the contractor can provide valuable input while gaining a better understanding of the client's program and budgetary constraints.

Many firms are cautious about using the word *estimate* in their discussions with clients and in their agreements. They substitute *opinion of probable cost*, a term that might help clarify the intent. If you do use the term *cost estimate*, define it in the Definitions section of your agreement. (See *Definitions*.) Either way, insert language into your contract that states your limitations in providing an estimate. Such a clause might read:

OPINIONS OF PROBABLE CONSTRUCTION COST

In providing opinions of probable construction cost, the Client understands that the Consultant has no control over the cost or availability of labor, equipment or materials, or over market conditions or the Contractor's method of pricing, and that the Consultant's opinions of probable construction costs are made on the basis of the Consultant's professional judgment and experience. The Consultant makes no warranty, express or implied, that the bids or the negotiated cost of the Work will not vary from the Consultant's opinion of probable construction cost.

As a further protective measure, attach a cover letter to your cost estimate when you deliver it to your client, using much the same language to remind the client that you make no warranty as to the accuracy of your opinion of probable cost.

Finally, you might consider offering to redesign the project as a sole remedy in the event that the construction bids vary from your estimate by a certain predetermined percentage (perhaps 10 or 15 percent). You might offer to do this on the condition that these services be performed prior to the award of the construction contract. As an example, the following language could be added to the clause above:

In the event the bids or negotiated cost of the Work exceed the Consultant's opinion of probable construction cost by more than ___ percent, the Consultant, upon notice from the Client and prior to the award of the construction contract, agrees to modify, at the Consultant's sole expense, the Consultant's contract documents (or those portions of the documents where bids exceeded the stipulated percentage). This redesign effort shall constitute the Consultant's sole responsibility with respect to its opinions

Opinions (Estimates) of Probable Construction Costs

of probable construction cost, and the Client agrees to cooperate with the Consultant in revising the Project scope and quality in order to reduce the bids or negotiated price so that they do not exceed the Consultant's opinion of probable construction costs.

By limiting your responsibility to performing this redesign, you may be able to cut off claims of any other responsibility for inadequacy of your opinions of probable construction cost.

SEE ALSO:

Contingency Fund
Definitions
Excluded Services
Scope of Services
Subconsultants
Value Engineering

RELEVANT STANDARD FORM AGREEMENT PROVISIONS:

AIA B141-1997:	Articles 1.3.1; 2.1.7; 2.3.1; 2.4.2.1; 2.4.3.2; 2.4.4.1; 2.8.3.16
EJCDC 1910-1 (1996 edition):	Article 5
	Exhibit A 1.01A.5; 1.02A.4; 1.03A.3
	Exhibit B 2.01J
	Exhibit F 5.02

PROTOTYPE DESIGNS

Designs that are intended to be built over and over again have a special set of risks associated with them. For instance, an engineer may design a prototype of a warehouse that will be reiterated many times in different geographic or climatic conditions. Or an architect might design the models for a tract of 500 homes. In a perfect world, the owner would want the consultant involved every time a building is reproduced. The reality, however, is that the consultant may never be involved when his or her design is constructed.

In related situations, a consultant who modifies pre-engineered buildings is also at risk, as is the consultant who agrees to site-adapt "package plans." In both cases, without specific contract safeguards, the consultant may incur substantial liability for defects in someone else's plans.

THE PROBLEM

The risk you incur from prototype designs or the reuse of your plans can be enormous. To put the problem in perspective, let's suppose you are asked to design a prototype restaurant for a new fast-food chain, Mr. Tofu. If the chain is successful, the owner might want to reuse your plans all over the country — conceivably hundreds of times at hundreds of new Mr. Tofu sites, and all without your involvement. Now, imagine your potential liability for a single design error — multiplied dozens or even hundreds of times. If you haven't protected yourself by contract, the possible damages could be staggering. (See *Ownership of Instruments of Service* for more information.)

If you are not allowed to provide construction phase services, you are deprived of your most effective loss prevention tools just when you need them most. Even the best-designed prototype buildings require some code, site and geographic adaptation, but you are not likely to be allowed to provide them. You will not usually be hired to perform normal jobsite observation nor will you be asked to provide necessary interpretation of your plans and specifications. (Refer to **Design Without Construction Administration** and **Requests for Information** for related discussions.) Furthermore, as the owner and contractors acquire experience by repeatedly constructing a structure, they could begin to cut corners, make changes or modify your drawings to save money — without consulting you. (See **Unauthorized Changes to Plans**.)

Prototype Designs

If you design changes or additions to a pre-engineered building — such as interior partitions, facades or even site adaptation — you could incur liability for defects in the design of the building, perhaps even in portions not affected by your work.

Finally, some popular magazines and catalogs advertise package designs — plans for everything from A-frame vacation cottages to 20-room mansions. Be aware, however, that if you put such a design over your title block and sign or add your seal (perhaps only to help a client obtain a building permit), you might be placing yourself at risk. The plans could be seriously flawed and the builder may be incompetent or worse. You could find yourself assuming liability — or at least having to defend yourself — for claims of defects in someone else's work. There also may be serious problems under your state's licensing laws regarding signing plans prepared by others.

THE SOLUTION

If you design a structure you know or suspect will be used as a prototype — to be rebuilt without your involvement — you'll want broad contractual protection. Your contract should contain a waiver of claims (an agreement that your client will not sue you) and a strong indemnity for third-party claims arising from the reuse of your documents:

PROTOTYPE DESIGNS

It is understood that the Client intends to reuse the construction documents produced by the Consultant under this Agreement on other sites. The Client has requested that the Consultant not provide construction phase services in connection with any of these reuses. In recognition of the risks to the Consultant, therefore, the Client agrees to waive all claims against the Consultant that might be contributed to or caused in any way by the Consultant's exclusion from the construction phase, and any claims that might, with reasonable certainty, have been avoided or mitigated had the Consultant provided construction phase services on these projects involving the reuse of the construction documents.

In addition, the Client agrees, to the fullest extent permitted by law, to indemnify and hold harmless the Consultant, its officers, directors, employees and subconsultants (collectively, Consultant) against all damages, liabilities or costs, including reasonable attorneys' fees and defense costs, arising out of or in

any way connected to the reuse of the construction documents on any other project or site without the involvement of the Consultant in the construction phase services normally provided on such projects, excepting only those damages, liabilities or costs attributable to the sole negligence or willful misconduct by the Consultant.

Be certain your contract also has provisions that protect you from changes to your plans without your approval. (See *Unauthorized Changes to Plans*.)

PRE-ENGINEERED BUILDINGS

If your client hires you to specify, site-adapt or modify a pre-engineered building, you need to protect yourself from the inadvertent assumption of someone else's liability. After all, the structure was designed and manufactured by others and you should not be responsible for anything beyond your own negligent acts. Your agreement should have a waiver and indemnity against claims arising out of the design, fabrication or installation of any pre-engineered or prefabricated structures.

PRE-ENGINEERED BUILDINGS

The Client acknowledges that it has requested the Consultant to specify a pre-engineered building otherwise identified as a *{model number or other specification}*. **The Client further acknowledges that the Consultant will not engineer, design, manufacture, assemble or erect said building and is not responsible in any way for defects or deficiencies in the building. Therefore, the Client waives all claims against the Consultant arising in any way from the specification of the building or for any defects, deficiencies, errors or omissions in the design, fabrication or erection of the building.**

In addition, the Client agrees, to the fullest extent permitted by law, to indemnify and hold harmless the Consultant, its officers, directors, employees and subconsultants (collectively, Consultant) against all damages, liabilities or costs, including reasonable attorneys' fees and defense costs, arising out of or in any way connected with the specification, design, fabrication,

Prototype Designs

erection or use of the buildings, excepting only those damages, liabilities or costs attributable to the sole negligence or willful misconduct by the Consultant.

PACKAGE PLANS

To avoid liability associated with "package plans," your best defense is simply to decline to provide this service. If you do provide such services, however, first make sure that you are operating within the licensing laws of your state if you review, stamp and sign plans prepared by others not employed by you nor acting under your direct supervision. You should also take appropriate measures to protect yourself. Start with a thorough discussion of risk allocation with your client, assuming you have carefully pre-selected him or her. Include reasonable waiver and indemnity clauses in your agreement (modify the above clauses as appropriate), along with provisions for Limitation of Liability, Attorneys' Fees, Dispute Resolution and any other **Deal-Maker** clauses that pertain to your project. (Refer to these sections for suggested sample clauses.) Insist on adequate fees and time to enable you to check the plans carefully — just as if you had created them yourself. If all of this is not possible, then pass the job on to someone less mindful of his or her professional responsibilities.

SEE ALSO:

Attorneys' Fees
Copyrights
Design Without Construction Administration
Dispute Avoidance and Resolution
Indemnities
Limitation of Liability
Ownership of Instruments of Service
Requests for Information

THERE ARE NO RELEVANT PROVISIONS IN THE AIA OR EJCDC STANDARD FORM AGREEMENTS.

QUALITY CONTROL STANDARDS

Some owner-written contracts require the design or environmental professional to have written quality control standards and procedures for the performance of the project. Sometimes a contract will go further and require the consultant to adhere strictly to these procedures and may even dictate that they be submitted for the owner's review and approval. While such conditions probably seem reasonable to the owner, they may put the consultant in a risky position.

THE PROBLEM

If you agree by contract to follow a set of rigid rules and guidelines, you may be changing the standard of care by which you are judged. (See *Standard of Care* for a related discussion.) In fact, you could be agreeing to abide by yet another set of standards and procedures — in addition to the standards of your profession you are legally obliged to follow.

No one objects to the need for well-defined quality control procedures. Most good design and consulting firms will already have such programs in effect if they want to remain competitive and reduce claims. Your office may have written quality control manuals that you and your staff refer to continually. But such procedures — even if they were developed in-house — are by definition generalized and are written to fit all kinds of situations. They are intended as guidelines, examples of how you might approach a given situation. It makes little sense to try to impose by contract inflexible rules and procedures on what is, in truth, a creative process. Each project you undertake is unique. You cannot know, when you begin an assignment, what difficulties you will face or what decisions you will need to make. You might follow the guidelines to the letter 99 percent of the time, but ultimately, you must rely on your professional experience and judgment to make the right decisions. You must retain the prerogative to depart from "standard operating procedures" and to do what your professional expertise tells you is best for your client and to protect the health and safety of the public.

Quality Control Standards

THE SOLUTION

If a client-written contract requires you to maintain and adhere to written quality control procedures and standards, your best approach is to delete the clause. Find out what your client really expects. If your client simply wants assurance that you intend to provide quality professional services, explain that you are already legally obligated to uphold a high standard. The law requires you to perform your services in a manner consistent with the degree of skill and care used by other competent practitioners of your discipline under similar circumstances. (Refer to *Standard of Care* for a sample clause you can offer your client.)

Certainly, it would be helpful if you could demonstrate to your client that your firm is vitally concerned about quality — with a formalized Total Quality Management program, for instance. (See *Further Reading* for resources on TQM.) Or perhaps you are ISO 9000 certified or certified under quality programs established by large industrial clients (such as The Big Three auto makers).

Many firms find that having been peer reviewed impresses quality-conscious clients — a side benefit to a peer review's main purpose of improving your in-house procedures. (For information about available peer-review programs, contact your professional society or your professional liability insurance specialist. DPIC Companies strongly advocates peer review and offers incentives to its insureds who participate in this process.)

If, however, your client insists that your contract specify that you have quality control procedures in place, you may agree — with certain limitations. Be sure the provision allows you to use your best judgment as a professional to apply or not apply those procedures as appropriate. Here is a sample clause:

QUALITY CONTROL

The Consultant agrees to maintain written quality control procedures for the general guidance of its staff in providing services under this Agreement. Such procedures may be modified by the Consultant from time to time as appropriate to the Consultant's professional practice. The Consultant shall utilize these quality control procedures to the extent practicable in rendering services in accordance with the standard of professional care.

We suggest that you not agree to submit your procedures to your client for review and approval. This tends to carve them in stone. Quality manuals are "living documents" and are subject to change. If you were required to submit them for client approval, you could find yourself locked into a set of procedures that are static instead of growing and changing along with your experience and practice. As a fallback, you might offer to maintain a current set in your offices and make them available to your client in your offices for review at reasonable times.

You are retained by your client to be his or her professional advisor and you are licensed in order to protect the public health and safety. To fulfill these obligations, you must be able to rely on your best judgment and experience. It is neither appropriate to your profession nor in the best interest of your client or the public to be bound by an uncompromising set of rules.

SEE ALSO:

Code Compliance
Non-Negligent Services
Standard of Care

THERE ARE NO RELEVANT PROVISIONS IN THE AIA OR EJCDC STANDARD FORM AGREEMENTS.

II-22

Retaining Subconsultants

During the course of a project, it may become necessary for a consultant to retain additional expertise or subconsulting services. Hiring subconsultants may have been assumed by the design team when the proposal was submitted, or it may not have been contemplated at all. In any event, the freedom to retain subconsultants is desirable and necessary.

On the other hand, this freedom is compromised when a client selects certain subconsultants or specifies that they be added to the design team.

The Problem

As the design or environmental professional on a project, you'll want the ability to hire any subconsultants that you believe, in your professional judgment, are necessary to properly carry out the assignment and fulfill your scope of services. But some client-drafted contracts attempt to restrict your right to hire subconsultants by requiring you to obtain the client's prior consent. If subcontracting restrictions are too severe, you might not be able to hire appropriate subconsultants. In such a situation, you might have to contact the client repeatedly to obtain consent and prepare extensive paperwork to document this process. This slows progress and could create a technical breach of contract should you have to call in a subconsultant in an emergency when there is no time to obtain the client's prior consent.

Quite another problem arises if a client demands that you hire a specific subconsultant to perform part of the services. You may not know (or like) the firm's reputation, capabilities, business practices, insurance or financial situation. When you hire a firm, you depend on it to perform its services in a competent, technically sound and professional manner. All of this is questionable if your client foists an unfamiliar (and possibly unqualified) subconsultant on you. Your reputation, your exposure to liability, your financial resources and the success of the project may be in jeopardy.

The Solution

The best approach is to delete any restrictive clauses requiring the client's prior consent. If there is no prohibition in your agreement, you are free to subcontract any part of the

Retaining Subconsultants

services you deem appropriate. Professional services agreements are not personal services contracts or employment agreements. Your status is that of an independent contractor and this presumes your authority to get the job done however you deem fit, including subcontracting to whatever subconsultants you may require.

The next best solution is to add a provision to your contract that specifically addresses retaining subconsultants and gives you sufficient leeway to do so, as necessary. If your client wants some control, list the subconsulting disciplines you may need on the project, thus eliminating the need for prior consent:

RIGHT TO RETAIN SUBCONSULTANTS

The Consultant may engage the services of any subconsultants when, in the Consultant's sole opinion, it is appropriate to do so. Such subconsultants may include: *{list any subconsulting disciplines you may need, such as land surveyors, testing laboratories, geotechnical engineers}* **and any specialized consulting services deemed necessary by the Consultant to carry out the scope of the Consultant's services.**

If the client wants a greater degree of control over those whom you hire, you could append a list of specific consultants you believe may be needed to fulfill your duties. You could give your client an opportunity to voice objection to any additional firms not on your list.

RIGHT TO RETAIN SUBCONSULTANTS

The Consultant may retain the services of any subconsultants listed in Exhibit ____ of this Agreement, when, in the Consultant's professional opinion, it is appropriate to do so. If the Consultant desires to retain subconsultants not listed in Exhibit ___, the Consultant shall notify the Client in writing prior to engagement of that subconsultant. If the Client has any objection, the Client shall notify the Consultant within five (5) calendar days of receiving notice. Nothing herein shall prevent the Consultant from engaging any subconsultants that the

> Consultant, in its sole opinion, deems necessary in an emergency situation, and the Consultant shall notify the Client as soon as practicable after the emergency.

If there is a possibility that you might be asked to hire, say, the client's "consultant" brother-in-law, you might want to add some language that prohibits the client from forcing you to take on unwanted subconsultants. Such language could read:

> **The Consultant shall not be required by the Client to retain any subconsultant not fully acceptable to the Consultant.**

Failing that, you have a few options — none of which is particularly attractive. First, you can flat-out refuse to hire a subconsultant that the client wants you to take on. You could, instead, insist that the client hire the consultant directly. Although this will probably result in some resentment from your client and require you to negotiate for additional fees for coordination with the client's consultant, at least you would not assume the vicarious liability for the acts of the client's consultant.

If you do succumb and hire the client's "recommended" subconsultant, remember that the normal standard of care rules apply: if you hire someone, you are responsible for his or her acts. Insist on a good subconsultant agreement with a clear scope and a strong indemnity and be sure to check to see that the subconsultant is properly insured, particularly for professional liability. (See *Subconsultants*.)

A caution: be sure to use consistent terminology throughout your contract. For example, if you refer to "subconsultants" in one clause, don't switch to "subcontractor" in another. (For further discussion, refer to *Contractual Reference to the Consultant*.)

SEE ALSO:

Assignment
Contractual Reference to the Consultant
Extension of Protection
Standard of Care
Subconsultants

RELEVANT STANDARD FORM AGREEMENT PROVISIONS:

AIA B141-1997:	Articles 1.1.3.5; 1.2.3.1
EJCDC 1910-1 (1996 edition):	Article 6.01C

Right of Entry

When a client owns the building site that the design or environmental professional has been retained to evaluate, granting a right of entry is a simple matter. Sometimes, however, clients might have only an option to purchase the property — and that purchase might hinge on the consultant's studies or evaluation. Sometimes, too, it is necessary for the consultant to enter a neighboring parcel of land, and permission is needed from the adjacent owners — not necessarily a given if they are unaware of or oppose the project.

The Problem

The typical Right of Entry clause used by many clients calls for you to obtain all the permits and licenses necessary in order to enter the project site. (See *Permits and Approvals*.) But these permits may also require that the project or land be restored to its original condition following any testing you may have to perform. The result: not only could you spend considerable time and energy in obtaining the permits, but you also assume additional liability just by being on the property.

The Solution

Your agreement needs to be specific about who makes the legal arrangements, who bears the cost of the permit and who assumes the cost of repairing anything damaged in the course of providing your services on the site.

The cost and difficulty of obtaining entry permits is more properly borne by the client. The best solution may be a Right of Entry clause similar to the following:

Right of Entry

The Client shall provide for the Consultant's right to enter the property owned by the Client and/or others in order for the Consultant to fulfill the Scope of Services included hereunder.

Right of Entry

> Although the Consultant will exercise reasonable care in performing its services, the Client understands that use of testing or other equipment may unavoidably cause some damage, the correction of which is not part of this Agreement. The Client agrees, to the fullest extent permitted by law, to indemnify and hold harmless the Consultant, its officers, directors, employees and subconsultants (collectively, Consultant) against any damages, liabilities or costs, including reasonable attorneys' fees and defense costs, arising or allegedly arising from procedures associated with testing or investigative activities or connected in any way with the discovery of hazardous materials or suspected hazardous materials on the property.

Make sure you coordinate the language of this clause with that in your Permits and Approvals clause.

Your contract should have a broad indemnification regarding the unanticipated discovery of hazardous materials. (See *Hazardous Materials* for suggested language.) The use of an indemnification is important. Just a suspicion of the presence of hazardous materials could result in rumors that might lower a property's value. And even if that suspicion is incorrect and no such materials are found, you might face a claim from someone who argues that your actions resulted in a lowering of property values. (See *Indemnities*.) If you do discover hazardous materials, you will be glad that you have contractual protection should you have to report their existence to government authorities. (See *Confidentiality* and *Public Responsibility*.)

SEE ALSO:

Confidentiality
Hazardous Materials
Indemnities
Permits and Approvals
Public Responsibility

RELEVANT STANDARD FORM AGREEMENT PROVISIONS:

AIA B141-1997:	Article 2.6.2.3
EJCDC 1910-1 (1996 edition):	Exhibit B 2.01F

SCOPE OF SERVICES

A comprehensive scope of services consists of three separate parts: 1) services that the design or environmental professional will perform for a basic fee; 2) services that are available to the client for an additional fee; and 3) services that are specifically excluded because the client has refused them, has agreed to have them performed by another party or because the consultant does not provide them.

THE PROBLEM

Sometimes client-written contracts attempt to use broad, general language in their workscope provisions. They may ask you, for instance, to "provide *any and all* engineering services necessary for the completion of the project." Or they may ask you to provide "*complete* architectural services." Such language makes your services difficult to quantify, to price or even to know when you are done with your duties. What may be *complete* to your client may not be complete to you.

Unless your scope is carefully defined, you may not be able to differentiate included services from extra services that are not contemplated in your basic fee. This makes it difficult to charge for any additional services you are required to perform.

Furthermore, even under the best of circumstances, it is impossible to know up-front all the services that might be needed because of changed or unanticipated conditions or required by new codes or regulations. So be wary of any client-developed language that asks you to state that the scope described is "adequate for the project" or give any other broadly worded or open-ended description of the completeness of your services.

THE SOLUTION

Work with your client to develop a comprehensive scope of basic services. Help your client define his or her needs and expectations and explain how these expectations can be met. This step will give your client a better understanding of your role in the construction process. It will also provide an opportunity for you to outline all of your services available to the client and to explain additional services[1] and how they will be charged. You may find

---

[1] *The new 1997 AIA agreements refer to additional services as "Changes in Service."*

Scope of Services

that detailed checklists of all potential services can help you avoid overlooking scope items. You can use the basic services lists in the AIA, EJCDC or other professional association agreements, or you may want to develop your own matrix or checklist. However you develop your workscope, make certain you review with your client those services you will provide, those you can provide for an additional fee and those you will not provide.

If your contract does not embody a detailed workscope, you can append your checklist or matrix to the agreement. You and your attorney might consider language such as:

SCOPE OF SERVICES

The Client and the Consultant have agreed to a list of Basic Services the Consultant will provide to the Client, listed on the appended Scope of Services, Exhibit A.

If agreed to in writing by the Client and the Consultant, the Consultant shall provide Additional Services, which shall be labeled as Exhibit B, appended hereto. Additional Services are not included as part of the Basic Scope of Services and shall be paid for by the Client in addition to payment for Basic Services, in accordance with the Consultant's prevailing fee schedule, as provided for in Section ____, Compensation, or as agreed to by the Client and the Consultant.

If you do not have a separate contract provision on Excluded Services, you could add the following paragraph to the above clause:

Services not set forth above as Basic Services and not listed in Exhibit A of this Agreement are specifically excluded from the scope of the Consultant's services. The Consultant assumes no responsibility to perform any services not specifically listed in Exhibit A.

The best way to protect from liability arising from not performing Excluded Services is to provide a list or attachment of specific services that are not included in your scope.

By stating "what's in and what's out" of the workscope, there should be no room for confusion. (See *Excluded Services* for a complete discussion and contract wording.)

If your client asks you to provide additional services not in your original scope and you don't wish to provide those extra services (they may, for example, be outside your expertise or just too risky), or if you cannot reach agreement with your client on equitable adjustments to your fee or schedule, you will need protection. A reasonable Termination clause should be included in every agreement you sign. This clause should include provision for termination if you and your client cannot agree on changes in the scope of services or the resulting changes in compensation and schedule. Although terminating your contract is harsh, if you and your client cannot agree on such basics as equitable fees and adequate time to perform, your relationship is probably already on the rocks. Having the power to terminate in your pocket may help you negotiate reasonable terms. (See *Termination*.)

Delete any client-drafted clauses that ask you to agree (or even certify) that the scope of services proposed will be "adequate to meet the project needs," that you will "provide any and all professional services necessary for completion of the project" or similar sweeping language. Instead, describe in detail exactly which services you will provide and which you will not provide and negotiate this scope to your mutual satisfaction. If the complexity of the project defies definition, you should consider performing your services on an hourly basis until both you and your client can get a better idea of what will be required. This is not only fiscally prudent, but it's also the professional approach to solving a problem with many uncertainties. Reasonable clients would do nothing less in their own businesses and should understand your need to do likewise.

SEE ALSO:

Changed Conditions
Excluded Services
Termination

RELEVANT STANDARD FORM AGREEMENT PROVISIONS:

AIA B141-1997:	Articles 1.2.3.1; 1.4; 2
EJCDC 1910-1 (1996 edition):	Article 1.01
	Exhibit A

II-32

SUBSTITUTIONS

No matter how carefully a project is designed, detailed and specified by a consultant, contractors may propose substitute materials, products or equipment they would like to use in the project.

Bidding instructions normally establish rules for contractors to follow in proposing substitutions prior to the receipt of bids. Public-agency clients generally are required to consider proposed substitutions if they are equivalent to what was specified in the bidding documents. Some private clients, however, may be opposed to substitutions at any time and want the bid documents to so state. Others may encourage substitutions by permitting a kind of open-ended "value engineering" throughout the construction process.

THE PROBLEM

Substitutions proposed well in advance of the bid date and accompanied by appropriate performance information, test data and other materials necessary for evaluation are not the problem. The trouble lies instead with the substitution that is proposed too late, without necessary information or during construction-requiring additional research and changes to already-completed design documents. All of this eats into your profits and creates potential liability traps. Contractors propose substitutions for their own advantage — to reduce their costs, to shorten material lead-times, for ease of installation, because of their familiarity with the product or availability — and seldom for the client's benefit or yours.

You may find yourself caught between your client and the contractor. If you object to a substitution, the contractor may protest that you are stifling cost savings or are too defensive about your original design decisions. Indeed, although most clients want a project that is functional and durable, cost is always a significant consideration. By proposing substitute materials or equipment, the contractor may indeed show initial cost savings. But if the materials or equipment are inferior to those originally specified, costs to the client may increase over the life of the project. If the substitution causes higher maintenance or operating costs or has a shorter life span, you could be subject to claims long after the general contractor has gone. And, as usual, if you take too long to review the request, the contractor may claim for delays.

Substitutions

Late substitutions often involve a great deal of your time and effort to properly research and review to determine their acceptability. They can result in RFIs or unidentified or uncoordinated work if the need for additional drawings or specifications was not anticipated and provided for when the substitution was proposed. (See *Requests for Information*.)

Your procedures when specifying materials, products or equipment may also create a problem. If you specify *xyz* product "or equal" without spelling out the required criteria for that product, you may find yourself open to claims from a contractor because you refused to accept a substitute that was "equal" according to the contractor's criteria.

THE SOLUTION

If substitutions are to be allowed on a project, there should be specific procedures in the bidding documents regarding the form, content and timing of proposed substitutions. Make certain these procedures are included in the contract documents and review them with the contractor during the pre-bid conference. There must be sufficient time for you to review the proposed substitutions and, if they are approved, to notify all other bidders via an addendum so that they have the opportunity to consider the substitutions in their bids, too. To assure that the quality, appearance and the functionality you intended in the original drawings and specifications are at least met, the final decision as to acceptability of substitutions must be yours.

Try to discourage substitutions after the bid is accepted. Educate your client about the problems created by allowing substitutions during construction, including the additional time and effort that will be required to integrate the changes into the original design. The owner must realize that by the time you are compensated for necessary design changes and coordination, hoped-for savings may not be realized. There are exceptions: if an extended delivery time of the material originally specified would seriously delay the project, if a specified item is no longer manufactured or if the substitution offers such significant savings to the owner without a major change in scope or quality of the project, then you may have to consider a late substitution.

Your contract should anticipate the additional effort required by providing time and compensation for these additional services. Here is a sample clause:

SUBSTITUTIONS

Upon request by the Client, the Consultant shall evaluate and make recommendations regarding substitutions of materials, products or equipment proposed by the Client's consultants or contractors. The Consultant shall be compensated for these services, as well as any services required to modify and coordinate

> the construction documents prepared by the Consultant with those of the Consultant's subconsultants and the Client's consultants, as Additional Services. The Consultant also shall be entitled to an adjustment in schedule caused by this additional effort.

Some firms use a Substitution Approval Request Form and provide for its use by the contractor with appropriate language in the contract documents. (See *Exhibit 4* for a sample form you can adapt for use in your firm.) This form requires the contractor to justify the substitution and provide information necessary for the consultant to properly evaluate the request. A request for substitution should be accompanied by (as appropriate) drawings, independent laboratory data, performance data, cost and schedule considerations and any other pertinent documentation you may need.

SEE ALSO:

Delays
Requests for Information
Value Engineering

RELEVANT STANDARD FORM AGREEMENT PROVISIONS:

AIA B141-1997:	Articles 2.5.4.4; 2.5.5.4; 2.8.2
EJCDC 1910-1 (1996 edition):	Exhibit A 1.04A.11; 2.01A.13

Substitutions

Exhibit 4

SUBSTITUTION APPROVAL REQUEST FORM

Contractor requests for substitutions will be considered upon receipt of this completed Substitution Request Form and all required supporting documentation. Substitutions made without completion of this form and the Consultant's approval will be considered defective work.

Project _____

The Contractor proposes the following substitution in accordance with the requirements of the Contract Documents:

Scope of substitution _____

Specification references _____

Drawings references _____

Reasons for proposed substitution _____

Impact on project schedule _____

Impact on guarantees and warranties _____

Coordination required with adjacent materials and related systems _____

Deviations from specified requirements _____

Attachments _____ yes _____ no *(Attach supporting documentation sufficient for the Consultant to evaluate substitution. Substitution Request Forms submitted without adequate documentation will be returned without review.)*

Response date _____ *(Date by which response by the Consultant is requested in order to maintain project schedule and allow sufficient time for inclusion of proposed substitution.)*

Authorized Signature _____ Date _____
 (Contractor)

Firm name/address/phone number/fax number _____

_____

CONSULTANT'S RESPONSE

The Consultant's response is based on information submitted by the Contractor. Changes to the contract sum or changes of project schedule shall be processed using appropriate Change Order forms.

Signed _____ Date _____
 (Consultant)

Approved _____ Approved as noted _____

Revise and resubmit _____ Rejected _____

Returned without review _____

Part III

Construction Administration

Claims Arbiter Service
Construction Observation
Inspection
Jobsite Safety
Record Documents
Requests for Information
Shop Drawing Review
Stop Work Authority

III-2

CLAIMS ARBITER SERVICE

Professional service agreements will sometimes include a clause that requires the consultant to interpret and render decisions on questions of performance or obligations of both the contractor and the client. Such a clause is contained in both the AIA B141-1997 and the EJCDC 1910-1 (1996 edition) and is occasionally found in client-written contracts. It is interesting to note that this clause is one that owners frequently delete from association standard form agreements.

THE PROBLEM

If you serve as an arbiter, you may well expedite resolution of certain project issues, but this can also make you vulnerable to claims and lawsuits — or at least require you to spend a considerable amount of time in rendering this service or defending your decisions. It isn't that you don't want to provide a needed service to your client, but that you don't want to be drawn into disputes with contractors who will contest your decisions at the drop of a hard hat.

Furthermore, at the time you are writing your agreement with your client, there is no way to anticipate how much time might be required to perform this service.

THE SOLUTION

One solution is to avoid performing the service of claims arbiter altogether. Many consultants who consistently render other construction phase services, such as submittal review and construction observation, and who are comfortable with their roles as agents of the owner, do not wish to serve as claims arbiters. They believe that doing so may create a conflict of interest, put them at odds with the client who pays their fees and, in the event of an adverse decision, may even result in a claim from their client.

If you do provide arbiter service, you may want to do so as an Additional Service. Protect yourself with appropriate language in your agreement with your client and require your client to insert a similar provision in the client's contract with the contractor. Both provisions should address the fact that you will act impartially. Even though you are being paid by your client, the language must make clear that when performing this "arbiter" service you are stepping out of your role as the agent of the client and are obligated to perform objectively. You are being called upon to act as a "judge" and you need the freedom to act accordingly without fear of recrimination. The provisions should also state that your decisions are to be based on what is authorized in (or reasonably inferred from) the contract documents. Here is some sample language to accomplish this:

CLAIMS ARBITER SERVICE

On written request of either the Client or the Contractor, the Consultant shall interpret and render decisions on matters concerning performance of the Client and the Contractor under the requirements of the Contract Documents. The Client will pay the Consultant for these services in accordance with the Additional Services provisions of this Agreement. Decisions of the Consultant shall be consistent with the design concepts and information contained in the Contract Documents and reasonably inferable therefrom and shall be made with reasonable promptness. The Consultant shall attempt to ensure that both the Client and the Contractor faithfully perform their contractual obligations, and the Consultant shall not be partial to either. The Consultant shall not be liable to either the Client or the Contractor for the results of interpretations or decisions rendered by the Consultant in good faith.

Accordingly, the Client agrees, to the fullest extent permitted by law, to indemnify and hold harmless the Consultant from any damages, liabilities or costs, including reasonable attorneys' fees and defense costs, arising out of or in any way connected with the Consultant's service as a claims arbiter.

In addition, the Client agrees to make no claim and hereby waives, to the fullest extent permitted by law, any claim or cause of action of any nature against the Consultant arising out of or in any way connected with the Consultant's service as a claims arbiter.

SEE ALSO:

Confidential Communications
Excluded Services
Public Responsibility
Scope of Services

RELEVANT STANDARD FORM AGREEMENT PROVISIONS:

AIA B141-1997:   Article 2.6.1.7-9
EJCDC 1910-1 (1996 edition):   Exhibit A 1.05A.13

III-6

CONSTRUCTION OBSERVATION

Construction observation is a powerful weapon in the loss prevention arsenal of the architect, engineer or environmental professional. Only by visiting the jobsite at appropriate intervals can the consultant see if the Work is progressing in general conformance with the contract documents and according to the design concept. Site observation allows the consultant to answer questions or clarify and interpret documents for the contractor on the spot, and it may enable him or her to identify trouble spots early on — less costly by far than fixing problems after the project is completed.

If construction observation is so important, why isn't it done on every project? There are a number of reasons. First, some owners regard construction observation as costly and unnecessary. If the client cares little about the quality of the project, he or she may view construction observation as a needless front-end expense and not consider the high repair costs that might follow. This is typically the client who builds on "spec" and is primarily interested in the build-it-and-sell-it-fast dollar. Another type of client, only slightly more quality-conscious, may hire a project or construction manager, believing a consultant's observation of the project is redundant. Yet another sort is the inexperienced client who thinks that a completed set of plans and specifications is a perfect product, like the directions for assembling a bicycle on Christmas morning. If the contractor just follows the plans, the client reasons, the result will be a perfect structure. That these plans may contain errors or ambiguities or may need interpretation during construction doesn't occur to this client.

For all these reasons, it may seem obvious that consultants could have done a better job educating their clients on the merits of full construction observation. But design professionals began to retreat from construction phase responsibilities in the 1960s because they felt these services were too risky. This impression may have come in part from the layperson's misuse and the courts' interpretation of the words *inspect* and *supervise* when used to describe a consultant's services. (See **Inspection** for discussion.) Both terms suggested that the consultant was responsible for a great deal more than was intended and, accordingly, consultants were blamed for anything and everything that went wrong on a construction site.

Construction Observation

THE PROBLEM

Some clients seem to want things both ways. They are unwilling to pay the fee you need to perform construction observation, but they want you to take full responsibility for the problems created by your not doing it. Or they may hire someone else to do the observation more cheaply. They don't understand that another consultant, unfamiliar with your design concept or the assumptions you made in preparing your plans, is less likely to recognize problems or know what to do about them.

On the other hand, if you are not performing construction observation because you think it will increase your exposure to risk, think again. True, when you visit a jobsite, you may have an increased risk for claims of site safety. But that risk (which is largely manageable) should be weighed against another — and bigger — issue. When you design a project, you assume the associated liability, whether or not you visit the project. In avoiding observation, you forfeit the opportunity to satisfy yourself that construction is proceeding as it should. No matter how detailed or near perfect your plans are, even the best contractor can't build from them without some degree of interpretation. It is far better to protect your interests and those of your client by being there to provide clarification and interpretation. (See *Jobsite Safety*.)

Even if your client does agree to construction observation services, some client-written contracts contain onerous language that needs judicious editing. For instance, a client contract may state that the purpose of construction observation is to "guard the owner against all defects" or to "assure complete conformance with the contract documents." Both phrases can be construed as warranties or guarantees. Agreeing to such overstated provisions furnishes your client with an additional cause of action against you (for breach of warranty) and jeopardizes your professional liability insurance coverage. (See *Certifications, Guarantees and Warranties* for further discussion.)

Also troublesome are limited services agreements in which you are asked to provide only limited construction observation services. Your client may ask you to provide project observation on an on-call basis, meaning your services may or may not be requested. You will probably not be asked to visit the project often enough to perform adequate observation. Most likely, you'll only be called after a major problem develops, sometimes with a suggestion that you bring along your checkbook. Certainly, there is no assurance that you will be called upon at critical stages in the work. (See *Design Without Construction Administration* for more information.)

Finally, when construction observation is performed, some consultants assign their less experienced people, who may not have adequate training in proper field procedures. Perhaps worse, sometimes people are sent to observe construction outside their own fields of expertise — an electrical engineer, for example, to look over a mechanical system. A related problem arises when subconsultants are not retained to observe construction of their design work. (See *Subconsultants*.)

THE SOLUTION

The best approach may be to offer your client expanded construction phase services — full-time, on-site project representative services — as a first option. (The AIA document B352-1993 and the EJCDC 1910-1 (1996 edition), Exhibit D, are good starting points for developing such a workscope.) This client is provided with a choice: accept expanded services and increase the odds of discovering defects in the work, or choose observation at "appropriate intervals" only, with a corresponding reduction in the level of on-site representation on the client's behalf. Many firms consider this an opportunity to offer expanded services. Explain the trade-offs between levels of service and quality and fee — and insist that your client make the decision. If your client chooses not to go with full-time project representative services, document your offer and the client's refusal.

We believe that every architectural or engineering services agreement should include the scope and fees necessary to provide adequate construction observation services as a part of Basic Services. If your client is unwilling to accept expanded services, you should, as always, settle for nothing less than a level of service you believe will provide reasonable protection from defects before they develop into major problems. Your contract should clearly describe the extent of these services. State what it is you will and will not be responsible for when providing observation and describe the purpose of your site visits. You'll also want to set forth the contractor's responsibilities regarding performance, safety and quality. The following sample provision describes a basic level of construction observation:

CONSTRUCTION OBSERVATION

The Consultant shall visit the site at intervals appropriate to the stage of construction, or as otherwise agreed to in writing by the Client and the Consultant, in order to observe the progress and quality of the Work completed by the Contractor. Such visits and observation are not intended to be an exhaustive check or a detailed inspection of the Contractor's work but rather are to allow the Consultant, as an experienced professional, to become generally familiar with the Work in progress and to determine, in general, if the Work is proceeding in accordance with the Contract Documents.

Based on this general observation, the Consultant shall keep the Client informed about the progress of the Work and shall endeavor to guard the Client against deficiencies in the Work.

Construction Observation

> If the Client desires more extensive project observation or full-time project representation, the Client shall request that such services be provided by the Consultant as Additional Services in accordance with the terms of this Agreement.
>
> The Consultant shall not supervise, direct or have control over the Contractor's work nor have any responsibility for the construction means, methods, techniques, sequences or procedures selected by the Contractor nor for the Contractor's safety precautions or programs in connection with the Work. These rights and responsibilities are solely those of the Contractor in accordance with the Contract Documents.
>
> The Consultant shall not be responsible for any acts or omissions of the Contractor, subcontractor, any entity performing any portions of the Work, or any agents or employees of any of them. The Consultant does not guarantee the performance of the Contractor and shall not be responsible for the Contractor's failure to perform its Work in accordance with the Contract Documents or any applicable laws, codes, rules or regulations.

It is also important that the General Conditions of the construction contract reflect your duties and responsibilities accurately. If your contract says you will not perform construction phase services, make certain the General Conditions also state this fact to avoid confusion and unwarranted assumptions on the part of the owner and contractor about your duties and your liability.

Note that some professionals think the word *observation* is too weak and may convey the image of a "drive-by" site visit. For this reason, the 1997 edition of the AIA B141 deleted the word *observation* and substituted the title "Evaluations of the Work."

On the other hand, it is crucial that you avoid the words *inspect* and *supervise* in your agreement and workscope and in all your correspondence, notes and logs. Unfortunately, a layperson may believe that an "inspector" will examine things in detail and will uncover each and every error, unsafe condition and violation of law. (See **Inspection** for more information.) The term *supervise* may imply control of the contractor, his or her employees and the jobsite — which would have serious liability implications. Make every reasonable effort to delete these terms in reference to your services. If your client is determined to use them, you should insist on defining these words in a Definitions section of your contract. (See **Definitions**.)

Another word you should avoid when describing the frequency of your project visits is *periodic*, which, according to the dictionary, means "at regular intervals." Unless you intend to visit regularly — once a day or once a week — even if your presence is not required, don't agree to periodic visits.

To keep from making any inadvertent guarantees in your agreement when you are describing the purpose of your visits to the site, delete or modify phrases like *shall protect* or *guard the client against defects* or *ensure that the Work is in strict compliance with the Contract Documents* or similar language. Use less binding language such as "shall *endeavor* to guard," which is not an outright warranty and implies you will use reasonable efforts or will attempt to protect the client. (See **Certifications, Guarantees and Warranties**.)

Almost as important as appropriate contractual protection and a comprehensive scope of services is the effort you put into performing construction observation. Develop a field manual that sets forth procedures and protocols for site observation. Assign qualified field personnel and make certain they are properly trained and equipped to do the job. (See **Exhibit 5** for other loss prevention pointers.)

If the client refuses to allow you to do construction observation or other appropriate construction phase services, make certain that you get adequate contractual protection. (See **Design Without Construction Administration** for a sample paragraph.)

SEE ALSO:

Certifications, Guarantees and Warranties
Claims Arbiter Service
Definitions
Delays
Design Without Construction Administration
Information Provided by Others
Inspection
Jobsite Safety
Shop Drawing Review
Stop Work Authority
Subconsultants
Supplanting Another Consultant

RELEVANT STANDARD FORM AGREEMENT PROVISIONS:

AIA B141-1997:	Articles 2.6.2; 2.8
(See also: AIA B352-1993)	
EJCDC 1910-1 (1996 edition):	Exhibit A 1.05.6a&b
	Exhibit D

Exhibit 5

LOSS PREVENTION POINTS FOR CONSTRUCTION OBSERVATION

- Carefully describe your construction phase duties in your workscope — and then adhere to that workscope.

- Add a precise definition of *construction observation* to the Definitions section of your contract.

- Avoid words such as *inspect* and *supervise* in all your agreements, correspondence and documentation.

- Use your best people for construction observation, and make certain they are properly trained.

- Develop a field manual with proper procedures and require that your field personnel follow these procedures. (The *PLAN Project Representative's Manual* is a good model to build upon. See **Further Reading**.)

- If you are the prime consultant, require all your subconsultants to observe their portion of the project.

- Keep proper documentation of each project visit by using logs, videotapes, reports and photographs.

- Caution field representatives not to give direction to contractor personnel on construction means, methods, sequences or any safety procedures. That's the contractor's responsibility.

- Make sure your client is kept informed about the progress of the project. Provide copies of your project visit reports to your client and all other appropriate parties.

- Work to promote good relationships and communications with the contractors — they may be more likely to tell you if there are problems.

INSPECTION

The dictionary tells us that to "inspect" something is to examine it carefully and critically for flaws. In the construction industry, an inspection is a comprehensive, detailed examination of the work in progress. It is a common misconception, however, that the purpose of a consultant's project visit is to "inspect" the contractor's work to uncover any code violations or construction defects. Because the words *inspection* and *construction observation* have been widely and inaccurately used to describe the same function, they are often confused. Many clients — and more than a few juries — don't understand that, unlike inspection, construction observation is generally quite limited in scope and purpose.

There are times when a client truly needs the services of an inspector — and many of these services can be provided by architects or engineers. A client may want a full-time resident inspector on a complex construction project, or may need a building inspected before purchase to fulfill a lender's requirements or to determine whether it is safe for occupancy following an earthquake or other disaster. Sometimes a consultant contracts with a municipality as a city building inspector. Sometimes special inspection services are mandated by municipal or state code to assure the integrity of certain structural elements of a building. Whatever the nature of the inspection, however, these are higher-risk services and require special contractual protection.

THE PROBLEM

The words *inspect* and *inspection* imply a much more detailed examination than mere observation of a project. Inappropriate use of these words in contracts, correspondence or even in conversation can establish obligations you never intended. A layperson may believe that an "inspector" should uncover each and every defect, unsafe condition and violation of law. If you had unknowingly misused the word *inspect*, it could be alleged you are responsible for any defects that were not discovered. In fact, agreeing to provide inspection services raises the standard of care to which you must perform. The liability implications are immense. What's more, if you are "inspecting" a project, it also could be claimed you failed to detect unsafe conditions on the site — and you could be held responsible, at least in part, for workers' injuries. (Refer to *Jobsite Safety*.)

Inspection

A simple "walk-through inspection" of a building for lenders, potential buyers or for owners requiring a survey under ADA legislation may seem straightforward enough. The time spent and the corresponding fee received hardly seem to merit the trouble of getting a written contract. But if a financial decision or safety determination is based — even partially — on your inspection report and troubles surface later, your losses could amount to hundreds of times your fee.

THE SOLUTION

Unless you intend to provide actual inspection services, you should avoid the use of the word *inspect* to describe your basic observation role. If a client-written contract contains the offending word, delete it and replace it with *observation*. If that is not possible, carefully define *inspect* in the Definitions or Scope of Services section of your contract to describe exactly what service you will provide. (You may want to refer to the current AIA document B352 for a well-defined scope of services for resident inspectors or project representatives. Also refer to *Construction Observation*, *Definitions* and *Scope of Services*.)

If your client asks you to provide inspection services, first determine if he or she truly wants an inspector or is misinterpreting the term and really intends a normal level of contract administration and project visits instead. If a full-time, on-site inspector is what is required, your client should contract with a qualified inspector directly. The vicarious liability you could assume for subcontracting with an inspector is significant and should be avoided. If you must retain an inspector, however, get an indemnification from your client and make certain the inspector is adequately insured. You should also consider this greater risk when negotiating your fee. (See *Indemnities*, *Insurance* and *Subconsultants* for related discussions.)

Whatever the purpose, when inspecting existing buildings, always make sure that you have a provision that protects you in the event unexpected hazardous materials are discovered. (See *Hazardous Materials* for recommended language.) We also recommend that you include a clause that addresses your right to rely upon information given to you concerning the condition of the building. (See *Information Provided by Others* for a sample clause.)

BUILDING INSPECTION SERVICES

Whatever the inspection is of — no matter how small — insist on some form of written contract. Even if it's a quick "walk-through" building survey, at least obtain a signed letter of agreement or a short-form contract. The Coalition of American Structural Engineers (CASE), the AIA and EJCDC all have limited services standard form agreements. (Refer to *Further Reading* for information on contacting these organizations.)

When providing visual, on-site inspection services of an existing building — whether to verify compliance with codes, to check the integrity of a building for potential lenders or to ascertain the quality of a structure for prospective buyers — you will be making certain assumptions about the building and its condition. Without extensive invasive and destructive testing, you cannot know certain facts about the building. Therefore, you should protect yourself with a strong contractual provision. If you are not using a standard contract, such as one from CASE or AIA, you might, at the very least, consider this language in a letter agreement:

BUILDING INSPECTION SERVICES

Because evaluation of the existing structure requires that certain assumptions be made regarding existing conditions, and because some of these assumptions cannot be verified without expending additional sums of money or destroying otherwise adequate or serviceable portions of the building, the Client agrees, to the fullest extent permitted by law, to indemnify and hold harmless the Consultant, its officers, directors, employees and subconsultants (collectively, Consultant) against all damages, liabilities or costs, including reasonable attorneys' fees and defense costs, arising out of or in any way connected with this Project, excepting only those damages, liabilities or costs attributable to the sole negligence or willful misconduct by the Consultant.

EMERGENCY INSPECTION SERVICES

Only a few states have enacted "Good Samaritan" laws to provide some protection to design or environmental professionals who, at the request of a public agency, inspect buildings to determine if they are safe for occupancy in the event of a natural disaster. Check with your attorney and your professional society. If your state does not yet have such a law, you and your professional society should urge your state legislators to pass one. In the meantime, protect yourself by contract. (See *Emergency Services* and the sample Emergency Services Agreement in *Appendix I*).

MUNICIPAL INSPECTION SERVICES

Many states have statutes that provide immunity and defense to their public employees when they are sued for damages arising in the course and scope of their duties, even if they were negligent. If your firm provides contract municipal services as a building inspector, public works engineer or other type of building official, you can attempt to wrap yourself in whatever municipal immunity might be available. You also might want to use such phrases as "appointed by the City" and "authorized representative of the City" in your contracts and reference appropriate sections of the Uniform Building Code pertaining to the duties and powers of a building official. The following example could be inserted in the agreement between you and a municipality for whom you provide contract professional services:

MUNICIPAL INSPECTION SERVICES

The Consultant, acting as the City Building Inspector *(or other applicable title)*, **when acting in good faith in the discharge of its duties, shall not thereby render itself liable personally and is, to the maximum extent permitted by law, relieved from all liability for any damage that may accrue to persons or property by reason of any act or omission in the discharge of its duties. Any suit brought against the Consultant because of the acts or omissions performed by it in the enforcement of any provisions of the City Building Code shall be defended by the legal department of the City until final termination of the proceedings. The Consultant shall be entitled to all defenses and municipal immunities that are, or would be, available to the City if the same services were provided by City employees.**

SPECIAL INSPECTORS

Finally, if you are to provide services as a Special Inspector to review certain structural components of a building (such as special welding, concrete or connection details), there are specific contracts available for such services. (CASE publishes one such contract for Special Inspection Services. See *Additional Resources*.)

SEE ALSO:

Appendix I
Americans with Disabilities Act
Construction Observation
Definitions
Emergency Services
Excluded Services
Hazardous Materials
Indemnities
Information Provided by Others
Insurance
Jobsite Safety

Scope of Services
Stop Work Authority
Subconsultants

Relevant standard form agreement provisions:

AIA B141-1997:	Articles 1.2.2.5; 2.6.6.1; 2.6.6.2; 2.8.1.3; 2.8.1.4
EJCDC 1910-1 (1996 edition):	Exhibit A 1.05A.2; A 1.05A.16&18
	Exhibit B 2.01P

III-18

JOBSITE SAFETY

Among the most dangerous of all industrial workplaces, construction project sites are hazardous for consultants, too. Roughly one in every ten liability claims against architects and engineers is related to safety on the site. Moreover, the Secretary of Labor, through the Occupational Safety and Health Administration (OSHA), increasingly seeks to impose substantial and uninsurable fines on architects and engineers for construction worker injuries. Jobsite safety is such a vital concern that it is imperative that consultants understand the issues thoroughly. They must be able to explain them to their clients and, more importantly, conduct their practices prudently by training their field employees and avoiding contract language that could make them responsible for safety on the site.

The courts are continually looking at the issue of jobsite safety. Two recent cases are worth noting. In one, the structural engineer was telephoned by the contractor for the engineer's opinion about the adequacy of temporary shoring supporting a concrete deck. A subsequent collapse resulted in injuries to several construction workers — and a claim by OSHA that the engineer was responsible for enforcement of the federal construction safety regulations, although the contract disclaimed responsibility for jobsite safety and means and methods of construction. The court ultimately held the engineer was not responsible because the contractor, not the engineer, had physical control and contractual responsibility for activities on the jobsite.[1] One telephone conversation was not enough to hold the engineer responsible for the construction means and methods.

In a more recent New Jersey case, a state court held a civil engineer's inspector responsible in the death of a contractor's employee resulting from the collapse of a trench that was not properly shored. Even though the engineer's contract also disclaimed responsibility for means, methods and safety, it was found that the engineer's inspector was present at the site and observed the collapse, had observed a similar collapse only a week before and had taken no action to protect the worker in a situation of *imminent* danger. Although the inspector claimed it was not his job, the court found otherwise, noting that the inspector had both the opportunity and ability to alleviate the risk of harm.[2]

---

[1] <u>Secretary of Labor v. Simpson Gumpertz</u>, 3 F.3d 1 (1st Cir. 1993)
[2] <u>Carvalho v. Toll Brothers & Developers</u>, 143 N.J. 565, 675 A.2d 209 (N.J. 1996)

Jobsite Safety

What these seemingly contradictory rulings appear to mean is that although it is important to have contractual protections, a consultant cannot ignore his or her duty as a licensed professional — or a human being — to step forward in the face of imminent threats to life or safety.

THE PROBLEM

When a contractor's employee is injured, he or she generally cannot sue the contractor and must accept as sole remedy from that employer the state-mandated workers compensation benefits. Of course, these benefits rarely cover full medical costs and lost time and are certainly lower than awards one might hope for through successful litigation against a third party. This inequity can set into motion a search for "deep pockets" and an attempt to impose responsibility on a source other than the employer — in other words, you.

But jobsite safety is not just an issue for employees of the contractor. Subcontractor employees, invitees, passers-by, even trespassers can be exposed to hazards on the site. And virtually anyone who is injured in connection with a project may make claim against the contractor, the owner and, once again, you.

Jobsite safety normally — and rightly — is the primary responsibility of the general contractor. The contractor has actual (physical) control of his or her employees and of the site, and is the overall coordinator of the Work. Assuming any responsibility for safety programs and safety procedures, either by contract or by your actions, can have serious economic consequences. Certainly, design-build and construction management projects may change your responsibilities and roles, and increase your liability for safety on the site, but this *Guide* is primarily focused on contract issues involved with traditional delivery projects. (See *Construction Management* and *Design-Build* for more information.)

THE SOLUTION

You must do everything you can to ensure that nothing in your contract or your actions implies that you will in any way assume jobsite safety responsibilities. Under no circumstances should you accept a contract clause that makes you responsible for any losses or injuries that occur at the jobsite. Such clauses should be considered **Deal Breakers**.

Carefully negotiate agreements so that they accurately reflect the responsibilities you intend to assume. Make it clear to the owner and the contractor that you are not responsible in any way for the means, methods, sequence, procedures, techniques or scheduling of construction activities — nor for jobsite safety. These duties belong with the general contractor, who has control of the jobsite and responsibility for constructing the project. Delete any language in an owner-drafted agreement that calls for your "supervision" on a jobsite. (See *Construction Observation* for more information.) Likewise, do not accept any extreme contract language that calls for you to "assure strict compliance" with plans and specifications. Your observation of the Work is meant only to determine general conformance of the contractor's work with the design concept and information contained in the contract documents.

(See *Stop Work Authority* for a related discussion.) If you are not using AIA or EJCDC standard agreements, consider the following clause:

JOBSITE SAFETY

Neither the professional activities of the Consultant, nor the presence of the Consultant or its employees and subconsultants at a construction/project site, shall relieve the General Contractor of its obligations, duties and responsibilities including, but not limited to, construction means, methods, sequence, techniques or procedures necessary for performing, superintending and coordinating the Work in accordance with the contract documents and any health or safety precautions required by any regulatory agencies. The Consultant and its personnel have no authority to exercise any control over any construction contractor or its employees in connection with their work or any health or safety programs or procedures. The Client agrees that the General Contractor shall be solely responsible for jobsite safety, and warrants that this intent shall be carried out in the Client's contract with the General Contractor. The Client also agrees that the Client, the Consultant and the Consultant's subconsultants shall be indemnified by the General Contractor and shall be made additional insureds under the General Contractor's policies of general liability insurance.

As noted in the provision, have the client make sure you are named (along with your client and your subconsultants) under the general contractor's general liability policy. This allows you to tender back to the contractor any claims from an injured worker in the event you are named in a jobsite injury suit. In addition, you should ensure the client has a provision in the General Conditions to the construction contract requiring the contractor to indemnify your client, your subconsultants and you for any claims arising from the performance of the contractor and the subcontractors. It is important that you consult with knowledgeable legal counsel and your professional liability insurance specialist to develop such language and to make certain it is insurable and enforceable in your jurisdiction.

When you and your client develop your scope of work, carefully define your field or construction phase services to avoid inadvertently assuming responsibility for site safety, especially if you are offering full-time resident representatives or expanded field services. (See *Scope of Services*.)

Watch out for overreaching indemnity language from your client that seeks to have you indemnify for "any and all damages or claims that arise from or in connection with the project" or "in connection with your services." Again, this broad language could have you inadvertently assuming jobsite safety responsibilities (along with other horrendous liabilities). (See *Indemnities*.)

Finally, you and your employees must work cautiously and safely, especially on or about a project site. Develop a field manual for your project representatives that establishes standard procedures to be followed if they observe an unsafe condition on a project site. Reinforce these procedures by requiring that your field personnel receive periodic training, and be certain to insist on adequate documentation of your project representative's visits to the construction site. Finally, field personnel should be informed on a project-specific basis as to the limitations of their authority and involvement with respect to safety-related issues, based on your workscope and specific contract terms for each project.

SEE ALSO:

Certifications, Guarantees and Warranties
Construction Management
Construction Observation
Design-Build
Indemnities
Inspection
Insurance
Scope of Services
Stop Work Authority

RELEVANT STANDARD FORM AGREEMENT PROVISIONS:

AIA B141-1997:	Articles 2.6.2.1; 2.6.2.5; 2.6.4.1
EJCDC 1910-1 (1996 edition):	Article 6.01I&J

RECORD DOCUMENTS

Design and environmental professionals are often required to provide what used to be called "as-built" drawings and "corrected specifications" at the completion of a project to depict what was actually constructed. Clients may want to use these documents for facility maintenance or future remodeling of the structure. Whatever the ultimate intended purpose, the consultant must make clear that such documents are compiled by the consultant based on information supplied by the contractor — information that is unverified, unverifiable and, in some cases, unreliable.

THE PROBLEM

Clients often do not realize that Record Documents are created from input over which you have no control. And while consultants bemoan the confusion, they continue to add to the problem by calling such documents *as-builts*. To an unsophisticated owner or a jury, the term "as-built" can only mean "as it was built" — or why would consultants call it that?

In addition, some clients want your Record Documents on CADD files. But electronic files are unsuitable for archival purposes because they will deteriorate over time. (See *CADD/Electronic Files* for a discussion and sample contract clauses.)

THE SOLUTION

Be sure your client understands the limitations of Record Documents and just how they are compiled. Refrain from using the term *as-built* drawings, a phrase that tends to imply "plans without error." Stress instead *Record Document*s, a term that is more accurate and can help reduce misunderstandings. Use it in all your contracts, correspondence and drawing stamps.

Some firms offer to provide Record Documents to their clients; some do not. Some include provision of Record Documents in their basic services; others consider it an additional service. EJCDC documents call for it as an Additional Service and require the client's prior written authorization. The 1997 AIA documents make it an Optional Additional Service, which a client can request, if desired.

Record Documents

Many firms feel it is more appropriate for the general contractor to prepare (and take responsibility for) Record Documents — especially if they have not provided normal on-site construction observation services. If you are to provide the Record Documents, make certain that in the General Conditions the client and the contractor understand their duty to provide you with complete and accurate information on the location of all work and any deviations from your drawings and specs. (See *Information Provided by Others* for further discussion.) Make sure your agreement reflects the source of and responsibility for information provided by others. Consider the following:

RECORD DOCUMENTS

Upon completion of the Work, the Consultant shall compile for and deliver to the Client a reproducible set of Record Documents based upon the marked-up record drawings, addenda, change orders and other data furnished by the Contractor. These Record Documents will show significant changes made during construction. Because these Record Documents are based on unverified information provided by other parties, which the Consultant shall assume will be reliable, the Consultant cannot and does not warrant their accuracy.

As an additional precaution, make sure each page of your Record Documents bears a warning stamped onto it. Such a stamp could read:

WARNING

These Record Documents have been prepared based on information provided by others. The Consultant has not verified the accuracy and/or completeness of this information and shall not be responsible for any errors or omissions that may be incorporated as a result of erroneous information provided by others.

There are some alternative solutions. You can delete altogether the Record Documents provision from a client-developed agreement but use your warning stamp on individual sheets of record plans and specifications.

If you need to soften the contract language, include an explanation of Record Documents in the Definitions section of your agreement instead. (See *Definitions*.) You could strengthen the contract clause by including an indemnification in addition to your stamped warnings on the Record Documents. (See *Indemnities*.) You could also reword your Information Provided by Others clause to add a reference to Record Documents.

SEE ALSO:

CADD/Electronic Files
Definitions
Indemnities
Information Provided by Others
Renovation/Remodeling

RELEVANT STANDARD FORM AGREEMENT PROVISIONS:

AIA B141-1997:	Article 2.8.3.20
EJCDC 1910-1 (1996 edition):	Exhibit A 2.01A.18

III-26

REQUESTS FOR INFORMATION

An engineer we know says that during the construction phase of a project he sometimes feels like a defensive cornerback in a strange game of football. "It's the fourth quarter, we've played defense for 55 minutes, and the offense has thrown a 'Hail Mary' pass almost every single down," he sighs. "On each play we have to cover the split end and run down the ball until the whistle blows. And even if we intercept or hold on downs, we have to give the ball back."

It's easy to see why he feels that way. During a construction project, a design or environmental professional has to scramble to respond to a constant barrage of requests for information (RFIs) from the contractor, all the while facing a tight schedule and very high stakes.

Granted, the RFI process is a normal and necessary element of the construction phase of a project. It allows the consultant to clarify the construction documents by providing answers to reasonable questions from the contractor. When used by competent and well-meaning parties for its intended purpose, the procedure works very well.

Unnecessary RFIs are another story. Commonly, these result from such factors as incomplete or poorly coordinated documents, product substitutions (see *Substitutions* for more information) or inadequate staffing by the contractor. But far more ominous is the contractor who intentionally abuses the RFI process in order to pave the way for claims for extras and delays.

THE PROBLEM

Although valid RFIs are a part of every construction project, many a contractor will generate them at the drop of a hard hat, often when a simple perusal of the construction documents and other available data would reveal the necessary information. This is an attempt to shift legitimate contractor duties to the consultant — an unfair and unwelcome burden. If the contractor is in a severe time or money squeeze, he or she may look to the RFI process for financial salvation. The desperate contractor may attempt to build a case for delays and extras by issuing urgent RFIs for every reason imaginable. In so doing, the contractor buries the consultant in paper and forces him or her into "unacceptably" long response times. By the end of the project, the total number of RFIs (valid or otherwise) may reach into the hundreds or even thousands. A jury could interpret this to indicate flawed design documents and substandard performance by the consultant. Why else, the jurors will say, would the poor contractor have had to ask so many questions?

There are many reasons. And design or technical professionals and owners can sometimes be responsible. Poorly prepared documents and uncoordinated last-minute changes during the final preparation of construction documentation can cause RFIs. Unscheduled owner-generated activities, such as value engineering and scope changes at the tail end of document preparation, often lead to incomplete or poorly coordinated construction documents and can prompt valid requests for information.

Another reason can be the ineffective use of progress meetings and the failure of both the consultant and the contractor to establish an open line of communications to ask questions and resolve problems.

But there are also contractor-caused RFIs. If the contractor's key staff is inadequate, under qualified or frequently reassigned, the consultant is somehow expected to pick up the slack. When there are frequent turnovers, new contractor employees may lack the continuity and the historical perspective to know how or where to find answers. Often, the information already shows on the construction documents. Some RFIs are requests for dimensional information that is available only through knowledge of field conditions. And some RFIs are requests for guidance in the means or methods of construction. All of these are strictly the contractor's responsibility. If the contractor had provided adequate, qualified and stable staffing, he or she wouldn't need to ask the consultant for answers.

THE SOLUTION

Is there really an answer to the RFI dilemma? Not completely, but you can substantially reduce the problem by adopting clear-cut RFI procedures backed up by the authority of your agreement. Include appropriate contract language in your agreement with your client and in the construction contract documents to focus the attention of both the client and the contractor on unnecessary RFIs. You must insist on contractor compliance with specified procedures and steadfastly require resubmittal of vague or incomplete RFIs.

Of course, your best protection is always to work with quality contractors and subcontractors, people who share the common goal of a project built on schedule, on budget and without disputes. Another important safeguard is a carefully coordinated, high-quality set of construction documents. You need to make certain that you allot adequate time for the proper preparation and coordination of your design documents.

Make sure there is open communication between your project representative and the contractor's staff. Many minor issues can be resolved more quickly in progress meetings and during site visits than by the more formal and time-consuming RFI procedure.

That's all fine in theory, of course, but in the real world, you may be faced with RFI excesses and abuse every day. Repeat after us: *an RFI should be issued only when information is either missing from the construction documents or is ambiguous.* These requests should specify which drawings and details need clarification and exactly what information is required. Ideally, a formal RFI would be the last measure taken by the contractor — issued only after the contractor's reasonable review of the construction documents and field conditions fails to come up with an answer. Many questions can be answered with a phone call or jobsite conversation between the superintendent and your field representative; without resorting to the RFI process. (As always, though, your staff should keep careful records of all such conversations.)

It is not asking too much to require the contractor to demonstrate that an honest effort was made to look for answers and work out a solution based on the information shown. This effort should include working with its subs to resolve coordination or cross-trade issues. The contractor should be required to prioritize RFIs and to present them in a timely and organized manner to facilitate your response.

To address these issues, recommend that the client add a provision to the contract documents that requires a thorough review of the construction documents and field conditions by the contractor prior to submitting an RFI. For example:

REQUESTS FOR CLARIFICATION OR INTERPRETATION

The Contractor may, after exercising due diligence to locate required information, request from the Consultant clarification or interpretation of the requirements of the Contract Documents. The Consultant shall, with reasonable promptness, respond to such Contractor's requests for clarification or interpretation. However, if the information requested by the Contractor is apparent from field observations, is contained in the Contract Documents or is reasonably inferable from them, the Contractor shall be responsible to the Client for all reasonable costs charged by the Consultant to the Client for the Additional Services required to provide such information.

In your own agreement with the client, add a provision regarding fees for additional services for responding to RFIs if adequate information already exists on the construction documents or is apparent and available to a reasonably competent contractor by observation of field conditions.

Requests for Information

REQUESTS FOR CLARIFICATION OR INTERPRETATION

The Consultant shall provide, with reasonable promptness, written responses to requests from the Contractor for clarification and interpretation of the requirements of the Contract Documents. Such services shall be provided as part of the Consultant's Basic Services. However, if the Contractor's requests for information, clarification or interpretation are, in the Consultant's professional opinion, for information readily apparent from reasonable observation of field conditions or a review of the Contract Documents, or are reasonably inferable therefrom, the Consultant shall be entitled to compensation for Additional Services in accordance with Section _____, Compensation, for the Consultant's time spent responding to such requests.

A knowledgeable client is a big part of the solution. Your clients must understand that they will encounter unexpected costs due to changes during construction. Encourage the client to plan for these extra costs by setting up a contingency allowance. (See *Contingency Fund* for more information and a sample clause.)

Your client also needs to understand that his or her own eleventh-hour decisions to have value engineering or make a sudden major change to the program requirements can adversely impact the documentation process. Your contract should provide for these by calling for additional compensation and time for the completion and the coordination of all documents after such disruptions.

Make clear to the client that the contractor is obliged to adequately staff the job with enough people who are qualified to properly plan, schedule, direct, monitor and perform the construction. You (and the client) have a right to rely on the contractor to staff and carry out the project competently when you compute your fee and schedule for construction administration services.

In your agreement with the client, you may want to address the additional services that you will provide in the event the contractor fails to provide adequate staff or carry out the Work properly. Consider the following sample clause:

ADDITIONAL SERVICES[3]

The Consultant shall provide, without advance authorization from the Client, the Additional Service(s) listed below. The Consultant shall notify the Client promptly in writing upon providing such services:

1. Services made necessary by the default of the Contractor or Client under the Contract for Construction or by deficiencies, defects or delays in the Work by the Contractor.

2. {Other Additional Services items to be covered.}

Ideally, contractors for either bid or negotiated jobs should be carefully pre-qualified. A contractor's reputation for staffing jobs with trained and experienced key personnel should count heavily in his or her favor. If the contractor cannot be pre-selected because of procurement laws applying to public work, both you and the owner need to be aware of the problems (and costs) associated with selecting the contractor solely on the basis of lowest bid. When working with a low-bid contractor, you will probably experience higher costs and longer schedules due to the additional and more experienced field personnel you'll need to assign to such projects, as well as the additional documentation you'll need to provide for the contractor's inadequate staff.

Finally, remember, you also have an obligation in the RFI process: to respond to valid RFIs in a reasonable time and to keep accurate and complete records (date in/date out and response given) as part of the project file. By obligating the contractor to perform the work as described in the contract documents, by having an RFI submittal form and procedures, and by responding to RFIs in a careful and timely manner, you can greatly reduce your exposure to claims for delays or extras resulting from misuse of the RFI process. If you believe the contractor is papering the project with invalid RFIs, tell the contractor, citing his or her obligations, when you return the submittal form.

SEE ALSO:

Contingency Fund
Shop Drawing Review
Substitutions
Value Engineering

---

[3] *The 1997 edition of the AIA standard forms of agreement has changed the term "Additional Services" to "Changes in Service."*

Requests for Information

RELEVANT STANDARD FORM AGREEMENT PROVISIONS:

AIA B141-1997: Articles 1.3.3; 2.6.1.5
EJCDC 1910-1 (1996 edition): Exhibit A 1.05.8

SHOP DRAWING REVIEW

Of all the design professional's duties, the review of shop drawings and submittals is one of the most demanding and tedious. Perhaps that's why it is also a task that is often not performed well — sometimes with serious consequences.

THE PROBLEM

Because today's construction process is so complex, shop drawings have become a major source of claims against architects and engineers. These claims can result from procedural failures (delays) and technical failures (not catching discrepancies or errors in details).

In truth, the fundamental problem is often that none of the parties involved (owner, contractor, as well as consultant) understand exactly where the responsibility for shop drawings should lie. But many architects and engineers continue to contractually assume levels of responsibility beyond those intended or required, review drawings unnecessarily or perform aspects of drawing review rightly the responsibility of the contractor. The problem is magnified when consultants give insufficient attention to the timely processing of shop drawings or assign the job to under-qualified people. Lack of precision in contract terms, inadequate internal procedures and failure to treat submittal review as a critically important task can prove costly to a design firm.

THE SOLUTION

One school of thought holds that cautious wording on your shop drawing stamp and in your agreement can somehow lessen the risk you face when you review shop drawings. The reality is that no matter how carefully you and your attorney craft your stamp and contract language, you will still be held to the professional standard of care; you are obligated to use the reasonable degree of skill and judgment in performing the review function that other professionals would have used under similar circumstances. (See *Standard of Care*.) Conservative language on your shop drawing stamp may not protect you. If you call for a submittal, then review and return it to the contractor without objection, a court may well say you "approved" it regardless of the language you use on your stamp.

Your best course, therefore, is to precisely define your role in the review process and to establish and follow strict procedures for handling submittals. Consider the following suggestions:

1. Seek to limit your responsibilities by appropriate contract language. Clearly and precisely describe your duties in reviewing submittals. Spell out, too, those items for which you are not responsible but that are instead the contractor's duty, such as dimensions, gauges, quantities, weights and construction means and methods. (See *Jobsite Safety*.) This language may need to be customized to your practice and the particular project:

SHOP DRAWING REVIEW

The Consultant shall review and approve or take other appropriate action on the Contractor submittals, such as shop drawings, product data, samples and other data, which the Contractor is required to submit, but only for the limited purpose of checking for conformance with the design concept and the information shown in the Construction Documents. This review shall not include review of the accuracy or completeness of details, such as quantities, dimensions, weights or gauges, fabrication processes, construction means or methods, coordination of the work with other trades or construction safety precautions, all of which are the sole responsibility of the Contractor. The Consultant's review shall be conducted with reasonable promptness while allowing sufficient time in the Consultant's judgment to permit adequate review. Review of a specific item shall not indicate that the Consultant has reviewed the entire assembly of which the item is a component. The Consultant shall not be responsible for any deviations from the Construction Documents not brought to the attention of the Consultant in writing by the Contractor. The Consultant shall not be required to review partial submissions or those for which submissions of correlated items have not been received.

---

2. Identify shop drawings by type and define for the contractor exactly which ones you will review. It may be contrary to your nature, but don't yield to the temptation to review more drawings than necessary to protect the integrity of your design. Of course,

this will depend on the type of project and your own professional judgment. If you receive uncalled-for submittals from the contractor, they should be stamped "Not Required for Review" and returned at once.

3. Give the contractor a list of the submittals you will require prior to construction. Require the contractor to provide a schedule of submittals and insist the contractor adhere to it. Inform the contractor in writing when delays in submittal cause delay in your processing. But as the contractor is expected to stick to the submittal schedule, you, too, must abide by your promised turnaround time. Allow yourself sufficient leeway to perform your own review and return the submittals according to your promised schedule.

4. Insist that the contractor do his or her job — that all contractor and subcontractor submittals be reviewed and approved by the contractor before being sent to you. Never accept submittals directly from a subcontractor or vendor. If you believe the contractor has not reviewed a submittal carefully but has merely "rubber-stamped" it, and if it contains obvious errors, return it immediately with a note of explanation and insist that it be properly checked. Keep a record of the errors or discrepancies you find to facilitate your review of the resubmittal.

5. Assign people who are experienced and well qualified to check shop drawings. Insist on a thorough review. You are generally responsible for checking for conformance with the overall design concept. Is the shop drawing compatible with the rest of the design? Does it fit and is it coordinated with the requirements of that portion of the overall project designed by you? If possible, have another qualified member of your firm double-check the review prior to returning the shop drawing to the contractor. On the other hand, don't assume responsibility that is not yours. For example, if you have not agreed to check dimensions, don't do so.

6. Establish within your firm a logging, tracking and follow-up system for shop drawing and submittal processing — and appoint reliable people to maintain it. Document each step of the process in writing, using standardized logs, transmittals and checklists.

7. Use a shop drawing stamp to indicate you have reviewed the submittals. (Two examples follow in *Exhibit 6*.) Whatever language you choose, be certain it is consistent with your agreement with your client and with the General Conditions of the construction contract.

8. Insist on a clause in the General Conditions of the construction contract that requires the contractor to provide you with written notice of deviations of any type from the requirements of the contract or from the Construction Documents. Such a clause should state that the contractor remains liable for any deviations unless you review and acknowledge such changes in writing.

9. Work with your client in advance to ensure the owner-contractor contract is consistent with the language and intent of your own agreement with the owner. Review all logs, correspondence, stamps, transmittals and miscellaneous documentation to make

certain that the language is also consistent with your agreement and the intent of all parties.

10. As a general rule, don't review shop drawings or other submittals concerning the proposed implementation of means, methods, procedures, sequences or techniques or other temporary aspects of the construction process. Those are the sole responsibility of the contractor, and review of these submittals could subject you to responsibility not normally assumed by a design professional.

SEE ALSO:

CADD/Electronic Files
Construction Observation
Delays
Inspection
Jobsite Safety
Requests for Information
Standard of Care

RELEVANT STANDARD FORM AGREEMENT PROVISIONS:

AIA B141-1997:	**Articles 2.6.4; 2.8.1.1; 2.8.2.1**
EJCDC 1910-1 (1996 edition):	**Exhibit A 1.05A.10**

Exhibit 6
Shop Drawing Stamps

❏ Reviewed ❏ Furnish as Corrected
❏ Rejected ❏ Revise and Resubmit
 ❏ Submit Specified Item

This review is only for general conformance with the design concept and the information given in the Construction Documents. Corrections or comments made on the shop drawings during this review do not relieve the contractor from compliance with the requirements of the plans and specifications. Review of a specific item shall not include review of an assembly of which the item is a component. The Contractor is responsible for: dimensions to be confirmed and correlated at the jobsite; information that pertains solely to the fabrication processes or to the means, methods, techniques, sequences and procedures of construction; coordination of the Work with that of all other trades and performing all Work in a safe and satisfactory manner.

{Name of Consulting Firm} _____

Date _____

By _____

❏ Approved ❏ Furnish as Corrected
❏ Rejected ❏ Revise and Resubmit
 ❏ Submit Specified Item

This review is only for general conformance with the design concept and the information given in the Construction Documents. Corrections or comments made on the shop drawings during this review do not relieve the contractor from compliance with the requirements of the plans and specifications. Approval of a specific item shall not include approval of an assembly of which the item is a component. The contractor is responsible for: dimensions to be confirmed and correlated at the jobsite; information that pertains solely to the fabrication processes or to the means, methods, techniques, sequences and procedures of construction; coordination of the Work with that of all other trades and performing all Work in a safe and satisfactory manner.

{Name of Consulting Firm} _____

Date _____

By _____

III-38

STOP WORK AUTHORITY

Some clients want to give the design or environmental professional the contractual authority — and responsibility — to reject the work of a contractor or to stop the work altogether if corrections are not made.

THE PROBLEM

If you take on the right to stop work, you create a substantial exposure for yourself. With the right goes a duty. Having the right to stop work can be and often is construed as having the duty to stop work. Several liability issues arise. For instance, if you have a duty to stop the work because of poor construction quality, don't you also have a duty to stop the work if jobsite safety is in question? And who is responsible for consequential damages if delays result from your stop work order?

The economic impact of stopping work on a project can be massive when you take into account all the costs of contractor mobilization, equipment expenses and delay claims. A client, contractor or subcontractor who questions the wisdom of your stop work order could very well sue you for huge costs associated with such delays.

Perhaps even more important, the contractual right to stop work is a significant factor for the courts when determining whether you might be subject to civil, criminal or OSHA penalties if a site worker is injured.

THE SOLUTION

Given everything at stake, the owner — and only the owner — should make the decision to stop work. Delete any client-provided contract clause that gives you such stop work authority. You can, however, with proper contractual protection, reject (not stop) work that does not, based on your site observations and judgment, conform to the construction documents or work plans (in the case of environmental consultants).

Be certain you have a clause in your agreement that clearly states what your responsibilities are. Consider the following example:

Stop Work Authority

REJECTION OF WORK

The Consultant shall have the authority to reject any Work that is not, in the judgment of the Consultant, in conformance with the Construction Documents or work plans. Neither this authority nor the Consultant's good-faith judgment to reject or not reject any Work shall subject the Consultant to any liability or cause of action to the Contractor, subcontractors or any other suppliers or persons performing work on this project.

If you and your attorney feel you need stronger protection, you can insert an indemnity in the agreement with your client and require your client to insert a similar provision in the owner-general contractor agreement. (See *Indemnities*.)

Bear in mind that there is always some risk involved when you reject portions of the contractor's work. However, the courts have generally upheld the authority of the consultant to reject portions of the work — so long as it is based on a good-faith professional opinion.

If you want even more protection — and many firms prefer this more conservative approach — consider changing "reject" to "recommend to the client rejection of" in the above clause. With this approach, it would be up to the client to reject the work. You can give your client all the input needed — your observations and your reasons along with your recommendations to reject portions of the work. But, remember, the right to stop work — and the awesome responsibility it entails — must remain squarely on the owner's shoulders.

SEE ALSO:

Claims Arbiter Service
Confidential Communications
Consequential Damages
Construction Observation
Delays
Indemnities
Inspection
Jobsite Safety

RELEVANT STANDARD FORM AGREEMENT PROVISIONS:

AIA B141-1997:	Article 2.6.2.5
EJCDC 1910-1 (1996 edition):	Exhibit A 1.05A.7

Part IV

Schedule, Payment and Termination

Billing and Payment
Changed Conditions
Pay-When-Paid
Retainage
Retainers
Suspension of Services
Termination
Timeliness of Performance

IV-2

BILLING AND PAYMENT

How and when the consultant will be paid usually is set forth in the agreement or in the fee proposal. The more precisely design or environmental professionals define the details of these payment terms, the greater the likelihood of prompt payment and the fewer the opportunities for fee-related disputes.

THE PROBLEM

Money issues are at the root of most disputes and claims, including those that seem to stem from technical causes. Poorly written contracts that do not set forth when payment is due, what the penalties are for late payment, and what your rights are in the event of nonpayment just invite collection problems. They also encourage liability claims, as clients attempt to avoid paying you by alleging negligence or design error. The worst — and most ironic — scenario finds you forced to sue to collect your fees from a client, only to have him or her countersue you, with little or no basis, merely as a legal maneuver to avoid payment. In the process, you lose a client, you endure the litigation process and you stand to spend some or all (or more) of what you have already earned just to collect your legitimate fees — a no-win proposition.

THE SOLUTION

Professionalism rarely offends good clients. Without compromising your client relationships or your professional stature, you can follow sound business practices and get paid for your services. Well-managed businesses, vendors with whom you trade, even your clients — all have developed and use these proven methods to collect what is rightfully owed them. You must use the tools — legal and contractual — available to you and do so in a consistent and impartial manner. Retainers, interest, collection costs, suspension, termination, lien rights, dispute resolution and litigation are implements you should have available to use as needed. Use these terms on all billings you render, including Basic Services, reimbursables and Additional Services. The advice of your attorney on how each of these can help and how they can be provided for in your agreements will be invaluable to your firm's financial health.

Billing and Payment

Develop and follow a consistent collection strategy for your firm. Consider the following sample contract provisions as building blocks or tools of the collection trade. They can be linked together, mixed-and-matched, to make as strong a collection clause as you wish to negotiate into your agreement.

SAMPLE BILLING AND PAYMENT TERMS

RETAINER. The Client shall make an initial payment of ____ dollars ($___) (retainer) upon execution of this Agreement. This retainer shall be held by the Consultant and applied against the final invoice.

PAYMENT DUE. Invoices shall be submitted by the Consultant *{monthly, bimonthly, weekly, upon completion of each phase}*, are due upon presentation and shall be considered past due if not paid within ___ (___) calendar days of the due date.

INTEREST. If payment in full is not received by the Consultant within ___ (___) calendar days of the due date, invoices shall bear interest at one-and-one-half (1.5) percent (or the maximum rate allowable by law, whichever is less) of the PAST DUE amount per month, which shall be calculated from the invoice due date. Payment thereafter shall first be applied to accrued interest and then to the unpaid principal.

COLLECTION COSTS. If the Client fails to make payments when due and the Consultant incurs any costs in order to collect overdue sums from the Client, the Client agrees that all such collection costs incurred shall immediately become due and payable to the Consultant. Collection costs shall include, without limitation, legal fees, collection agency fees and expenses, court costs, collection bonds and reasonable Consultant staff costs at standard billing rates for the Consultant's time spent in efforts to collect. This obligation of the Client to pay the Consultant's collection costs shall survive the term of this Agreement or any earlier termination by either party.

SUSPENSION OF SERVICES. If the Client fails to make payments when due or otherwise is in breach of this Agreement, the Consultant may suspend performance of services upon _____ (__) calendar days' notice to the Client. The Consultant shall have no liability whatsoever to the Client for any costs or damages as a result of such suspension caused by any breach of this Agreement by the Client. Upon payment in full by the Client, the Consultant shall resume services under this Agreement, and the time schedule and compensation shall be equitably adjusted to compensate for the period of suspension plus any other reasonable time and expense necessary for the Consultant to resume performance.

TERMINATION OF SERVICES. If the Client fails to make payment to the Consultant in accordance with the payment terms herein, this shall constitute a material breach of this Agreement and shall be cause for termination of this Agreement by the Consultant.

SET-OFFS, BACKCHARGES, DISCOUNTS. Payment of invoices shall not be subject to any discounts or set-offs by the Client, unless agreed to in writing by the Consultant. Payment to the Consultant for services rendered and expenses incurred shall be due and payable regardless of any subsequent suspension or termination of this Agreement by either party.

If your client objects to these provisions, you should seriously question his or her intent to pay you on time or to pay you at all. Carefully weigh the client credit risks before you take on the project or finalize your fee.

Still another measure you might consider is a provision that states your client's payment will be taken to mean that he or she is satisfied with your services and is unaware of any defect. (See *Defects in Service* for more information.) Consider the following example:

Billing and Payment

SATISFACTION WITH SERVICES

Payment of any invoice by the Client to the Consultant shall be taken to mean that the Client is satisfied with the Consultant's services to the date of payment and is not aware of any deficiencies in those services.

If your client tries to insert language to permit him or her to withhold fees for disputed invoices, refuse. Don't accept any client-written provision that gives the client power to withhold your fees or to make unilateral determinations of fault or of your responsibility for damages. If you must address this issue, though, you might use language similar to the following:

DISPUTED INVOICES

If the Client objects to any portion of an invoice, the Client shall so notify the Consultant in writing within ___ (___) calendar days of receipt of the invoice. The Client shall identify in writing the specific cause of the disagreement and the amount in dispute and shall pay that portion of the invoice not in dispute in accordance with the other payment terms of this Agreement. Any dispute over invoiced amounts due which cannot be resolved within ten (10) calendar days after presentation of invoice by direct negotiation between the parties shall be resolved within thirty (30) calendar days in accordance with the Dispute Resolution provision of this Agreement. Interest as stated above shall be paid by the Client on all disputed invoice amounts that are subsequently resolved in the Consultant's favor and shall be calculated on the unpaid balance from the due date of the invoice.

Note that this provision is tied to your Dispute Resolution clause. You could insert the dispute resolution method here by adding it to this clause, especially if you choose a different method of resolution for payment disputes (fast-track arbitration, for example.)

If you do agree to this type of clause, note the importance of putting definite time limits on the steps to get resolution. If you don't enforce these limits and don't have the right to suspend, resolution can get stretched out until your services are complete and you have lost your best leverage to get paid.

Additionally, you should discuss with your attorney the availability of lien rights for services by design or environmental professionals in your jurisdiction and, if available, the procedures and documents necessary to institute and enforce such rights. Usually, you should establish lien rights within a very short time of providing services, so check with your attorney and promptly follow the required procedures if you want to preserve these rights. If the client wants you to waive your lien rights, we strongly suggest you refuse to do so. If your legislature has given you this protection to secure your right to payment, why give it up?

Finally, one of the best methods many consulting firms have to ensure they get paid is to withhold submission of their documents for plan check or permit approval or for use by the client until they are fully paid. This takes some bravado to carry out but is one of the most effective collection devices available. (Refer also to the *Ownership of Instruments of Service* provision that ties any transfer of ownership rights to receipt of full payment, if that is part of your agreement.)

By using contract language that has "teeth" and by following a consistent, well-designed billing and collection system, you can minimize the risks of write-offs and slow-to-pay accounts as well as threats of retaliatory liability claims.

SEE ALSO:

Attorneys' Fees
Contingency Fund
Defects in Service
Dispute Avoidance and Resolution
Ownership of Instruments of Service
Pay-When-Paid
Retainers
Suspension of Services
Termination

RELEVANT STANDARD FORM AGREEMENT PROVISIONS:

AIA B141-1997:	Articles 1.5; 1.3.3; 1.3.9
EJCDC 1910-1 (1996 edition):	Article 4
	Exhibit C, Appendix 1&2

IV-8

CHANGED CONDITIONS

During the course of a project, conditions may become apparent that differ significantly from those assumed to exist when the workscope, fee and schedule were first developed. These conditions may require substantial additional services, may impact the schedule, may increase construction or remediation costs, may greatly increase the architect's, engineer's or environmental consultant's risk, or may even necessitate services that he or she cannot provide.

In construction contracts, owners and contractors usually address the possibility of encountering differing site conditions by incorporating remedy-granting provisions. The same should hold true for design or environmental professional service contracts.

THE PROBLEM

Some clients seem to believe that if you agree to a specific workscope, you are obligated to do anything and everything necessary to complete the project. If difficulties arise, the thinking goes, that is your problem, not your client's.

The discovery of asbestos or PCBs in a renovation project; the enactment of new codes, laws or regulations after the contract is executed; a negative development in the financial condition of the client; a switch of key client personnel involved in the project; a radical change in the nature or use of the project — all are examples of changed conditions that would adversely affect you and might cause you to reevaluate workscope, schedule, fees, risk allocation terms, or even question your continued involvement with the project. Unless the possibility of changed circumstances is discussed and provided for in the agreement with your client beforehand, the situation could easily result in misunderstandings — and litigation.

THE SOLUTION

Since your agreement cannot possibly anticipate all changes that may occur, it is important to establish a procedure for identifying and handling them. Be sure that identification involves your professional judgment and that the method of handling change is mutually agreed upon. The following clause may be effective in providing for changed conditions:

Changed Conditions

CHANGED CONDITIONS

If, during the term of this Agreement, circumstances or conditions that were not originally contemplated by or known to the Consultant are revealed, to the extent that they affect the scope of services, compensation, schedule, allocation of risks or other material terms of this Agreement, the Consultant may call for renegotiation of appropriate portions of this Agreement. The Consultant shall notify the Client of the changed conditions necessitating renegotiation, and the Consultant and the Client shall promptly and in good faith enter into renegotiation of this Agreement to address the changed conditions. If terms cannot be agreed to, the parties agree that either party has the absolute right to terminate this Agreement, in accordance with the Termination provision hereof.

If the client is reluctant to give you blanket license to call for renegotiation, explain that no design or environmental professional wants to alienate a good client or stop working on a project that is both challenging and profitable, and that you have no incentive to do so. Show your client that your contract has (or should have) a Termination clause that gives you the right to terminate the contract due to any material changes. (See *Termination* for specific language.) However, if it helps your client, you could end the second sentence in the above clause at "Agreement" and then insert the following language to include reference to your fee schedule for additional services:

> . . . enter into renegotiation of this Agreement. In establishing fees for any additional services to be performed, the Consultant shall utilize the same fee schedule already agreed upon, as shown in Exhibit ____. If terms cannot . . .

If your client is unwilling to agree to a Changed Conditions clause, ask what his or her response would be to various eventualities that may occur, such as the examples given earlier, or other situations you find particularly relevant to your project. If your client's responses are what you would hope for, suggest that this understanding be committed to writing. If your client expects you to assume the risks of unexpected changed conditions, you must seriously ask yourself if you want to work for this client. Regardless of the answer, examine your contract Termination clause closely and make sure you always have a way out should you and your client be unable to reach reasonable agreement.

SEE ALSO:

Code Compliance
Excluded Services
Hazardous Materials
Renovation/Remodeling
Scope of Services
Suspension of Services
Termination
Timeliness of Performance

RELEVANT STANDARD FORM AGREEMENT PROVISIONS:

AIA B141-1997:	Articles 1.1.6; 1.3.3; 1.5.2-3; 2.6.1.4
EJCDC 1910-1 (1996 edition):	Exhibit A 2.01A.3
	Exhibit B 2.01D

IV-12

PAY-WHEN-PAID

When one design or environmental professional is a subconsultant to another, the subconsultant may be asked to accept a Pay-When-Paid provision. Such a clause usually says that when the owner/client pays the prime consultant, then the prime will pay the subconsultant.

Pay-When-Paid clauses vary. Some will say that receipt of payment by a prime consultant from the client is a strict condition to a prime's obligation to pay the subconsultant. Other clauses may state that the prime will pay the subconsultant when paid by the client but will then provide that if payment is not received from the client, the prime will ultimately pay the sub after a stated period of time. The question remains: who will bear the risk of the owner/client not paying the prime consultant? The answer is the subject of much debate and negotiation between primes and subconsultants.

THE PROBLEM

At best, a Pay-When-Paid provision can significantly delay the receipt of a subconsultant's fees. At worst, it can preclude the subconsultant from ever collecting those fees. What happens if the owner/client goes out of business? If the prime becomes involved in a dispute with the client? If the prime is a poor bill collector or for some other reason does not receive payment? Courts generally have held that a Pay-When-Paid provision does not relieve the prime of responsibility to pay the subconsultant if his or her client defaults, unless the provision specifically and explicitly provides that if the prime does not get paid, the consultant does not get paid either.

Another subject of debate between the professions is how soon (or how long) after the prime receives payment from the owner should the prime pay the subconsultant. If the prime is perceived to be "sitting on" the cash and not remitting it promptly, the subconsultant will naturally feel abused.

THE SOLUTION

Of course, both the prime and the subconsultant want to be paid — everyone does! One solution is to delete any type of Pay-When-Paid provision and include standard payment terms in the prime/sub agreement.

Pay-When-Paid

IV-14

If, however, the prime insists on a Pay-When-Paid provision and if the subconsultant agrees to it, the subconsultant should attempt to secure an outer time limit by which the sub must be paid, whether the prime has been paid or not. Suggested language, which could be incorporated into the other Billing and Payment provisions of the prime consultant/subconsultant agreement, might read:

PAYMENT TERMS

The Subconsultant shall submit invoices monthly to the Consultant, who shall review them promptly. The Consultant shall either approve these invoices or notify the Subconsultant of any invoices not approved. The Consultant and Subconsultant shall confer and attempt to resolve such disputed invoices.

The Consultant shall promptly invoice the Client for the Subconsultant's service in accordance with the billing terms of the Consultant's agreement with the Client and shall use reasonable and diligent efforts to collect payment from the Client. The Consultant shall pay the Subconsultant within ___ (___) calendar days after receiving payment from the Client. Regardless of whether or not the Client pays the Consultant in full, the Consultant shall pay the Subconsultant for all undisputed invoices within a reasonable period of time after the completion of the Subconsultant's services under this Agreement.

If payment is not received by the Subconsultant for undisputed invoices within ten (10) calendar days after the Client pays the Consultant for such services, or within forty-five (45) calendar days after the Subconsultant submits its invoices for such services, whichever occurs first, then such invoices shall bear interest at one-and-one-half (1.5) percent (or the maximum rate allowable by law, whichever is less) of the PAST DUE amount per month, which shall be calculated from the tenth or forty-fifth day, as above, whichever occurs first. Payment to the Subconsultant shall first be applied to accrued interest and then to the unpaid principal.

Unless the prime consultant and subconsultants intend to share in the risks and rewards of working for the project owner (as in a joint venture, for instance), or unless the subconsultant has built into his or her fee a sufficient sum to cover the risk of never getting paid, the subconsultant has the right to expect to be paid within a reasonable time for professional services on behalf of the prime consultant. Banks, credit-card companies and department stores all charge something to extend credit and to cover losses due to defaulting customers. Consultants and subconsultants should do no less, whether it is factored into their fees or computed as interest for late payment.

How diligent primes are when collecting fees from their clients and how promptly they pay their consultants is a sore point between prime professionals and subconsultants. These are factors each firm must take into consideration in deciding with whom to team and what the payment terms will be.

Although it is a matter to be negotiated between primes and subconsultants, in the interests of good interprofessional relations, it is generally not advisable to require a strict "condition precedent" form of Pay-When-Paid provision. Prime consultants may very well find themselves acting as subconsultants on some future project and will not like it when the shoe is on the other foot.

SEE ALSO:

Billing and Payment
Subconsultants
Suspension of Services
Termination

RELEVANT STANDARD FORM AGREEMENT PROVISIONS:

AIA C141-1997:	Article 12.5
EJCDC 1910-10 (1985 edition):	Article 5.3.1
1910-14 (1985 edition):	Article 5.4.2

IV-16

RETAINAGE

In owner-contractor agreements, retainage is often used in lieu of a performance bond. (See *Performance Bonds*.) Retainage is usually a fixed percentage (frequently 5 to 10 percent) withheld from each payment to the contractor to ensure proper completion of the Work. Problems arise, however, when a client attempts to impose such a contractor-oriented provision on a consultant who performs a professional service rather than delivers a physical product or construction work.

THE PROBLEM

Some clients try to impose a retainage provision on their consultants. This makes no sense. Your client isn't technically qualified to judge whether or not your professional service is satisfactory and how the retainage would be used to correct deficiencies.

A contractor's work is — and should be — reviewed by someone else for correctness and degree of completion. It is usually the engineer or architect who reviews the contractor's work and recommends client approval of the contractor's payment requests. If that review reveals that significant rework is necessary and the contractor fails or refuses to correct the problems, the contractor can be dismissed and corrections can be made using the retainage withheld from his or her fee.

Your professional work is not normally reviewed by anyone else on the project. It may be safe to say that clients who demand a retainage from you have not considered how it could be applied. If the retainage is intended to offset costs resulting from your negligent performance, negligence would have to be decided first by a competent judicial forum. This is impractical. And if your client intends to use the retainage to correct *any and all* problems with your work, then the client would be attempting to hold you to perfection — a standard of performance far in excess of that required by law — and doing so without the benefit of fair legal process. You are not required to be perfect. (See *Standard of Care*.)

THE SOLUTION

Don't confuse *retainage* with *retainer*. Although there are some instances where you should insist on a *retainer* (a payment up-front) from your client to mitigate a credit risk (see

Retainage

Retainers), any contract clause requiring *retainage* from you by your client should be deleted from your agreement. If he or she persists, insist that the client identify typical scenarios indicating specifically when and how the retainage would be applied. If the client cannot do this, or if the examples are unsatisfactory, it may be best not to undertake the project. Retainage is simply not appropriate in professional service agreements.

SEE ALSO:

Billing and Payment
Performance Bonds
Retainers
Standard of Care

THERE ARE NO RELEVANT PROVISIONS IN THE AIA OR EJCDC STANDARD FORM AGREEMENTS.

Retainers

A design or environmental professional deserves to be paid promptly and in full for services he or she provides. By anticipating payment difficulties before beginning contract negotiations, a consultant can add provisions that may reduce collection problems later. One excellent option is to require a retainer from the client. While "retainage" or holdbacks imposed on the consultant by the client are inappropriate, many architects, engineers and environmental consultants feel a "retainer" deposit payment up-front from a client is not only fitting but advisable. (See *Retainage*.)

The Problem

It is not unusual to have difficulty obtaining timely payment for your services from certain types of clients. This can happen for a variety of reasons. Some clients are just slow to pay their bills. Others seem to expect that you will, in essence, finance the front-end costs of a project by forcing you to carry your accounts receivable for several months. Add in the lagtime between payroll and billing, and your firm's cash flow is easily stretched to the limit.

Some clients are often most reluctant to pay your final invoice. When a client's capital is tight, he or she may have far greater incentive to pay the contractor than to pay you. After all, the thinking goes, you have completed most of your services while the contractor has yet to finish construction and the client "needs" the contractor more than client "needs" you at that moment. Then, too, some unscrupulous clients simply choose to not pay the final bill as a unilateral way of discounting your fees.

A significant number of professional liability claims result from collection efforts. If you press a client for payment, you may get your answer in the form of a threat or even an actual lawsuit. A client who, for whatever reason, has no intention of making that last payment has a splendid justification — he or she will claim there were errors in your plans and specifications. These countercharges are often inflated and used to make your collection efforts so costly that the idea of writing off that last invoice starts to look good.

THE SOLUTION

First and most obviously, try to choose clients who have a history of paying their bills on time. If this is a new client, check his or her credit and payment history with other consultants or with a credit service. Any well-run business calls for a credit report before opening a new account, so why shouldn't yours? You can spare yourself a lot of problems later. In addition, make certain your client has realistic budget expectations, that he or she truly understands what can be achieved with the available funding and, in fact, that he or she has the necessary funds. Be particularly wary of highly speculative projects and over-leveraged clients. If the client has a history of litigation or if the budget is completely inadequate, do not hesitate to turn down the project.

If you do decide to accept the project, even in the knowledge of financial risk, there are several good reasons to try to get some (or perhaps all) of the fees paid in advance. If a client has a history of late payment, and if you want to maintain a positive cash flow, explain to your client that you need to make certain you will be paid. It is not unreasonable to ask for a partial payment before work commences and for regular payments as the project progresses. Consider requiring a retainer in an amount equal to at least two months of projected fees. Be sure to provide that the retainer be credited only against your final invoice. In this way, you will be working on the client's capital — not your own — all the way through the project.

Your contract should reflect your understanding with the appropriate language in the Billing and Payment section. Consider the sample version below:

RETAINER

The Client shall make an initial payment of _____ dollars ($____) as a retainer, upon execution of this Agreement. Upon receipt of this retainer payment, the Consultant shall commence services as provided for under this Agreement. The retainer shall be held by the Consultant and shall be applied against the final invoice. In the event the amount of the retainer exceeds the final invoice, the Consultant shall refund the balance with the final invoice. If the final invoice exceeds the retainer, the Client shall promptly remit the amount due. As services are performed, invoices will be submitted monthly by the Consultant to the Client, and are payable on receipt. *{Add additional payment terms such as provisions for interest, suspension of services, attorneys' fees and collection costs and other appropriate items.}*

If you are forced to suspend your services because your client has failed to pay you, you may choose to apply the retainer against outstanding billings. That amount could easily eat up most, if not all, of your retainer. Therefore, before you resume services, remember to require your client to replenish the full amount of the retainer. (See *Suspension of Services* for sample clause language.)

If a client's payment history concerns you but the project and the client are otherwise acceptable, or if your client is located in a country where there is a question of political stability, funding availability or currency fluctuation, resolve to work on the client's nickel whenever possible. Ask for payment up front — perhaps for all prescribed services that are approved by the client. (See *International Projects*.)

Design or environmental professionals are often reluctant to ask for a retainer. But consider this: with a retainer, you have leverage. If you are working on the client's money, and if he or she stops paying you, you can stop providing services. It is as simple as that. The retainer is your buffer, your assurance that you will be paid for your most recent services. Make sure, though, you resist the temptation to continue providing services when you are not being paid, most especially when the value of the services would amount to more than the retainer you hold. If you find yourself thinking, *Maybe, if we do a little more work, the client will come through and pay us* — stop and think again. Can you imagine a loan officer having this thought when deciding whether or not to raise the credit line of a deadbeat customer?

In addition to having a retainer provision in your contract, it is important to address other payment issues in your agreement. You need a provision that allows you to suspend or terminate your services in the event of nonpayment as well as an attorneys' fees provision. Armed with these, and your client's dollars in your pocket, you have a better chance to collect for the services you have provided.

SEE ALSO:

Attorneys' Fees
Billing and Payment
International Projects
Retainage
Suspension of Services
Termination

THERE ARE NO RELEVANT PROVISIONS IN THE AIA OR EJCDC STANDARD FORM AGREEMENTS.

IV-22

SUSPENSION OF SERVICES

There are times when a project needs to be suspended or delayed during design or construction for various reasons: client convenience, funding delays, regulatory holdups or even natural disasters or strikes.

Suspension of a contract is different from termination. Suspension keeps the basic terms and conditions of a contract in force while the duty to perform is held in abeyance for a period of time. It allows the parties to resume those duties at the point the project was suspended and continue toward completion of the contract.

If the suspension lasts for more than a few days, a consulting firm will incur extra expenses in stopping and restarting services. It may become necessary to reassign staff and reschedule other projects. There may be costs associated with not being able to proceed in the expected manner on which fees were established.

The owner and consultant need a clear understanding: how long may a suspension continue before the consultant is entitled to additional fees? For what costs is the consultant entitled to reimbursement? If the suspension is even more lengthy, at what point can the consultant terminate the contract?

On the other hand, the consultant should also have the right to suspend services for cause, especially for a client's breach of certain contract terms, such as failure to pay.

THE PROBLEM

Stop-and-start projects cause big headaches for consulting firms. If you must significantly alter your schedules and reassign personnel and facilities, you lose continuity, efficiency and profitability. A suspension could impact other projects for other clients. If a project sits suspended for a long period, memories fade, details may be lost, and it takes time to get your staff back up to speed. Unless your agreement provides for it, you may not be compensated for expenses incurred in the interruption and resumption of your services.

If there are too many stops and starts, or if the suspension goes on too long, you might not be legally entitled to terminate, absent some specific contract provision. You could find

Suspension of Services

yourself "put on hold" indefinitely or repetitively and then be expected to resume services at the snap of a client's finger under the original terms, fees and schedule. This would not only cause you economic hardship, it could be a source of liability claims. (See *Termination* for a related discussion.)

Realize, too, that if your contract has a fixed schedule or completion date, you could be held to that schedule if you do not provide for an extension of time caused by any suspension of the project. (See *Timeliness of Performance* for a discussion.)

Failure by a client to pay you is considered a breach of a material term and therefore a cause for you to terminate, but if you also want the right to suspend, you have to provide for it in your contract. You may not want to use the ultimate "hammer" of termination; you may want to be able to suspend and withhold your services in hopes of forcing the client to cure the breach but keep the contract in force. You need the right, therefore, to suspend your services without breaching the contract yourself or incurring liability for delay. Granted, if the nonpayment continues for a sufficient time after you have made demand and given proper notice of the breach, you may ultimately wish to terminate. But in the meantime, you at least want to avoid increasing your receivables. (See *Billing and Payment* and *Retainer* for related discussions and suggested contract clauses.)

THE SOLUTION

One solution is to allow your client to suspend the contract for a defined but relatively short period of time without any additional cost. For a longer suspension, you should be compensated for the expenses of interrupting and resuming your services. And, for an excessive period of client-ordered suspension, you need the option to terminate the agreement; you may need to step back and renegotiate the entire deal.

In addition, give yourself the right to suspend your services without risk or liability for delay in the event of nonpayment of your fees, or for any other breach by your client of terms you consider critical to the progress of your services. Here is a sample suspension provision:

SUSPENSION OF SERVICES

If the Project or the Consultant's services are suspended by the Client for more than thirty (30) calendar days, consecutive or in the aggregate, over the term of this Agreement, the Consultant shall be compensated for all services performed and reimbursable expenses incurred prior to the receipt of notice of suspension. In addition, upon resumption of services, the Client shall compensate the Consultant for expenses incurred

> as a result of the suspension and resumption of its services, and the Consultant's schedule and fees for the remainder of the Project shall be equitably adjusted.
>
> If the Consultant's services are suspended for more than ninety (90) days, consecutive or in the aggregate, the Consultant may terminate this Agreement upon giving not less than five (5) calendar days' written notice to the Client.
>
> If the Client is in breach of the payment terms or otherwise is in material breach of this Agreement, the Consultant may suspend performance of services upon five (5) calendar days' notice to the Client. The Consultant shall have no liability to the Client, and the Client agrees to make no claim for any delay or damage as a result of such suspension caused by any breach of this Agreement by the Client. Upon receipt of payment in full of all outstanding sums due from the Client, or curing of such other breach which caused the Consultant to suspend services, the Consultant shall resume services and there shall be an equitable adjustment to the remaining project schedule and fees as a result of the suspension.

We have chosen 30, 90 and five days as examples of time periods for this provision. You may wish to insert different times; you and your client should negotiate periods that are reasonable and acceptable to both of you. Note that we suggest counting calendar — and not working — days of suspension and stipulate days in the aggregate. Otherwise, in theory, your client could suspend for 29 days, order you to resume work on the 30th and then suspend for another 29, leaving you with no recourse. (See *Notices*.)

If your agreement calls for a retainer from your client and you suspend services because of nonpayment, you will want to be able to apply the retainer against outstanding billings. If you do, it is important to ensure that the client replenishes the retainer before you resume services. In that case, the following language could be added to the above language as a final paragraph: (See *Retainers*.)

> In the event the Client has paid a retainer to the Consultant, the Consultant shall be entitled to apply the retainer to cover any sums due from the Client up to the date of suspension. Prior to

Suspension of Services

resuming services after such suspension, the Client shall remit to the Consultant sufficient funds to replenish the retainer to its full prior amount.

Be sure to coordinate your Suspension of Services clause with the Billing and Payment, Retainers, Changed Conditions and Termination provisions in your agreement. (See those sections for suggested contract language.) While some contracts combine Suspension with a Termination clause, we suggest separating them so that if a court rejects one provision, the other might remain in force.

Consider this clause a **Deal Maker** — a must-have in every contract. And it is just as important whether you're a prime or a subconsultant. If you are a subconsultant, it is critical that the prime also include similar language in its agreement with the owner. If the prime has not done so and it is too late to fix it, you must recognize that you are at a greater risk of not getting paid and factor that in when negotiating your fees and other contract terms.

SEE ALSO:

Billing and Payment
Changed Conditions
Definitions
Delays
Notices
Retainers
Severability and Survival
Termination
Timeliness of Performance

RELEVANT STANDARD FORM AGREEMENT PROVISIONS:

AIA B141-1997:	Articles 1.3.8.1; 1.3.8.2; 1.3.8.3
EJCDC 1910-1 (1996 edition):	Articles 3.01; 3.02; 4.02B; 6.06A.1b.2

Termination

When a consultant and a client sign an agreement for services, the consultant is promising to employ his or her professional skills, knowledge, capital and reputation for the benefit of the client under certain terms and conditions in exchange for a stipulated fee. Should either party fail to perform its part of the bargain, should the circumstances of the project materially change or should insolvable disagreements arise, both the consultant and the client need the right to terminate the agreement.

While the client may argue it should be entitled to more freedom to terminate than the consultant, the consultant can and should insist on several causes for which it may terminate, including the client's breach of any material condition (nonpayment of fees, for example), inability to reach agreement on additional services, changes in the parties or substantially changed conditions. Under any of these circumstances, the consultant should have the absolute right to terminate the contract upon appropriate notice. (See *Assignment*, *Billing and Payment*, *Changed Conditions* and *Scope of Services* for related discussions.)

The Problem

If your agreement does not address (or does not adequately address) the subject of termination, it is an invitation to a dispute. Beware, too, of a client-written contract with one-sided language that permits only your client to terminate. Any agreement that gives just one party the right to terminate is onerous and inequitable — and speaks volumes about the author.

Recognize also that your firm will incur substantial shutdown costs if you are terminated prematurely from a project to which you have heavily committed your resources. Beware, too, of a provision hidden in a termination clause that transfers the ownership of documents. This might allow the client to terminate you early from the project just to obtain ownership of your plans. (See *Ownership of Instruments of Service* for more information.)

The Solution

Every contract should have a termination clause. This is a **Deal-Maker** provision — a must-have. The termination clause should define the circumstances under which either party

Termination

may end their legal relationship and, depending on who initiates the action, specify the rights that each party has when the termination occurs.

The following clause allows your client to terminate with or without cause but to be held responsible for any costs you incur associated with stopping the project. It gives you the right to terminate for specified causes and offers you protection when you quit for justifiable cause.

TERMINATION

In the event of termination of this Agreement by either party, the Client shall within fifteen (15) calendar days of termination pay the Consultant for all services rendered and all reimbursable costs incurred by the Consultant up to the date of termination, in accordance with the payment provisions of this Agreement.

The Client may terminate this Agreement for the Client's convenience and without cause upon giving the Consultant not less than seven (7) calendar days' written notice.

Either party may terminate this Agreement for cause upon giving the other party not less than seven (7) calendar days' written notice for any of the following reasons:

- Substantial failure by the other party to perform in accordance with the terms of this Agreement and through no fault of the terminating party;

- Assignment of this Agreement or transfer of the Project by either party to any other entity without the prior written consent of the other party;

- Suspension of the Project or the Consultant's services by the Client for more than ninety (90) calendar days, consecutive or in the aggregate;

> • Material changes in the conditions under which this Agreement was entered into, the Scope of Services or the nature of the Project, and the failure of the parties to reach agreement on the compensation and schedule adjustments necessitated by such changes.
>
> **In the event of any termination that is not the fault of the Consultant, the Client shall pay the Consultant, in addition to payment for services rendered and reimbursable costs incurred, for all expenses reasonably incurred by the Consultant in connection with the orderly termination of this Agreement, including but not limited to demobilization, reassignment of personnel, associated overhead costs and all other expenses directly resulting from the termination.**

Some consulting firms insist on compensation for all costs associated with early termination and, in the event of a termination for the client's convenience, they require the anticipated profit on those services they were not allowed to perform. (This is the position of the AIA B141-1997.) The issues of termination expenses and payment for loss of anticipated profits are quite complex. How they are addressed in your agreement will vary depending on the size and complexity of the project, the allocation of economic risks and the relative bargaining power of the parties.

Some consultants also include stricter provisions concerning ownership of instruments of service in the event they are terminated early, in order to prevent clients from walking off with complete or near-complete construction documents and forgoing construction administration services.

Under some circumstances of breach by the client, such as for nonpayment of your fees, you may not want to terminate immediately. You might prefer to have the option to suspend, i.e., temporarily withhold, your services and keep the contract in force until the client cures the breach. For this reason, we recommend a separate Suspension of Services provision be included in all your agreements. (See *Suspension of Services*.)

While in some jurisdictions courts might construe overly onerous one-way termination provisions as bilateral, don't rely on this as protection. Negotiate for explicit and reasonable termination rights that work for both you and your client.

Termination

IV-30

SEE ALSO:

Assignment
Billing and Payment
Changed Conditions
Delays
Ownership of Instruments of Service
Pay-When-Paid
Retainers
Supplanting Another Consultant
Suspension of Services
Unauthorized Changes to Plans

RELEVANT STANDARD FORM AGREEMENT PROVISIONS:

AIA B141-1997:	Articles 1.3.8.1; 1.3.8.3-7
EJCDC 1910-1 (1996 edition):	Articles 6.06; 6.10F

TIMELINESS OF PERFORMANCE

Perhaps because they do not appreciate the nature of a consultant's services, clients (or, more accurately, their attorneys) often attempt to insert a phrase into agreements that states, "time is of the essence." Such imprecise, boilerplate language is the sort of thing that is taught to first-year law students as suitable when more specificity is impossible. This seemingly innocuous phrase can do a design or environmental professional serious harm, however, especially if specific completion dates are stated in the agreement. In fact, it might be interpreted to mean that the professional's services must be completed in strict accordance with the schedule. Even a minor delay could be cause for a client to terminate the contract and/or make a claim for delay damages.

THE PROBLEM

Just as no one would tell a surgeon how quickly to complete a delicate operation, you, too, must be given adequate time to do a competent, professional job. In the contract formation stage, it is impossible to tell with certainty how long you will need to complete the various phases of the project. Unanticipated problems, site conditions, client delays, uncertainty in the scope and scale of the client's program, acts of God — all of these variables and more can render any estimation of a schedule for your services pure guesswork.

Fuzzy language, such as "time is of the essence," could lead to claims in which even minor deviations from the client's unstated expectations could mean that you either breached the contract (which could result in a refusal by the client to pay your fees) or caused delay damages (for which you could be liable since you had acknowledged the importance of time in your agreement).

It is also possible that your professional liability insurance does not cover you for claims arising from late delivery of drawings and specifications absent any allegation of negligence. While DPIC does provide such coverage in its policies, several insurers do not.

THE SOLUTION

Delete any "time is of the essence" language in client-drawn contracts. Your best approach is either to remain silent on the issue of timeliness or to address the problem with language that describes the uncertain nature of the construction process, such as the following:

Timeliness of Performance

TIMELINESS OF PERFORMANCE

The Client and Consultant are aware that many factors outside the Consultant's control may affect the Consultant's ability to complete the services to be provided under this Agreement. The Consultant will perform these services with reasonable diligence and expediency consistent with sound professional practices.

If the client demands a definitive project schedule in the contract, you'll need a different approach. Be sure, before you commit to it, that the appended schedule is reasonable and that you can meet its deadlines with time to spare before you commit to it. Such a schedule must have allowances for the owner and public authorities to perform their necessary reviews and give approvals, and for other delays outside your control. Such a clause might read:

SCHEDULE FOR RENDERING SERVICES

The Consultant shall prepare and submit for Client approval a schedule for the performance of the Consultant's services. This schedule shall include reasonable allowances for review and approval times required by the Client, performance of services by the Client's consultants, and review and approval times required by public authorities having jurisdiction over the Project. This schedule shall be equitably adjusted as the Project progresses, allowing for changes in scope, character or size of the Project requested by the Client, or for delays or other causes beyond the Consultant's reasonable control.

The time needed to perform pre-design activities and construction administration is especially difficult to estimate. For this reason, many design firms and environmental consultants insist that their contracts provide for open-ended schedules for stages of a project not within their control. Some firms will not agree to closed-ended schedules for anything other than the construction document phase of a project. Instead, they insist on an hourly or direct-labor type of contract for the pre-design programming, research and preliminaries and for construction phase and close-out services, where the schedule is largely dependent on the contractor's performance and the responsiveness of the owner and public officials.

Your contract also should contain a solid, no-responsibility-for-delays provision. (See *Delays* for sample language and a related discussion.) And, of course, no professional services agreement should contain even a hint of Liquidated Damages. (See that section for discussion.)

One last option: if your client wants notice of impending slippage in the schedule, you might agree to add to the above clause some notification language such as:

NOTICE OF DELAY

If the Consultant becomes aware of delays due to time allowances for review and approval being exceeded, delay by the Contractor, the Client, the Client's consultants or any other cause beyond the control of the Consultant, which will result in the schedule for performance of the Consultant's services not being met, the Consultant shall promptly notify the Client. If the Client becomes aware of any delays or other causes that will affect the Consultant's schedule, the Client shall promptly notify the Consultant. In either event, the Consultant's schedule for performance of its services shall be equitably adjusted.

SEE ALSO:

Billing and Payment
Consequential Damages
Delays
Liquidated Damages
Public Responsibility

RELEVANT STANDARD FORM AGREEMENT PROVISIONS:

AIA B141-1997:	Articles 1.1.2.6; 1.2.3.2; 1.3.3.2; 2.1.2
EJCDC 1910-1 (1996 edition):	Articles 3.01V; 6.01F
	Exhibit A

IV-34

PART V

ALLOCATION OF RISK

Certifications, Guarantees and Warranties
Consequential Damages
Contingency Fund
Defects in Service
Delays
Extension of Protection
Indemnities
Information Provided by Others
Insurance
Interpretation
Limitation of Liability
Liquidated Damages
Non-Negligent Services
Performance Bonds
Standard of Care
Third-Party Beneficiaries
Unauthorized Changes to Plans

V-2

CERTIFICATIONS, GUARANTEES AND WARRANTIES

Architects, engineers and environmental consultants are often asked to certify, warrant or guarantee that something has been accomplished or that certain conditions exist. Such certification requirements may lurk in unsuspected places: in a client-drafted contract, a document from the owner's lender or a form from a governmental agency. Although certifications, guarantees and warranties may be commonplace in a constructor's contract, they have no place in a design or environmental professional's agreement.

THE PROBLEM

By definition, the words *certify, warrant* or *guarantee* mean to assure the total accuracy of something or to confirm absolute compliance with a standard. Legally, these words and their derivatives are virtually synonymous. Therefore, if you certify or warrant something, you are guaranteeing that something is unequivocally true or correct or perfect.

If pushed, you can certify known facts, such as your name, for instance, and your professional registration number. You can certify that you visited a jobsite on a certain date and that you observed certain conditions during your visit — things you know for sure. What you should not do, however, is guarantee something you do not positively know as fact.

This also means avoiding the use of extreme or absolute wording, such as *all* or *every*. For instance, you cannot certify that a contractor has correctly placed *all* the rebar in a foundation. Even if you were looking over the contractor's shoulder day and night, you couldn't absolutely guarantee that the contractor had completed *all* aspects of the Work without defect. Similarly, you cannot warrant that a site is free of all toxic materials, even if your Preliminary Site Assessment uncovered no indications of hazardous materials. No matter how thorough you were, you could not have observed or tested every cubic inch of that site. (See *Hazardous Materials* for more information.) You cannot certify without qualification that a building complies with the ADA, since that is a legal determination, not an architectural or engineering finding. (See *Americans with Disabilities Act*.) Nor can you certify that a building was constructed in strict accordance with your plans and specifications. You simply do not know that every detail conforms in every respect to your design.

Certifications, Guarantees and Warranties

You cannot certify that the building was designed and constructed in conformance with all applicable laws, codes and ordinances. It is entirely possible that codes, regulations and rules of various overlapping jurisdictions will conflict with each other, so that compliance with one will mean noncompliance with another. (See *Code Compliance*.)

By certifying or warranting something, you are assuming a level of liability well beyond the standard of care required by law. As a design, geotechnical or environmental consultant, all you need do is conform to the standard of care as practiced by your peers. And that's what your professional liability insurance covers. By certifying something, you raise that standard of care. If you certify someone else's work, you may be assuming that person's liability too. Under the law, you do not have to guarantee your work or the work of others. (See *Standard of Care* for more information.) It is important to remember that your professional liability insurance is not intended to cover breach of contract or breach of warranty, the assumption of someone else's liability, or a promise to perform to a higher standard of care than required by law. (See *Insurance* and *Non-Negligent Services* for more information.) What's more, claims against you involving alleged breaches of contract or warranty may be subject to a longer statute of limitations period than would be applicable to claims involving allegations of negligence.

When you certify or warrant or guarantee that something is perfect, you also hand your client an effective weapon to use against you. The smallest error — even if caused by someone else — could produce another cause of action for breach of warranty, which is somewhat easier to prove than professional negligence.

For the same reasons, beware of the "sure" words: *insure, ensure* or *assure*. Once again, if you ensure something is true, you might be setting yourself up for a breach of contract and/or a breach of warranty claim. Even the innocent-sounding words *state* or *declare* (for instance, "I hereby state that the building was constructed in conformance with . . .") may be interpreted as a warranty. An unequivocal declaration that something is true is tantamount to guaranteeing it.

THE SOLUTION

There are several possible solutions available to you. If your client has drafted a contract that requires you to certify, guarantee or warrant anything, or has absolute declarations or statements, your first line of defense is to delete those provisions. Explain why you cannot and should not be expected to expand your liability and jeopardize your insurance coverage. If your client or a lender thrusts a certification form in front of you for signature, you have the right (and should maintain it) to modify the form sufficiently to be insurable. Here is an example of a bad (and uninsurable) client certification form that has been made reasonably acceptable:

Certifications, Guarantees and Warranties

V-5

CONSULTANT'S ~~CERTIFICATION~~ OPINION

I hereby certify that I am a licensed architect in the State of _____. ~~I further certify~~ <u>To the best of my knowledge, information and belief</u>, the building was constructed in ~~strict~~ <u>general</u> conformance to the plans and specifications and insert, <u>in my professional opinion</u>, is in compliance with ~~all~~ <u>applicable</u> laws, codes and ordinances.

A more aggressive approach is to add a clause to your contract that prevents your client from requiring certifications proposed by anyone. Some clients use fee payments as leverage to force you to sign unexpected certification documents after your contract has been signed and sealed. The following wording would protect you from an attempt to withhold your fees because of your refusal to certify something:

CERTIFICATIONS, GUARANTEES AND WARRANTIES

The Consultant shall not be required to sign any documents, no matter by whom requested, that would result in the Consultant's having to certify, guarantee or warrant the existence of conditions whose existence the Consultant cannot ascertain. The Client also agrees not to make resolution of any dispute with the Consultant or payment of any amount due to the Consultant in any way contingent upon the Consultant's signing any such certification.

A different strategy is to include a contract provision that prohibits any action that would jeopardize your professional-liability insurance coverage. This would also protect you from being forced to sign any documents for the client's lender without your review and consent. (To avoid duplication or conflict, coordinate the following clause with any Lenders' Requirements provision in your agreement.)

Execution of Documents

The Consultant shall not be required to execute any documents subsequent to the signing of this Agreement that in any way might, in the sole judgment of the Consultant, increase the Consultant's risk or the availability or cost of its professional or general liability insurance.

If your contract gives you the right to refuse to sign certification documents that are unreasonable or too risky, you are then in a position to substitute acceptable language. For instance, although you can "certify" facts you know to be true, you cannot sign most broad certification forms because you cannot be certain of all the facts. One way to handle this is to add the words "in my professional opinion" or "to the best of my information, knowledge and belief." This reduces much of the risk of a certification form. After all, as a professional, you are trained and paid to render professional opinions — not to be a guarantor or a surety. This approach is used in the *Application and Certificate for Payment (AIA Form G702)*.

Another way to dilute a dangerous guarantee or warranty is to define the offensive terms with the precise meanings you intend. You can either define these dangerous words as they appear or include them in a Definitions section in your contract. (See *Definitions*.) Carefully explain the meaning of *certify* or *declare* or *state* in acceptable terms. For instance:

Definition of "Certify"

As used herein, the word *certify* shall mean an expression of the Consultant's professional opinion to the best of its information, knowledge and belief, and does not constitute a warranty or guarantee by the Consultant.

Some public agencies, lenders or owners may insist that the wording on their forms is non-negotiable and must be signed "as is." Most, however, are willing to listen to reasonable explanations of why you cannot "certify" or "warrant" something. A client unwilling to make such an obviously necessary and reasonable change is going to be difficult to work with.

Finally, the federal EPA and several states' civil codes have defined *certification* by law to give some protection to architects and engineers. This may or may not apply to your jurisdiction or project, however, and you should not depend on such protection. Check with your state professional association or knowledgeable local counsel.

We consider a client's requirement for inappropriate certifications, warranties and guarantees to be a **Deal Breaker**. If you cannot delete or change the clause to your satisfaction, consider walking away from the project.

SEE ALSO:

Americans with Disabilities Act
Code Compliance
Definitions
Hazardous Materials
Insurance
Lenders' Requirements
Non-Negligent Services
Standard of Care
Year 2000

RELEVANT STANDARD FORM AGREEMENT PROVISIONS:

AIA B141-1997:	Articles 1.3.7.8; 2.63
EJCDC 1910-1 (1996 edition):	Article 6
	Exhibit A 2.01A.21
	Exhibit E

V-8

CONSEQUENTIAL DAMAGES

As used in a professional agreement, consequential damages are indirect expenses — such as the loss of profit or the loss of use of a facility — that are remotely connected to a failure by a design or an environmental professional. For instance, a client may allege that delays by an architect in reviewing shop drawings caused a toy store to be completed too late for the Christmas shopping season. Or major costs may be claimed if a minor error by an electrical engineer resulted in a system failure that interrupted factory production for a month.

THE PROBLEM

If you are to be held responsible for consequential damages, you could be sued for damages totally out of proportion to your fee or grossly exceeding the cost of repairing the actual damage. The problem is the *indirect* nature of consequential damages; they can be very remote and therefore unforeseeable.

Some client-drafted agreements even go so far as to specifically say that you will be held responsible for consequential damages, either in an indemnity or elsewhere. If your contract remains silent about consequential damages, however, you can still be sued for them.

THE SOLUTION

Today, in many commercial contracts and transactions such as equipment sales, waivers for consequential damages are becoming commonplace. Certainly, your professional practice deserves equal protection.

Start by deleting any language in a client-drafted contract that would make you responsible for consequential damages. Typically, this might appear in an indemnity clause. But don't stop there. You need to go a step further and add a provision that makes it clear that neither you nor your client will be held responsible for consequential damages because of any alleged failures by either party. Both the *AIA B141-1997* and the *EJCDC 1910-1 (1996 edition)* contain mutual waivers of consequential damage clauses. By making it mutual, you improve the likelihood of client acceptance. Such language could read:

Consequential Damages

CONSEQUENTIAL DAMAGES

Notwithstanding any other provision of this Agreement, and to the fullest extent permitted by law, neither the Client nor the Consultant, their respective officers, directors, partners, employees, contractors or subconsultants shall be liable to the other or shall make any claim for any incidental, indirect or consequential damages arising out of or connected in any way to the Project or to this Agreement. This mutual waiver of consequential damages shall include, but is not limited to, loss of use, loss of profit, loss of business, loss of income, loss of reputation or any other consequential damages that either party may have incurred from any cause of action including negligence, strict liability, breach of contract and breach of strict or implied warranty. Both the Client and the Consultant shall require similar waivers of consequential damages protecting all the entities or persons named herein in all contracts and subcontracts with others involved in this project.

Even if you have (and you should) a Limitation of Liability clause in your contract, you could still be held responsible for the entire negotiated limit of liability, despite the size of your fee or the price tag on the actual damage. (See *Limitation of Liability* for discussion.) Having a negotiated limit of liability does not take the place of the additional protection against liability for consequential damages. You'll need to be sure the Limitation of Liability and Consequential Damages clauses are coordinated with each other and are enforceable in your jurisdiction; talk to your attorney about this. Remember, too, that both of these clauses apply only to claims between you and your client. Third-party claims will not be subject to these protections.

- You may well find that your private-sector clients are used to discussing consequential damage issues. Many of them may ask for this protection when they are the sellers of products or services, so requesting the same protection for yourself is rarely offensive to a sophisticated client. Your clients should appreciate that you are willing to assume direct responsibility for your services and in reasonable measure, but you will not accept unlimited liability that is too remote, indirect or grossly out of proportion to your fee.

SEE ALSO:

Delays
Limitation of Liability
Timeliness of Performance

RELEVANT STANDARD FORM AGREEMENT PROVISIONS:

AIA B141-1997:	Article 1.3.6
EJCDC 1910-1 (1996 edition):	Exhibit I 6.11B.2

V-12

Contingency Fund

No one is perfect. While it's true that professionals strive for perfection in their work, it's also true that perfection is impossible to attain. Every architect and engineer knows that the perfect set of drawings and specifications has yet to be produced. Even the best prepared documents probably contain minor errors or deficiencies that may result in change orders and additional costs.

Most clients understand that they will encounter some unexpected costs caused by hidden site conditions and contractor construction problems. Experienced clients will anticipate these costs by having contingency reserves set aside in their project budgets. Design and environmental professionals must also educate their clients about the realities and uncertainties of the design process. If clients learn to expect and plan for some changes due to errors and omissions, they are less likely to file claims later.

The Problem

Architecture and engineering are considered such exacting professions that the public has difficulty understanding the potential for human error. Professionals do little to dispel this expectation. Even your clients often have unrealistic expectations and presume your services will be error-free. Clients with such expectations can subject you to liability claims when errors or omissions — no matter how minor — result in change orders and additional costs. (Refer to *Standard of Care* for a related discussion.) Unless you plan for and anticipate by contract the reasonable level of defects, errors, omissions and ambiguities that are a normal part of every project, your client may expect you to pay for the resulting change orders.

The Solution

Your client must understand that even though you provide competent and professional services, there will be minor errors and omissions in your documents. Show your client that these errors and omissions can be managed effectively — and that your goal is to find problems and fix them quickly. You can do this by establishing a procedure by which you handle problems as they arise.

Contingency Fund

First, implement an early-warning system to identify any difficulty as soon as possible. This is accomplished by establishing quality control and design review procedures within your office and by obligating the owner, contractor and subcontractors to advise you immediately of any deficiencies they discover. Insist on a provision in your contract with your client (and a parallel clause in the client's agreement with the contractor) that requires the client and all contractors and subcontractors to promptly report any defects they discover. (Refer to *Defects in Service* for suggested contract language and *Appendix II* for a sample General Conditions provision.)

Second, make the document corrections and negotiate costs of extras at the earliest possible moment. The sooner these are done, the less likely that memories will fade and costs will escalate. It's also a good idea to document these discussions and actions for your files.

Third, incorporate an alternative dispute resolution clause into each of your client agreements. Such a provision would provide for mandatory nonbinding mediation as the first formal step in resolving any dispute, including a disagreement over change orders and extras. If you make certain the owner has a similar provision in his or her contract with the general contractor, you will frustrate those contractors who bolster their profits by claiming extras for "design deficiencies." (See *Claims Arbiter Service, Dispute Avoidance and Resolution* and *Requests for Information* for more information and *Further Reading* for additional resources.)

Fourth, educate the owner about the possibility that he or she will be required to assume the financial risk of a certain "threshold" percentage of errors and omissions, and encourage the owner to plan for the resultant extra costs by setting up a contingency fund. Such a fund establishes a certain percentage of the project budget to cover the costs due to errors and omissions, which the owner should expect to incur despite your adherence to the required standard of care. Your contract should include an agreement that your client will not sue you for extra costs resulting from design errors that are within the contingency amount. The percentage set aside for a design contingency reflects the professional standard of care required under the circumstances and should take into account all of the relevant factors, including the scope, limitations and other pertinent provisions of your agreement with your client, as well as the size, complexity and duration of the project and any "innovative" or other unusual features of the project design.

Successfully negotiating a contingency provision may be easier if you and your client follow a plan such as the one suggested above. Here is a sample provision:

Contingency

The Owner and the Consultant agree that certain increased costs and changes may be required because of possible omissions, ambiguities or inconsistencies in the drawings and specifications prepared by the Consultant and, therefore, that the final construction cost of the Project may exceed the estimated construction cost. The Owner agrees to set aside a reserve in the amount of __ percent of the Project construction costs as a contingency to be used, as required, to pay for any such increased costs and changes. The Owner further agrees to make no claim by way of direct or third-party action against the Consultant or its subconsultants with respect to any increased costs within the contingency because of such changes or because of any claims made by the Contractor relating to such changes.

See Also:

Appendix II
Betterment
Claims Arbiter Service
Defects in Service
Dispute Avoidance and Resolution
Non-Negligent Services
Requests for Information
Standard of Care

Relevant standard form agreement provisions:

AIA B141-1997:	Articles 1.2.2.2; 1.3.1.2; 2.1.7.3
EJCDC 1910-1 (1996 edition):	Exhibit F 5.02B

V-16

DEFECTS IN SERVICE

The perfect set of drawings has yet to be produced. Despite the best efforts of the design or technical professional, minor errors, omissions, inconsistencies, gaps and overlaps do occur in drawings, specifications and reports. An enlightened client understands the likelihood of minor defects in the documents and also understands that the contractor may be in the best position to spot these defects before they are quite literally cast in concrete. The client should assist the consultant by requiring the contractor and subcontractors to identify and report these deficiencies as soon as possible so that they can be remedied.

THE PROBLEM

The price tag on a minor defect can rise dramatically if it is not promptly called to your attention so you can make immediate corrections. The cost of removing and reinstalling work after the fact is often a good deal more expensive than doing the work correctly in the proper construction sequence. Sometimes, however, contractors may remain silent about defects they discover so they can inflate the cost and number of change orders or set up a delay claim. Your client may then make claim against you because of these defects, even though they were not reported to you when they could have been corrected at little or no cost.

THE SOLUTION

The best solution is to work with clients who will select their contractors carefully and require those contractors and their subcontractors to "play straight" by alerting you as soon as they are aware of any problems. Ideally, the client, consultants, contractor and subcontractors work together in a partnership to identify and solve problems as they appear. You can encourage this kind of teamwork by means of contract language that obligates the owner and his or her constructors to advise you promptly of any deficiency they discover. You may also want to discuss with your client the merits of project partnering. (See *Dispute Avoidance and Resolution*.)

There is another important reason for such a clause. Claims of design defects often are made in response to your attempt to press your client for payment. Frequently, a client will use a lawsuit, or the threat of one, as a lever to delay payment further or to reduce the amount he or she owes you. By means of a Defects in Service clause, however, the client

Defects in Service

would be responsible for any defects of which he or she was aware but did nothing to mitigate. It is well worth adding such a clause to your contract. Consider the following model:

DEFECTS IN SERVICE

The Client shall promptly report to the Consultant any defects or suspected defects in the Consultant's services of which the Client becomes aware, so that the Consultant may take measures to minimize the consequences of such a defect. The Client further agrees to impose a similar notification requirement on all contractors in its Client/Contractor contract and shall require all subcontracts at any level to contain a like requirement. Failure by the Client and the Client's contractors or subcontractors to notify the Consultant shall relieve the Consultant of the costs of remedying the defects above the sum such remedy would have cost had prompt notification been given when such defects were first discovered.

If you cannot negotiate this or similar wording into your contract, you might send an occasional notice to clients (perhaps with your invoices) that requests a report of any defects or asks them if they are satisfied with your performance on the project up to that point. Having clients on record as satisfied with your services — or at least not expressing dissatisfaction when they had opportunity to do so — may help you in defending spurious claims of defects. You can also accomplish this by writing a letter to your client that incorporates such language when drawings and specifications are completed and delivered.

As mentioned in the section on Billing and Payment, you also can add language to that clause that suggests that payment of any invoice by the client shall be taken to mean that the client is satisfied with your services and is not aware of any deficiencies in those services. Alternatively, you can use a contract clause that prohibits the withholding of any sum of money from payments due you unless you have been found legally liable for some discrepancy or costs of changes in the work. (See *Billing and Payment*.) Consider the following:

Defects in Service

V-19

PAYMENTS TO THE CONSULTANT

Payments to the Consultant shall not be withheld, postponed or made contingent on the construction, completion or success of the project or upon receipt by the Client of offsetting reimbursement or credit from other parties who may have caused Additional Services or expenses. No withholdings, deductions or offsets shall be made from the Consultant's compensation for any reason unless the Consultant has been found to be legally liable for such amounts.

See *Appendix II* for a sample clause you can offer to your client to include in the owner/general contractor agreement or General Conditions. The clause obligates the contractor to report any defects of which he or she has knowledge. You'll note that the sample language seeks to establish realistic expectations regarding the standard of care by the consultant. (See also *Standard of Care*.)

SEE ALSO:

Appendix II
Billing and Payment
Construction Observation
Dispute Avoidance and Resolution
Non-Negligent Services
Pay-When-Paid
Standard of Care

RELEVANT STANDARD FORM AGREEMENT PROVISIONS:

AIA B141-1997:	Article 1.2.2.7
EJCDC 1910-1 (1996 edition):	Exhibit B 2.01D

V-20

Delays

Construction projects can be delayed for a long list of reasons. There might be severe weather, earthquakes, fires, strikes or shortages of materials. Slow decisions by regulatory agencies or owners, or the inability of the contractor to meet schedule can also hinder progress, as can the discovery of toxic materials on site, errors in the drawings or delay in processing change orders or RFIs by the consultant.

Some delays, such as those caused by defective or delayed work, are directly attributable to the contractor. The owner, too, may be responsible for delays caused by its belated decisions or last-minute changes. Still other situations are beyond anyone's control but are risks that may be borne by either the owner or the contractor. Into this category fall natural or manmade disasters, for instance, delays in approval of permits by public authorities, strikes or labor shortages, discovery of hazardous site conditions or unavailability of materials.

Delays that are totally within the control of the environmental or design professional are rare and have but a single cause: failure by the consultant to complete his or her services on time and with reasonable accuracy.

The Problem

Delay claims by contractors against owners and consultants are frequent, complex and expensive. They may be exacerbated by the pressures on the contractor caused by low-bidder selection, unrealistic time and budget requirements, liquidated damages contract provisions and owner or regulatory-agency inefficiencies. But even though the client or the contractor may suffer damages as a result of delays, it would be grossly unfair for you to be held accountable for a delay you did not cause.

In addition, if your services and your ability to perform your duties in an orderly and efficient manner are made difficult or are delayed due to some fault of the client, the contractor, public authorities or anyone else not under your control, you are entitled to a reasonable increase in your time for performance and probably in your compensation as well.

The Solution

Your agreement should address the issue of delays in two ways: by stating you are not responsible for delays caused by others and by requiring equitable adjustment in your compensation and schedule. Such a clause might read:

Delays

The Client agrees that the Consultant is not responsible for damages arising directly or indirectly from any delays for causes beyond the Consultant's control. For purposes of this Agreement, such causes include, but are not limited to, strikes or other labor disputes; severe weather disruptions or other natural disasters; fires, riots, war or other emergencies or acts of God; failure of any government agency to act in timely manner; failure of performance by the Client or the Client's contractors or consultants; or discovery of any hazardous substances or differing site conditions.

In addition, if the delays resulting from any such causes increase the cost or time required by the Consultant to perform its services in an orderly and efficient manner, the Consultant shall be entitled to an equitable adjustment in schedule and/or compensation.

Such a clause is not the only place in your agreement to discuss adjustments in your fee and schedule. You should coordinate this clause with other contract provisions concerning your scope of basic services, additional (or changes in) services, changed conditions and with your billing and payment terms. (See *Billing and Payment*, *Changed Conditions*, *Excluded Services*, *Hazardous Materials* and *Scope of Services* for additional discussion and sample clauses.) You may be entitled to additional time for delays resulting from a number of causes beyond your control: changes to codes, laws and regulations; late changes of instructions or approvals by the client; defective or delayed work by the contractor; the need to review an excessive number of claims, unnecessary RFIs or change orders; participation in unanticipated value engineering, constructibility review or project peer-review required by the client; evaluation of substitutions and the resultant revision of construction documents after their completion; or other significant changes made by the client to the program, budget, schedule, delivery system or procurement method. (See *Code Compliance*, *Requests for Information*, *Substitutions*, *Timeliness of Performance* and *Value Engineering*.)

There are some other steps you can take to help avoid delay claims. First, you should recommend that before signing the construction contract, your client review each prospective contractor's dispute history and look for a record of delay-related claims. Also, explain to your client the importance of making decisions and rendering approvals in a timely manner to prevent slowing progress on a project. On more complex projects, urge your client to decide in advance if there is to be a constructibility review or value engineering, so it can be planned for and not disrupt the orderly progress of your services (including revising your drawings and specifications to respond to these reviews). Your client should also understand that the contractor must adhere to the submittal schedule and be held responsible for the costs of unwarranted RFIs.

SEE ALSO:

Billing and Payment
Changed Conditions
Code Compliance
Consequential Damages
Construction Observation
Contingency Fund
Excluded Services
Fast Track Projects
Hazardous Materials
Liquidated Damages
Requests for Information
Scope of Services
Shop Drawing Review
Substitutions
Timeliness of Performance
Value Engineering

RELEVANT STANDARD FORM AGREEMENT PROVISIONS:

AIA B141-1997:	Articles 1.1.6; 1.2.2.5; 1.2.3.2; 1.3.3.2; 1.3.8.1-2
EJCDC 1910-1 (1996 edition):	Articles 3.01A&B; 3.02A&B; 6.01D-F
	Exhibit A 2.01A.3; 2.02A.4

V-24

EXTENSION OF PROTECTION

The protections provided under certain contractual clauses — such as indemnities and limitations of liability — can be passed downstream to subconsultants if prime design or environmental professionals specifically provide for it in their client agreements.

THE PROBLEM

You have negotiated your agreement masterfully, albeit painfully, with your client to allocate the risks of a project. You have won for your efforts a limitation of liability or an indemnity for, say, unexpected hazardous conditions. But, you still may not have obtained the hoped-for protection. If you haven't included your subconsultants, for example, and your client sues your subconsultant, your sub may in turn make claim against you for the amount of its liability to your client. This would result in needless expense, time and ruptured relationships with your subconsultants.

THE SOLUTION

If you succeed in negotiating some form of contractual protection (such as the client indemnifying you or limiting your liability) in your client agreement, we recommend that you extend this protection to your subconsultants. Having obtained these provisions from your client, you can reduce the likelihood of a "rear-guard action" by simply extending the protective language in your client contract to include those to whom you subcontract — not a great stretch for your client. The best solution may be a clause such as the following:

EXTENSION OF PROTECTION

The Client agrees that any and all limitations of the Consultant's liability and indemnifications by the Client to the Consultant shall include and extend to those individuals and entities the Consultant retains for performance of the services under this Agreement, including but not limited to the

Extension of Protection

V-26

> Consultant's officers, partners and employees and their heirs and assigns, as well as the Consultant's subconsultants and their officers, employees, heirs and assigns.

Note that included in this clause is an extension of protection to your own officers or partners and to your employees. This may prove valuable if you are not able to obtain a Corporate Protection provision in your agreement. (See *Corporate Protection*.)

If you are unable to negotiate this provision, you might be able to accomplish much the same thing by listing your subconsultants among those parties to be indemnified by your client or those whose liability is to be limited if you are able to get either of these clauses included in your agreement. (See *Indemnities* and *Limitation of Liability*.)

SEE ALSO:

Corporate Protection
Indemnities
Limitation of Liability
Subconsultants

THERE ARE NO RELEVANT PROVISIONS IN THE AIA OR EJCDC STANDARD FORM AGREEMENTS.

INDEMNITIES

Of all the provisions in an agreement for consulting services, indemnities have the most far-reaching liability implications. They are also the most difficult clauses to negotiate, especially if a client (or a client's attorney) is not inclined to be reasonable. Furthermore, enforceability, restrictions and interpretations vary widely from state to state. Some states prohibit many forms of indemnities while others allow broadly written, mutually agreed upon provisions. For these reasons, it is critical that consultants understand the issues and work closely with their attorneys and professional liability insurance specialists to review and negotiate any contract indemnification language.

Pared down, the concept of indemnification (or hold harmless) is simple: it is an agreement to assume a specific liability in the event of a loss. It may mean a shifting of risk from one party to another, a kind of insurance. When a consultant indemnifies a client, he or she may be assuming some of the client's potential or actual legal liabilities, thereby acting as an insurer, of sorts, for that client.

When a contractor takes over control of an owner's property and occupies it for the purpose of constructing something on it, it's reasonable to ask the contractor to hold the owner of the property harmless from liability for virtually anything that happens on the site. The same logic does not apply to architects or engineers. Consultants do not occupy or exercise constructive control over the jobsite. They are not building something tangible on a site. Instead, they're rendering their professional and rather intangible services (planning, collecting data, designing, rendering opinions and observing construction) for the benefit of the client. It makes no sense, therefore, for consultants to have to provide the same kinds of indemnity protection as contractors. What's more, clients themselves are not simply passive parties to the construction process. They are in the inherently risky business of construction.

It is only logical that all parties (owner, contractor and consultant) be responsible for their own risks or those they can best control. If no one can control a risk, then it must remain with the owner. In some instances, a project may be so hazardous or the consulting services so risk-prone that it would make more sense to reverse the situation and have the owner indemnify the consultant for those risks in return for the benefit the owner derives from the professional services provided under such risky circumstances.

Indemnities

Two points must be kept in mind. First, lawmakers generally disfavor indemnities and the courts tend to follow their lead. There is no guarantee that a particular jurisdiction will necessarily enforce an indemnity in a consultant's favor, given the great disparity in the enforceability and interpretation of indemnity clauses resulting from various state anti-indemnity statutes and court decisions. When it comes to indemnities, consultants should expect the worst of both worlds — that a client's indemnity might be enforced and the consultant's might not. This is why good legal advice is especially important on any indemnity language. (See *Interpretation*.)

Second, many of the sample clauses offered throughout this book include specific indemnifications simply because each contract topic is considered separately. Many attorneys believe that a contract should have as few indemnities as possible (although everything for which a consultant seeks indemnification should be included). This often can be accomplished by combining all the issues, causes or situations for which the consultant wants to be indemnified into one general indemnity clause. Overall, the agreement should allocate project risks clearly and unambiguously (specify who is responsible for what risks).

A consultant may encounter at least four different types of indemnity situations:

1. WHEN YOUR CLIENT WANTS AN INDEMNITY FROM YOU

In that cleverly crafted agreement sent to you by your client's attorney probably lurks one or perhaps a dozen clauses requiring you to indemnify the client. The language may be short and innocuous-sounding, or it may be pages long, convoluted and confusing. In either case, proceed with caution. With the help of your attorney, your professional-liability insurance specialist and the suggestions below, you can unravel even the most offensive legal verbiage and, if you can't dispose of the provision altogether, perhaps you can negotiate to make it more equitable.

THE PROBLEM

The biggest problem is the existence of the clause itself. By including this indemnity, your client is attempting to transfer some or perhaps all of his or her risk to you — and likely demanding that you take on more liability than law or custom requires. If you doubt this, ask yourself: without this indemnity, whose risk would it be? Almost invariably, it would be the client's.

Several other critical factors must be examined:

- Client-drafted indemnities often ask you to pay for the client's own negligence. Your client has control over the budget and the workscope. During design and construction, he or she frequently participates in discussions and may make decisions intended to save money but which also increase your risk — approving cheaper grades of materials, for instance, or a shortcut construction method. This is especially dangerous if your contract has you indemnifying the client and bearing all the risk — including the risk for your client's negligent decisions. Typically, a client requests indemnity for *any claims caused in whole or in part by the consultant, except for the sole negligence of the client*. The inference is clear: the client intends that you pay the entire amount of any loss jointly caused by you and the client, even if he or she is 99 percent at fault and you are a mere 1 percent negligent. Keep in mind that even the most inept lawyer can convince a jury that you are 1 percent at fault for just about anything.

- Most client-drafted indemnities are uninsurable. If you sign a client's indemnity that is not limited to just your negligence (indemnifying for "any act" or for "all claims arising from the project"), you are accepting liability beyond that required by law and beyond that for which you are insured. Your professional liability policy may include such language as "This insurance does not apply to liability assumed by you under any 'contract'; but this exclusion does not apply if you would have been liable in the absence of such 'contract,' due to your own negligent act, error or omission." However it is worded, check with your professional liability insurance specialist or knowledgeable legal counsel to determine if a proposed indemnity clause would be covered or if your policy would exclude certain aspects of it.

- Client-drafted indemnities frequently contain onerous, overreaching language. For instance, a client may ask for indemnity for your "*intentional* acts." The truth is, virtually everything you do could be interpreted by an enterprising attorney as intentional. (It is possible your client means *willful* or *malicious* instead. Keep in mind, however, that malicious acts are not insurable.) Sometimes clients want you to indemnify against *allegations* or *claims* of your negligence. That, too, is excessive language, because anyone can allege or claim anything, and you could conceivably find yourself indemnifying someone simply on the strength of those allegations. Beware, also, of any extreme phrasing, such as *at any time, from any cause whatsoever* or *any or all claims*. These only serve to broaden your liability and may render the clause uninsurable.

- Client-drafted indemnities frequently ask you to *defend* the client. If an indemnity is not tied directly to your negligence (see the following sample clause), this provision could be interpreted as an obligation on your part to retain an attorney for your client and pay for his or her defense — even before your legal liability for actual negligence (if any) has been established. You might find yourself having to pay for your client's defense attorney from your own pocket even if you're proven to be non-negligent because your professional liability carrier is not responsible for paying such expenses. (In most instances, your insurer will reimburse for defense costs after the fact if they are part of your client's damages and after your negligence has been proven.) Again, discuss the terms of your coverage with your insurance specialist.

- Client-drafted indemnities sometimes attempt to include inappropriate parties as *indemnitees* (parties to be indemnified). Such clauses often contain a long list of indemnitees, some of whom can be indemnified and others who cannot. For example, it is not unusual to indemnify a client's partners, principals, officers, directors and employees. However, you should not agree to indemnify a client's agents, contractors, attorneys, contract employees, lenders, volunteers or anyone else who is not directly part of the client entity. You do not owe these parties the same obligations, and they can always seek their own legal remedies should they somehow be damaged by your negligence.

THE SOLUTION

At all times, your guiding principle should be: *unlimited liability is not an option*. Refuse to accept it. The goal is to keep the risk in the hands of the party who is in the best position to control or transfer it. If the risk cannot be reasonably controlled or transferred, it should remain with the client. Many consulting firms adhere to a strict policy: "If we can't insure a risk, we won't assume it."

Your best solution? Delete any provision that requires you to indemnify the client. Explain that under the law, you already have an obligation to perform your services in a non-negligent manner and, if you fail to do so, the client has recourse in tort. (Assuming you make the changes we suggest to the client's indemnity language, the client will gain very little, if any, additional protection anyhow.) Accordingly, your professional liability insurance covers you against damages resulting from your negligent professional acts, errors or omissions. To prove negligence, a claimant must establish the professional standard of care, establish your duty to adhere to that standard of care, establish your failure to do so — and then prove that this failure proximately resulted in injury or damage to the claimant. Your client may be more agreeable if you can show that the clause as presented is uninsurable and, therefore, too great a liability for you to accept.

Second best, if your client insists on some form of indemnification, counter with a mutual indemnity, in which each of you indemnifies the other — but only for the direct result of your own negligent acts. This should seem equitable to a fair-minded client. Consider:

INDEMNIFICATION

The Consultant agrees, to the fullest extent permitted by law, to indemnify and hold harmless the Client, its officers, directors and employees (collectively, Client) against all damages, liabilities or costs, including reasonable attorneys' fees and defense costs, to the extent caused by the Consultant's negligent performance of professional services under this Agreement and that of its subconsultants or anyone for whom the Consultant is legally liable.

The Client agrees, to the fullest extent permitted by law, to indemnify and hold harmless the Consultant, its officers, directors, employees and subconsultants (collectively, Consultant) against all damages, liabilities or costs, including reasonable

> attorneys' fees and defense costs, to the extent caused by the Client's negligent acts in connection with the Project and the acts of its contractors, subcontractors or consultants or anyone for whom the Client is legally liable.
>
> Neither the Client nor the Consultant shall be obligated to indemnify the other party in any manner whatsoever for the other party's own negligence.

As a final — and by far, least desirable — alternative, you may be forced to give your client some kind of unilateral indemnity. (We're assuming, of course, that you have fought valiantly and have used every known negotiating technique without success.) However, you should, if at all possible, limit the indemnity to that which is insurable. Make certain the indemnity is tied to *your* negligence and purge the clause of any client-generated onerous language. Include the concept of comparative negligence, which holds you liable for only the portion of the damages for which you are responsible (unless your state law has an even more protective provision) and, finally, see that the indemnity is limited to the services called for under the agreement. These concepts are reflected in the following suggested language:

INDEMNIFICATION

> The Consultant agrees, to the fullest extent permitted by law, to indemnify and hold harmless the Client against damages, liabilities and costs arising from the negligent acts of the Consultant in the performance of professional services under this Agreement, to the extent that the Consultant is responsible for such damages, liabilities and costs on a comparative basis of fault and responsibility between the Consultant and the Client. The Consultant shall not be obligated to indemnify the Client for the Client's own negligence.

If your client tries to force you to sign an unfair indemnity, you may want to suggest that he or she is using *disparate bargaining power*; that is, adopting a "take it or leave it" stance occasionally used by those in a superior bargaining position. This constitutes a refusal to bargain in good faith and results in what courts may call a *contract of adhesion*. Under certain circumstances, this may allow you to claim that the clause is unenforceable. Public

Indemnities

officials are becoming more sensitive to this issue, so it may be worthwhile to raise it if you feel the client is refusing to negotiate on an indemnity. If you do nothing else, at least document your concerns and objections in a letter to the client and keep complete records of your negotiation efforts for your files. This may come in handy if the client tries to unfairly enforce the indemnity.

We regard onerous or inappropriate indemnities as **Deal Breakers**. A client who insists on unfair and one-sided indemnity provisions has an obvious agenda: to lay all or most of the project risk at your feet. If you cannot either delete the provision or negotiate a more equitable indemnity, you must consider walking away from the project.

2. WHEN YOU WANT AN INDEMNITY FROM YOUR CLIENT

There are some types of projects for which your client should indemnify you and even some in which it is appropriate for your client to go a step further and waive his or her rights against you. High-risk assignments may expose your firm to liabilities out of all proportion to your potential profit from the project. Unless you use protective contract language, such extraordinary risks could be yours.

THE PROBLEM

Certain situations are so risk-prone or hazardous to the health of your business that it is imperative your client keep all the risk. Such instances may involve hazardous waste, asbestos, condominiums, renovations or the possible unauthorized reuse of your documents. (See *Condominiums*, *Hazardous Materials*, *Ownership of Instruments of Service* and *Renovation/Remodeling* for further discussion on these topics.)

THE SOLUTION

These are times when indemnity by your client from third-party claims is the only approach that seems to make sense. After all, you didn't create the hazardous condition — you are there to help your client deal with it. In high-risk projects, you should consider such a clause a **Deal Maker**; if your client won't give you indemnity protection, consider not accepting the project. But remember that an indemnity is only as good as your client's net worth. If your client doesn't have the financial resources or appropriate insurance to back up the indemnity or if he or she refuses to indemnify you, also consider declining the project.

There is an additional step you might take to protect your firm. On very risky projects or on projects you cannot properly insure, you should also ask your client to agree not to sue you. This is called a *waiver*, and it is different from and in addition to asking your client to indemnify you against claims by other parties. Although an important protection, it is one of the most difficult provisions to obtain and to enforce. You and your attorney must be extremely cautious in its wording and presentation, since there are wide variations in state statutes pertaining to waivers. When drafting your contract, keep the waiver and indemnity in separate paragraphs. If a court declares the waiver invalid, you don't want the indemnity thrown out as well. (This is a good reason to insist on a Severability provision in your contracts. Refer to *Severability and Survival* for sample language.) Finally, to avoid any conflict, you and your attorney should coordinate the waiver with any Limitation of Liability provision. Consider the following sample waiver and indemnity provisions:

WAIVER

In consideration of the substantial risks to the Consultant in rendering professional services in connection with this Project, the Client agrees to make no claim and hereby waives, to the fullest extent permitted by law, any claim or cause of action of any nature against the Consultant, his or her officers, directors, employees, agents or subconsultants, which may arise out of or in connection with this Project or the performance by any of the parties above named of the services under this Agreement.

INDEMNIFICATION

In addition, and notwithstanding any other provisions of this Agreement, the Client agrees, to the fullest extent permitted by law, to indemnify and hold harmless the Consultant, its officers, directors, employees and subconsultants (collectively, Consultant) against all damages, liabilities or costs including reasonable attorneys' fees and defense costs, arising out of or in any way connected with this Project or the performance by any of the parties above named of the services under this Agreement, excepting only those damages, liabilities or costs attributable to the negligent acts or negligent failure to act by the Consultant.

Remember, you will need the help of your attorney on these waiver and indemnity protections; they are very tricky and must be carefully crafted to comply with the laws of each jurisdiction.

Indemnities

3. WHEN YOU AND YOUR CLIENT WANT INDEMNITY FROM THE CONTRACTOR

More and more often, consultants are being sued for jobsite accidents in which injured third parties, including construction workers, claim that the architect or engineer had an obligation to monitor safety precautions or provide a safe jobsite.

THE PROBLEM

When someone — a worker or a passerby — is injured on the jobsite, the search for "deep pockets" takes a predictable course. Whether triggered by the contractor's insolvency or inadequate Workers Compensation, the search usually turns to the architect or engineer, even if the consultant's share of the blame is minimal or nonexistent.

THE SOLUTION

To protect yourself against third-party claims, add language to your contract with the owner that requires the owner to include provisions in the owner/general contractor agreement requiring that all contractors indemnify you, your subconsultants and the owner for claims by the contractor's employees. You also will want to have the contractor name you and the owner as additional insureds on the contractor's general liability policy. (See *Insurance* and *Jobsite Safety*.) In addition, you should require the contractor to procure contractual liability coverage sufficient to cover the indemnity obligations being assumed and to provide evidence of this coverage to all indemnified parties.

CONTRACTOR INSURANCE AND INDEMNITY REQUIREMENTS

The Client agrees, in any construction contracts in connection with this Project, to require all contractors of any tier to carry statutory Workers Compensation, Employers Liability Insurance and appropriate limits of Commercial General Liability Insurance (CGL). The Client further agrees to require all contractors to have their CGL policies endorsed to name the Client, the Consultant and its subconsultants as Additional Insureds and to provide Contractual Liability coverage sufficient to insure the hold harmless and indemnity obligations assumed by the contractors. The Client shall require all contractors to furnish to the Client and the Consultant certificates of insurance as evidence of the required insurance prior to commencing work and upon renewal of each policy during the

> entire period of construction. In addition, the Client shall require that all contractors will, to the fullest extent permitted by law, indemnify and hold harmless the Client, the Consultant and its subconsultants from and against any damages, liabilities or costs, including reasonable attorneys' fees and defense costs, arising out of or in any way connected with the Project, including all claims by employees of the contractors.

Note that when providing construction-management services and under some forms of design-build contracts, there may be a greater than normal responsibility for jobsite safety. This increased risk can be partially managed by allocating it through appropriate indemnification and insurance provisions. (See *Construction Management* and *Design-Build* for discussion and more information.)

4. When You Want an Indemnity from Your Subconsultants

Prime consultants often require indemnities from their subconsultants to protect themselves from damages and costs arising from claims due to the actions of these subconsultants.

The Problem

If your subconsultant is sued for negligence, you, as the prime consultant, will almost certainly be named in the suit. Even if you are blameless, the very act of defending yourself may well cost you your deductible (if you are insured) besides your time and the staff costs expended in your own defense — a considerable sum.

The Solution

We recommend that in your subconsultant agreements, you use a reasonable indemnity clause that is both mutual and insurable and that allows you to recover your costs in the event of a claim. That it be mutual is a matter of equity; each party retains responsibility for its own negligence. That it be insurable is important for the reasons discussed in Section 1 of this chapter. Put yourself in the subconsultant's position (and you may be from time to time). Consider the following:

INDEMNIFICATION

The Consultant and the Subconsultant mutually agree, to the fullest extent permitted by law, to indemnify and hold each other harmless against all damages, liabilities or costs, including reasonable attorneys' fees and defense costs, arising from their own negligent acts in the performance of their services under this Agreement, to the extent that each party is responsible for such damages, liabilities and costs on a comparative basis of fault.

Another approach would be to adapt the mutual indemnity in Section 1 of this chapter and modify it to fit your consultant/subconsultant situation.

Indemnities are extremely complex and have enormous liability implications. Have your lawyer examine any indemnity language with respect to the laws of the governing jurisdiction to determine exactly what your rights and exposures may be. Work, too, with your professional liability insurance specialist to determine the insurability of any indemnities you intend to sign.

SEE ALSO:

Condominiums
Construction Management
Design-Build
Hazardous Materials
Extension of Protection
Governing Law and Jurisdiction
Insurance
Interpretation
Jobsite Safety
Non-Negligent Services
Ownership of Instruments of Service
Renovation/Remodeling
Severability and Survival
Standard of Care
Subconsultants

RELEVANT STANDARD FORM AGREEMENT PROVISIONS:

AIA B141-1997:	No applicable provisions.
EJCDC 1910-1 (1996 edition):	Article 6.11

Information Provided by Others

Design and environmental professionals are often required to rely on data and documents prepared or collected and provided by other parties. Such information might range from client program requirements to soils and survey data, to the location of underground utilities, to the original plans and specifications for an older building being renovated. (See *Renovation/Remodeling* and *Underground Improvements*.)

The Problem

For the consultant, the starting point of most projects is existing information. Some you collect yourself, some is available from public sources and some is given to you by your client or by contractors or consultants working for your client. Client-provided information can include historical records, financial or technical data developed by the client, the client's program requirements as well as plans, reports and surveys prepared by other consultants. Such information may be in hard copy or in electronic files. (See *CADD/Electronic Files* for discussion and sample contract language.)

You are expected to accept all this information and use it as the basis for your designs or services without checking its accuracy or completeness. Although any errors in the information provided can very well cause errors in your services, a client will seldom pay you to spend the time verifying what the client — or someone on its behalf — delivers to you. Nevertheless, you should not be held liable if indiscernible errors exist in these documents or data.

The Solution

One solution is to have an express understanding that, for purposes of expediency and economy, you are entitled to use and rely on information supplied or produced by others, including the client, and its consultants and contractors, and that the client will bear the resulting risk. A clause that accomplishes this could read:

Information Provided by Others

INFORMATION PROVIDED BY OTHERS

The Client shall furnish, at the Client's expense, all information, requirements, reports, data, surveys and instructions required by this Agreement. The Consultant may use such information, requirements, reports, data, surveys and instructions in performing its services and is entitled to rely upon the accuracy and completeness thereof.

If you are to provide Record Documents, it is especially important to be able to rely on all reports and information provided to you by the client's contractors. You are expected to incorporate into your Record Documents the reported location and details of work performed by others without being able to check or verify the information. (See *Record Documents* for more information.)

SEE ALSO:

CADD/Electronic Files
Record Documents
Renovation/Remodeling
Underground Improvements

RELEVANT STANDARD FORM AGREEMENT PROVISIONS:

AIA B141-1997:	Articles 1.2.2.1; 1.2.3.7; 2.2.1.1; 2.2.1.2; 2.6.4.3
EJCDC 1910-1 (1996 edition):	Articles 6.01B; 6.01E; 6.04B&C

INSURANCE

Almost every professional service agreement contains detailed and often confusing insurance requirements, usually phrased in mind-numbing "insurancespeak." To make sense out of these requirements and know how to deal with them, consultants must master some insurance basics. They need to understand what the various types of policies are, what they cover, and what extra coverages and endorsements are available. Most importantly, consultants must be able to spot unattainable or ambiguous insurance requirements in client-written contracts and negotiate reasonable alternatives.

THE PROBLEM

Perhaps because some clients are used to specifying insurance requirements for contractors, they think design and environmental professionals should carry the same types of coverage. Often, agreements drawn up by clients or their attorneys will specify insurance requirements that are impractical or impossible for you to meet.

A quite different set of insurance issues arises if your firm provides design-build, construction management, facility operations or maintenance, or any of a myriad of non-traditional or expanded services. Some of these may require coverages or products (such as bid or performance bonds) unfamiliar to most design and environmental consultants. (See *Performance Bonds* for more information.)

THE SOLUTION

Your best source for insurance assistance and information is a specialized professional liability insurance agent or broker who is knowledgeable about the architecture and engineering professions and the construction industry. (Refer to *Further Reading* for information on how to obtain a listing of specialized agents and brokers.) These individuals can help you analyze contractual requirements for the types of insurance discussed in this section and advise you on insurability issues. Certainly, before you assume any non-traditional or expanded role, be sure to seek the advice of a qualified insurance professional.

If you are providing or thinking about providing design-build or construction management services, more information can be found in the *Design-Build* and *Construction Management* sections of this *Guide*, as well as in DPIC's handbooks on those subjects. (See *Further Reading*.)

Sometimes the best approach when dealing with contractual insurance requirements is to take the initiative. Offer a paragraph that in simple, straightforward language states you will attempt to maintain appropriate policies with reasonable limits of coverage and list the coverage you have on an addendum attached to your contract. (See *Exhibit 7* at the end of this section for a sample format.) If you offer such a paragraph up front, you may head off drawn-out negotiations with your client over insurance requirements:

INSURANCE

During the term of this Agreement, the Consultant agrees to provide evidence of insurance coverages as listed on Addendum _____, attached hereto.

PROFESSIONAL LIABILITY INSURANCE

Professional liability insurance protects you from claims arising from your negligent acts, errors or omissions in the performance of your professional services. Because this coverage is specific to licensed professionals, few clients fully understand its function and limitations.

Professional liability policies have several unique features that narrowly define coverage:

- First, policies are written on either a *claims-made* or a *claims-made and reported* policy form. Both policies cover claims made against you during the policy period and require that claims be reported to your carrier in accordance with the policy terms. To be covered, such claims must have arisen from acts, errors or omissions occurring after the retroactive date stated in your policy.

- Second, in order to keep your *retroactive date* and to have your *prior acts* covered, you normally must continue to renew your policy every year. In other words, if you break the chain of continuous coverage and later take out a policy, you may not have coverage for projects you designed while you were previously insured.

- Third, professional liability policies have *aggregate limits*. The policy limit you purchase is the total amount your insurer will pay for both defense costs and indemnity, regardless of the number of claims made during the policy period.

- Fourth, professional liability policies are *expense within the limits* policies. This means that after you pay your deductible, any additional defense costs paid on that claim by your insurer will decrease the policy limits available for payment of that claim or other claims.

Because of these features and because the insurance market for this coverage is somewhat volatile — in both price and availability — it would be unwise to agree to a contract requirement to maintain specific levels of professional liability coverage for any extended time. You might not be able to comply in the future.

Instead, you could soften a client's absolute requirements for professional liability insurance with a clause similar to this:

> **The Consultant agrees to attempt to maintain professional liability coverage for the period of design and construction of the Project, and for a period of ___(__) years following substantial completion, if such coverage is reasonably available at commercially affordable premiums. For the purposes of this Agreement, "reasonably available" and "commercially affordable" shall mean that more than half the consultants practicing the same professional discipline in the state where the project is located are able to obtain such coverage.**

Clients often confuse professional liability with general liability insurance (discussed later in this section) and try to specify the same coverage they require of contractors. Because of this, it is important to review and negotiate client-drawn contracts and to delete unattainable or unreasonable requirements, such as the inclusion of "additional insureds" on your professional liability policy. Despite a client's demands, there often are provisions to which you simply cannot or should not agree. (Some of those provisions are listed in *Exhibit 8* at the end of this section.)

Professional liability insurance is written by relatively few insurance carriers. While there are some similarities among them, there are also significant differences in their underwriting, policy language and claims services. Once again, the advice of a professional liability insurance specialist can be invaluable when you are seeking insurance coverage designed to suit your firm's needs and when you are selecting or changing carriers.

PROJECT INSURANCE

One solution to the limitations of professional liability practice policies (such as duration of coverage and aggregate limits) is to obtain a professional liability project policy. Project

Insurance

policies provide *extended coverage* for the design and construction period of a single project, plus a pre-selected *discovery period* after substantial completion of the project. These policies provide a separate project limit so claims on other projects will not erode the limits available for this project. And because they are written on a multi-year basis and are guaranteed noncancelable under most circumstances, there is less administrative burden on you and your client to ensure continuous and adequate coverage.

Another advantage to project coverage is that the entire consulting team — including all the subconsultants — can be covered under a single policy by a single insurance carrier. This cuts down on intramural conflict or finger pointing among project team members if a claim arises, and it can also help reduce lawsuits, counterclaims and blame shifting within the project team, which in turn reduces overall liability costs.

Because of the significant advantages of project insurance, owners often will pay the cost — or some part of it. Sophisticated owners recognize project insurance as a solution to many of their liability concerns and will treat it as a normal project cost in much the same way they treat insurance required of contractors. Project insurance also is an excellent solution in those instances where your client wants a higher limit than your practice policy offers.

Check with your professional liability insurance specialist to see if coverage is available or to obtain a quote for your projects. If you feel that project insurance is appropriate, you may be able to negotiate with your client to include the cost as a direct reimbursable item under your agreement. Here is a sample provision that incorporates these ideas:

PROJECT INSURANCE

The Consultant agrees to obtain professional liability project insurance specifically to cover this Project. This project policy will cover the design and construction period and will include a discovery period of ___(__) years after substantial completion. The policy will provide a project aggregate limit of $____ and a deductible of $____. The cost of this coverage shall be paid by the Client as a Direct Reimbursable Cost in accordance with paragraph ____, Reimbursable Expenses, hereof.

COMMERCIAL GENERAL LIABILITY

Another frequently required insurance is commercial general liability (also called comprehensive general liability, CGL, or public liability). It insures your firm for liability claims for bodily injury and property damage sustained by others arising from your nonprofessional activities and your business operations. Claims arising from your professional acts, errors or omissions are excluded. For instance, this policy would provide coverage should a visitor slip and fall while in your offices. Because, as an architect, engineer or environmental professional, almost everything you do — attending a planning commission meeting, drawing plans or observing work at the jobsite — is considered a professional act, there is little risk of a general liability claim. You might find it difficult to obtain general liability insurance if you do not also maintain professional liability insurance.

Many coverage endorsements (amendments to your policy) that cannot be added to your professional liability policy can be provided under your general liability policy. Your clients might ask for endorsements they believe will give them additional protection under your policies, such as *Waiver of Subrogation*, *Severability of Interest* or *Cross Liability* provisions or being named an *Additional Insured*. Depending on the insurer, these endorsements are usually available under your general liability policy.

General liability also differs from professional liability in that it is written on an *occurrence* basis instead of a claims-made form. This means that if an insured event (say, a visitor tripping in your office) takes place while the policy is in force and later results in a claim — perhaps years later and even after the policy had been dropped — coverage would still be provided under that policy.

General liability insurance is occasionally combined with property insurance (furniture/fixtures/real property) in what is sometimes called an "office package policy." Such packages often include additional coverages for valuable papers and other exposures common to a professional practice. This may be the most economical form of coverage for smaller firms or those without complex contractual requirements. Larger firms usually need specifically tailored general liability policies as well as property coverages appropriate to their unique operations and exposures.

Workers Compensation

Workers compensation is a no-fault insurance that protects employers and employees when workers are injured, become ill or are killed on the job as a direct result of their employment. It is paid for by the employer and provides benefits set by law for medical costs and lost wages. Although required by statute in every state, your clients' contracts usually require proof that you carry workers compensation coverage.

Once again, clients may confuse you with contractors and specify endorsements to be added to your workers compensation policy that may or may not be attainable. Before agreeing to provide more than basic statutory coverage, ask your professional liability insurance specialist to be sure you can meet your clients' requirements. Availability of endorsements like Waiver of Subrogation and Additional Insureds varies from state to state and insurance carrier to carrier. Check with your broker and negotiate your contract language to provide only coverage that is available from your insurers and is appropriate to your role.

AUTOMOBILE LIABILITY

Clients often require that you provide evidence of automobile liability insurance, whether or not you are likely to use any vehicles on the project. If you do have a business automobile insurance policy, this is usually not a problem; you can provide certificates of insurance to your clients. Many firms, however, in which employees drive and insure their own personal automobiles sometimes face a dilemma because private passenger auto insurance companies often are reluctant to issue certificates or to name your clients as additional insureds. Some firms have solved the problem by having one vehicle — the company delivery truck or the president's car — owned (or leased) and insured by the firm so that there is a business automobile policy for which they can provide evidence of coverage.

NON-OWNED AUTOMOBILE LIABILITY

Often, there is a contract requirement to provide evidence of *non-owned and hired auto coverage*. This is insurance carried by the firm for automobiles it does not own — such as your employees' cars — but that are used on company business. It provides liability coverage for your firm in addition to the primary limits carried by the car owner. This coverage often is attached to your firm's owned automobile policy (discussed above), but in some states it may be possible to obtain a freestanding Non-Owned Auto Policy.

INTERNATIONAL PROJECTS INSURANCE

Special problems may arise if a project is in another country. Many insurance policies are limited to providing coverage in the United States (and perhaps U.S. territories and Canada). If the job is in a country where coverage is not provided under your existing policies, separate foreign coverage insurance may be needed for workers compensation, general liability or automobile liability. Professional liability policies often provide, or can be endorsed to provide, international or worldwide coverage. Before undertaking any projects abroad, check with your professional liability insurance specialist to review your exposures and to determine the international projects coverage available under each of your insurance policies. (See *International Projects* for more information.)

Remember, it is crucial that you review and negotiate the insurance terms of any contract before you sign it. You must be sure you can obtain the required coverage, and you need to know the costs of having special endorsements added to your policies. Often, by contract or practice, clients will withhold your fees until you provide the required insurance certificates. If you can't get an insurance certificate that satisfies your contract requirements, your fees may be held up.

It's just not good business to promise to provide insurance coverages you can't obtain. Lawyers earn high fees extricating people from contract promises they later realize are impossible to keep.

Nor should you give advice to your clients about insurance or surety (bonding) matters; claims arising out of such advice are typically excluded under most professional liability policies. Instead, refer your clients to their own insurance agents or brokers to obtain needed insurance counsel.

If you are interested in learning more about insurance, **Further Reading** includes information on available resources.

SEE ALSO:

Certifications, Guarantees and Warranties
Consequential Damages
Construction Management
Design-Build
Indemnities
International Projects
Limitation of Liability
Subconsultants
Third-Party Beneficiaries

RELEVANT STANDARD FORM AGREEMENT PROVISIONS:

AIA B141-1997:	Articles 1.2.2.6; 1.3.7.4; 1.3.9.2.6
EJCDC 1910-1 (1996 edition):	Article 6.05
	Exhibit G

Exhibit 7

If you use a contract provision that references an Insurance Addendum listing coverages you intend to provide, you might start with this as a model. In consultation with your professional liability insurance specialist, you should develop specific wording to correspond to the coverages you intend to carry and that are available in your locale.

Addendum to Agreement Between Consultant and Client

SCHEDULE OF INSURANCE

In accordance with the terms of this Agreement, the Consultant shall attempt to obtain and maintain the following insurance policies with coverages and limits as indicated:

- ❑ **Professional Liability Policy** with limits of $ _____ per claim and $ _____ aggregate.

    or

- ❑ **Professional Liability Project Policy** with limits of $ _____ per claim and $ _____ project aggregate. This policy shall remain in force for the period of design and construction (estimated to be _____ years, _____ months) but not beyond {date} and shall include a discovery period of _____ years, _____ months, to commence upon substantial completion of the project.

- ❑ **Commercial General Liability Insurance** with limits of $ _____ each occurrence and $ _____ aggregate. This policy shall be written or endorsed to include the following provisions:

    - ❑ {*Client*} shall be named as an additional insured.
    - ❑ Waiver of Subrogation.
    - ❑ Severability of Interest (Separation of Insureds).
    - ❑ Cross Liability Endorsement.
    - ❑ Other (specify): _____.

- ❑ **Workers Compensation Insurance** as required by statute, including **Employers Liability**, with limits of:

    $ _____ each accident.

    $ _____ disease, _____ each employee.

    $ _____ disease, _____ policy limit.

- ❑ **Automobile Liability Insurance** with limits of $ _____ each accident, combined single limits.

- ❑ **Non-Owned Automobile Liability Insurance**, including coverage for hired and leased vehicles, with limits of $ _____ each accident, combined single limit.

The indicated coverages shall be subject to all of the terms, exclusions and conditions of the policies.

Exhibit 8

PROFESSIONAL LIABILITY INSURANCE LIMITATIONS

Your professional liability insurance policy:

... cannot be written on an **Occurrence** basis.

... cannot name the client as an **Additional Insured**.

... cannot contain a **Severability of Interest** clause.

... cannot be written to cover claims beyond the terms of the policy.

... cannot cover "any act" of the consultant.

... cannot cover the client for his or her own negligence.

Furthermore, you should not agree by contract to:

... maintain coverage for any extended period of years (unless it's a project policy).

... maintain a deductible with a not-to-exceed amount.

... provide insurance coverages, endorsements or certificates you are unsure of without checking with your qualified professional liability insurance specialist.

V-48

INTERPRETATION

Most lawsuits against design and environmental professionals allege multiple causes of action or theories under which a consultant is being sued. For example, if a client claims the architect omitted something from the plans or specifications, the architect will be sued for negligence. But the client might also claim breach of contract if the architect had agreed in his or her contract to perform services according to the standard of care — and failed to do so. Furthermore, the client could charge breach of warranty, alleging that there was an implied warranty that the architect would perform the services without defect. Of course, if the architect had neglected to remove such onerous words as *warrant* or *guarantee* from the contract, the client might also claim breach of express warranty. The client might even throw in a claim for breach of some sort of fiduciary duty. The theory goes that if the client doesn't prevail on one cause of action, perhaps another will work.

THE PROBLEM

Although the number of causes of action under which you can be sued may not alter the total amount of damages to which you may be exposed, the plaintiff will have more leeway and better odds and more discovery will be created (not to mention billable hours for the lawyers) the greater the number of cases. It could be likened to a shotgun. The plaintiff fires off several rounds, hoping that at least one pellet will find its mark — which, in this case, is your pocketbook. In some instances, this may simply be an attempt to obviate some legal obstacle the plaintiff may face. For example, the statute of limitations for simple negligence is normally much shorter than that for breach of contract.

Courts vary widely in their acceptance and interpretation of indemnities and other limitations of a design or environmental professional's liability. Some courts may narrowly interpret these protective clauses and apply them under very limited circumstances. If, for instance, your client agrees by contract to limit your liability to $50,000, a court may nevertheless decide this limitation applies only to your negligence. Such a ruling would leave the way open for a plaintiff to sue for a higher amount under a variety of other legal theories, such as breach of contract, warranty or strict liability — despite the intent of your agreement with your client to have the limit apply to any and all claims. (See *Limitation of Liability*.)

The Solution

Add a provision to your contract that makes it clear that any protective clauses you've agreed upon (limitations of liability, indemnities, waivers of claims, limits on consequential damages) apply not only to claims in tort (negligence) but also to any other cause of action except willful misconduct or sole or gross negligence. If you and your client have already agreed on the allocation of the risk, this clause merely carries out your intent and gives guidance to a court if there is ever a question. The provision may serve to avoid narrow interpretations by the courts and may help to strengthen your protective clauses, too. Consult with your attorney about including contract language such as the following:

INTERPRETATION

Limitations on liability, waivers and indemnities in this Agreement are business understandings between the parties and shall apply to all legal theories of recovery, including breach of contract or warranty, breach of fiduciary duty, tort (including negligence), strict or statutory liability, or any other cause of action, provided that these limitations on liability, waivers and indemnities will not apply to any losses or damages that may be found by a trier of fact to have been caused by the Consultant's sole or gross negligence or the Consultant's willful misconduct. The parties also agree that the Client will not seek damages in excess of the contractually agreed-upon limitations directly or indirectly through suits against other parties who may join the Consultant as a third-party defendant. "Parties" means the Client and the Consultant, and their officers, directors, partners, employees, subcontractors and subconsultants.

The above clause encompasses not only your firm but also your officers, partners, employees and subconsultants, and it further strengthens your indemnities and limitations of liability. However, if your client won't agree to include those other parties and you need a fallback position, you could agree to omit reference to your subconsultants in the last line. It also might be worthwhile to insert a similar provision in any agreements with your subconsultants if those contracts contain indemnities in your favor.

The provision also contains language that attempts to prevent your client from coming "in through the back door" and suing other parties who, in turn, might sue you for amounts over your limitation of liability.

Interpretation

As a caution, if your contract doesn't have a limitation of liability, a waiver of claims or an indemnification in your favor, then you will want to eliminate reference to that provision. Some attorneys suggest you place this Interpretation clause at the very end of a contract so it could be construed to apply to all foregoing clauses in the agreement.

SEE ALSO:

Certifications, Guarantees and Warranties
Consequential Damages
Extension of Protection
Indemnities
Limitation of Liability
Subconsultants
Third-Party Beneficiaries

THERE ARE NO RELEVANT PROVISIONS IN THE AIA OR EJCDC STANDARD FORM AGREEMENTS.

LIMITATION OF LIABILITY

Limitation of Liability (LoL) is a provision in an agreement between the design or environmental professional and the client to establish the maximum liability the consultant will be responsible for if there is a claim by the client on the project. The purpose is simple: to allocate risk in some reasonable proportion to the profits and other benefits to be derived by each party. In other words, if the professionals obtain a small benefit (their profit) while helping their clients achieve a much larger one, the risk these professionals must bear should rightfully be in proportion to their benefit.

To place this in a construction industry context, it may be helpful to consider a simple hypothetical project. An owner who plans to build a $10 million office building expects a minimum of 10 percent return per year over perhaps 20 to 40 years — a substantial sum — and still have a saleable building at the end of that time. The general contractor bids $10 million to construct it and expects to earn a profit of perhaps 10 percent of that $10 million — or $1 million. The architect who designs the building might charge perhaps a 7 percent fee — or $700,000. With luck, and assuming he or she doesn't have to pursue the client to collect the fee, the designer hopes for a 10 percent profit on that fee — or $70,000. And yet, should problems develop with the building, this same designer would be subject to legal costs or damages far in excess of the fee, despite his or her modest profit. It is the inequity of this situation that limitation of liability seeks to address.

THE PROBLEM

The standard of care for design or environmental professionals requires only that you provide your services with that degree of skill and care that would be used by other reasonably competent practitioners of your profession in the same locale under similar circumstances. The word *perfection* is nowhere to be found in the standard of care. Yet clients often expect and demand perfection from you. If perfection is not attained (and, truthfully, it never can be), litigation frequently follows.

Today's construction projects have a high degree of complexity and sophistication, involve numerous participants in the design and construction process and are done under greatly compressed time schedules. Simply put, a lot of things can go wrong, and even though you may not be primarily at fault, you will probably be brought into the dispute.

Limitation of Liability

In our sue-first, ask-questions-later society, litigation — even the threat of litigation — is so costly that without some limit to the damages, a single protracted lawsuit can put a small consulting practice out of business. Any professional firm that continually accepts unlimited risks can expect huge losses eventually and, perhaps, financial disaster. To make matters worse, in some circumstances, a firm's principals also could face personal bankruptcy.

THE SOLUTION

Your survival in the marketplace may depend as much on effective risk management as anything else. This means a resolute refusal to accept unlimited liability. You need to balance your risk in proportion to your return, and insist that the lion's share of the risk remain with the party who stands to profit the most — the owner.

You can start to manage your risks by placing Limitation of Liability provisions in all your contracts. Not only is LoL always an important provision, we consider it a **Deal Maker** — a must-have — when the risk of a project increases. Jobs involving hazardous materials, asbestos, condominiums, design without construction administration, renovation, or any other assignment that increases risk and the cost of your insurance — all these demand strong Limitation of Liability language.

Keep in mind, however, that since LoL clauses do not apply to third-party claims, they are only effective in claims against you by your client. Although attorneys representing design or technical professionals often recommend clauses to protect from third-party claims, such clauses are not foolproof. Discuss with your attorney whether such clauses can help. (See *Indemnities* and *Third-Party Beneficiaries*.)

Obtaining LoL in all or most of your agreements is not an unrealistic goal. True, in the past, clients and even some design or environmental professionals have resisted the idea. But the climate is changing. There are now many firms who routinely ask for and get Limitation of Liability clauses in all their contracts. These firms have come to realize and are convincing their clients that LoL is a reasonable way to set the level of responsibility to which a consultant will be held in the event something should go wrong. They recognize, too, that there are many instances in which fault may not originate with the consultant (or may to a very minor degree) but that the consultant will most likely be brought into a costly suit regardless.

Your success in negotiating LoL with your client depends on several factors. Your first step must be a frank discussion of risk-allocation concepts — and specifically LoL — to help the owner understand and accept that building a project is a risky business and that a major portion of that risk rightly belongs with him or her. To help your client see the issue in a different light, ask, "How can you ask me to assume risk that is rightfully yours?" Demonstrate that as a practical matter your liability is always limited anyhow: you don't have unlimited resources or unlimited insurance. Nor is insurance the answer. Clients must understand that professional liability insurance carries an aggregate policy limit, is not always available for a particular risk, is expensive and does not assure future coverage.

You may have more success in obtaining LoL if you use a preprinted contract that contains an LoL provision. Several professional societies have come to recognize this (and the importance of LoL) by including the clause in the body of their standard agreements. Other societies also recognize LoL as an important risk-management tool and provide Limitation of Liability clauses as a standard addendum. Whether or not you use a professional society contract, you should develop your own "preferred" contract language that includes an LoL clause.

An important factor in enforcing a Limitation of Liability provision is to be able to show that the provision was negotiated or at least was negotiable.[1] You and your client should discuss and decide on an equitable limit to your liability. We suggest clauses that provide a blank in which you can insert an agreed-upon liability dollar cap. Some firms believe, however, they have greater success in obtaining LoL provisions if they offer contracts with a dollar figure preprinted in the body of the contract. If you decide to use a preprinted liability cap, bear in mind that you may weaken the premise that the clause was negotiated, so you should offer to discuss and negotiate the terms of the agreement.

Many firms choose $50,000 or $100,000 as a preselected liability limit; some use the amount of their fees. Just be sure to select a limit that is meaningful and that takes into account potential damages on a project.[2] If your client demands a higher dollar cap, at least you are negotiating for some limit — rather than leaving your liability unlimited. Any limitation is better than none. Talk with your attorney. He or she can help you decide which is the better course in your jurisdiction.

There are some clients who insist on equating the dollar cap to the amount of professional liability insurance you carry. If you agree to this, make certain the wording reflects "insurance coverage available at the time of settlement or judgment" in the event your policy limit has been reduced by a prior claim. (This provides an excellent opportunity to raise the issue of project insurance with your client. See *Insurance* for more information.)

Depending on your attorney's advice, and considering your jurisdiction, you may want to highlight the clause in some manner. Some prefer that the clause be printed in bold, large-type, capital letters, or with space provided for both parties to initial. Still others include a paragraph just before the signature line of the agreement that states the contract contains a Limitation of Liability clause and that the client has read and consents to all terms. You could also place the LoL clause at the very end of the contract, immediately above the client's signature line.

---

[1] A 1991 California appellate court decision, (<u>Markborough v. Superior Court</u>, 227 Cal.App.3d 705 1991) held that a Limitation of Liability clause in a preprinted contract was valid, even though it was not specifically negotiated or initialed. An important consideration for the court was the existence of an opportunity to negotiate, which was present in the form of a cover letter from the design professional, giving the client the option to accept, reject or modify any element of the contract. Another consideration was the relative bargaining power of the parties.

[2] A 1996 Oregon Supreme Court decision (<u>Estey v. Mackenzie Engineering Inc.</u>, 324 Ore. 372, 927 P2d 86, 1996) invalidated a Limitation of Liability clause, in part because the specified limit was so low ($200 — the engineer's fees) when compared to the actual damages ($340,000).

Limitation of Liability

Some standard form agreements — such as those published by the AIA or EJCDC — offer Limitation of Liability clauses as addenda or amendments, which are coordinated with the rest of the contracts. If you don't use these forms, are using your client's contract or would like another option, there are several alternatives, beginning with the following:

LIMITATION OF LIABILITY

In recognition of the relative risks and benefits of the Project to both the Client and the Consultant, the risks have been allocated such that the Client agrees, to the fullest extent permitted by law, to limit the liability of the Consultant to the Client for any and all claims, losses, costs, damages of any nature whatsoever or claims expenses from any cause or causes, including attorneys' fees and costs and expert-witness fees and costs, so that the total aggregate liability of the Consultant to the Client shall not exceed $____, or the Consultant's total fee for services rendered on this Project, whichever is greater. It is intended that this limitation apply to any and all liability or cause of action however alleged or arising, unless otherwise prohibited by law.

The above clause is a reasonable provision that incorporates most of the features necessary to give you sufficient protection and may be acceptable to your clients.

To make certain the client understands the LoL is negotiable, some firms add language to the above that gives the client the opportunity to increase the limit for an additional fee. For example:

Additional limits of liability of $___ may be made a part of this Agreement for a fee of ____ percent (___%) of the total fees included herein.

Some consulting firms use a simplified version of LoL. Although not as broad or protective as the above clause, it may be easier to obtain. These firms believe that the client who agrees to a basic form of LoL clause has agreed to the principle of reasonable risk-allocation and will be more willing to work out problems as they occur on the project. Such a clause might read:

Limitation of Liability

LIMITATION OF LIABILITY

To the maximum extent permitted by law, the Client agrees to limit the Consultant's liability for the Client's damages to the sum of $____ or the Consultant's fee, whichever is greater. This limitation shall apply regardless of the cause of action or legal theory pled or asserted.

In higher risk projects — condominium design, renovation, PSAs and other jobs that may involve hazardous materials — where obtaining an LoL provision is a **Deal Maker** (a must-have) or in instances where you are less than comfortable with the client, contractor or other design-team members, you may prefer a clause that gives you more protection. Note that this clause limits your liability not only to your client but also to the contractor and his or her subs. Because some courts may interpret this as an indemnity, the clause is presented in two paragraphs. If the second paragraph is challenged, your Limitation of Liability clause may survive intact:

LIMITATION OF LIABILITY

To the fullest extent permitted by law, and not withstanding any other provision of this Agreement, the total liability, in the aggregate, of the Consultant and the Consultant's officers, directors, partners, employees and subconsultants, and any of them, to the Client and anyone claiming by or through the Client, for any and all claims, losses, costs or damages, including attorneys' fees and costs and expert-witness fees and costs of any nature whatsoever or claims expenses resulting from or in any way related to the Project or the Agreement from any cause or causes shall not exceed the total compensation received by the Consultant under this Agreement, or the total amount of $____, whichever is greater. It is intended that this limitation apply to any and all liability or cause of action however alleged or arising, unless otherwise prohibited by law.

Limitation of Liability

CONTRACTOR AND SUBCONTRACTOR CLAIMS

The Client further agrees, to the fullest extent permitted by law, to limit the liability of the Consultant and the Consultant's officers, directors, partners, employees and subconsultants to all construction contractors and subcontractors on the Project for any and all claims, losses, costs, damages of any nature whatsoever or claims expenses from any cause or causes, including attorneys' fees and costs and expert witness fees and costs, so that the total aggregate liability of the Consultant and the Consultant's subconsultants to all those named shall not exceed $___, or the Consultant's total fee for services rendered on this Project, whichever is greater. It is intended that this limitation apply to any and all liability or cause of action however alleged or arising unless otherwise prohibited by law.

Note that the above clause limits your liability — and that of your subconsultants — to the owner to a certain sum not only for your negligence but also for any joint negligence. By including your subconsultants, you preclude the possibility of paying for joint-liability claims — and may even prevent the subconsultant from later seeking damages against you.

DPIC Companies, as well as several professional associations, has been advocating and recommending limitation of liability for more than 20 years. In fact, DPIC feels so strongly about LoL that it offers substantial premium credits to its insureds who implement LoL in their contracts. (If you want more information about LoL, see *Further Reading* for suggested resources. Your professional liability insurance specialist and professional society also can offer assistance.)

Limitation of liability may not be attainable in every one of your contracts, but it is a worthy goal. The important thing is to start the education process for both yourself and your clients. Remember that no firm ever got Limitation of Liability without asking for it.

SEE ALSO:

Condominiums
Design Without Construction Administration
Hazardous Materials
Indemnities
Information Provided by Others

Limitation of Liability

V-59

Insurance
Interpretation
Renovation/Remodeling
Standard of Care
Subconsultants
Third-Party Beneficiaries

RELEVANT STANDARD FORM AGREEMENT PROVISIONS:

AIA B511-1996:	Articles 2.1.7.6; 12.2
EJCDC 1910-1 (1996 edition):	Article 6.11A.5
	Exhibit I

V-60

LIQUIDATED DAMAGES

Liquidated damages are specified sums of money, agreed upon in advance by the parties to a contract to represent damages for breach of contract, usually due to delay. They are used in situations where quantifying the exact amount of damages would be too difficult, imprecise, time-consuming or downright impossible. An owner and contractor may simply agree by contract that delay in completion of their project will cost the contractor so much per day. For example, an owner and a contractor might agree that if the contractor failed to complete construction of a toy store by November 1, the owner would stand to lose substantial holiday season profits. They could stipulate that $500 per day would represent those lost profits. If the contractor is 10 days late in completing the toy store, he or she will forfeit $5,000 as liquidated damages.

THE PROBLEM

While the use of liquidated damages is commonplace with contractors and subcontractors, professional services do not customarily lend themselves to strict schedules. As a design or environmental professional, you provide an intellectual service; you do not provide a tangible product or perform a physical task. During the proposal and contract negotiation stages of a project, it is impossible to know precisely how much time you will need to complete your services professionally and competently. Nor do you have any control over the responsiveness of the owner, the contractor or public agency staff. It would be unreasonable, therefore, to expect you to accept liability for delays in the completion of your services. (For more discussion, see *Timeliness of Performance*.)

If you agree by contract to pay liquidated damages, those damages may not be fully covered by your insurance. All professional liability insurers exclude coverage for penalties and fines and any type of liability assumed by contract that is not the result of your negligence. While some insurance companies do not cover any claims for late delivery of drawings and specifications and reports, many other insurance companies cover the direct, provable damages that result from late delivery of your design or report. For instance, if you have agreed to $500 per diem in liquidated damages, but it is only possible to prove $300 of real damage per day, the $200 balance may be considered to be a penalty and would not, therefore, be covered by your professional liability insurance.

Liquidated Damages

And what about the contractor? While these penalty clauses or liquidated damages are relatively commonplace in the General Conditions of the contractor's contract, are they a good idea? Whether or not these provisions are appropriate or even justified in the construction contract in order to motivate the contractor could be the subject for another book. Certainly, the pressures generated by liquidated damages can cause a good deal of trouble for the consultants on the project. Some contractors, saddled with penalty clauses, begin to protect themselves from the first day of the project, with the intent of proving later that the completion date was not met because of the failure of others (read: *you*). In addition to the extra costs caused by the delays themselves, some contractors even claim that they are entitled to significant extended overhead costs as a result.

If the contractor is able to demonstrate that his or her progress was impeded by your failure to respond in a timely manner to RFIs, failure to prepare bulletins promptly and failure to issue change orders expeditiously, he or she will not only avoid liquidated damages but also demand a significant extra for delay costs including extended overhead. The owner will then attempt, often successfully, to lay this off on you.

THE SOLUTION

Your best solution is to delete any reference to liquidated damages in your agreement with your client. Explain that such a provision is inappropriate for contracts for professional services. Tell the client that you cannot control many of the factors that influence project completion. Furthermore, it is industry standard not to include liquidated damages in any form of professional services agreement. And because they are uninsurable, they represent unacceptable risk to you anyway.

For all these reasons, we regard the inclusion of a liquidated damages clause as a **Deal Breaker**. If a client-written contract contains a liquidated damages provision and you cannot persuade your client to delete it, give serious consideration to walking away from the project.

If presented with a Liquidated Damages provision, substitute a Standard of Care provision in which you agree to do what is expected of you as a professional: to perform your duties in a manner consistent with the ordinary degree of care and skill practiced by your peers. (See *Standard of Care* for discussion and specific clause suggestions.) Or you might agree — if absolutely necessary — to a Timeliness of Performance clause, using language that suggests that your work toward an established schedule must be governed by sound professional practices. One such sample clause appears below. (For more information, refer to *Timeliness of Performance*.)

TIMELINESS OF PERFORMANCE

The Consultant acknowledges the importance to the Client of the Client's project schedule and agrees to put forth reasonable efforts in performing the services under this Agreement with due diligence in a manner consistent with that schedule, as provided in Exhibit ____ hereto. The Client understands, however, that the Consultant's performance must be governed by sound professional practices.

In addition, if you know *before* you sign your agreement with your client that the contractor's contract will include liquidated damages, in recognition of the increased risk and additional burden, you might request an increase in your fee — or consider turning the project down. Otherwise, you may want to include a provision in your contract that would increase your fee in the event your client elects to include penalties or liquidated damages in his or her agreement with the contractor. Here is one example:

STANDARD FORM GENERAL CONDITIONS

The Consultant's scope of services and compensation for Basic Services under this Agreement are based on the assumption that the construction Contractor will be hired under the standard terms of General Conditions {*insert AIA-A201, EJCDC Form 1910-8 or other standard form*}. **If the Client elects not to use this standard form, it is understood and agreed that the Consultant shall be entitled to reasonable adjustments in compensation and schedule caused by the additional efforts required to work with the Contractor under nonstandard terms and conditions. Specifically, and in addition, if the Client employs a Liquidated Damages or other time penalty provision in the construction contract, the Consultant's fee for Basic Services shall be increased by ____ percent.**

This clause puts the client on notice that it is more expensive and time-consuming for you to work with nonstandard documents. In addition, it quantifies the increased difficulty,

Liquidated Damages

based on your firm's experience, of working with contractors who are under the gun of liquidated damages.

Liquidated damages clauses are intended to motivate nonperforming contractors. Contractors who are doing the job, however, ought not to have to work under a cloud of onerous penalties. So, help your client select a reputable contractor based on qualification rather than lowest bid and encourage your client to develop General Conditions that won't put the contractor in the position of being squeezed for money. Here, too, is a perfect opportunity to introduce the subject of Partnering to your client. (See *Dispute Avoidance and Resolution*.) By anticipating problems and working on them together, you, your client and the contractor can often ease the contractor's defensive attitude and even end up with a mutually profitable project. Remember, a successful project allows all parties to earn a fair and reasonable profit for their efforts.

SEE ALSO:

Consequential Damages
Delays
Dispute Avoidance and Resolution
Requests for Information
Standard of Care
Timeliness of Performance

THERE ARE NO RELEVANT PROVISIONS IN THE AIA OR EJCDC STANDARD FORM AGREEMENTS.

NON-NEGLIGENT SERVICES

Sometimes clients will include a phrase in their contracts that states the design or environmental professional will "perform services in a non-negligent manner." The phrase seems harmless enough. After all, isn't that what the law requires and what a design or environmental professional intends to do anyhow?

THE PROBLEM

The clause may seem innocuous, but it is not. We are all obligated to perform non-negligently in whatever we do, or we are responsible for damages under tort law. By agreeing specifically by contract to perform your services in a non-negligent manner, however, you could aggravate your liability exposure. With such a clause in your agreement, performing a negligent act could now also be called a *breach of contract* or perhaps even a *breach of warranty*. In many jurisdictions, the statute of limitation to bring suit for negligence is several years shorter than the statute governing breach of contract suits. In addition, claims for breach of warranty are excluded from coverage under all professional liability policies. Why agree to such a clause and expose yourself unnecessarily to greater liability for a longer period of time? (See *Insurance*.)

THE SOLUTION

You should delete any "non-negligent" clause and be frank with your client about the liability issue. If consultants could guarantee perfection and always perform in a non-negligent manner, the professional liability insurance industry would be far smaller. But perfection is simply not attainable nor should your client expect it.

You could go one step further in distancing yourself from this sort of problem by adding a disclaimer of warranty to your Standard of Care provision. Consider the following:

Non-Negligent Services

Standard of Care

In providing services under this Agreement, the Consultant will endeavor to perform in a manner consistent with that degree of care and skill ordinarily exercised by members of the same profession currently practicing under similar circumstances.

The Consultant makes no warranty, either express or implied, as to the professional services rendered under this Agreement.

For more information, refer to *Certifications, Guarantees and Warranties* and *Standard of Care*.

See Also:

Certifications, Guarantees and Warranties
Defects in Service
Insurance
Standard of Care
Statutes of Repose and Limitation

There are no relevant provisions in the AIA or EJCDC standard form agreements.

PERFORMANCE BONDS

Normally required of the contractor, a performance bond is a financial guarantee that he or she will complete a project. If the contractor defaults, the surety is obligated to step in and see that the job is finished. Although such bonds may be costly, many owners find them worthwhile because of the financial instability of some constructors. Performance bonds are rarely required of design or environmental consultants.

THE PROBLEM

Although some clients (particularly those in the public sector) may ask you to obtain a performance bond, such a bond is almost never available for architectural or engineering services. First of all, you do not deliver a product; you provide a professional service. The nature of this service can be defined only in somewhat general terms, which makes it difficult to determine whether or not the service has been fully performed. For instance, is an error or omission considered a performance failure, thereby rendering the contract incomplete?

Since there is no such thing as a *perfect* set of drawings and specifications, errors and omissions *will* happen. A surety company is not likely to agree to serve as guarantor of perfection if no such perfection can be guaranteed. Therefore, few, if any, sureties would be willing to issue performance bonds for the services you normally provide.

In addition, consulting firms do not usually accumulate the assets bonding companies require as collateral for performance bonds. Retained earnings, buildings, equipment and cash are just not normally found on consulting firms' balance sheets. And without such security (and usually personal guarantees from the firm's principals and their spouses) bonding companies are reluctant to issue bonds, even if they get past the error and omission problem.

THE SOLUTION

The truth is, there are very few instances in which consultants fail to complete their assigned tasks. They tend to act responsibly and professionally, and the need for financial security to guarantee completion is almost nonexistent. The integrity of most licensed professionals is sufficient to assure performance of their services. In fact, some would argue that, at least in the private sector, it is the consultant who should require surety of the client to guarantee his or her performance (i.e., payment of fees) rather than the other way around!

Delete any clause that requires you to obtain a performance bond. Explain to your client why such bonds are unnecessary and very difficult for architects and engineers to obtain. You can remind your client, however, that as a licensed professional, you remain personally responsible long after the project is completed — in contrast to a contractor who might disappear overnight. A performance bond would not only increase your client's expense but, in reality, would serve no useful purpose. While bonding may be appropriate and necessary for contractors, you are not a contractor and requiring bonding is just not the solution.

There are a few exceptions. If you assume the lead role in a design-build project (see Scenario Two in *Exhibit 12* on page X-10) or set up a design-build entity with a contractor (see Scenario Three in *Exhibit 12*), then the owner may want assurance that various types of surety (bid bonds, performance bonds and payment bonds) have been secured. But, as we've pointed out, because surety companies generally require high collateral, it may be extremely difficult for you to find bonding. If that is the case, you should probably not be in a lead role. Alternatively, you may rely on the bonding capacity of your contractor/partner, who may already have bonding capability established with a surety company. If neither is possible, you may need to make some other financial arrangements to give your client the assurance needed (such as a letter of credit or assignment of other collateral).

SEE ALSO:

Design-Build
Insurance
Standard of Care

RELEVANT STANDARD FORM AGREEMENT PROVISIONS:

AIA B141-1997:	Article 2.6.6.4
EJCDC 1910-1 (1996 edition):	Exhibit A 1.05A.15b
	Exhibit B 2.01I.1

STANDARD OF CARE

What was the applicable standard of care? Was it met? These are the first questions asked when a design or environmental professional is accused of negligence. The legal definition of the professional standard of care, however, may vary widely from the public's perception — and a client's expectations.

All that is expected or required of design or environmental professionals is that they render their services with the ordinary degree of skill and care that would be used by other reasonably competent practitioners of the same discipline under similar circumstances, taking into consideration the contemporary state of the art and geographic idiosyncrasies. This concept dates from English Common Law doctrine, which holds that the public has the right to expect that those providing services will do so in a reasonably careful and prudent manner, as tested or established by the actions of their own peers under like circumstances. Nowhere in this doctrine or definition is there any mention of "perfection." Being perfect isn't required or even contemplated for design or environmental consultants. The only test is the quality of the consultant's actions: are they reasonable, normal and prudent under the given circumstances?

THE PROBLEM

Perhaps because architecture and engineering are perceived as exacting professions and sciences, the public has difficulty acknowledging your potential for human error. Clients, too, have expectations, sometimes unrealistic, of you as a design or technical professional. And it is unmet expectations — not technical error — that most often lead to liability claims.

Some clients will attempt to revise the standard of care language in their contracts to require consultants to "perform to the highest standard of practice." If you accept such a clause — or any language that seeks to raise the customary standard — you are agreeing to be judged by far more than the ordinary standard of practice. This increases your risk, and your professional liability insurance will not cover you for this increased exposure, since it represents an assumption of additional liability for which you would not otherwise be responsible.

Standard of Care

You also may be leaving yourself open to heightened risk and difficulty in negotiating realistic contract terms with your client if you tend to puff up your firm's abilities in exaggerated terms ("the best" or "most qualified") in your correspondence, promotional literature or project proposals.

Some client-written contracts contain a provision that would have you agree to perform your services in a non-negligent manner. This could be construed as a warranty, with all the related issues of insurance and statutes of limitation. (See *Non-Negligent Services*.)

THE SOLUTION

While it's true that most design and environmental professionals strive for perfection in their work, it is also true that perfection is impossible to attain. Nor is it expected of you under the law: you are not required to be perfect. In fact, the perfect set of plans has yet to be produced by a consulting firm. The best way to protect yourself is to ensure that your client has realistic expectations of you and your services. Tell your client that perfection is unattainable at any price.

If your client drafts a contract clause that purports to raise the standard of care to a higher level, you must delete the offending words and revise the standard to an "ordinary" or "normal" or "reasonable" level. It is a good idea to have a clause in your contracts that affirmatively defines the standard of care to which you will perform. Consider the following:

STANDARD OF CARE

In providing services under this Agreement, the Consultant will endeavor to perform in a manner consistent with that degree of care and skill ordinarily exercised by members of the same profession currently practicing under similar circumstances.

Should you feel it necessary or helpful, you may want to consider offering to correct defective services without an additional fee. Note, however, that this offer does not include any of the costs to perform construction or to add items that may have been omitted from the original design. You might add to the previous clause:

> . . . similar circumstances. Upon notice to the Consultant and by mutual agreement between the parties, the Consultant will without additional compensation, correct those services not meeting such a standard.

Some might argue that if your contract says you will perform to a certain standard, it might give rise to an additional cause of action against you for breach of warranty. They suggest you soften the provision with qualifiers like *attempt to* or *strive to*. The courts disagree. A 1992 decision[3] expressly found that contract language stating that the engineer "*will* use that degree of care and skill ordinarily exercised under similar conditions by reputable members of our profession practicing in the same or similar locality . . . " simply incorporated the professional standard of care and did not create any express or other warranty obligation. (See *Certifications, Guarantees and Warranties*.)

Delete any warranty-like language (such as promising to perform in a "non-negligent manner") that could create insurance-coverage problems or extend the applicable statute of limitation. In fact, you could turn this around by adding to your Standard of Care clause, additional wording such as:

> . . . under similar circumstances. The Consultant makes no warranty, express or implied, as to its professional services rendered under this Agreement.

You can go even further to make certain everyone understands you do not have to be perfect. You can insert language in the General Conditions of the Owner/Contractor contract (the AIA document A201 or the EJCDC 1910-8, if you are using association standard documents) that sets reasonable expectations of the design or environmental professional for both the owner and the contractor, making it clear that the instruments of service may well contain conflicts, errors, omissions and other slight imperfections. (See *Appendix II* for suggested language.)

You should also add a Contingency Fund provision to your contract or, if there is going to be a contingency fund in the owner/contractor agreement, you should attempt to include in the list of contingencies those costs resulting from discrepancies in your construction documents. (See *Contingency Fund*.)

---

[3] *Gibbes Incorporated v. Law Engineering*, 960 F 2d 146 4th Cir. 1992.

See Also:

Appendix II
Certifications, Guarantees and Warranties
Code Compliance
Contingency Fund
Defects in Service
Indemnities
Non-Negligent Services

Relevant standard form agreement provisions:

AIA B141-1997:	Article 1.2.3.2
EJCDC 1910-1 (1996 edition):	Article 6.01

THIRD-PARTY BENEFICIARIES

The legal obligations of architects, engineers and environmental consultants to others are sometimes difficult to interpret. The concept of "privity of contract" once held that people owed a duty of care only to those with whom they had a contract. However, that duty has been extended by some court decisions to anyone who predictably could be harmed by the actions of consultants even if no contract exists.

Certainly, those who suffer direct bodily injury and/or property damage because of a consultant's negligence can demand compensation. But what about those who claim an architect's negligence caused them economic loss? Does the law hold that a third party is entitled to consequential damages if an engineer's negligence deprives him or her of a profit? Frankly, the jury is still out. Some states hold that a design or technical professional owes no duty of care to a third party for economic loss, since no contract exists between them. Other jurisdictions have ruled that a contract is not a prerequisite to claiming damages for economic loss because of negligence. In still other states, courts have decided in both directions, further muddying the legal waters.

THE PROBLEM

With so much variance in the courts, it is difficult to know where your responsibilities lie. Virtually everyone — from the general contractor to vendors to future owners — can claim that you knew or should have known that they could have been economically harmed by your negligence and sue you for damages. Their chances of prevailing depend on several factors, including the jurisdiction in which the claim is filed and, perhaps, any preventive steps you and your client may have taken to avoid third-party claims. If your contract is silent on the matter, a court may follow what it believes to be precedent or it may make new law based on its predilections.

THE SOLUTION

Parties to a contract can establish many of their own rules to guide judicial interpretation. You and your client can — and should — address the issue of third-party claims in your agreement. At the very least, such a provision will clearly define your intentions and responsibilities and may help defeat claims in some jurisdictions where the case law is

Third-Party Beneficiaries

not settled or compelling on this issue. Many defense attorneys believe this is an important provision that should be included in every professional service agreement. Consider the following as a starting point:

THIRD-PARTY BENEFICIARIES

Nothing contained in this Agreement shall create a contractual relationship with or a cause of action in favor of a third party against either the Client or the Consultant. The Consultant's services under this Agreement are being performed solely for the Client's benefit, and no other party or entity shall have any claim against the Consultant because of this Agreement or the performance or nonperformance of services hereunder. The Client and Consultant agree to require a similar provision in all contracts with contractors, subcontractors, subconsultants, vendors and other entities involved in this Project to carry out the intent of this provision.

Your client should have no objection to such a clause, since it does not compromise either party's position and may be of some benefit to both of you.

The final sentence of the provision requires you and your client to include a similar third-party provision in all agreements with other parties to the project. If your client is hesitant to agree to this, you could omit the sentence, but the clause would not provide nearly as much protection. Remember, if you agree to include such language in your agreements with subconsultants, you must take care to do so.

SEE ALSO:

Public Responsibility
Statutes of Repose and Limitation
Subconsultants

RELEVANT STANDARD FORM AGREEMENT PROVISIONS:

AIA B141-1997:   Articles 1.3.7.5; 2.6.2.5
EJCDC 1910-1 (1996 edition):   Article 6.08C.2

UNAUTHORIZED CHANGES TO PLANS

Sometimes changes are made to construction documents by the owner, a contractor or even a building department official without the knowledge and approval of the consultant. In a few states, if an architect's or engineer's design is changed without his or her knowledge by the contractor or owner, and if those changes result in damages, a statute gives the consultant protection from liability. This is not true in many jurisdictions, however. In most states, absent some contractual safeguards, the consultant may well become liable — or at least have to bear the costs of his or her defense — because of someone else's unauthorized changes.

THE PROBLEM

It is so easy — and so common — for someone else to make changes to your design. A contractor who is having difficulty making a detail in the plans work might decide on a minor (and what he or she thinks is a harmless) field change without consulting you. The danger increases if you are performing only limited construction phase services or none at all. (See *Construction Observation* and *Design Without Construction Administration*.) Perhaps your contract is terminated after the construction documents are complete, leaving the construction phase to another consultant — who makes modifications to your design. (Refer to *Supplanting Another Consultant*.) Consider the building inspector who, being a helpful sort of person, makes an offhand suggestion to a contractor about an alternate approach to a problem. If you aren't there to intercede, the contractor probably will defer to the building inspector. Then there is the owner who asks for a copy of your plans on computer disk and has his or her own in-house designers make modifications without your knowledge. While simple to do, the changes may be virtually undetectable by anyone else. (See *CADD/Electronic Files*.) Or think about the developer of a residential project who asks you to design five model houses and then makes changes to accommodate site differences when building out the development. (See *Prototype Designs*.) Unless you have adequate protection from liability, you are subject to claims in all these instances.

Unauthorized Changes to Plans

THE SOLUTION

Your best bet is to add a provision in your contract that absolves you of responsibility and protects you if changes are made without your authorization. You also want the owner to include a provision in the contractor's contract (to be passed on to the contractor's subcontractors) prohibiting anyone from making any changes without your knowledge and consent. Such a paragraph might read:

UNAUTHORIZED CHANGES

In the event the Client, the Client's contractors or subcontractors, or anyone for whom the Client is legally liable makes or permits to be made any changes to any reports, plans, specifications or other construction documents prepared by the Consultant without obtaining the Consultant's prior written consent, the Client shall assume full responsibility for the results of such changes. Therefore the Client agrees to waive any claim against the Consultant and to release the Consultant from any liability arising directly or indirectly from such changes.

In addition, the Client agrees, to the fullest extent permitted by law, to indemnify and hold harmless the Consultant from any damages, liabilities or costs, including reasonable attorneys' fees and costs of defense, arising from such changes.

In addition, the Client agrees to include in any contracts for construction appropriate language that prohibits the Contractor or any subcontractors of any tier from making any changes or modifications to the Consultant's construction documents without the prior written approval of the Consultant and that further requires the Contractor to indemnify both the Consultant and the Client from any liability or cost arising from such changes made without such proper authorization.

If at all possible, retain ownership of your plans and specifications, including your electronic files. (See *Ownership of Instruments of Service*.)

As always, you should work closely with your attorney to ensure the above provision is coordinated with any other clauses in your contract that address CADD/Electronic Files,

Copyrights, Design Without Construction Administration, Ownership of Instruments of Service, Prototype Designs, Supplanting Another Consultant and Termination. (Please see these sections for suggested language and discussions.)

SEE ALSO:

CADD/Electronic Files
Changed Conditions
Construction Observation
Copyrights
Design Without Construction Administration
Ownership of Instruments of Service
Prototype Designs
Supplanting Another Consultant
Termination

THERE ARE NO RELEVANT PROVISIONS IN THE AIA OR EJCDC STANDARD FORM AGREEMENTS.

V-78

Part VI

Dispute Avoidance and Resolution

Attorneys' Fees

Betterment

Corporate Protection

Dispute Avoidance and Resolution

Frivolous Lawsuits

VI-2

Attorneys' Fees

In the absence of some agreement to the contrary, each party to a lawsuit usually must pay his or her own legal expenses, including attorneys' fees, court costs, expert-witness fees and other related expenses. Unlike the "English Rule," under which the "loser" pays the prevailing party's legal fees, courts in the United States simply do not award legal costs to the prevailing party unless a specific statute or contractual provision allows for recovery of these costs. While there are jurisdictions that have enacted attorney fee-shifting statutes, these tend to favor the plaintiff in actions brought against "bad guys," such as violators of EPA regulations, or landlords who refuse to release security deposits.

But what of the design or environmental professional who is named in a lawsuit of little or no merit? Very often, merely the threat of the huge expense of a legal squabble is enough to make a consultant throw in the towel and offer to settle — even if he or she is not at fault. This form of "legal" blackmail can be prevented.

The Problem

It's a sorry commentary on our times, but it is not uncommon for unprincipled clients to use threats of lawsuits against consultants to reduce the fees they owe. These clients also know that if you are forced to sue them to get your last invoice paid, your legal costs will likely amount to more than the invoice so a suit is often not worth the trouble. They consider a lawsuit against you — or even the threat of a lawsuit or a counterclaim — an effective means of getting a "discount" on your fees.

If your client sues you, claiming negligence, your defense costs could be astronomical. You might spend several years and thousands of dollars just to prove you weren't at fault. Insurance helps, of course, but you still bear the cost of your deductible and your staff time. Defending a lawsuit, no matter how unmeritorious or irresponsible it may be, is costly, time-consuming and detracts from your ability to do productive work. No wonder it is sometimes tempting to cave in to clients, who threaten a lawsuit and pay them, or write off your fee just to make the lawsuit go away. Often the legal cost of investigation and defense may equal or exceed the amount in dispute.

Attorneys' Fees

Even more frustrating is being forced to sue a client to collect fees you have already earned. The prospect of spending thousands of dollars to collect your receivables without the possibility of recovering the legal costs may weaken your resolve and cause you to just forget the whole thing and chalk it up to experience.

If your agreement is silent on the issue, you are generally responsible for your own legal fees even if you "win." Even worse is a client-written Attorneys' Fees clause that is one-way, giving only your client the right to recoup attorneys' fees. Agreeing to such an obviously biased and onerous clause would be downright foolish.

THE SOLUTION

The solution is simple: delete any unilateral Attorneys' Fees provisions and include in every contract a bilateral clause stating that the prevailing party is entitled to recoup his or her legal expenses from the loser. While in some states, a clause that is unilateral would be construed both ways by the courts, it is not true in all jurisdictions. You should not depend on the courts to interpret this in your favor.

As a starting place, here is a sample clause you might consider:

ATTORNEYS' FEES

In the event of any litigation arising from or related to this Agreement or the services provided under this Agreement, the prevailing party shall be entitled to recover from the non-prevailing party all reasonable costs incurred, including staff time, court costs, attorneys' fees and all other related expenses in such litigation.

Will your client agree to such a clause? Or does your client expect a one-sided Attorneys' Fees clause — tilted in his or her favor? Your client's reaction to this question is a good indication of the caliber of person you are dealing with. If possible, try inserting an additional clause — Certificate of Merit — that is intended to discourage nonmeritorious lawsuits. (See *Frivolous Lawsuits*.)

Note that neither the AIA nor EJCDC standard documents contain an Attorneys' Fees clause in their owner/consultant agreements. True, such clauses are double-edged swords. If you have such a clause and a court finds you responsible for negligence as charged, you would have to pay the other party's legal expenses in addition to the damages you caused (although such legal fees should be a compensable damage under your professional liability insurance). On the other hand, consultants do tend to prevail more often when they are the plaintiffs — in collection actions, for instance. If you sue your client for fees and win, the court will award you attorneys' fees in addition to your unpaid professional fees if you have such a contractual provision. If you don't have an Attorneys' Fees clause, courts will not award the "winner" legal costs.

There is an honest difference of opinion as to whether it helps more than it hurts to have a "prevailing party" provision in your agreements. We recommend such clauses in all professional service agreements because so few liability claims proceed through the entire legal system to a verdict. Having such a provision can sometimes strengthen your bargaining position when negotiating a claim settlement. Talk to your attorney and your insurance company about whether you should have an Attorneys' Fees clause.

Because so few cases go the entire legal distance, it would be helpful to define what it means to "prevail" in a case that is settled before going to trial. You could add the following language to the above Attorneys' Fees clause:

> **In the event of a non-adjudicative settlement of litigation between the parties or a resolution of a dispute by arbitration, the term "prevailing party" shall be determined by that process.**

Some firms prefer to call for attorneys' fees in their billing and collection provisions and only apply it to suits for fees. (See *Billing and Payment*.) In doing so, they avoid the duty to pay (as well as the right to collect) attorneys' fees in other types of litigation. Such a clause might read:

COLLECTION COSTS

> **In the event legal action is necessary to enforce the payment terms of this Agreement, the Consultant shall be entitled to collect from the Client any judgment or settlement sums due, plus reasonable attorneys' fees, court costs and other expenses incurred by the Consultant in connection therewith and, in addition, the reasonable value of the Consultant's time and expenses spent in connection with such collection action, computed according to the Consultant's prevailing fee schedule and expense policies.**

Attorneys' Fees

VI-6

A word of warning, however. If you are able to obtain an Attorneys' Fees clause, make sure your client's lawyers can't come at you through the "back door" via poorly worded indemnity language. Don't agree to "defend" or to indemnify someone for "claims, suits, demands or allegations." Such phrases seek to have you pay for your client's legal fees and defense costs, even if you are not at fault. Never agree to indemnify your client for anything other than your actual proven negligence. (See *Indemnities* for discussion and sample language.)

SEE ALSO:

Billing and Payment
Dispute Avoidance and Resolution
Frivolous Lawsuits
Indemnities
Limitation of Liability

THERE ARE NO RELEVANT PROVISIONS IN
THE AIA OR EJCDC STANDARD FORM AGREEMENTS.

BETTERMENT

In law, the concept of *betterment* or *unjust enrichment* means that a person who is damaged because of another's mistake should be entitled to recoup losses caused by that mistake but not to gain an advantage or profit because of it.

To illustrate, let's use a simple example: the architect of a post office omitted the restrooms for postal employees from her plans. It was not until the construction of the post office was nearly complete that someone finally noticed the omission. Clearly, it had to be corrected, and the government demanded the bathrooms be installed at the architect's expense.

What were the architect's obligations? Bathrooms were required; the contractor would have included the cost in the bid sum, and the government would have paid for them if they had been designed, included in the bid documents and installed in the first place. Because the post office was nearly complete, however, the restrooms would now cost more to install. There might be demolition costs, materials and labor might now be more expensive, concrete would have to be sawed, drain lines brought in, plumbing installed and porta-potties rented. What's more, the contractor would doubtless claim for profit and overhead on the resulting change orders.

Under the concept of betterment, the architect is legally responsible only for the "delta" — the costs over and above what it would have cost had the bathrooms been designed, specified and constructed in the first place. This extra cost is the *premium* that must be paid to add the omitted item out of normal sequence. The post office would have to pay what the cost of labor and materials would have been if the restrooms had been built in the proper sequence during the original construction. The post office is not entitled to get the benefit of the bathrooms for free.

THE PROBLEM

Your client, when confronted with an unexpected contractor's change order for something you neglected to specify, is going to blame you. If you made a mistake, your client may expect you to pay whatever it takes to make it right — even if it means the entire cost of an omitted item would come out of your pocket. If tempers were cooler, you could explain that your client would have had to pay for the item anyway, had it been in the plans. But he or she isn't going to want to hear a lesson on the legal concept of *unjust enrichment* just then.

Unless you have paved the way for just such an eventuality, both in talks with your client and in contract language that makes your mutual expectations crystal clear, this kind of situation can escalate from a minor dispute to full-scale litigation.

THE SOLUTION

The best solution is to explain the concept of betterment to your client when you are drafting your agreement. Your goal is to avoid any misunderstandings should problems occur and to have your client acknowledge understanding of the concept. (It is the law anyway, the way a court would usually apportion the damages if it came to that.) Then, with a contract clause that reflects that understanding, both of you will know what to expect if a glitch arises. Such a clause could be added to a Standard of Care clause or it could stand alone. Here is a sample clause:

BETTERMENT

If, due to the Consultant's negligence, a required item or component of the Project is omitted from the Consultant's construction documents, the Consultant shall not be responsible for paying the cost required to add such item or component to the extent that such item or component would have been required and included in the original construction documents. In no event will the Consultant be responsible for any cost or expense that provides betterment or upgrades or enhances the value of the Project.

By defining your responsibilities under the concept of betterment and having your client acknowledge that there is "no free lunch," you will have gone a long way toward preventing a major source of misunderstanding and disputes.

You can start by talking to your clients and educating them on the possible pitfalls and imperfections of the design and construction process. Such a discussion offers the perfect opportunity to suggest that your client plan on a contingency fund for unexpected costs related to design. (See **Contingency Fund** and **Standard of Care** for more information and sample clauses.)

SEE ALSO:

Code Compliance
Contingency Fund
Defects in Service
Standard of Care

RELEVANT STANDARD FORM AGREEMENT PROVISIONS:

AIA B141-1997:   No applicable provisions.
EJCDC 1910-1 (1996 edition):   Exhibit I 6.11B.3

VI-10

CORPORATE PROTECTION

Of all the parties to a construction or remediation project, the architect, engineer and environmental professional are most at risk. That's because, in virtually every state, licensed professionals can be held personally liable for their professional acts. While the owner and contractors can shield themselves from personal liability for their business activities by forming corporations, such protection is unavailable to the licensed professional. Even if the design or environmental firm closed its doors and went out of business, the individual licensed professional who signed and sealed the plans or wrote the Phase I report would remain personally accountable for damages. That liability can extend for years — perhaps even after the professional's death — to his or her estate. And that liability, in most jurisdictions, stretches to virtually anyone to whom the professional owes a duty of care. (See *Standard of Care* and *Statutes of Repose and Limitation* for discussion.)

THE PROBLEM

Persons making claims against consultants frequently try to bring added emotional and legal pressure to bear by suing not only the consulting firm but also the individual licensed professionals or consultants. In other words, if you are incorporated, the claimant might name not only the corporation but also you personally and any other licensed professionals who provided services on the project. The claimant might even name your corporation's officers and directors, claiming that they managed or directed the firm's allegedly negligent activities.

Being named as an individual in a lawsuit, whether negligence is eventually proven or not, can be devastating. Not only must you spend a great deal of money and time defending yourself, but your personal assets — your home, your savings, your children's college education — might be placed in jeopardy. It is an unfair and unwarranted tactic since it is the consulting firm that contracted with the client to provide the service and realized the profit on those services.

THE SOLUTION

Professional liability insurance policies generally cover not only your firm but also its employees, partners and principals, and its officers and directors for claims arising from the normal scope and course of their employment. Even if an ex-employee is sued for professional acts he or she performed while in your employment, most policies also would provide them protection. Check with your professional liability insurance specialist to determine the specific terms of your professional liability policy that apply to both present and former employees. In particular, there is cause for real concern if your firm drops its coverage or if a new carrier does not provide as broad a coverage for all these potential defendant parties.

Some states have laws that require a corporation to indemnify its employees from claims arising from the normal scope of their employment. However, this is not true in every state, and even where it exists, it applies only to firms that are incorporated. If you operate as a partnership or proprietorship, employees may not be protected by such laws. (Check with your lawyer to see if your state has this kind of statutory corporate protection.)

Is there any other protection available to you? Perhaps. It may be possible, depending on applicable state laws, to limit your exposure to first-party suits — claims by those with whom your firm has a contract. Since more than half of all professional liability claims are made by clients, this may be a significant protection.

In the agreement with your client, you could include a clause providing that, in the event of a claim, your client would sue only your firm and would not name any individual employee, officer or director. Some consultants have been successful in obtaining such a provision. Discuss the use and wording of this clause with your attorney to see if it is enforceable in your jurisdiction. If you are not a corporation, check to see if it can be adapted to a partnership or a proprietorship.

CORPORATE PROTECTION

It is intended by the parties to this Agreement that the Consultant's services in connection with the Project shall not subject the Consultant's individual employees, officers or directors to any personal legal exposure for the risks associated with this Project. Therefore, and notwithstanding anything to the contrary contained herein, the Client agrees that as the Client's sole and exclusive remedy, any claim, demand or suit shall be directed and/or asserted only against the Consultant, a {insert state} **corporation, and not against any of the Consultant's individual employees, officers or directors.**

If you are successful in negotiating such a provision, bear in mind that while it might protect you from claims by your client, you are still vulnerable to third-party suits. (See *Third-Party Beneficiaries*.) In some special situations, nevertheless, you might be able to combine the above clause with an indemnity in which your client holds you harmless for third-party suits. This is an innovative measure, however, and may be attainable only in high-risk situations where you are in a strong bargaining position. Work closely with your attorney in drafting and negotiating this provision to make it as enforceable as possible.

In the end, if your client doesn't agree to a Corporate Protection clause, it may still serve as a good springboard for discussing risk allocation and may help you in negotiating Limitation of Liability and Indemnification provisions for your contract. (Refer to *Indemnities* and *Limitation of Liability* for discussions and sample clauses.)

SEE ALSO:

Indemnities
Limitation of Liability
Standard of Care
Statutes of Repose and Limitation
Third-Party Beneficiaries

THERE ARE NO RELEVANT PROVISIONS IN THE AIA OR EJCDC STANDARD FORM AGREEMENTS.

VI-14

DISPUTE AVOIDANCE AND RESOLUTION

Being involved in a lawsuit is one of the most traumatic events a design or environmental professional can face. When a claim is filed, it signals the beginning of an exceedingly rough journey that will, in all probability, last several years. The impact can be devastating. The costs in lost staff time, the uninsured expenses associated with defending oneself, the insurance deductible, the bad publicity and the emotional wear and tear on staff and family — all can be ruinous to a professional practice.

There is encouraging news, though. In recent years, contractors, design and environmental professionals and their clients (and, yes, even many lawyers) began adding up the costs of construction litigation — costs to the "winners" and "losers" alike — and were appalled by the bottom line. It became obvious that no one really *wins* in a lawsuit. They began to search for ways to prevent or minimize disputes and to improve techniques for resolving the disputes that do arise.

It was also apparent that once a dispute was put into the hands of a third party, the costs in time, money and anguish escalated. So there began a quest for techniques in which the parties to a dispute could devise their own solutions. The results have been striking. We have seen the emergence of project partnering and a resurgence of jobsite dispute resolution techniques. (See Parts One and Two of this section, *Partnering* and *Jobsite Dispute Resolution*.) Non-binding mediation, almost unheard of just a decade ago, has become relatively commonplace in construction disputes. (See Part Three, *Mediation*.) Similarly, disputants have begun to turn to other innovative, non-adjudicative dispute resolution techniques, such as minitrials, mediation/arbitration and advisory arbitration. (See Part Five, *Other Dispute Resolution Methods*.) International projects have adopted their own alternatives to litigation. (See Part Six, *Resolving International Disputes*.) On the other hand, mandatory binding arbitration, once the industry dispute resolution (DR[1]) standard, has been increasingly rejected as too expensive, time-consuming, and often apt to lead to inequitable, non-appealable results. (See Part Four, *Arbitration*.)

---

[1] *While many refer to this as Alternative Dispute Resolution or ADR, we at DPIC like to think of it as DR. Litigation is the alternative and a poor one at that.*

Dispute Avoidance and Resolution

As warm and fuzzy and "90s" as a lot of these new techniques may seem when compared to the let's-sue-the-rascals attitude of the last few decades, they still require a hardheaded approach. Problems on the jobsite must be anticipated and their resolution provided for up front. Contract formation is the ideal time to discuss with a client the many options available for keeping litigation at bay. At the very least, consultants should insist on a dispute resolution provision that calls for mediation as the first step in formal dispute resolution. But they can go a lot further. Consultants can use contract discussions as an opportunity to educate their clients. The client may not understand the benefits of partnering, for instance, or may believe that arbitration is the most efficient way to avoid litigation. Many in the construction industry are coming to see the advantages of dispute avoidance and resolution. Remember: it is a lot easier to convince a client of the benefits of mediation during contract negotiation than after a lawsuit has been filed.

PART ONE: PARTNERING

Given all the fanfare that project partnering has been receiving over the past few years, one might be tempted to dismiss the process as just the latest fad to come along in the construction industry. But a closer look reveals an intriguing trend. Thousands of construction projects have been successfully completed by creating a positive dispute prevention atmosphere through the use of project partnering.

Partnering is hardly a new idea. Rather, it is an old precept restated — the affirmation of the good faith and fair dealing that somehow have been lost sight of by many in the construction industry. It is the pledge to work together to enhance quality, efficiency, and on-time performance, and to improve relationships and communications with a fair profit for all participants. In short, it is a promise to work towards the best of all forms of dispute resolution: dispute *avoidance*.

The concept is simple: to dispel the adversarial us-versus-them approach all too commonly found on today's construction and remediation projects and to promote instead a let's-all-pull-together attitude. While the actual steps may vary, they usually involve facilitated team-building activities that help define common goals, improve communication and cultivate a problem-solving attitude among key representatives of the design or remediation and construction teams *before* work on a project begins. Most often, the participants draft a pledge or charter stating their commitment to deal fairly with one another. They may then meet regularly to weigh their progress. Many partnering arrangements make it a point to renew and reaffirm their commitment once the project has been underway for some time.

The benefits realized by consultants who participate in partnering can be significant. Their role in the decision-making process may be enhanced, for example. Their liability and thus exposure to litigation is reduced. Their participation in construction phase services is more likely. (See ***Construction Observation*** and ***Design Without Construction Administration*** for more information.) What's more, the process may help reduce cost overruns, as well as help minimize project delays and resulting delay claims. As a bonus, design or environmental professionals who suggest partnering to their clients may also find it an effective sales tool because it sets them apart from other firms.

THE PROBLEM

Given all the benefits, why aren't owners, consultants and contractors rushing to implement partnering on all their projects? Most likely, many clients — and design and environmental professionals — don't yet understand the process and its potential benefits. Some owners may believe that a partnering arrangement requires more energy and up-front costs than they are willing to invest or may regard it as nothing more than a "touchy-feely" waste of time. What's more, although many public entities and large firms are beginning to incorporate partnering into larger projects, thus far the process has not been widely used on smaller projects. Often, consultants do not realize that the precepts of partnering can be successfully applied to projects of all sizes and descriptions.

Some consultants are also concerned that entering into a partnering arrangement might constitute a contractual relationship between the contractor and the consultant and would, in those few states where privity of contract is required in order to sue somebody, give the contractor standing to sue the designer. (See *Third-Party Beneficiaries*.) Some also worry that partnering might increase their liability for construction-related and jobsite safety problems.

There is one more dilemma. Some projects that do employ partnering may only involve the owner and the contractors and exclude the design and technical professionals from the process. This makes little sense. To exclude the very parties who can best interpret design documents and reports and suggest ways to mitigate problems would seem contrary to the partnering idea.

THE SOLUTION

Learn the fundamentals of partnering. Although it is not a panacea for all construction problems, partnering has been shown to be well worth the effort. The American Consulting Engineers Council, the Army Corps of Engineers, the American Institute of Architects, the Associated General Contractors of America, the Construction Industry Institute and many state agencies and other organizations — including DPIC — believe partnering represents an important cost-effective method by which to manage projects more efficiently and achieve quality results. The difficulties mentioned above are largely based on misconceptions that can be readily debunked.

For instance, if you or your client think that the costs associated with partnering (a one- or two-day facilitated workshop, tailored to the size and complexity of the project, and follow-up meetings) might be too high, take a moment to consider the cost of giving a one-day deposition in a lawsuit, not to mention the loss of good working relationships. Even most smaller projects can effectively and inexpensively implement partnering. If necessary, a properly run, half-day workshop held in your lunchroom can use the same team-building techniques and generate the same spirit as a full-blown two-day retreat.

As for increased liability for jobsite safety and construction claims, we believe — partnered project or not — that every design, geotechnical or environmental professional should perform construction phase services. While this may increase the chances of involvement in site issues, the possible increase in risk should be more than offset by better project results. In any case, your contract should have a strong Jobsite Safety provision — we consider it a **Deal Maker** — that makes clear that responsibility for site safety and construction means and methods remains with the contractor. (See *Jobsite Safety*.) You can also insist that the client add to his or her agreement with the contractor a provision stating that partnering in no way relieves the contractor of his or her safety responsibilities or responsibilities to perform the Work in accordance with the requirements of the Contract Documents.

How do you ensure that partnering is implemented on a project — and that you are included? The best solution is the most straightforward. Explain to your client your commitment to the partnering ideals and ask for a similar resolve on his or her part. This is important. In order for partnering to work, it must be owner-driven. The owner must be committed to the concept, be willing to incorporate the concept of partnering into the bid solicitations, and be ready to take the necessary steps to ensure that the process actually takes place, that the parties don't just go through the motions.

Resolve to negotiate with your client a solid, *fair* contract. You must have an agreement in which the risk is shared equitably; any agreement that gives one party an undue portion of the risk will truly undermine the essence of partnering.

Then, you and your client should set forth your mutual expectations in your agreement. Whether or not partnering is anticipated, we think every contract should contain in the Preamble — the "whereas" section — an affirmation of your mutual commitment to deal with one another in good faith. One public entity regularly uses the following wording:

PREAMBLE

This Agreement is based upon a mutual obligation of good faith and fair dealing between the parties in its performance and enforcement. Accordingly, the Client and the Consultant, with a positive commitment to honesty and integrity, agree to the following:

That each will function within the laws and statutes that apply to its duties and responsibilities; that each will assist in the other's performance; that each will avoid hindering the other's performance; that each will work diligently to fulfill its obligations; and that each will cooperate in the common endeavor of the contract.

This is a good start — and establishes an atmosphere of trust and cooperation in which problems are likely to get solved. But don't stop there. We suggest you go on to include a clause in your agreement with your client stating that partnering will be employed on the project and that you will be included in the process. This accomplishes several things. First, it serves to introduce the concept of partnering and educates a client who may not be familiar with it — or gives a little push to an undecided client. It tells your client and the world that you embrace and practice the concept of teamwork. The clause is a mechanism by which you can make certain that partnering is addressed in the client/contractor contract. Finally, it ensures you will be part of the partnering process. Here is a sample partnering clause:

VOLUNTARY PARTNERING

The Client will encourage participation in a formalized Partnering process that involves the Client, the Consultant and its subconsultants, and the Contractor and its principal subcontractors and suppliers. This Partnering relationship will be structured to draw on the strengths of each organization to identify and achieve common goals. The objectives are effective and efficient contract performance and completion of the Project within budget, on schedule, in accordance with the drawings and specifications, and without litigation.

Participation in Partnering will be totally voluntary and all participants will have equal status. Any cost associated with implementing Partnering will be agreed to in advance by all parties and will be shared equally.

Does placing a partnering clause in your contract undermine the spirit of volunteerism necessary to successful partnering? We think not. Participation in an active partnering procedure is, after all, still voluntary. But such a clause also says to your client that you are first and foremost interested in working in a non-adversarial atmosphere that is dedicated to dispute avoidance — and asks your client to retain contractors who are like-minded. Finally, it may set the stage to introduce mediation provisions into your agreement. (Refer to *Mediation* in this section.)

It has not been shown that entering into a partnering agreement in any way constitutes a contractual agreement or supersedes or negates your contract with your client. If you are concerned, you and your attorney may want to add an additional sentence to the above clause (and perhaps to your partnering pledge or charter as well) making clear your intent:

> By engaging in Partnering, the parties do not intend to create a legal partnership, or to create additional contractual relationships, or to alter in any way the intent of this Agreement between the Client and the Consultant.

Just because your project is partnered does not mean you and your client are not obligated to adhere to the terms of your contract. On most jobs, once you stumble home from contract negotiations, you will put your agreement away and may never have to look at it again. If you do need it, though, it is right there in its file, setting forth your legal rights and duties as well as those of your client. Your partnering arrangement in no way undermines that agreement.

Participants in a partnering workshop typically determine how they will resolve problems quickly and at the lowest possible level of management. They may decide to establish a dispute review board, if the project is large enough to warrant it, or some other mechanism. Mediation or another form of dispute resolution may be decided upon for conflicts that cannot be solved by the participants. We offer a caveat here, however. You will want to be sure that any reference to *formal* dispute resolution in the partnering pledge is consistent with any dispute resolution provision in your contract with your client.

You have nothing to lose. By introducing the concept of partnering to your clients and by placing it in your agreement and in the General Conditions, you are creating an opportunity to educate your client about the process and to set reasonable expectations of all participants in the project. If nothing else, you may be able to ferret out an owner (or contractor) whose value system is different from yours. After all, if they balk at the basic concepts of good faith and fair dealing of partnering, is this really your kind of client?

THERE ARE NO RELEVANT PROVISIONS IN THE AIA OR EJCDC STANDARD FORM AGREEMENTS.

Part Two: Jobsite Dispute Resolution

Recent research by the Construction Industry Institute (CII) underscores once again the value of preventing problems and resolving disputes at the jobsite level. Every lawsuit starts as a mere *problem*, explain the authors of the three-year study. If the problem cannot be solved quickly, it grows into a *disagreement*. If the parties can't immediately resolve the disagreement, it becomes a *dispute*, which still could be resolved at the project site. However, if the dispute cannot be resolved, it grows into a *conflict*, moves off the jobsite, out of the hands of the disputants, and enters the traditional dispute resolution arena. If not settled through dispute resolution techniques, such as mediation or arbitration, it then moves to a courtroom by way of the ritualistic game of "chicken" called *litigation*.

The study confirmed that if difficulties can be resolved on the project site during the construction phase, the costs of resolution and the levels of hostility remain relatively low. Once the dispute moves off the jobsite and into the hands of others (read: *the lawyers*), the expenses and enmity begin to escalate. Clearly, the best and least expensive way to avoid litigation is to have a project-wide commitment that, at the first indication of a problem, participants will work together to resolve it and not allow it to escalate into a conflict where third-party resolution is required.

There are several techniques to accomplish this. Along with project partnering (see Part One of this section, **Partnering**), two of the most effective — step negotiations and dispute review boards — are often implemented together.

Step negotiations really amount to a commitment to resolve a problem as soon as possible at the lowest possible level of management. If parties directly involved cannot resolve a problem at the jobsite, their supervisors then meet to work out a solution. If they, in turn, cannot agree, then the problem will be passed on to higher management in both organizations in a step-by-step process up the management ladder. Often each of these levels is identified at the beginning of the project, and there should be a predetermined time limit for resolving an issue at each given level. For instance, if a problem cannot be fixed in two days at the first level, then it is passed to the next decision-making level, which meets and has four days to find a solution. Because passing on a problem means having to report a failure to the boss, everyone has an incentive to settle disputes very quickly.

On other construction projects, the parties have adopted the concept of *standing neutral.* This is formalized in an agreement between the owner, contractor and (usually) the design team to select an independent dispute resolver to be at hand throughout construction. Generally consisting of one or more industry experts, this resolver is commonly known as a *dispute review board* (DRB). A dispute review board (also called a *standing mediator* or a *standing arbitrator*) has several advantages over conventional dispute resolution processes. A DRB is set up at the beginning of a project and continues throughout the project's lifetime. Because the board frequently visits the jobsite, there is continuity and familiarity with the parties and the specific project at hand. Disputes are often resolved quickly while the facts are still fresh in everyone's mind. Complaints without merit are discouraged by this process. Everyone involved on the project is encouraged to communicate openly and to resolve problems on-site and at the lowest possible decision-making level without resorting to the DRB. In fact, parties to projects where DRBs are established have found that the very existence of a board tends to encourage participants to resolve problems themselves — through step negotiations or similar mechanisms — before referring them to the board. The success of DRBs is impressive. Since the late 1970s, when the first boards came into existence, hundreds of projects have instituted DRBs. Of the completed projects, very few have had any litigation.

THE PROBLEM

All too often, design and environmental professionals and their clients fail to establish a mechanism for dealing with the inevitable problems and difficulties that arise on any project. But unless you and your client have agreed beforehand on how to handle such issues — and memorialize this agreement in your contract — you may find it difficult to implement DR techniques once a problem comes up.

There is another reason for addressing these issues during contract formation. Having a procedure for you and your client to solve your disagreements as soon as possible is only part of the picture. You also want your client to obligate the contractor, subcontractors and vendors to do the same. If such a requirement is not inserted into the General Conditions of the owner/contractor agreement by your client, the contractor is under no such obligation.

THE SOLUTION

You and your client should decide at the beginning of the project what steps you will take during construction to resolve problems as soon as they arise. It is important to put this in your agreement and to have the owner put a similar clause in his or her contract with the contractor. Here is a sample DRB clause:

DISPUTE REVIEW BOARD

In an effort to resolve any conflicts that arise during the design or construction of the Project, the Client and the Consultant agree to the establishment of a dispute-review board, chosen by _____. It is intended that all jobsite disputes that cannot be

**Part Two:
Jobsite Dispute
Resolution**

resolved by direct negotiation between the parties involved shall be submitted to this board prior to resorting to mediation or any other form of formal dispute resolution.

The Client and Consultant further agree to include a similar provision in all agreements with independent contractors and consultants retained for the Project and to require all independent contractors and consultants to include a similar provision in all agreements with their subcontractors, subconsultants, suppliers and fabricators.

THERE ARE NO RELEVANT PROVISIONS IN
THE AIA OR EJCDC STANDARD FORM AGREEMENTS.

PART THREE: MEDIATION

When an architect or engineer is a party to litigation, chances are the case will never get as far as a courtroom. More than 95 percent of all lawsuits involving professional liability are settled before they go to trial — but often only after years of interrogatories, depositions, countersuits, legal maneuvering and mounting legal fees. No wonder parties to construction disputes have come to see the litigation process as a frustrating waste of productive time and massive sums of money. It makes one ask, if the chances are that a dispute will eventually end at the negotiating table, why not start there in the first place?

In fact, there is already a process that allows disputing parties to do just that — a comparatively inexpensive and quick process, with established structure and rules. It is called *mediation.* It is a voluntary method of helping disputing parties reach agreement among themselves, thus maintaining or reopening communications between client and consultant. The approach involves a mediator, an impartial third party who helps resolve conflicts. By direct and informed negotiation, consultation with each side and "shuttle diplomacy" between them, the mediator works with (and on) the parties until they are able to reach their own settlement. Unlike arbitration, mediation is usually not binding on the parties. But no matter. If the parties choose their own solution, they are likely to carry it out.

There are other advantages to mediation. For instance, in some situations, when facing a claim that is so new or in which the issues are so complex or unclear, opposing parties are loathe to agree to mediate until they learn more. In litigation, the usual response to this situation is to spend a lot of money, in the form of all-out discovery warfare: subpoenas for document production, expert opinions and depositions. It is not unheard of for attorneys to hire a service to copy, catalog and index a truckload of the opposing party's records, even though the key pieces of information may actually be contained in a single file.

Mediation offers an alternative to this costly blanket discovery. A technique called mediated or facilitated discovery allows the parties to learn what the case is all about — to define and narrow the issues — without spending a lot of money up front. They and their attorneys can sit down with a mediator and agree that the case may actually turn on the depositions of, say, two people, instead of a dozen. They may decide that the key documents are actually few in number. With the help of a mediator, they may choose to share the cost of a single, neutral expert. Then, when the agreed-upon information has been collected and the issues made clearer, the parties can either go back to the mediation table, decide to litigate or pursue another dispute resolution method.

In a 1994 survey on dispute avoidance and resolution within the construction industry, attorneys rated mediation as the most effective dispute resolution technique for reducing the time necessary to resolve disputes. Respondents thought that mediation led to more equitable resolutions to disputes. They also felt it was the most effective technique for reducing the cost of dispute resolution; the best process for identifying the strengths and weaknesses of one's case and for minimizing future disputes; and, along with early neutral evaluation, the most effective method for opening channels of communication on the jobsite.

If total resolution of all issues cannot be reached through mediation, the parties can try advisory arbitration, a minitrial or another consensual method of dispute resolution in which the parties continue, in a voluntary and nonbinding way, to work out their solutions to the remaining issues. (See Part Five, *Other Dispute Resolution Methods*, of this section.) If methods such as these are not successful, then the parties can proceed to an adjudicative form of dispute resolution, in which someone else renders a binding decision — arbitration, or, as a last resort, litigation. (See Part Four of this section, *Arbitration*.)

THE PROBLEM

Unless you and your client have agreed beforehand to handle conflicts through mediation, you may miss the chance to resolve your differences this way. It is difficult to explain the benefits of mediation to an angry client and persuade him or her to try it after a claim has been made, a lawsuit filed and relationships ruined. Sadly, once a dispute becomes hostile, as it does in litigation or arbitration, it is unlikely that you will be able to preserve your relationship with your client or work on future projects together.

Most professional association standard contract forms now provide for mediation. The AIA 1997 documents call for mediation as the first step before arbitration for resolving disputes. The EJCDC 1910-1 (1996 edition) calls for good faith direct negotiations of disputes for 30 days and, if the dispute is not resolved, then Exhibit H gives a choice of mediation or arbitration as agreed upon during contract formation. The EJCDC General Conditions (1910-8) says disputes will be resolved by whatever method is agreed upon in the Supplementary Conditions. Both CASE Contract Document 2 (1991) and ASFE Standard Forms of Agreement provide for mediation as well.

THE SOLUTION

Provide for mediation in all of your contracts. Mediation has a remarkable track record, especially when it is employed at the appropriate stage of the dispute. (In one study, fully three-fourths of more than 2,000 claims against design professionals were resolved to the disputants' satisfaction through mediation.) Discuss the problems and expense of senseless litigation with your client during contract formation and explain your wish to have in place a mechanism to resolve conflicts and possibly avoid litigation altogether.

By including such a provision in your agreement, you and your client will have on tap a proven means by which you can inexpensively settle most disputes and very likely emerge from the process with your business relationship intact. Such a clause might read:

MEDIATION

In an effort to resolve any conflicts that arise during the design and construction of the Project or following the completion of the Project, the Client and the Consultant agree that all disputes between them arising out of or relating to this Agreement or the Project shall be submitted to nonbinding mediation unless the parties mutually agree otherwise.

The Client and the Consultant further agree to include a similar mediation provision in all agreements with independent contractors and consultants retained for the Project and to require all independent contractors and consultants also to include a similar mediation provision in all agreements with their subcontractors, subconsultants, suppliers and fabricators, thereby providing for mediation as the primary method for dispute resolution between the parties to all those agreements.

We recommend you and your client select the mediation service together when a dispute arises rather than have a mediator predetermined in the contract. There are several local and national organizations that provide mediation services for design and/or construction industry disputes. Generally, they each have their own detailed set of rules and procedures. When you and your client agree on the mediation service, you have agreed to be guided by their rules. Check with your attorney, professional liability insurance specialist or insurance carrier for the names of recommended mediation services in your area. They should be able to commend a service to you.

There are many other alternatives for dispute resolution available to you. (See Part Five of this chapter.) Start with mediation, however, and provide for it in your agreements. Because the cost in time and dollars for mediation is so low and the success ratio so high, mediation is an effective problem-solving device and worth a try as a first step. Although you'll need some legal representation in most mediation and alternative dispute processes, your legal fees should be substantially less than those involved in a full-blown court or arbitration proceeding. You have everything to gain and nothing to lose by trying the process. In fact, DPIC Companies believes so strongly in mediation that we consider this clause a **Deal Maker** — a must-have — in all your agreements.

RELEVANT STANDARD FORM AGREEMENT PROVISIONS:

AIA B141-1997:	Articles 1.3.4-5
EJCDC 1910-1 (1996 edition):	Article 6.09
	Exhibit A 2.01A
	Exhibit H

Part Four: Arbitration

Arbitration remains the best known formal dispute resolution alternative to litigation. It can take several forms; it can be voluntary or mandatory, binding or non binding, specialized or expedited, or one of several variations of mediation-arbitration (see Part Five of this section, *Other Dispute Resolution Methods*).

The focus here is on binding arbitration as it is sometimes used in design and environmental professional agreements. This is a formal dispute resolution technique in which the opposing parties present their cases before one or more neutral individuals who are empowered to render a binding and court-enforceable decision. Although this procedure was originally intended to offer significant benefits over litigation by providing a forum in which disputes could be resolved without the spending of large amounts of time and money, today this is not always the case.

The Problem

Until recently, many standard professional association contracts (including AIA documents) contained an arbitration clause that called for mandatory binding arbitration in the event of a dispute. Under this type of contract, you must submit disputes to arbitration even if circumstances suggest that other dispute resolution methods would be more appropriate in resolving the conflict. Newly revised AIA forms, however, provide for mediation as the first step in dispute resolution, and then arbitration if mediation does not work.

You should be aware that although arbitration may be an effective dispute resolution tool in some limited situations, there are several drawbacks to the process that can render it an unsatisfactory, and sometimes disastrous, remedy.

First, unless specifically provided for, discovery proceedings are not generally allowed in arbitration. This means you may not be able to obtain documents and other information that could be vital to your case. You cannot subpoena documents, and you cannot require sworn testimony (depositions) from witnesses.

Second, arbitration does not follow the rules of evidence found in civil litigation, and this can result in proceedings that may or may not be focused on relevant issues. Arbitrators can refuse to accept documentary evidence, for example, and even permit hearsay testimony — something not permitted even on a TV courtroom show.

Third, arbitrators are not required to apply legal principles or even the terms of your contract in reaching their decisions. In fact, they are generally not required to state the grounds or reasons for their decisions. You might even say they can act "arbitrarily."

Fourth — and this is a major drawback — it is difficult to obtain knowledgeable, qualified arbitrators through some arbitration services. Even the venerable American Arbitration Association recently found it necessary to raise the standards of its construction industry arbitrators, and trimmed its numbers from more than 20,000 to about 4,000 panel members.

Finally, unless arbitrators are found to have acted with bias, prejudice or fraud, you generally cannot appeal their decisions.

In spite of these limitations, there are a few situations in which you may wish to use arbitration or some form of tailored arbitration as a problem-solving forum and perhaps arrange it so that the above drawbacks do not come into play. For instance, small, two-party disputes may lend themselves to arbitration. Consider a fee dispute with your client. Typically, claims by consultants for unpaid fees result in cross claims for huge amounts by the client. However, if fee disputes are decided by mandatory arbitration, such cross claims may be forestalled. Claims involving relatively small sums also lend themselves to arbitration. Some firms stipulate in their agreements that they will arbitrate disputes involving less than $10,000 or $20,000, while others will arbitrate disputes up to $50,000. Some international disputes can be readily (although not necessarily inexpensively) resolved through arbitration. (See *International Projects* and Part Six of this section, ***Resolving International Disputes***.) You and your attorney need to weigh the pros and cons. If the conflict involves only two parties and your evidence is readily available to you, arbitration may be the right method. If, however, there is a chance other parties might be brought in, or if the amount involved is significant, then you, your attorney and your insurer will want to look at other dispute resolution methods.

THE SOLUTION

When faced with a contract that calls for mandatory binding arbitration, your best course is to delete the clause and replace it with a paragraph that calls for some form of mediation as the first step in resolving a dispute. (See Part Four of this section, ***Mediation***, for discussion and suggested contract language.) If your client is adamant about retaining the arbitration clause, however, then insist on changing the language from "shall be decided by arbitration . . ." to "may, with the consent of both parties, be decided . . ." Regardless of the modifications you make, we recommend that you always make a concerted effort to add a provision for mediation as the first step in dispute resolution.

Some consulting firms prefer to specify in their contract that certain types of disputes or disputes involving less than a specified dollar amount are to be settled by mandatory binding arbitration. If you and your attorney believe arbitration might be an acceptable solution for some simple disputes involving small sums, you will want to insert an arbitration provision in your contract. Again, make certain you have provided for mediation elsewhere in your contract as a first step in conflict resolution, as well as for other options for dispute resolution. (See Part Five of this section, ***Other Dispute Resolution Methods***.)

Part Four: Arbitration

ARBITRATION

In the event the parties to this Agreement are unable to reach a settlement of any dispute involving an amount of less than $_____, arising out of this Agreement or related to the services under this Agreement, in accordance with Paragraph _____ (Mediation), then such disputes may, with the consent of both parties, be settled by binding arbitration in accordance with the **rules of** *{insert appropriate reference to a specific arbitration service's rules, such as the Construction Industry Arbitration Rules of the American Arbitration Association, or the arbitration rules of the International Chamber of Commerce or the Center for Public Resources or such other arbitration rules as you may choose}* **current as of the date of this Agreement then pertaining.**

Be sure to check with your attorney and your insurer's claims staff regarding whose rules you should reference. They may have suggestions regarding which arbitration service they recommend in a particular locale or for the type of project you are undertaking.

Instead of specifying a dollar limit, you could change the language to limit arbitration to certain kinds of issues, such as fee disputes.

Because appeal of an arbitrator's decision is so difficult, it is important that you retain some control over the selection of the arbitrators, no matter what set of rules you select. You could work with your attorney to develop wording that either gives you and your client the power of mutual agreement over choice of an arbitrator or specify a set of rules that gives you some measure of veto.

Arbitration is only one option in the array of dispute resolution techniques available. As with any tool, it works well when used correctly and for the right task. Even if your contract does not call for arbitration, it is a procedure that is always available to you and your client, even if only to help you focus on the solvable issues in a dispute before proceeding — if all else fails — to litigation.

RELEVANT STANDARD FORM AGREEMENT PROVISIONS:

AIA B141-1997:	Article 1.3.5
EJCDC 1910-1 (1996 edition):	Exhibit H 6.09A.1-4

PART FIVE: OTHER DISPUTE RESOLUTION METHODS

In addition to the more common methods we've discussed, there is a whole array of creative dispute resolution (DR) techniques available. Some of the best are minitrials, mediation/arbitration, mediation-then-arbitration, voluntary nonbinding arbitration, summary jury trials and private litigation.

A *minitrial* is actually more a private nonbinding settlement method than a trial. Procedures vary but usually allow the legal counsel for the disputants to briefly present their cases before a panel of top management representatives of each party and, usually, a neutral legal or technical advisor, in a confidential trial-like setting. The procedure may provide for some limited testimony, document production or both; these details are agreed upon beforehand. Management can hear both sides of the issues, see the strengths and weaknesses of their respective cases and get a sense of the likely outcome of litigation. Often this persuades both sides to settle their differences rather than move to all-out litigation. Following the case presentation, the executives may negotiate by themselves, without counsel, although they may confer with counsel at any time. For a minitrial to succeed, the executives who participate should not be directly involved in the project, must possess excellent negotiating skills and must have full authority to settle the dispute for their firm.

Mediation/arbitration, as might be surmised, is a combination of mediation and arbitration. The technique, often called med/arb, requires one person to act as both mediator and arbitrator. This person, agreed upon by the parties before construction begins, is selected on the basis of his or her objectivity, honesty and knowledge of the industry.

If a dispute arises, the parties involved attempt to solve it on their own. Failing that, the mediator is brought in to attempt to settle the dispute. If these efforts fail, the role of the mediator switches to that of an arbitrator and a binding decision will be made based on his or her findings. Because the parties will be required to use the med/arbitrator throughout the project on additional disputes, the range of conflict usually narrows, and the entire resolution process can be accelerated significantly. Some critics of med/arb point out that, whereas mediation is a conciliatory process, arbitration is an adversarial process. They also object to the fact that the med/arbitrator learns information during the mediation process that prevents the parties from maximizing their outcome. Proponents argue that this knowledge actually permits the med/arbitrator to construct an equitable solution should arbitration be required.

Mediation-then-arbitration is very similar to mediation/arbitration, except that the arbitration following mediation is conducted by a different neutral who has also been preselected but does not participate in the mediation discussions. This sidesteps some of the controversial factors of the med/arb method but requires that two individuals be agreed upon.

Voluntary nonbinding arbitration, also known as *advisory arbitration*, is typically used to stimulate agreement before parties resort to a more binding DR procedure. Advisory arbitration is most successful when the resolution of a claim is riding on only a few critical issues. Disputants can make their own rules. They can hear for themselves the decision of a neutral party and discover how their testimony and expert witnesses might hold up in court or another forum.

Rent-a-judge, a form of private litigation, refers to a process in which a retired judge is retained to preside over a faster, more confidential proceeding than regular litigation. Retired justices are not limited to courtroom procedures, however, and may be willing to preside over many other types of DR proceedings as well.

A *summary jury trial* is usually ordered by the court to get an advisory opinion from a "hired" jury (paid for jointly by the parties) as to the probable decision in a case. A summary jury trial gives both parties a "sneak preview" of a jury trial without the expense required for a full-blown court proceeding. Although the jury's decision is not binding, it usually encourages settlement. If the parties proceed with the litigation, the outcome of the summary jury trial is not normally admissible in court. In this method, as well as the previously discussed rent-a-judge, the parties can agree upon their own rules.

THE PROBLEM

DPIC believes that formal dispute resolution — for those disputes that cannot be resolved at the jobsite or by direct negotiation between the parties — should start with formal nonbinding mediation (see Part Three of this chapter). If that process is not successful or only partially successful, you and your client can always resort to any of the other DR processes available. But how do you choose which technique would be most appropriate for your needs?

THE SOLUTION

There are three possibilities. First, you could specify in your contract a previously agreed-upon step process of DR techniques to be invoked if a dispute arises. Obviously, no matter which you choose to write into your agreements, you and your client can agree to another procedure at any time.

STEPPED DISPUTE RESOLUTION

In the event of a dispute arising out of or relating to this Agreement or the services to be rendered hereunder, the Client

> and the Consultant agree to attempt to resolve such disputes in the following manner:
>
> First, the parties agree to attempt to resolve such disputes through direct negotiations between the appropriate representatives of each party.
>
> Second, if such negotiations are not fully successful, the parties agree to attempt to resolve any remaining dispute by formal nonbinding mediation conducted in accordance with rules and procedures to be agreed upon by the parties.
>
> Third, if the dispute or any issues remain unresolved after the above steps, the parties agree to attempt resolution by submitting the matter to _____ {insert name of preferred alternative dispute resolution procedure}.
>
> {If the process selected in step three is binding upon the parties, such as med/arb, you need to go no further. If the process is advisory or nonbinding, you may need a fourth step, such as arbitration, rent-a-judge or civil litigation, in order to obtain final resolution of the dispute.}

This approach commits you and your client up-front to a definite set of steps to try to avoid litigation and may give pause to a litigation-prone client.

Second, you and your client could try mediation, but if you don't succeed in resolving the dispute, you could agree in advance to allow the mediator to help you select an alternative resolution method.

Third, you and your client could have a panel decide on the DR method best suited to your dispute. In this novel approach, you and your client can each choose a champion, and the two chosen will in turn, agree on a third panel member. This panel will then review the aspects of the conflict and decide on the appropriate resolution technique. Although impaneling three people to choose a DR process might sound cumbersome, it does provide a definitive method that you and your client can rely upon if you can't agree on anything else.

THERE ARE NO RELEVANT PROVISIONS IN THE AIA OR EJCDC STANDARD FORM AGREEMENTS.

Part Six: Resolving International Disputes

While it is true that litigation is still not as common overseas as it is in the United States and Canada, there are signs that some countries are becoming more litigious. International commercial arbitration is on the upswing. And this arbitration doesn't come cheap. We know of one case that was arbitrated before the International Chamber of Commerce (ICC) for which the ICC demanded a deposit of $100,000 up front for fees and costs. Such fees are not unusual.

Just as in the United States, there are alternatives to arbitration and litigation. Some creative techniques are being employed to resolve disputes all around the world.

The *referee system*, for instance, as used in some countries, can be compared to dispute review boards — but with hand grenades. It works like this: neutral private referees are engaged in advance by parties to a contract to adjudicate disputes that arise over the course of a project. These individuals or panels preside over (usually) informal proceedings, evaluate evidence and try to get the parties to resolve their differences. Failing that, the referees will issue a decision that is generally binding and enforceable unless a decision of an arbitration panel or a court is sought, in which case the referees' decision is usually still admissible in evidence.

Conciliation, a technique used in some Pacific Rim countries, is similar to advisory arbitration, because the conciliator plays a role in investigating the dispute and proposing solutions. Under the ICC's rules, when a party requests conciliation, the ICC appoints a committee of three conciliators, one from each party's country and a chairperson from a neutral country. The committee hears from the parties and then submits its settlement terms to the parties for their acceptance. Parties who cannot reach a settlement can take their dispute into arbitration or litigation, and because conciliation is confidential, the proceedings do not affect the parties' legal rights if they choose another resolution.

The Problem

International litigation is no faster, cheaper or fairer than domestic litigation. However, dispute avoidance or resolution techniques that are more familiar to us — partnering, mediation, dispute review boards or minitrials — have not yet attained the acceptance abroad that they have in the United States and Canada. Absent some agreement between you and your client in advance, there is little chance you will be able to resolve your international disputes outside the courts.

THE SOLUTION

You and your client can and should discuss the disadvantages of and alternatives to litigation and agree by contract to try to settle your disputes using some form of DR. As a first step, put a mediation clause in your agreement. If your client needs convincing, the ICC and the United Nations Commission on International Trade Law (both located in New York) have available rules for mediation.

SEE ALSO:

Construction Observation
Delays
Design Without Construction Administration
Governing Law and Jurisdiction
International Projects
Jobsite Safety
Third-Party Claims

RELEVANT STANDARD FORM AGREEMENT PROVISIONS:

Engineers working internationally might wish to refer to the FIDIC standard agreements, available either directly from FIDIC or from the ACEC. Refer to *Additional Resources* **for information on how to contact these organizations.**

VI-36

FRIVOLOUS LAWSUITS

Have you heard the one about the drunk driver? He careened down a road, past several well-marked detour signs and crashed. When he finally sobered up, the fellow sued the engineering firm that designed the road, along with the road's general contractor, subcontractors and several others. Five years later, all of the defendants settled for $35,000. But just getting to that settlement cost a 15-person engineering firm more than $200,000 in legal fees.[2]

Is this kind of suit unusual? Just how serious the frivolous (or *non-meritorious*, as trial lawyers prefer to have them called) lawsuit problem is depends on whom you ask. A 1996 survey of California lawyers found that while only 5 percent of them would admit to filing a frivolous suit, 64.9 percent said they had defended one. Over half of the lawyers felt that frivolous and unfounded suits were ruining the economy.[3]

THE PROBLEM

The truth is, there are frivolous claims against architects, engineers and environmental consultants all the time. These are usually "shotgun" lawsuits, cases in which a plaintiff's attorney names everyone who had anything to do with a project in hopes that some have either assets or insurance. Often these people are named without proof of how or even *if* they contributed to the problem. Although this is sometimes done unwittingly by an attorney who is unfamiliar with the facts, very often shotgun suits are filed intentionally, with the purpose of finding someone who can be intimidated into paying something just to get out of the lawsuit. It is a subtle form of legalized blackmail. Who is to blame? The "system?" Judges? Insurance companies? Certainly, both plaintiffs and their lawyers play a major role.

Thankfully, they don't always get away with it. In really egregious cases, attorneys can be sued for malicious prosecution. But, while there might be a certain satisfaction in seeing the plaintiff's attorney suffer in kind, these actions are difficult to prove, and the entire process can cost the original (blameless) defendant years of frustration and stress.

---

[2] *American Civil Engineers Council and the American Tort Reform Association.*
[3] *California Lawyer*, October 1996.

THE SOLUTION

Unfortunately, there is no complete protection against frivolous lawsuits. There are, however, some measures you can take. One answer is an Attorneys' Fees clause, which entitles the prevailing party in a lawsuit to recoup his or her legal expenses from the loser. We repeat the language here (see *Attorneys' Fees* for further discussion):

ATTORNEYS' FEES

In the event of any litigation arising from or related to this Agreement or the services provided under this Agreement, the prevailing party shall be entitled to recover from the non-prevailing party all reasonable costs incurred, including staff time, court costs, attorneys' fees and all other related expenses in such litigation.

But an Attorneys' Fees provision is not enough, because this provision is triggered only if one party actually *prevails*. In other words, if your client sues you, the suit would have to go through the whole legal process and then a court of competent jurisdiction would have to decide the case in your favor before you could recoup your legal fees. Until then, you would have to foot your own bills, a very expensive and lengthy process. Many people decide at some point that it is not worth the time and trouble and may opt to settle — even though they are blameless. Because many settlements are the result of mediation or other non-adjudicative processes or resolution by arbitration, you could add a provision to the above clause that lets the process determine who the "prevailing party" is, such as:

In the event of a non-adjudicative settlement of litigation between the parties or a resolution of dispute by arbitration, the term "prevailing party" shall be determined by that same process.

There is another solution. A growing number of jurisdictions have enacted — or are currently considering — legislation called *Certificate of Merit* laws.[4] These laws oblige a potential plaintiff to demonstrate that a case against a design or environmental professional has legal merit. Some jurisdictions require that another consultant licensed in the same

---

[4] *As of December 1997, California, Colorado, Georgia, Hawaii, Kansas, Minnesota and New Jersey all had some form of Certificate of Merit law.*

discipline declare whether or not a case should proceed through the civil system. In other jurisdictions, a screening panel of knowledgeable persons gives its opinion. In most Certificate of Merit jurisdictions, if the required Certificate has not been filed by the plaintiff, the law will allow the defendant to file a motion for summary judgment, a relatively quick and inexpensive means of getting out of a lawsuit.

A Certificate of Merit requirement accomplishes two things: First, it might discourage a client from suing you without justification. Second, if the client does obtain such a Certificate, that tells you that there is at least one member of your profession who believes the case against you is worthwhile and may be prepared to testify to that in court.

If you live or work in a jurisdiction that does not have such a law, or if the existing Certificate of Merit law in your state is not working well, it is certainly possible for you and your client to write your own Certificate of Merit contract provision. Just as you can set your own statute of limitation by contract (see *Statutes of Repose and Limitation*), you can agree on a provision to set up a procedure to pre-screen disputes for probable cause before litigation can be filed. Consider the following sample provision:

CERTIFICATE OF MERIT

The Client shall make no claim for professional negligence, either directly or by way of a cross complaint against the Consultant unless the Client has first provided the Consultant with a written certification executed by an independent consultant currently practicing in the same discipline as the Consultant and licensed in the State of ____. This certification shall: a) contain the name and license number of the certifier; b) specify the acts or omissions that the certifier contends are not in conformance with the standard of care for a consultant performing professional services under similar circumstances; and c) state in detail the basis for the certifier's opinion that such acts or omissions do not conform to the standard of care. This certificate shall be provided to the Consultant not less than thirty (30) calendar days prior to the presentation of any claim or the institution of any arbitration or judicial proceeding. This Certificate of Merit clause will take precedence over any existing state law in force at the time of the claim or demand for arbitration.

Frivolous Lawsuits

The last sentence of the above clause is appropriate so long as the requirements of this paragraph are at least as broad or demanding as the existing laws, if any, of your jurisdiction.

If your state has a Certificate of Merit law, it applies to *all* parties who might sue you: a client, a contractor or an injured passerby. Unfortunately, if your state does not have such a law, any Certificate of Merit clause you negotiate into your contract would only apply to claims by your client, because a contract is binding only on the parties who sign it.

This is why, even if you are able to negotiate a Certificate of Merit clause into every one of your contracts, if your state does not have such a law, you and your colleagues should be trying to change that. A number of state professional associations are working to enact or improve existing Certificate of Merit laws. The American Consulting Engineers Council (ACEC) has developed model law language and will help local professional organizations get this legislation on the books. (See *Additional Resources* for information on how to contact the ACEC.)

In the meantime, add Certificate of Merit clauses to your contracts. Your clients may be hard-pressed to refuse. It is difficult, especially in the formative stages of a contract, for clients to argue against putting a provision in a contract that would require them to do something they ought to do in the first place!

SEE ALSO:

Attorneys' Fees
Dispute Avoidance and Resolution
Statutes of Repose and Limitation

THERE ARE NO RELEVANT PROVISIONS IN THE AIA OR EJCDC STANDARD FORM AGREEMENTS.

Part VII

Statutes, Codes and Regulations

Americans with Disabilities Act (ADA)

Code Compliance

Copyrights

Hazardous Materials

Permits and Approvals

Public Responsibility

Specification of Materials

Statutes of Repose and Limitation

VII-2

AMERICANS WITH DISABILITIES ACT (ADA)

The Americans with Disabilities Act of 1990 is federal legislation aimed at providing Americans with disabilities full and equal access to employment, goods and services in commercial and public facilities. One-sixth of the American populace is considered affected by the ADA, which defines disability as a "physical or mental impairment that substantially limits one or more of the major life activities of an individual."

That the ADA greatly affects the design professions is evident. Less clear, however, are the precise obligations imposed upon architects and engineers. The Act is not another set of building codes. Instead, it is civil rights legislation that carries with it the full weight of the United States Department of Justice. Anyone who believes he or she has been discriminated against can file a complaint with an appropriate federal agency or file a civil lawsuit in Federal District Court against the party who owns, leases or operates a facility. The court can levy stiff penalties against a building owner or operator and can order the facilities be made accessible.

Title III of the ADA mandated the removal by January 1992 of architectural and communications barriers in all existing public accommodations, including facilities that are privately owned and operated but that serve the public. For example, restaurants, theaters, sports arenas, stores, professional offices, other service establishments, galleries, lodgings and places of recreation are all considered public accommodations. The 1990 Act does not apply to single or multifamily housing.

Removal of barriers is required if it is "readily achievable." The guidelines to the Act define that as "easily accomplished and able to be carried out without much difficulty or expense." What is "readily achievable" is supposed to be determined on a case-by-case basis by weighing the nature and cost of the modifications against the financial resources of the facility, as well as a variety of other factors. In other words, the courts are expected to hammer it out, and consultants can anticipate conflicting interpretations of the Act.

If public accommodations are out of compliance, the owner or operator will be subject to punishment under the law. The law applies to new and pre-1992 public accommodations.

Americans with Disabilities Act (ADA)

If immediate barrier removal proves too difficult for some public accommodations, the development of an action plan for compliance and a real effort to implement it may be considered a demonstration of a good-faith effort. In these cases, the ADA recommends the removal of barriers in a certain order of priority. Commercial facilities are also affected when an alteration is made to a part of the facility.

The Act affects design professionals in several ways. First, architects and engineers should have already evaluated their own offices to make certain they conform to ADA guidelines. Next, designs for alterations or new construction must comply with the ADA. Finally, architects and engineers will need to keep current with what could be significant changes — depending on where they practice — to state and local codes as they are brought up to ADA standards.

THE PROBLEM

Because the ADA is civil rights legislation and not a building code, it will be the courts, not the legislators, who emerge as the true authors of the Act. The concept of universal accessibility is not the problem; that is a sensible and desirable goal for the design and construction of all facilities. The problem is the lack of clarity. Congress has passed a bill so vague in its language that the true meaning of the ADA and its Accessibility Guidelines (ADAAG) will only be determined through the less predictable process of administrative interpretation and litigation, case by painful case.

What this means to you and your peers is that there is — and will continue to be — much uncertainty and confusion surrounding requirements under the ADA. Until a body of published interpretations, regulations and case law evolves, your obligations and the extent of your liability will not be established. For example, in 1996, the Federal District Court for the District of Columbia held that architects cannot be sued directly under the ADA unless they both designed and constructed the facility.[1] Undeterred, the U.S. Department of Justice itself filed an expanded suit in federal court in Minnesota against the same A/E firm alleging the same violation already dismissed by the District of Columbia court. The court in Minnesota has refused to grant the architect a dismissal in this case. Yet the Federal District Court in Florida said the architect might be subject to enforcement proceedings under the Act and also refused to grant a dismissal, but the case was later dropped. Clearly, the courts have been neither clear nor consistent on the ADA.

You could be subject to civil rights prosecution should something you designed be involved in a charge of discrimination by a person with disabilities. On the other hand, even if you cannot be directly named, your client can — and probably will — seek a defense and indemnity from you should a complaint be filed against him or her. But the difference between direct and indirect action against you could be significant: a direct civil rights action against you seeking fines and penalties is not insurable under most professional-liability policies written today.

[1] _Paralyzed Veterans of America v. Ellerbe Beckett Architects and Engineers, PC_, U.S. District Court for the District of Columbia, 945 F. Supp.1 (DDC 1996).

Because building codes and interpretations by local building officials are not binding for ADA purposes unless the code has been "certified" by the Justice Department, buildings designed and constructed in compliance with state codes could still be found in violation of the ADA. (Claiming budgetary reasons, however, Justice has not certified any local codes thus far.) In fact, the Accessibility Guidelines (ADAAG) occasionally have been found to be in conflict with local building codes. Although many states are moving to incorporate the Accessibility Guidelines into their building codes, there are no guarantees. Because there are no ADA inspectors and there is no such thing as ADAAG plan review or prior approval, designers and owners have no place to turn for clarification or binding interpretation. (You can discuss accessibility questions on an ADA "hotline," but you cannot get a binding decision you can rely upon. There is also an "assistance manual" that the Department of Justice has published, but a court has said the manual does not have the binding force of law; it is only for "assistance.") A design is always subject to later challenge by someone who feels he or she has been denied adequate accessibility. More than one frustrated design professional has been tempted to send his or her drawings to the United States Attorney General for review.

THE SOLUTION

The most important point to keep in mind — and underscore to your client — is that compliance with the Americans with Disabilities Act is a legal and economic problem, not an architectural or engineering issue. If a client wants you to inspect a property for ADA conformance, limit your services to evaluation of the property's noncompliance and the development of a range of possible solutions. You should not provide recommendations on which modifications are "readily achievable . . . in light of the resources available." Nor should you decide the priority or phasing of compliance measures. These are questions that must be answered by the owner and the owner's attorney and accountant. You are not licensed or insured to provide legal or accounting advice to your clients. (See *Opinions (Estimates) of Probable Construction Costs* for a related discussion.) Ironically, attorneys and accountants often seek opinions from architects or engineers regarding compliance or what is readily achievable. Tread carefully here: you will want to insist on a detailed workscope and solid contractual protection by way of disclaimers, waivers and indemnities when giving such advice.

Familiarize yourself with the provisions of the ADA and make certain your client understands its responsibilities; both of you are required to uphold the law, but it is the owner who has the ultimate control over the design and use of the project. You need to explain to your client why you cannot certify or guarantee that your design is in compliance with the ADA. (See *Certifications, Guarantees and Warranties*.)

Since compliance with the ADA still is being determined on a case-by-case basis, you cannot know whether your design or recommended modifications are in compliance. Accordingly, we recommend you always address the ADA in your contract with a clause that explains these limitations. Furthermore, you should delete any language that requires you to strictly comply with "all laws, codes, standards and regulations." (See *Code*

Compliance for a discussion and an alternative clause.) Also delete any provision that requires you to provide a certification, guarantee or warranty that a building is in full compliance with the ADA. (See *Lenders' Requirements*.)

ADA COMPLIANCE IN REMODELING PROJECTS

Alterations to commercial facilities must provide for accessibility to "the maximum extent feasible" if the costs are not disproportionate. According to the Accessibility Guidelines, improvements to provide handicapped-accessible paths of travel may be considered disproportionate when costs exceed 20 percent of the overall cost of the alterations. In theory, if the costs exceed that percentage, then paths of travel must be made accessible to the extent that the costs are not out of line. In reality, though, this formula rarely deters the Department of Justice in its enforcement actions.

Consider the following suggested contract provision:

ADA COMPLIANCE

The Americans with Disabilities Act (ADA) provides that alterations to a facility must be made in such a manner that, to the maximum extent feasible, the altered portions of the facility are readily accessible to persons with disabilities. The Client acknowledges that the requirement of the ADA will be subject to various and possibly contradictory interpretations. The Consultant, therefore, will use its reasonable professional efforts and judgment to interpret applicable ADA requirements and other federal, state and local laws, rules, codes, ordinances and regulations as they apply to the Project. The Consultant, however, cannot and does not warrant or guarantee that the Client's Project will comply with all interpretations of the ADA requirements and/or the requirements of other federal, state and local laws, rules, codes, ordinances and regulations as they apply to the Project.

If you and your attorney decide to use such a clause, make certain it agrees with any other provisions of the contract regarding code and standards compliance.

ADA COMPLIANCE ON NEW CONSTRUCTION

New construction must comply with the ADAAG. Here again, you should attempt to provide for contradictory interpretations of the ADA in your contract and be sure to coordinate such a clause with other provisions concerning codes and standards compliance. Consider the following language:

ADA COMPLIANCE

The Americans with Disabilities Act (ADA) provides that it is a violation of the ADA to design and construct a facility that does not meet the accessibility and usability requirements of the ADA unless it can be demonstrated that it is structurally impractical to meet such requirements. The Client understands that the requirements of the ADA will be subject to various and possibly contradictory interpretations. The Consultant, therefore, will use its reasonable professional efforts and judgment to interpret applicable ADA requirements and other federal, state and local laws, rules, codes, ordinances and regulations as they apply to the Project. The Consultant, however, cannot and does not warrant or guarantee that the Client's Project will comply with all interpretations of ADA requirements and/or requirements of other federal, state and local laws, rules, codes, ordinances and regulations as they apply to the Project.

Alternatively, you may prefer a more comprehensive provision that puts more emphasis on your client's obligations:

ADA COMPLIANCE

It is recognized that the Client faces certain obligations under the Americans with Disabilities Act (ADA) that could affect the design of the Project. It is further recognized that the ADA is federal civil rights legislation that is not part of, or necessarily compatible with, state or local law, codes, and regulations governing construction. Consequently, the Consultant will be

Americans with Disabilities Act (ADA)

unable to make recommendations or professional determinations that will ensure compliance with the ADA or guarantee that the design will conform to the ADA standard of "reasonable accommodation." The Consultant strongly advises the Client to obtain appropriate legal and financial counsel with respect to compliance with the ADA.

The Consultant will endeavor to design for accessibility by persons with disabilities in conformance with applicable provisions and references in applicable state or local building codes. The Consultant further agrees to include in the design such provisions for persons with disabilities as the Client may request in response to the ADA, provided such requests are timely made, technically achievable and in conformance with all other pertinent codes and regulations.

The Client will determine the full extent of its obligations under the ADA. The Client shall communicate design requests regarding compliance with the ADA to the Consultant in writing and in a timely manner to allow for incorporation into the construction documents.

As the ADAAG become more widely incorporated into state and local building codes and building officials have greater knowledge of how to handle ADA issues, you will be able eventually to rely on the traditional approval process once again. Until then, a good-faith effort by the client and consultant, with a well-documented compliance plan, will probably be looked upon favorably by the courts in the event of legal action.

SEE ALSO:

Certifications, Guarantees and Warranties
Code Compliance
Lenders' Requirements
Opinions (Estimates) of Probable Construction Costs
Renovation/Remodeling
Standard of Care

THERE ARE NO RELEVANT PROVISIONS IN
THE AIA OR EJCDC STANDARD FORM AGREEMENTS.

CODE COMPLIANCE

Many client-drafted agreements require the design or environmental professional to promise to comply with "all laws, codes and regulations." Many consultants readily agree to this provision, reasoning, *What's the big deal? After all, don't we already have a duty to obey the law?*

Yes they do. But although such an innocent-sounding clause may appear simply to state the obvious, it is a loaded, dangerous and perhaps unattainable goal.

THE PROBLEM

The major difficulty with such a provision is the inclusive word *all*. Thousands of laws, codes and regulations that relate to construction are on the books; all are subject to change and many are open to interpretation by public officials. It is not unusual to find that a given regulation may conflict with another, placing you in the untenable position of having to comply with two differing requirements. If you can only adhere to one — and you have agreed in your contract to comply with *all* requirements — you are in breach of contract. Consider the difficult position of an engineering firm that finds itself trying to satisfy both the Federal Highway Administration and the National Park Service requirements for a national park roadway.

As a design or environmental professional, you are already required to comply with laws, codes and regulations. Failure to design to the requirements of local building codes is negligence per se. In fact, designing to code is the very least you must do. Under certain circumstances, merely designing to meet minimum code requirements may still be negligence if the circumstances and the applicable standard of care dictate a design solution that clearly exceeds the code. (Refer to **Standard of Care** for discussion.)

There are other issues to consider: Who pays for design changes needed to conform to a new or revised code or regulation (when ADA or OSHA were enacted, for instance) that is put in force during the course of a project? If your contract does not provide for such eventualities (through a comprehensive Scope of Services, a Code Compliance clause or even a strong Changed Conditions provision), you may find yourself providing extensive redesign services to bring projects up to code and perhaps doing so without compensation.

Code Compliance

VII-10

Some consultants report that plan checkers, building inspectors or other building officials often disagree in their interpretations of what complies with code. Who pays for design changes if the inspector and the person granting the permit don't agree on what fire-protection systems comply with code or what code sections apply in an adaptive reuse situation?

THE SOLUTION

The best solution is to delete any all-encompassing language from a client-written clause on code compliance and, instead, carefully delineate your obligations in the Scope of Services. At minimum, if a client-written contract would have you "comply with *all* codes, laws and regulations," you should attempt to delete the word *all* and insert the word *applicable*. Remember that your obligation is not to *guarantee* that all codes and regulations will be met but that you will attempt to do so within the standard of professional care. The AIA B141-1997 document addresses this issue another way, by saying only that the "Architect shall *respond in the design*... to requirements imposed by governmental authorities...."

You will want to specify a date that establishes what code you are responsible for adhering to under Basic Services. A fair cutoff date would be the inception date of the contract; any design changes necessary after that date would then be considered Additional Services and could be billed for accordingly.

CODE COMPLIANCE

The Consultant shall put forth reasonable professional efforts to comply with applicable laws, codes and regulations in effect as of the date of {*the execution of this Agreement, submission to building authorities, or other appropriate date*}. **Design changes made necessary by newly enacted laws, codes and regulations after this date shall entitle the Consultant to a reasonable adjustment in the schedule and additional compensation in accordance with the Additional Services provisions of this Agreement.**

An alternative approach would be to reword a client's clause to tie your efforts to the standard of care, such as:

Code Compliance

VII-11

> **CODE COMPLIANCE**
>
> **The Consultant shall exercise usual and customary professional care in its efforts to comply with all laws, codes and regulations in effect as of the date of _____. Design changes made necessary by newly enacted laws, codes and regulations after this date shall entitle the Consultant to a reasonable adjustment in the schedule and additional compensation in accordance with the Additional Services provisions of this Agreement.**

Help your client understand the potential for conflict between codes and regulations at various levels of government or between different agencies having jurisdiction over the project. You might incorporate this concept into your contract, if possible, with language like the following:

> **In the event of a conflict between laws, codes and regulations of various governmental entities having jurisdiction over this Project, the Consultant shall notify the Client of the nature and impact of such conflict. The Client agrees to cooperate and work with the Consultant in an effort to resolve this conflict.**

Keep your client fully involved throughout the project by explaining design decisions that are based on certain assumptions of critical code interpretations. When a code official makes an adverse interpretation, you need to have your client participate in resolving the problem. Government agencies and employees generally cannot be held responsible for their acts or failures in reviewing and approving designs or construction work for compliance with building codes. Statutory immunities and court decisions generally hold building departments and regulatory agencies blameless, even if they are negligent in performing their duties. You cannot rely upon permit-issuing agencies or inspectors to catch code violations or notify you of design errors. It is not normally a defense (to a claim for negligent design) that a permit was granted or an approval was given by a public official.

If you provide renovation, alteration or preservation services, be particularly cautious regarding codes. Because these projects are so complex, it is difficult to preserve the structure's design integrity while adhering to current building codes. You may well find yourself conducting more research, working extensively with appropriate government officials and having to be more creative in coming up with alternative materials and methods

Code Compliance

to comply with the intent — if not the letter — of the code. All these factors increase your risk and underscore the need for caution in developing your contract language. (See *Renovation/Remodeling*.)

Once you have explained your professional obligation to comply with applicable laws, codes and regulations, reasonable clients should understand there is no need for an over-reaching contractual clause and will probably agree to delete or modify it.

SEE ALSO:

Americans with Disabilities Act
Renovation/Remodeling
Scope of Services
Standard of Care

RELEVANT STANDARD FORM AGREEMENT PROVISIONS:

AIA B141-1997:	Articles 1.2.3.6; 1.3.3.2.2
EJCDC 1910-1 (1996 edition):	Article 6.01D
	Exhibit A 2.01A.3

COPYRIGHTS

Copyright law defines "architectural work" as the design of a building as expressed in plans or drawings, but not individual standard features. The owner of a copyright to an architectural work has the exclusive right to reproduce it, to make derivative works from it, to grant licenses to use the work, to sell the work and to otherwise deal with the copyright. In general, these rights last throughout the life of the owner and extend fifty years beyond that.

Prior to 1990, design professionals had only limited protection under copyright laws. While the engineering plans or drawings for a building design could be protected, the building design itself could not. Anyone with a camera, a tape measure and a calculator could copy a structure without infringing upon the copyrights of the building's designer. However, the 1990 Architectural Works Copyright Protection Act amended the U.S. copyright laws to provide more extensive safeguards for the designs of architects and engineers. The Act prohibits unauthorized construction of buildings depicted in copyrighted drawings created on or after December 1, 1990. So in addition to the fact that an architect's or engineer's drawings are copyrighted as they are created, now, for the most part, the actual buildings are, too. The Act generally applies to architectural works intended for human use or occupancy. Housing, churches and commercial structures are copyrighted, for instance, but not roads, dams and bridges.

THE PROBLEM

Although your rights as a designer have been strengthened by the 1990 legislation, it is up to you to safeguard these rights. It is too easy to sign away all these valuable protections with the stroke of a pen. How? By agreeing, in a client-written contract, to give up your ownership and rights — including copyrights — to your client. For the most part, such a requirement is inappropriate for traditional design projects.

Be aware, too, that if you do contract away your copyrights, it is possible you might not be able to use derivatives of your own design — such as unique design features or possibly even your firm's standard design details — for another client. Be on the lookout as well for assignment clauses or documents from your client's lender, which might try to impose upon you language that transfers ownership of your documents and the copyrights to your

Copyrights

design to the lender if your client defaults. (See *Ownership of Instruments of Service* and *Assignment*.)

If you supplant another consultant on a project, you may have some different copyright concerns. Depending upon the terms and conditions of the supplanted consultant's contract, you may need his or her permission to take over complete or unfinished designs, or you could be liable for copyright infringement. This may be true even if you substantially change the original design. Be aware that your professional liability insurance may not cover claims for copyright infringement. (See *Supplanting Another Consultant*.)

THE SOLUTION

Although your copyright automatically exists as soon as you create your drawing or design — even if you do nothing — it is such a simple matter to mark your designs with a copyright notice that we recommend you do so on every copy of every document you create. There are several good reasons for this: marking your documents tells the world your work is protected by copyright, identifies the copyright owner and shows the year of first publication. Also, if your work is infringed, and you have put a proper copyright notice on it, a court will not allow a defendant to claim "innocent infringement."

For additional protection, you should also register your documents with the United States Copyright Office, a simple and inexpensive procedure that will assist you in the enforcement of your rights. (See *Additional Resources*.) If you file your registration within three months of the date you first create your design documents, you should be eligible for certain additional rights granted under federal law that are not otherwise available, such as the right to file for an injunction, to claim statutory damages, and perhaps to recoup your attorneys' fees should you confront someone who infringes upon your copyright.

Even if you delay registraton of your copyright, you still have some protection. Although by delaying registration you forfeit certain rights, you still have up to five years after publication to add or correct a copyright notice. It is far better, however, to appoint one person in your firm to see that all your designs are promptly copyrighted as a matter of office routine. In addition, consider requiring your employees to agree in writing in their employment agreements that they are employed on a "work-for-hire" basis, so that only your firm — and not your employees — can register the copyrights.

To avoid any misunderstandings, your client agreement should always address copyrights. It should clearly state that you will retain the copyrights to your drawings and design as well as the ownership of those documents. (Refer to *Ownership of Instruments of Service* for a related discussion.) We repeat the following suggested contract language:

Copyrights

VII-15

OWNERSHIP OF INSTRUMENTS OF SERVICE

All reports, plans, specifications, computer files, field data, notes and other documents and instruments prepared by the Consultant as instruments of service shall remain the property of the Consultant. The Consultant shall retain all common law, statutory and other reserved rights, including the copyright thereto.

Since any copying of your plans by the contractor without your express consent might be a technical copyright infringement, you might be willing to grant a limited license to contractors to use and copy applicable portions of your documents so they can go about their work. The AIA A201 General Conditions has such a provision, which also requires that each copy made bear the design professional's copyright notice. If the A201 is not used, you can provide for a limited license for the contractors in whatever document you are using.

Before you agree to sign away any right, seek qualified legal counsel. Copyright law is a highly specialized field, and you need a knowledgeable attorney to advise you on your ownership rights. If you do transfer copyrights, either from a consultant to you or from you to another party, you should record that transfer in an appropriate filing with the United States Copyright Office by sending in a copy of the instrument evidencing the transfer (or an abbreviated form to be used for this purpose) along with the required fee.

Should you decide to contract away your copyrights, you will need some additional protection. Your contract should have provisions that guard you against unauthorized reuse and unauthorized changes to your designs. (Refer to *Prototype Designs* and *Unauthorized Changes to Plans* for more information and suggested clauses.)

Ownership of documents created by subconsultants may be transferred to the prime or retained by the subconsultant. This is a matter of negotiation, however, and a point you and your attorney should carefully consider when drafting your subconsultant or prime consultant agreements. (Refer to *Subconsultants*.)

Finally, a related issue is worth noting. Another law, the Visual Artists Rights Act of 1990, prohibits any modification or destruction of a work of visual art (this would include sculptures, frescoes and other artwork incorporated into buildings) that would prejudice the reputation of the artist. This law has been used to prohibit certain types of renovation, for instance, and may be of concern to those involved in renovation projects. If this is the nature of your project, you'll need to specify who is responsible for obtaining the license or permission of the copyright owner in order to modify or destroy such works of art. Again, seek qualified counsel. (See *Renovation/Remodeling*.)

Copyrights

SEE ALSO:

Assignment
CADD/Electronic Files
Lenders' Requirements
Ownership of Instruments of Service
Prototype Designs
Renovation/Remodeling
Subconsultants
Supplanting Another Consultant
Unauthorized Changes to Plans

RELEVANT STANDARD FORM AGREEMENT PROVISIONS:

AIA B141-1997:	Article 1.3.2
EJCDC 1910-1 (1996 edition):	Article 6.04

HAZARDOUS MATERIALS

If you are not an environmental consultant, the existence of hazardous materials on or near the project site represents a serious risk to your practice. This section is intended to help you manage those risks in your agreements. Environmental professionals, of course, deal with hazardous materials every day. Their specialized contractual needs are addressed in DPIC's Contract Guide Supplement for Environmental Professionals.

Over the last century, literally thousands of toxic substances have been buried, released, dumped or otherwise deposited into our surroundings. Now, more and more often, architects and engineers are encountering these pollutants unexpectedly on the jobsite.

In addition, in less enlightened times, normal construction materials included substances now known to be highly hazardous. There are, for example, thousands of public and commercial buildings that still contain materials made with asbestos.

Of course, not all hazardous materials were put in place by man. Naturally occurring substances, such as radon and methane gases, are very real dangers too, not only to public health but also to the consultants who discover them.

THE PROBLEM

No one is immune to risk from environmental hazard claims. Any discipline in which you practice can expose you to some environmental liability. Consider the mechanical engineer who designs an adequate ventilation system according to code, but after occupancy there are allegations of *sick building syndrome*. Or the architect who faces claims that upholstery and wall coverings specified for an interiors job gave off poisonous fumes in a fire. Or a civil engineer whose design of a water-treatment plant did not anticipate the illegal dumping of heavy metals in the sewage system feeding the plant.

In a related problem, you face the very real probability of encountering asbestos in renovation and rehabilitation projects, especially in pre-1972 buildings. If your firm is not prepared for and does not react appropriately in such situations, you may face substantial civil or criminal repercussions. Even in jobs where you do not anticipate asbestos, its discovery could result in significant delays and increased costs. Conversely, you also could

Hazardous Materials

be held responsible under certain conditions for failure to discover asbestos on a site. (Refer to *Consequential Damages* and *Renovation/Remodeling*.)

Whether it is PCBs, asbestos, bacteria, fungus or some other unexpected, unidentified "gunk," it is not your job to locate and clean it up. You did not intend to include remediation work in your scope of services or even anticipate there would be toxic substances that needed to be cleaned up. But, because these substances might exist on the client's site, you could face delays, higher costs and increased risks.

THE SOLUTION

No matter how unlikely it seems that you will encounter toxic substances on a project, you must plan for that eventuality. This may be the most important provision in your agreement with your client. In every agreement you negotiate, insist on a clause that provides for the possibility of discovering hazardous materials on the jobsite. We consider this type of clause a **Deal Maker** — a must-have — and recommend that it become a standard part of all your contracts. There are several approaches you can take, each offering a degree of protection to your firm.

Your first step should be to define the terms. We suggest you include a definition of *hazardous materials* either in the Definitions section or in your contractual provision dealing with hazardous materials, to make certain it is interpreted as you intend. (See *Definitions*.) A model definition might read:

DEFINITION OF "HAZARDOUS MATERIALS"

As used in this Agreement, the term *hazardous materials* shall mean any substances, including but not limited to asbestos, toxic or hazardous waste, PCBs, combustible gases and materials, petroleum or radioactive materials (as each of these is defined in applicable federal statutes) or any other substances under any conditions and in such quantities as would pose a substantial danger to persons or property exposed to such substances at or near the Project site.

Next, provide for the right to suspend your services and keep your agreement in force while the owner has the site cleaned up. This is an important and minimal protection:

Hazardous Materials

VII-19

HAZARDOUS MATERIALS — SUSPENSION OF SERVICES

Both parties acknowledge that the Consultant's scope of services does not include any services related to the presence of any hazardous or toxic materials. In the event the Consultant or any other party encounters any hazardous or toxic materials, or should it become known to the Consultant that such materials may be present on or about the jobsite or any adjacent areas that may affect the performance of the Consultant's services, the Consultant may, at its option and without liability for consequential or any other damages, suspend performance of its services under this Agreement until the Client retains appropriate consultants or contractors to identify and abate or remove the hazardous or toxic materials and warrants that the jobsite is in full compliance with all applicable laws and regulations.

This approach only allows you to step aside to give the client a reasonable time to ascertain that the materials found are hazardous, remediate the site and certify to you that it is safe. If the client does not take care of the problem in a reasonable time, you'll need the contractual right to terminate the agreement. (See *Termination*.)

In addition to the right to suspend, you should try to include an indemnity provision in your agreement. Consider the following suggested language, which is an extremely protective indemnity, as an add-on to the above suspension clause:

HAZARDOUS MATERIALS INDEMNITY

The Client agrees, notwithstanding any other provision of this Agreement, to the fullest extent permitted by law, to indemnify and hold harmless the Consultant, its officers, partners, employees and consultants (collectively, Consultant) from and against any and all claims, suits, demands, liabilities, losses, damages or costs, including reasonable attorneys' fees and defense costs arising out of or in any way connected with the detection, presence, handling, removal, abatement, or disposal of any asbestos or hazardous or toxic substances, products or materials that exist

Hazardous Materials

> on, about or adjacent to the Project site, whether liability arises under breach of contract or warranty, tort, including negligence, strict liability or statutory liability or any other cause of action, except for the sole negligence or willful misconduct of the Consultant.

Alternatively, you could insert a general indemnity in your agreement that might be broad enough to provide the desired protection. (See *Indemnities* for discussion and suggested language.) But indemnities may not help you; some states have anti-indemnification laws or are very reluctant to enforce contractual indemnities. It is crucial that you obtain competent legal counsel familiar with local laws to help you write and negotiate any indemnity to ensure that the language you use is, to the maximum extent possible, enforceable in your jurisdiction.

Some firms prefer another approach — the right to terminate the agreement completely and renegotiate terms if hazardous substances are encountered when none were anticipated. It should be obvious to your client that under these new circumstances, the risks are substantially different. The workscope, schedule and fee may all need to be changed and, if not already a part of your agreement, appropriate indemnity protection is now imperative if you are to continue your services. (See *Changed Conditions*.)

In addition, it is important to include Interpretation, Public Responsibility, Severability and Survival, Specification of Materials and Confidentiality clauses in your agreement. (Refer to those sections for suggested language and discussion.) If you do use a Changed Conditions clause, be sure it is coordinated with your Hazardous Materials clause to avoid any ambiguity in your agreement.

If you are providing non-environmental professional services on a site where hazardous materials may be encountered and you have already factored in the risks and the appropriate schedule, scope and fee provisions, we strongly suggest your agreement include, in addition to the two previous clauses, a waiver of liability similar to the following:

WAIVER OF CLAIMS FOR HAZARDOUS MATERIALS

> In consideration of the substantial risks to the Consultant in rendering its services in connection with the Project due to the presence or suspected presence of hazardous materials at or near the jobsite, the Client agrees to make no claim and hereby waives, to the fullest extent permitted by law, any claim or cause

> or causes of action of any kind, including but not limited to negligence, breach of contract or warranty, either express or implied, strict liability or any other causes, against the Consultant, its officers, directors, partners, employees or subconsultants (collectively, Consultant), which may arise out of or may in any way be connected to the presence of such hazardous materials. The Client acknowledges that the Consultant is not and shall not be required to be in any way an "arranger," "generator," "operator" or "transporter" of hazardous materials present at or near the Project site, as these terms are defined in applicable federal or state statutes.

If you are unable to obtain the waiver language, you should at least obtain strong contractual language to limit your liability to a level you are willing to accept for the services you will perform. In addition to an indemnity, we recommend that you insist on a Limitation of Liability provision in every agreement you sign that may involve environmental hazards. (See *Limitation of Liability* for more information and suggested contract language.) The risks of toxic or hazardous substances should remain where they belong — squarely on the shoulders of the property owner. It is, after all, the owner who either polluted the property or owns the property on which the pollutants are located. In either event, because you didn't cause the problem, you should not be held responsible.

No reasonable amount of compensation could begin to cover your legal costs and lost billable time if you face a claim arising from hazardous materials. Before you enter contract negotiations, know precisely the protective terms you must have — and be prepared to walk away if your client is unwilling to agree to reasonable terms.

SEE ALSO:

Changed Conditions
Confidentiality
Corporate Protection
Definitions
Dispute Avoidance and Resolution
Excluded Services
Information Provided by Others
Interpretation
Limitation of Liability
Public Responsibility
Scope of Services
Standard of Care
Termination

Hazardous Materials

RELEVANT STANDARD FORM AGREEMENT PROVISIONS:

AIA B141-1997:	Articles 1.3.7.6; 2.8.3.8
EJCDC 1910-1 (1996 edition):	Articles 6.10; 6.11A.4; 7.01A.5, A.26-27, A.29-31
	Exhibit A 2.02A.4
	Exhibit B 2.01D

PERMITS AND APPROVALS

Client-provided contracts sometimes call for the consultant "to obtain all approvals and permits necessary to the performance of the services in the contract." Such vague wording could get the consultant into a lot of trouble. In some cases, this language is intended to apply only to permits and approvals necessary for the performance of the consultant's services; in others, it might apply to or be construed to apply to all permits and approvals needed for the overall project.

THE PROBLEM

The problem usually found in typical owner-drafted "permit" clauses comes down to two little words: *obtain* and *all*.

Keep in mind that it is always the owner's responsibility to actually obtain the permits and approvals needed for his or her project. The owner, and only the owner, bears the risk of whether or not his or her project receives approvals from whatever regulatory bodies have jurisdiction over the project. True, architects, engineers and environmental consultants often help their clients apply for permits and approvals normally required for construction by completing appropriate forms and providing necessary data. But regardless of how much you assist, you cannot promise to obtain something over which you have no control. Approval and permit procedures can be slow; it is impossible to guarantee the action or inaction of any governmental agency regarding the issuance of anything (except perhaps tax bills).

Agreeing to help obtain *all* permits establishes another broad condition that may be impossible for you to meet. You cannot know at the outset of a project just what permits will eventually be required, and you should not inadvertently agree to an open-ended requirement for any new permit requirements that might be imposed in the future, something not contemplated in setting your fee for your basic services.

THE SOLUTION

Find out exactly what clients really expect from you; they may not be expressing their true intentions by their contract language. Are they referring to permits and licenses you need

Permits and Approvals

in order to perform your work? If so, it is already your responsibility to maintain your professional and business licenses in any case, so there is no reason to include these in the contract. Do they really expect you to actually obtain all permits? As explained above, this is inappropriate. Only the owner can actually obtain the project permits. Or do your clients just want you to *assist* them (the more appropriate role) in obtaining the necessary approvals for construction to proceed? Consider the following clause, which more properly describes your role:

PERMITS AND APPROVALS

The Consultant shall assist the Client in applying for those permits and approvals normally required by law for projects similar to the one for which the Consultant's services are being engaged. This assistance shall consist of completing and submitting forms to the appropriate regulatory agencies having jurisdiction over the construction documents, and other services normally provided by the Consultant and included in the scope of Basic Services of this Agreement.

Sometimes additional services are needed — such as special research, documentation and reports, or attendance at more than a specified number of public meetings. These services should be compensated for as Additional Services at an additional fee. You can address this possibility in your contract by indicating what special services are not included under your basic scope and stating that you will discuss the scope and cost of these special services with the client and obtain client approval before you perform them. Consider adding the following:

. . . This assistance does not include, however, special studies, special research, attendance at more than ____ meetings with public authorities, special testing or special documentation not normally required for this type of project. The Consultant will provide such special services as Additional Services as authorized by the Client in accordance with the compensation provisions of this Agreement.

Permits and Approvals

You might want to consider listing just which permits and approvals you will assist the client in obtaining in your Basic Services fee proposal; some firms even specify which permits are *not* included. Still other firms prefer to put all permit assistance under Additional Services in order to avoid potential disagreement over which permits are "normal."

Be especially wary of the client who attempts to make your fee contingent upon obtaining the necessary permits and approvals. This is a gamble you needn't take and one that could cost you a great deal of time and money. If confronted with this, we strongly suggest you delete or modify such provisions to conform to the level of responsibility described in the above clauses.

SEE ALSO:

Certifications, Guarantees and Warranties
Code Compliance
Delays
Excluded Services
Requests for Information
Scope of Services

RELEVANT STANDARD FORM AGREEMENT PROVISIONS:

AIA B141-1997:	Articles 1.3.3.2.6; 1.3.9.2.2; 2.16
EJCDC 1910-1 (1996 edition):	Exhibit A 1.03A.2; 2.01A.1; 2.01A.7

VII-26

PUBLIC RESPONSIBILITY

In virtually all jurisdictions, design and environmental professionals are licensed for the purpose of protecting the public health and safety. This duty overrides any obligation to the client. Nothing in a professional services agreement should compromise a consultant's ability to carry out his or her responsibility to the public. In fact, the agreement should make it clear that the public duty takes precedence over all else.

THE PROBLEM

What happens when a client tells you to do something you believe is a violation of professional standards, laws, codes or regulations? What if your client fails to take a required action, and does not report unsafe conditions or the discovery of hazardous materials, asbestos or PCBs? The public health and safety implications are obvious. And if you are aware of the situation and you do nothing about it, you might be found liable or, worse, jeopardize your professional registration. At best, you would spend substantial legal fees for your defense.

But if you do report the situation to building officials, the EPA, OSHA or some other authority, an irate client may claim that no violation was involved and your "precipitous behavior" in "blowing the whistle" had caused significant financial loss. Faced with such a dilemma, you need the freedom to take reasonable and necessary action to fulfill what you believe to be your professional responsibility under your license and to do so without concern for future liability. (See *Hazardous Materials* and *Jobsite Safety*.)

THE SOLUTION

The best solution begins with careful client selection. If your client is as conscientious as you are about reporting any suspected situation and won't object if you act on the conservative side, you are indeed fortunate. On the other hand, if you're entering into an agreement worrying about whether or not your prospective client is likely to "do the right thing," you may have picked the wrong client.

You and your staff need a good working knowledge of applicable federal, state and local laws and a thorough understanding of your professional responsibilities. If you are at all

Public Responsibility

uncertain about your duties to the public under your license, consult with your attorney, your state licensing board, your professional association or appropriate regulatory agencies.

Plan for and decide upon appropriate course(s) of action should you discover or suspect the existence of hazardous materials or dangerous conditions. First, advise your client of the situation and carefully document your actions. If you make your concerns known verbally, follow them up in writing. You may want to suggest to your client that another qualified professional be retained in order to get an independent evaluation. Never knowingly violate building codes, even at the client's request. Doing so could expose you to tremendous legal liability, loss of your professional license and even criminal prosecution. Allow your client a reasonable amount of time, depending on the circumstances, to report to the responsible authorities. If your client fails to take the appropriate action, then you must do so.

Provide for your contractual protection if you must step in and take an action that is the primary responsibility of your client but for which you also have a duty.

You might also add a provision to your Termination clause that allows you to withdraw from the project if you believe your client's actions or continuing failure to act are in conflict with your public responsibility. (See *Termination*.)

The following clause addresses most of these concepts:

PUBLIC RESPONSIBILITY

Both the Client and the Consultant owe a duty of care to the public that requires them to conform to applicable codes, standards, regulations and ordinances, principally to protect the public health and safety. The Client shall make no request of the Consultant that, in the Consultant's reasonable opinion, would be contrary to the Consultant's professional responsibilities to protect the public. The Client shall take all actions and render all reports required of the Client in a timely manner. Should the Client fail to take any required actions or render any required notices to appropriate public authorities in a timely manner, the Client agrees the Consultant has the right to exercise its professional judgment in reporting to appropriate public officials or taking other necessary action. The Client agrees to take no action against or attempt to hold the Consultant liable in any way for carrying out what the Consultant reasonably believes to be its public responsibility.

Public Responsibility

VII-29

In addition, you might want some protection from claims by contractors whose work is delayed because you reported a dangerous situation to public authorities. Such protection might be gained by adding an indemnity to the above wording. Here is some model language:

> **The Client agrees the Consultant shall not be held liable in any respect for reporting said conditions. Accordingly, the Client agrees, to the fullest extent permitted by law, to indemnify and hold harmless the Consultant, its officers, directors, employees and subconsultants (collectively, Consultant) against all damages, liabilities or costs, including reasonable attorneys' fees and defense costs, arising out of or in any way connected with the Consultant's notifying or failing to notify appropriate public officials.**

In the absence of this type of clause, and if you just can't reach agreement with your client on if and when to report certain circumstances to public authorities, you'll need to rely on the dispute resolution or, possibly, the termination provisions of your agreement. (See *Dispute Avoidance and Resolution*.)

The bottom line: You should be familiar with the applicable laws, know your responsibilities under those laws and exercise your best judgment in carrying out your duties.

SEE ALSO:

Code Compliance
Confidential Communications
Confidentiality
Consequential Damages
Dispute Avoidance and Resolution
Hazardous Materials
Jobsite Safety
Permits and Approvals
Standard of Care
Termination

RELEVANT STANDARD FORM AGREEMENT PROVISIONS:

AIA B141-1997:	Article 1.2.3.4
EJCDC 1910-1 (1996 edition):	Article 6.10C

VII-30

SPECIFICATION OF MATERIALS

Some products that were widely used in the building industry just a few years ago — lead-based paint and asbestos, for example — were eventually determined to be hazardous. In most cases, these discoveries came only after these products had had many years of use. Like everyone else, architects and engineers were unaware of any serious risk and commonly specified these materials for their projects.

After these products were ultimately deemed hazardous, some claimants and their attorneys tried to hold consultants at least partially responsible for damages or injuries caused by these materials, even though they were considered safe, effective and standards of the industry at the time they were used. These claims were tantamount to insisting that architects and engineers should practice to a higher standard of care and have information unknown even to medical science and current technology.

THE PROBLEM

Although it's unfair to be held accountable for specifying materials widely thought to be safe and later discovered to be hazardous, it happens to consultants every day. And while a consultant may, in time, be absolved of liability, thousands of dollars and a great deal of time will be wasted in defending such claims. It is, after all, very easy to get dragged into litigation — and very, very tough to get out.

There are two separate but related issues concerning specifying building materials. Chances are you've run into at least one.

First, let's suppose you and your colleagues have been specifying an insulation product for many years and that current medical science and the building industry consider it to be effective and safe. You call for its use in an apartment building. Five years after the building is completed, a new scientific study shows the material to be carcinogenic. Can you be held responsible?

Another scenario finds you in a difficult dilemma: Your client suggests or even insists that you specify a product you feel may not be safe or reliable. Perhaps it's a product that while allowable under current building codes, contains material that is hazardous in other forms

Specification of Materials

or quantities. Or it might be new material or equipment that, in your opinion, has yet to undergo the test of time. Perhaps it is a product such as a new adhesive for carpeting or a wall paneling system that, although in general use, has never been proven in the high humidity application required by your project. If, against your better professional judgment, you agree to specify a product that later proves to be flawed or dangerous, can you be liable for damages?

THE SOLUTION

Fortunately, there are a few measures you can take to help avoid such claims. First, make it a practice to specify only those products and technologies that you know will do the job, that are time-tested and proven in a particular application. Ask yourself: what would other reasonable consultants do in these circumstances? (Refer to **Standard of Care** for a related discussion.) You might ask, too, how the scenario would play out in a deposition or on the witness stand.

If your client wants you to specify a new product or one with which you are unfamiliar, do your research. Your goal is to be able to demonstrate that you made a reasonable, professional effort to explore the suitability and reliability of the product. Collect brochures, product specification sheets, warranties and guarantees from the manufacturer and keep them for your records. Document your conversations with the suppliers and your client regarding the product and its application in the specific circumstance, including any reservations you might have raised. Require the manufacturers, suppliers and installers to give you assurances that the product is suitable for the intended application. Ask manufacturers' field representatives to be present during the installation to ensure that their product is installed properly and according to manufacturers' specifications.

If your client insists on your specifying an item that, although not life-threatening, is a product with which you are not comfortable — a question of quality or ease of maintenance or operation, for instance — put your objections in writing to your client. If the client overrules you, protect yourself by having this confirmed in writing. At a minimum, document these discussions and decisions well.

If the item in question involves health or safety issues, however, that is another matter altogether. If you cannot convince your client of the possible risks, you must look to the termination provisions of your contract rather than endanger the life or health of anyone. (See **Public Responsibility** and **Termination**.)

You could also address these issues in your agreement with a provision that spells out and limits your responsibility. Here's a sample clause:

SPECIFICATION OF MATERIALS

The Client understands and agrees that products or building materials that are permissible under current building codes and ordinances may, at some future date, be banned or limited in use in the construction industry because of presently unknown hazardous and/or defective characteristics.

The Client agrees that if any product or material specified for this Project by the Consultant shall, at any future date be suspected or discovered to be defective or a health or safety hazard, then the Client shall waive all claims as a result thereof against the Consultant.

The Client further agrees that if the Client directs the Consultant to specify any product or material after the Consultant has informed the Client that such product or material may not be suitable or may embody characteristics that are suspected of causing or may cause the product or material to be considered a hazardous substance in the future, the Client waives all claims as a result thereof against the Consultant and the Client agrees, to the fullest extent permitted by law, to indemnify and hold harmless the Consultant from any damages, liabilities or costs including reasonable attorneys' fees and defense costs, arising in any way from the specification or use of any products or materials which, at any future date, become known or suspected health or safety hazards.

Make sure you coordinate any such provision with your Code Compliance clause, as well as with the provision you have concerning toxic substances.

SEE ALSO:

Code Compliance
Hazardous Materials
Public Responsibility
Standard of Care
Termination
Year 2000

Specification of Materials

VII-34

THERE ARE NO RELEVANT PROVISIONS IN THE AIA OR EJCDC STANDARD FORM AGREEMENTS.

STATUTES OF REPOSE AND LIMITATION

Every state has a statute of limitation on the books and nearly all have a statute of repose. These statutes establish a maximum time period during which lawsuits of a particular kind can be brought against another party. Their purpose is to discourage stale claims and to expedite justice before memories fade and evidence is lost. Most statutes of repose or limitation are applicable to the construction industry. They vary widely as to what and to whom they apply, what the "trigger" or starting date is, and the time limits applicable to various types of claims.

The difference between the two types of statutes is important. Both limit the time for making a claim, but they differ on when the time period starts to run. A statute of limitation begins at the date of injury or discovery of the damage and thus may not be triggered for a very long time. For example, a typical statute of limitation might read:

Notwithstanding any other statute of limitation, an action against an engineer to recover damages for injury to a person, property or to any interest in property, including damages for delay or economic loss, regardless of legal theory, arising out of the preparation of drawings, maps, specifications or other design services must be commenced within two years after the date the injury or damage is first discovered or in the exercise of reasonable care should have been discovered.

More protective for consultants, however, is a statute of repose. This bars actions against architects and engineers after a fixed period of time following the completion of services or the completion of construction, and puts a final cap on the time during which the consultant is exposed to liability. Such a provision may be similar to the following:

In no event may an action arising out of the performance of services by a licensed architect be commenced more than 10 years after the date on which the final plans prepared by the architect are filed with the appropriate public agency having jurisdiction over the project or, if no final plans are filed, more than 10 years after the completion of the project.

Statutes of Repose and Limitation

THE PROBLEM

Every design or environmental professional confronts a similar dilemma: how long must I continue to be responsible for my projects? When, if ever, can I rest easy — even retire — without the threat of lawsuits and liability hanging over me?

Because the wording and interpretation of these statutes vary, and because most construction-related statutes continue to be challenged in the courts, simply relying on the current status of the courts and legislatures' whims makes it difficult to manage your liability exposure. For how much and for how long should you insure against the risk? What fee should you charge to compensate for that risk? It is difficult to know when you're "off the hook" if you cannot anticipate whether or not a particular statute of repose or limitation may bar a potential claim.

A related problem is trying to establish when a time period begins to run. In a construction defect situation, does the clock start when the alleged design error is committed, when construction is substantially or finally complete, when the defect is discovered, or at some other time? If the statutory time period is very long, or there is uncertainty about when the period starts (and therefore ends), you could have liability for a long, long time — possibly forever. This just isn't fair. There should be a moment when you can safely say "my project has withstood the test of time and performed well." After a certain reasonable amount of time, the risks of maintenance, use and deterioration should reside with the owner.

THE SOLUTION

You don't have to accept liability that extends to infinity. Just as you negotiate limits to your scope for a project, so, too, can you negotiate to limit your liability exposure as to time periods as well as dollar limits. (See *Limitation of Liability*.) It is certainly possible to establish by contract with your client your own time limits for legal action, even if your state legislature has not done so — or has failed to do so satisfactorily. While it will not affect third-party claims, you and your client can set your own ground rules for claims against each other by establishing in your agreement both the period of time in which the claim can be made and when that period begins. (See *Third-Party Beneficiaries*.) A clause that accomplishes both could read as follows:

TIME BAR TO LEGAL ACTION

All legal actions by either party against the other arising out of or in any way connected with this Agreement or the services to be performed hereunder shall be barred and under no circumstances shall any such legal action be initiated by either party after ____ (__) years from the date of Substantial Completion,

> unless this Agreement shall be terminated earlier, in which case the date of termination of this Agreement shall be the date on which such period shall commence.

You and your client can select an appropriate length of time and a date on which the time period begins, such as the date of substantial completion, final payment, completion of your services or some other date. The length of time you select must be reasonable and should not be longer than that established by applicable law, which could create an insurance problem if you contractually extended your liability. Check with your attorney and your professional liability insurance specialist on this point. If the project is insured by a project policy, you may want to tie the time period to the insurance policy's Extended Discovery Period, which normally begins upon substantial completion of the project. (See *Insurance*.)

Another approach is to not set the time period but to let the applicable statutes of limitation or repose control. You can set the date the statutes start to run. This type of clause might read:

STATUTES OF REPOSE AND LIMITATION

> All legal causes of action between the parties to this Agreement shall accrue and any applicable statutes of repose or limitation shall begin to run not later than the date of Substantial Completion. If the act or failure to act complained of occurs after the date of Substantial Completion, then the date of final completion shall be used, but in no event shall any statute of repose or limitation begin to run any later than the date the Consultant's services are completed or terminated.

Try to synchronize, if possible, the starting dates of all time periods (contractor's correction period, contractor's warranty, time bar to legal action and any other notice periods) by using the same trigger date for all parties involved in the project. In particular, make certain that the General Conditions of the construction contract reflect that date. The date of Substantial Completion is a date frequently used for this purpose.

Statutes of Repose and Limitation

SEE ALSO:

Code Compliance
Definitions
Indemnities
Insurance
Limitation of Liability
Severability and Survival
Standard of Care
Third-Party Beneficiaries

RELEVANT STANDARD FORM AGREEMENT PROVISIONS:

AIA B141-1997: Article 1.3.7.3
EJCDC 1910-1 (1996 edition): No applicable provisions.

Part VIII

General Terms and Conditions

Assignment

Authorized Representatives

Confidential Communications

Confidentiality

Contractual Reference to the Consultant

Definitions

Entire Agreement

Governing Law and Jurisdiction

Incorporation by Reference

Lenders' Requirements

Notices

Ownership of Instruments of Service

Severability and Survival

Titles

VIII-2

ASSIGNMENT

An assignment clause in a contract gives — or denies — one or both parties the ability to transfer their rights under the contract. If a client can assign the rights to a consultant's services to another party, the consultant could be forced to work for a stranger — someone with whom the consultant has never bargained and for whom the consultant may not want to work. The potential costs and risk can be perilous for the unsuspecting consultant.

THE PROBLEM

If your contract gives your client the unilateral right to assign the contract to others, you may not be able to object if the client sells your remaining obligations under contract as if your services were mere commodities. Such an assignment could be triggered by a merger, the sale of the project or a default by your client to the lender. Unless you have protected yourself, either by prohibiting assignment without mutual consent or by providing for your compensation for increased costs caused by the assignment, you could be asking for trouble. Instead of dealing with the experienced client with whom you originally contracted, you could find yourself suddenly working for the client's lender and trying to explain the details of the project to a freshly scrubbed MBA whose previous construction experience amounts to building a treehouse in the backyard. Worse, you might inherit a new client with insufficient funds to pay your fees. Even if you are willing to continue working with someone new, you will spend additional time bringing him or her up to speed, and you will face added construction observation services and meetings — all of which should be compensated for as Additional Services. (See *Scope of Services*.)

Another dilemma might arise if the contractor and owner have a dispute. If the contractor is prevented from suing you directly, because of the law in states with an "economic loss doctrine," a resourceful contractor might settle the claim with the owner and take an assignment of the owner's claim against you. If your agreement with your client does not prohibit assignment, this could prove costly.

If your contract contains no assignment clause — in other words, if the contract is silent on the issue — it may be presumed that your client has the right to "sell you" and all remaining rights under contract. A more obvious problem is the overreaching client who wants a provision that gives him or her the right to assign but prohibits you from doing the same.

Assignment

VIII-4

This client may be thinking about selling the project — along with your construction phase services — for a fixed price (presumably the unpaid balance of your compensation) despite increased costs to you. A client's insistence on such a unilateral provision is a good indication of how fair he or she will be in other matters.

THE SOLUTION

Have a strong, affirmative and two-way clause that prohibits both parties from assigning rights to another without mutual consent. Such a clause could read:

ASSIGNMENT

Neither party to this Agreement shall transfer, sublet or assign any rights under or interest in this Agreement (including but not limited to monies that are due or monies that may be due) without the prior written consent of the other party. Subcontracting to subconsultants normally contemplated by the Consultant shall not be considered an assignment for purposes of this Agreement.

Note that this clause makes clear that your normal subconsultant agreements do not require the consent of your client.

You should also review your agreement and delete any open-ended provisions that require you to "cooperate with the client's lender in every way" or to "sign all forms required by a lender." (See *Lenders' Requirements*.) Unless you have agreed to such a clause in your client agreement, you are under no legal obligation to comply with such a demand. Despite the lender's insistence that this is standard operating procedure, or your client's concern that his or her loan may be hanging in the balance, you must not give an unknown lender carte blanche to foist unreasonable documents on you (probably containing Indemnity, Ownership of Instruments of Service and Assignment clauses) after you have carefully and laboriously negotiated such provisions out of your client agreement. (Refer to the related discussions in *Indemnities* and *Ownership of Instruments of Service*.)

If you've protected yourself from assignment and duties to lenders, you may be willing to execute reasonable lender documents that have been purged of onerous clauses and that give you some basic protections. Supposedly unalterable standard lender forms (or forms from anyone who wants to take over the balance of your contract by assignment) can be negotiated and modified, if you understand and follow sound risk-management principles in negotiating your agreements. Above all, give yourself the time to get help from your attorney and your professional liability insurance specialist before you sign any seemingly onerous contract clauses.

SEE ALSO:

Indemnities
Lenders' Requirements
Ownership of Instruments of Service
Retaining Subconsultants

RELEVANT STANDARD FORM AGREEMENT PROVISIONS:

AIA B141-1997:	Article 1.3.7.9
EJCDC 1910-1 (1996 edition):	Article 6.08A&B

VIII-6

AUTHORIZED REPRESENTATIVES

A design or environmental professional will often need to communicate with key client representatives in order to make a report or get an immediate decision.

THE PROBLEM

Clear, effective and timely communication among authorized representatives of the various participants in a project is crucial. If your client or a key client representative is unavailable, a decision may have to be delayed, and problems could result or be aggravated. On the other hand, if you make a decision on behalf of a client without the client's approval, you may create serious problems involving economic risk or professional liability exposure.

Likewise, your client needs to know who in your organization is authorized to make decisions or receive official communications. Neither party wants a situation where a crucial communication is given to or a decision is made by someone who is not in a position of authority.

THE SOLUTION

To eliminate all uncertainty, consider including in your agreement — in a separate clause or an attachment — a listing of representatives who are authorized to receive notices and to make decisions on behalf of each party. You may even want to specify individuals who are authorized to make decisions at certain levels (for example, to approve change orders up to specified dollar amounts). The agreement should also include a provision for keeping the list current.

PROJECT REPRESENTATIVES

The Client and Consultant hereby designate their authorized representatives to act on their behalf with respect to the services and responsibilities under this Agreement. The following

Authorized Representatives

VIII-8

designated representatives are authorized to receive notices, transmit information and make decisions regarding the Project on behalf of their respective parties. They shall be called upon in the order listed:

For the Client:

1. Name _____ Work telephone _____

   Address _____ Home telephone _____

   _____ FAX telephone _____

   _____ E-mail address _____

2. Name _____ Work telephone _____

   Address _____ Home telephone _____

   _____ FAX telephone _____

   _____ E-mail address _____

Special provisions or limitations: _____

For the Consultant:

1. Name _____ Work telephone _____

   Address _____ Home telephone _____

   _____ FAX telephone _____

   _____ E-mail address _____

2. Name _____ Work telephone _____

   Address _____ Home telephone _____

   _____ FAX telephone _____

   _____ E-mail address _____

Special provisions or limitations: _____

In the event any changes are made to the authorized representatives or other information listed above, the Client and Consultant agree to furnish each other timely, written notice of such changes.

_____

Alternatively, you may state that the listing of authorized representatives is shown on a Schedule or Exhibit and appended to the contract. This clause and listing should be coordinated with the Notices provision in your Agreement or they could be combined. (See *Notices*.)

Should you urgently need to reach the specified contact and are unable to do so, it is important to keep a complete record of who was called and when, who was not available and what the subject of the call was. To help prevent misunderstandings and reinforce your documentation, send a letter, FAX or e-mail to your client, listing the contacts you attempted and outlining the substance of the calls — including any decisions made by the client's representative. Also send a copy to the person with whom you spoke, to give that person a chance to review and comment on your information.

SEE ALSO:

Assignment
Notices

RELEVANT STANDARD FORM AGREEMENT PROVISIONS:

AIA B141-1997:	Articles 1.1.3; 1.2.3.3; 1.2.2.3
EJCDC 1910-1 (1996 edition):	Article 6.02

VIII-10

CONFIDENTIAL COMMUNICATIONS

Architects, engineers and environmental consultants are expected to serve as their clients' professional advisors, candidly relating their observations, opinions and recommendations about the contractor and others. Such candor, however, can lead to problems if these remarks reflect negatively on another party.

THE PROBLEM

Like many consultants, you may find yourself advising your clients on the qualifications and performance of others. For example, your agreement may require you to make recommendations to your client about whether an apparent low-bid contractor is *responsive* (compared with the requirements of the bid package) or *responsible* (which may include financial or ethical responsibility as well as competence to do the job).

Contractors and suppliers, however, have been known to file — or threaten to file — libel or slander suits against design and environmental professionals in an attempt to either silence or influence such reports to their potential clients or obtain damages from the consultants if the owner acts upon the reports (such as by rejecting a low bid).

If you have knowledge that the apparent low-bid contractor is not responsible in some material way that would create undue risk, you have a responsibility to pass that information along to the client. On public projects, however, where the owner is required to accept the lowest qualified bid, what constitutes *qualified*? Suppose you've heard an apparent low-bid contractor is the town drunk. And is cheating on a spouse. Or has filed for bankruptcy twice in the last 15 years. Or has been late in completing several jobs. What are your responsibilities then?

THE SOLUTION

If you are about to offer recommendations to your client about another party's ability to perform, it is a good idea to get legal advice about what is germane. The reporting of drunkenness and the marital peccadilloes of our above hapless contractor may not be considered by a court sufficiently pertinent to the contractor's ability to do the job. On the other hand, the bankruptcies and late performance may be appropriate issues, assuming you have firsthand knowledge and can support your statements with facts.

You must be highly selective about the words you choose in reporting anything that could have a negative financial impact on another party. Report facts as facts, objectively, without embellishment or emotion; report opinions as opinions, carefully noted as such, and do your best to document the source of everything you say. Make sure others in your firm do the same. By taking this approach, you will make it difficult for the affected party to win a libel or slander suit against you, as well as the punitive damages that are also sometimes claimed. Remember that the best defense against a defamation action is the *truth.* But even with the truth as your shield, if you are forced to defend such a lawsuit, the process can be very expensive and time consuming.

Educate your clients. They must recognize that you cannot act as an effective advisor and help protect them if you face the threat of a lawsuit every time you state something negative about a bidder.

The best solution may be a contract clause through which the client agrees to protect you from slander or libel actions brought against you by parties about whose qualifications, performance or reputation you are required to render opinions and reports.

Consider this example:

CONFIDENTIAL COMMUNICATIONS

The Consultant may be required to report on or render confidential opinions about the past or current performance and/or qualifications of others engaged or being considered for engagement directly or indirectly by the Client. Those about whom reports and opinions are rendered may as a consequence initiate claims against the Consultant. To help create an atmosphere in which the Consultant may freely report or express such opinions candidly in the interest of the Client, the Client agrees, to the fullest extent permitted by law, to indemnify and hold harmless the Consultant against all damages, liabilities or costs, including reasonable attorneys' fees and defense costs, arising or allegedly arising from the rendering of such confidential opinions and reports by the Consultant to the Client or to the Client's agents.

Many consulting firms prefer, when they learn derogatory information about bidders or potential bidders, to simply refer their clients to the source of the information — a prior client whose projects were delayed, a newspaper article or public record containing negative information or other source documents not generated by the consultant. There is some legal debate over whether such negative reports and recommendations are more or less defensible if they are written or oral. Just remember: regardless of your course of action, stick to the facts — and only the facts.

SEE ALSO:

Claims Arbiter Service
Confidentiality
Construction Observation
Indemnities

THERE ARE NO RELEVANT PROVISIONS IN THE AIA OR EJCDC STANDARD FORM AGREEMENTS.

VIII-14

CONFIDENTIALITY

On occasion, a client may want a strict contract provision that requires the design or environmental professional to keep confidential the nature of any information developed and data related to a project. This may be for the protection of a marketing advantage or trade secrets, for public or political relations or for other legitimate client concerns. Such a provision may be acceptable and reasonable, if the terms are not so broad as to restrict the normal rights and obligations of the consultant in providing his or her professional services.

THE PROBLEM

If it is worded too tightly, a client-drafted confidentiality provision may cause you operational or legal difficulties. If the clause is too strict, it could prevent the normal sharing of vital information with subconsultants or even your own employees — clearly not the desired intent of such a provision.

Such a clause may also create a conflict between your contractual obligations to the client and certain laws and regulations. For instance, if you obey the law by reporting to appropriate agencies the discovery of hazardous materials, you may be breaching your contract with your client. But if you abide by the contract and don't report your findings, you may be violating the law. As discussed in *Public Responsibility*, your professional duty to protect the public health and safety goes beyond the duty owed to any client. (Refer to that section for further discussion.)

THE SOLUTION

Delete, if you can, any Confidentiality clause from your contract and offer to substitute the provision recommended in *Public Responsibility*. If your client insists on some confidentiality wording, however, you need to be clear on certain points, such as your obligation to meet government requirements and your rights regarding sharing information with legal counsel, employees and subconsultants. Such a clause, revised from a client-drafted version, might read:

Confidentiality

CONFIDENTIALITY

The Consultant agrees to keep confidential and not to disclose to any person or entity, other than the Consultant's employees, subconsultants and the general contractor and subcontractors, if appropriate, any data or information not previously known to and generated by the Consultant or furnished to the Consultant and marked CONFIDENTIAL by the Client. These provisions shall not apply to information in whatever form that is in the public domain, nor shall it restrict the Consultant from giving notices required by law or complying with an order to provide information or data when such order is issued by a court, administrative agency or other legitimate authority, or if disclosure is reasonably necessary for the Consultant to defend itself from any legal action or claim.

There are also times you may want your client to treat material you provide as proprietary. In that case, consider adding additional language, such as:

PROPRIETARY INFORMATION

The Client agrees that the technical methods, design details, techniques and pricing data contained in any material submitted by the Consultant pertaining to this Project or this Agreement shall be considered confidential and proprietary, and shall not be released or otherwise made available to any third party without the express written consent of the Consultant.

In addition, you might want to mark the technical and price sections of your documents CONFIDENTIAL. This clearly communicates that your proprietary information should not be circulated to others.

See Also:

Confidential Communications
Hazardous Materials
Ownership of Instruments of Service
Public Responsibility

Relevant standard form agreement provisions:

AIA B141-1997:   Articles 1.2.3.4; 1.3.7.7
EJCDC 1910-1 (1996 edition):   Article 6.10C

VIII-18

Contractual Reference to the Consultant

In agreements prepared by architects, engineers or environmental consultants, their firms are referred to by name (Smith, Doe & Associates), by acronym (SDA) or generically (Architect, Engineer, Environmental Professional or Consultant). In many client-prepared agreements, the consultant is often referred to as Contractor. Frequently, such contracts have been developed for contractors or suppliers and are not specifically intended for professional service firms.

The Problem

People who review or interpret a contract may not understand the difference between a construction contractor and a consultant under contract to a client. The importance of the words used can be significant, especially when a judge or jury does not comprehend that although you are being called a "contractor," you are not (or, with very few exceptions, should not be) responsible for jobsite safety, construction means and methods, warranties or a myriad of other things for which construction contractors are responsible. Lawyers thrive on confusion and misuse of terminology. In citing case law or statutes to a befuddled jury, a plaintiff's attorney might find it easy to blur the distinction between what law applies to construction contractors and what law applies to consultants who have carelessly allowed themselves to be called "contractors."

The Solution

The best solution is to identify the parties specifically by name, short name or acronym in a clause at the beginning of the contract. For example:

Contractual Reference to the Consultant

PARTIES TO THIS AGREEMENT

This Agreement for professional services has been entered into this _____ day of _____, ____ by Jones Widget Company (hereinafter referred to as JWC) and Smith, Doe & Associates (hereinafter referred to as Smith).

Another acceptable method is to define the parties generically in an introductory (preamble) clause as Client and Engineer, Architect, Design Professional or Consultant, as we have done throughout this book.

This Agreement is entered into this _____ day of _____, ____ by Jones Widget Company (hereinafter referred to as Client) and Smith, Doe & Associates (hereinafter referred to as Consultant).

Whether you call your firm Smith, Architect or SDA, be consistent. Make sure each time you or your client are referred to, it is exactly by the same designation. Before you send your contract to your client, perform a word search and have it checked for inconsistencies. If you have defined yourself as Architect, but in a few places Smith slips in, you have created an ambiguity. Typos and incorrect use of words in an agreement may have serious consequences. In this age of word processors and computers, it is a simple matter to customize contracts and use specific names or designations consistently throughout your documents.

If your clients, in their pre-printed contracts, insist on calling you Contractor and refuse to refer to you specifically by your firm name or by acronym, or to use a professional designation such as Engineer or Consultant, insist on including in the Definitions provision some language to mitigate the confusion and ambiguity of that terminology. (See *Definitions* for further discussion of that clause.) Consider adapting the following example to your situation:

Wherever used herein, the term Contractor shall mean Smith, Doe & Associates, (Smith), a professional corporation rendering professional architectural services. The term Contractor does not imply that Smith is engaged in providing construction contracting work, nor is Smith responsible in any way for the construc-

> tion means, methods, procedures, techniques or sequences nor for any aspect of jobsite safety. These duties are and shall remain the sole responsibility of the construction General Contractor.

Although this approach is less preferable than using a proper reference to your firm, it is better than being silent on the issue.

SEE ALSO:

Definitions
Design-Build
Jobsite Safety

THERE ARE NO RELEVANT PROVISIONS IN THE AIA OR EJCDC STANDARD FORM AGREEMENTS.

VIII-22

DEFINITIONS

Very often, words used in a professional services agreement have different meanings from those commonly understood by the public. If conflicts arise, such a difference in interpretation can cause confusion over the original intent of the parties to an agreement — and may even increase the consultant's liability if certain terms are left to laypersons (a jury, for instance) to interpret.

THE PROBLEM

Occasionally, a client may insist on using a word or term that you feel is misleading, such as by referring to you as a *contractor* (instead of a *consultant*, an *architect* or an *engineer*). (See **Contractual Reference to the Consultant** for further discussion.) Such usage idiosyncrasies can be baffling to a layperson, but there are other more dangerous words or terms that, when improperly used, may lead to confusion about your duties under the contract — thereby increasing your exposure to risk. These may include *cost estimate* as opposed to *opinion of probable*, *cost inspect* versus *observe* or *as-builts* instead of *record documents*. (See **Opinions (Estimates) of Probable Construction Costs**, **Construction Observation**, **Inspection** and **Record Documents** for more information.) Other confusing terminology might include abbreviations, acronyms, contractions or design and construction industry jargon. All of these can cause misunderstandings about what you and your client mean to say in your agreement.

THE SOLUTION

The best way to avoid misunderstandings — and lower your risk — is to draft a contract that uses well-defined or universally understood terms and phrases. Then look through your entire draft — starting with the Preamble (the "Whereas" section) and ending with the signature page and attachments — and highlight those words that might be misunderstood by average people on the street, passersby who would not be familiar with the design and construction or environmental consulting fields. (Those are, after all, the people who will be on a jury interpreting your contract.) As a cross-check, have a non-professional scan the contract draft and circle any words or phrases that are unclear. You'll probably come up with quite a list. Now, go back and decide whether you should collect those words into a Definitions section, keeping in mind that if a word is used only once or twice in the contract, you can define it right in the contract clause where it appears.

Next, develop standard definitions that you can plug into future agreements as appropriate. If you are using EJCDC or AIA documents, you can assume their definitions will be incorporated automatically. But you will find that many commonly used (and misused) words, such as *certify,* are not defined in the standard association documents.

If your client is adamant about using a particular word that you feel could be misunderstood or might increase your liability, you may find an appendix or contract clause clearly defining such words to be useful. This way, you can clear up ambiguities and misconceptions surrounding certain terms and further clarify "bad" words that your client (perhaps through his or her use of a pre-printed contract form) insists on retaining. Consider these examples:

DEFINITIONS

As used herein, the following words and their derivative words or phrases shall have the meaning indicated, unless otherwise specified in this Agreement.

CERTIFY, CERTIFICATION: A statement of the Consultant's opinion, based on his or her observation of conditions, to the best of the Consultant's professional knowledge, information and belief. Such statement of opinion does not constitute a warranty, either express or implied. It is understood that the Consultant's certification shall not relieve the Client or the Client's contractors of any responsibility or obligation they may have by industry custom or under any contract.

COST ESTIMATE: An opinion of probable construction cost made by the Consultant. In providing opinions of probable construction cost, it is recognized that neither the Client nor the Consultant has control over the costs of labor, equipment or materials, or over the Contractor's methods of determining prices or bidding. The opinion of probable construction costs is based on the Consultant's reasonable professional judgment and experience and does not constitute a warranty, express or implied, that the Contractor's bids or the negotiated price of the Work will not vary from the Client's budget or from any opinion of probable cost prepared by the Consultant.

DAY, DAYS: A calendar day of 24 hours. The term "days" shall mean consecutive calendar days of 24 hours each, or fraction thereof.

INSPECT, INSPECTION: The visual observation of construction to permit the Consultant, as an experienced and qualified professional, to determine that the Work, when completed by the Contractor, generally conforms to the Contract Documents. In making such inspections, the Consultant makes no guarantees for, and shall have no authority or control over, the Contractor's performance or failure to perform the Work in accordance with the Contract Documents. The Consultant shall have no responsibility for the means, methods, techniques, sequences or procedures selected by the Contractor or for the Contractor's safety precautions and programs nor for failure by the Contractor to comply with any laws or regulations relating to the performance or furnishing of the Work by the Contractor.

RECORD DOCUMENTS: Drawings prepared by the Consultant upon the completion of construction based upon the drawings and other data furnished to the Consultant by the Contractor and others showing significant changes in the Work made during construction. Because Record Documents are prepared based on unverified information provided by others, the Consultant makes no warranty of the accuracy or completeness of the drawings.

Alternatively, you could reference a glossary that contains all the terms you feel need defining in your agreement — such as the AIA Glossary or the EJCDC definitions. Check to be sure that any referenced document contains all the critical terms you want to nail down. You could also use language to incorporate that external document by reference. (See *Incorporation by Reference*.)

Another — but much less protective — method is to send the client a cover letter with the final form of the agreement, restating the definitions of words and terms you have previously reviewed with him or her.

Definitions

SEE ALSO:

Certifications, Guarantees and Warranties
Construction Observation
Contractual Reference to the Consultant
Incorporation by Reference
Inspection
Opinions (Estimates) of Probable Construction Costs
Titles

RELEVANT STANDARD FORM AGREEMENT PROVISIONS:

AIA B141-1997:   Article 1.3.7.2
Glossary of Construction Industry Terms
in Volume Three of the Architect's Handbook of
Professional Practice, published by the AIA.
EJCDC 1910-1 (1996 edition):   Article 7.01

ENTIRE AGREEMENT

Law books call it an "Integration" clause; EJCDC contracts refer to it as "Total Agreement." Whatever the name, this clause seeks to establish what lawyers call the "four corners of the agreement." In other words, *what is contained within the written contract is what the parties have agreed to.* The goal is to describe clearly and precisely exactly what makes up the agreement. Such a clause sometimes also specifies how and by whom the agreement may be modified.

THE PROBLEM

In all the pre-contract discussion and correspondence with your client, you both may form uncertain (and sometimes incorrect) expectations about what the other party will do. Certainly, after the heat of negotiations has cooled, memories tend to fade. It may be difficult to remember what scope items were discussed for what fee under what conditions. Pre-contract notes and memos may be unclear or even contradictory.

People also sometimes promise more than they can deliver. You may have implied you could design the best stadium in the world; your client may have hinted there would be an unlimited design budget to finance this miracle.

Unless your agreement specifically states otherwise, someone may later claim that the contract was supposed to say something it did not say, that you promised something additional in a discussion, or that a last-minute change was made in wording that sounded similar to what had been agreed to but in fact changed the intent substantially.

Unless it is clearly stated how and by whom an agreement may be changed or amended after it is signed, a confusing or an ambiguous situation may develop. Generations of lawyers have lived very well by sorting out the ambiguities created by mere mortals.

THE SOLUTION

You and your client should review the final written agreement in detail to assure that it contains everything you intend and understand regarding services to be performed and the terms and conditions of that performance.

Entire Agreement

VIII-28

In addition, we recommend you add an Entire Agreement clause to your contract. Such a clause generally appears near the end, just before the signature lines.

ENTIRE AGREEMENT

This Agreement, comprising pages ____ through ____, and Exhibits ____, ____ and ____, is the entire Agreement between the Client and the Consultant. It supersedes all prior communications, understandings and agreements, whether oral or written. Amendments to this Agreement must be in writing and signed by both the Client and the Consultant.

This type of clause will help prevent misunderstandings between you and the client about what constitutes your agreement and how the agreement may be modified. Such a clause is mutually beneficial and your client should readily accept it. It may have the additional benefit of helping to counter any overzealous statements that may have crept into your brochures and marketing materials. It makes clear that what you see in the agreement is what you (and your client) get.

SEE ALSO:

Authorized Representatives
Notices

RELEVANT STANDARD FORM AGREEMENT PROVISIONS:

AIA B141-1997:	Article 1.4.1
EJCDC 1910-1 (1996 edition):	Article 8.2

Governing Law and Jurisdiction

Suppose an architect in Miami contracts with a structural engineer in Atlanta to help design a project in Salt Lake City for a client headquartered in Vancouver. If there was a dispute, where would legal action be brought? What set of laws would govern the interpretation of the contract?

The general rule is that, absent an agreement to the contrary, a contract will be interpreted according to the law of the place the contract is to be performed. But statutes and their judicial interpretations vary from state to state and from country to country. It is possible that the laws in some jurisdictions will be more favorable toward design and environmental professionals than the laws in others, especially on such issues as statutes of repose and limitation, indemnification, limitation of liability, liens, responsibility for jobsite safety and certificates of merit.

The Problem

Difficulties can arise when you, your client and/or the project are located in different jurisdictions — whether in another state, province or country. (See *International Projects* for more information.) Should litigation become necessary, it is possible there could be two or three or more choices of jurisdictions. Will the courtroom be conveniently near you or a long distance away? Does the jurisdiction have a notoriously large backlog of cases awaiting trial? Will you benefit from a "home court" advantage or be subject to frontier justice and a "good ol' boy" judge? Will the applicable laws and rules of procedure be unfamiliar to you and your attorney? If you fail to specify a jurisdiction and set of laws to govern the interpretation of the contract, you may have created an ambiguity. You've also missed an opportunity to select a forum that may be more beneficial to you.

The Solution

Although the applicable building codes and standards of performance that govern a design or environmental consultant will be those of the location of the project, parties to a contract can generally choose the set of laws that govern the interpretation of the contract terms and

Governing Law and Jurisdiction

performance of the contract. They may also choose where the action can be brought. In the example above, the parties could agree that a lawsuit could be brought in Florida, Georgia, Utah or British Columbia. They could further specify that the laws of any one of those jurisdictions would govern the interpretation of the contract.

To avoid uncertainty, you and your client should agree in advance whose laws you wish to be applied and the location of the court where legal actions will be brought. The decision on these issues has to do with fairness, familiarity, convenience and economics. Talk to your attorney before making these choices. Generally, you may receive more favorable consideration in your "home" jurisdiction — where you and your employees live, do business, pay taxes and vote. Given a choice, you should specify a jurisdiction where, in your lawyer's opinion, you stand the best chance of winning a claim, given existing statutory law or court precedents. Your contract should be specific about which state's or country's laws will govern. If the client wants to rely on the laws of the state or country where it is situated or where the project is located, that may or may not be acceptable to you. While jurisdiction and governing law are two separate issues, they are closely related and may be addressed in one provision of a contract. Here is a sample clause:

GOVERNING LAW AND JURISDICTION

The Client and the Consultant agree that this Agreement and any legal actions concerning its validity, interpretation and performance shall be governed by the laws of {insert the principal place of business of the Consultant or other state, as appropriate}.

It is further agreed that any legal action between the Client and the Consultant arising out of this Agreement or the performance of the services shall be brought in a court of competent jurisdiction in {insert the principal place of business of the Consultant or other state, as appropriate}.

Note that there is a difference between substantive law (what the statutes, codes and precedents establish) and procedural law (how the court carries out its proceedings). You can attempt to specify a body of governing substantive law from a jurisdiction other than the one where an action is being heard. The court may or may not apply the substantive law of another state; there is no guarantee. A court will, however, normally use its own procedural law in carrying out its proceedings — rules of evidence, motions, discovery and the like.

It is interesting to note that both the AIA and EJCDC, in the latest editions of the B141 and 1910-1 standard documents, address Controlling Law but not Jurisdiction. The AIA stipulates as Controlling Law the architect's principal place of business while the EJCDC specifies the state where the project is located.

SEE ALSO:

Attorneys' Fees
Indemnities
International Projects
Jobsite Safety
Limitation of Liability
Statutes of Repose and Limitation

RELEVANT STANDARD FORM AGREEMENT PROVISIONS:

AIA B141-1997:	Article 1.3.7.1
EJCDC 1910-1 (1996 edition):	Article 6.07

VIII-32

INCORPORATION BY REFERENCE

Incorporation by reference is a contract term that says that the parties to a contract agree to be bound by the requirements, terms or conditions contained in another document that is neither quoted in its entirety nor appended to the contract. It may refer to a body of regulations or laws, a government agency or association standard, a section of code, the General Conditions of the contract for construction or the prime contract between the consultant's client and another party.

THE PROBLEM

Agreeing to incorporate and abide by the contents of another document without carefully reviewing it is just plain foolhardy, especially since the incorporated terms may increase your liability and/or may be uninsurable. In effect, agreeing to terms that you have not seen is like signing a blank check. You might be asked to agree to incorporate an entire agreement between your client and an owner, for instance, or between your client and a funding agency. Obviously, many portions of that agreement will simply not be applicable to the services of a consultant. This creates uncertainty, ambiguity and the possibility of an expensive struggle to untangle the legal consequences of what is written versus what you really intended.

THE SOLUTION

Before agreeing to be bound by the terms of any other document, either obtain the document yourself or insist that your client provide you with a copy of the referenced item or contract. Read it thoroughly and, if appropriate, have your attorney do the same.

It is always a good idea to append a copy (if it is reasonably possible) to your agreement with your client. This will prevent future misunderstandings or disputes caused by incorporating a document you did not anticipate or intend.

If you do not agree with the requirements of the entire document or if portions of it do not belong in your agreement, discuss this with your client and agree to delete or modify them.

If you and your client agree to incorporate most of the document but to delete certain articles or provisions, you could use the following clause to accomplish that:

Incorporation by Reference

INCORPORATION

It is understood and agreed that the provisions of {document} are incorporated herein and made a part of this Agreement by this reference, with the exception of:

Be as specific as possible when listing those portions of a larger document to which you will be bound — right down to chapter, section and paragraph (and the edition and date, if applicable) — or else you may be bound to something different than you had intended. You also could incorporate only certain sections of the referenced document that pertain to your agreement or to which you agree:

It is understood and agreed that certain portions of {document} **are incorporated herein and made a part of this Agreement by reference. Only the following** {clauses; articles; sections} **are incorporated:**

The Consultant shall not be bound by any other provision of said contract not specifically listed in this paragraph.

If you are a subconsultant and your client (the prime consultant) wants to incorporate his or her contract with the owner by reference into your subcontract, you may find the following sample provision useful:

The Consultant has an agreement with {client; owner}, **a copy of which is appended to this Agreement. The Subconsultant agrees to be bound by the terms and conditions contained therein to the same extent as the Consultant is bound.**

Incorporation by Reference

VIII-35

If you find certain provisions of the appended document unacceptable to you, the clause could be modified to read:

> **. . . contained therein to the same extent as the Consultant is bound, except as indicated through deletions or other modifications made therein, and initialed by both the Consultant and the Subconsultant.**

If your client doesn't wish to show you the entire contract, ask to see specifically those portions that would affect you and append or list the clauses and modify the above language:

> **. . . contained therein in only the following clauses:**
>
> **The Subconsultant shall not be bound by any other provision of said Agreement not specifically listed in this paragraph.**

Remember to ask to review the contract between the owner and the general contractor. You'll want to see that any references to you and your services are consistent with the terms and conditions of your own agreement with the client.

SEE ALSO:

Entire Agreement

RELEVANT STANDARD FORM AGREEMENT PROVISIONS:

AIA B141-1997:	Articles 1.4.1.3; 2.9.1
EJCDC 1910-1 (1996 edition):	Article 8
	Exhibit J

VIII-36

LENDERS' REQUIREMENTS

Client-drawn agreements sometimes call for the design or environmental professional to cooperate fully with the client's lender and to execute whatever documents that lender might demand. Such vague language can mean tremendous liability problems for the unwary architect, engineer or consultant.

THE PROBLEM

A provision that requires you to "cooperate in every respect" with the lender is overreaching and far too open-ended. Imagine what you might have to do to comply with that requirement! Lenders' attorneys stay up late at night planning for just such situations.

Even worse is the demand that you sign all documents required by a lender. Your clients' lenders might ask you to guarantee the absence of hazardous materials or asbestos. They might require you to guarantee that your designs or recommendations will achieve a specified level of quality, output or result. (See *Certifications, Guarantees and Warranties* and *Hazardous Materials* for more information.) They might require you to certify that your designs or deliverables are in *strict* compliance with *all* codes and standards. (See *Code Compliance*.) They might demand that you turn over ownership or copyrights to your drawings, specifications or reports to them. (See *Copyrights* and *Ownership of Instruments of Service*.) They might insist that you consent to Assignment clauses that would allow transfer of your clients' rights to the lender. (See *Assignment*.) Or they might impose additional insurance requirements on you without allowing you sufficient time to consult with your professional liability insurance specialist or attorney as to cost and availability.

Absent any contractual protection to the contrary, your clients' lenders could exert intense pressure on you to hurriedly sign documents you have never seen before and without opportunity or sufficient time to review or negotiate for liability and insurability implications. Even without such onerous contract clauses, it isn't unusual to be told that if you don't sign immediately, you could delay the funding of the project or even cause the loan to be denied, resulting in irreparable damage to your clients. No one should have to submit to this kind of commercial blackmail.

The Solution

Delete from contracts any language that would require you to *totally* or *fully* cooperate with the lender in every respect or to execute *any and all* documents the lender requests. If you refuse such a contractual requirement, you are then under no legal obligation to the lender later on. If you can't delete the provision entirely, at least modify it to state you will comply with only those lender requirements that are, in your judgment, reasonable and consistent with common law and with your agreement with your client. (Common law doesn't require that you certify or guarantee anything, that you indemnify anyone or that you turn over ownership of your documents to anyone. See *Standard of Care* for further discussion.)

Perhaps the best solution is an aggressive approach. Insert a clause that would exempt you from signing anything that might affect your insurance or increase your contractual or professional liability risk. Consider the following suggested clause:

LENDERS' REQUIREMENTS

The Consultant shall not be required to execute any documents subsequent to the signing of this Agreement that in any way might, in the sole judgment of the Consultant, increase the Consultant's contractual or legal obligations or risks, or adversely affect the availability or cost of its professional or general liability insurance.

Another solution is to include a provision that would obligate your client "prior to the effective date of the Agreement to append to the Agreement any document the Consultant will be required to sign during the course of the project." Because a lender probably will not have been selected before your contract negotiations, you then would be free to object and negotiate documents presented to you later if they are unreasonable or inequitable.

An alternative might be to require in your contract that you at least be given sufficient time to review and approve documents presented to you for execution by lenders. You should still reserve the right to change or negotiate any language that would alter your risks or insurance cost or availability, as we suggest in the preceding clause.

Discuss these alternatives with your attorney to be sure your agreement protects you from having to sign any onerous documents your clients' lenders may put in front of you. And when such documents are presented, review them carefully with legal counsel and your professional liability insurance specialist. You must make certain you are not increasing your risk and not jeopardizing your insurance coverage in the future.

SEE ALSO:

Assignment
Certifications, Warranties and Guarantees
Code Compliance
Copyrights
Hazardous Materials
Insurance
Ownership of Instruments of Service
Standard of Care

RELEVANT STANDARD FORM AGREEMENT PROVISIONS:

AIA B141-1997:	Articles 1.4.1.3; 2.9.1
EJCDC 1910-1 (1996 edition):	Article 8
	Exhibit J

VIII-40

NOTICES

Many contracts stipulate that notices given to the client are considered served only if sent by registered or certified mail to the address listed in the contract.

In addition, the word *days* is found throughout most contracts in describing a time period, such as a period of required notice, a period for performing a contractual duty or the period during which some rights exist. Several different and equally reasonable definitions or interpretations can be applied to the word.

THE PROBLEM

While such details may seem trivial, they are not. For instance, a provision that states that notices given to your client are only served if sent by certain kinds of mail is one-way and applies only to notices to the client. It also precludes other forms of communication that may be more convenient or effective. And it fails to stipulate just when a notice is considered to have been served — when it is sent or when it is received. The difference of a few days can be a major issue in some critical contractual matters.

The word *day* presents another problem. It could be taken to mean calendar day, work day (do you count holidays and, if so, whose?), days in the aggregate or consecutive days, or any period of 24 consecutive hours. (Consider problems you encounter with rental car agencies, airport parking lots and delivery schedules for consumer goods.)

If your agreement is not specific about when certain time periods begin or end, you may be setting yourself up for a dispute. Each party to a contract will choose the most favorable definition. But important issues revolve around a matter of a few days. For instance, how long can your client take to pay you without being considered in breach of contract? (See *Billing and Payment*.) How long a notice must either party give for suspension or termination of contract? (See *Suspension of Services* and *Termination*.) How long do you have to complete your agreed-upon scope of services? What is the time period for a party to perform acceptance tests on electronic files received from the other party? (See *CADD/Electronic Files*.) If your contract is not clear, your client could delay you or dispute your rights — or a court will tell you what it thinks you meant to say.

The Solution

The best solution is a clause that provides for delivery of notices by whatever means you and your client deem acceptable, taking into account ease of communication, security and the degree of certainty that messages sent will be received. Discuss this with your client. If you agree to transmit notices required in your agreement by e-mail, FAX, private courier or even smoke signal, that is acceptable. It is also important that you specify when a notice is considered served.

Notices

Any notice required under this Agreement shall be in writing, addressed as specified in this Agreement and sent by *[strike any that do not apply] electronic mail; facsimile; registered, certified, express or regular U.S. mail; by {name of} courier service* **to the address (or telephone number) listed in this Agreement. All notices shall be deemed delivered** *[strike those that do not apply] upon receipt; when transmitted; when received; ____ (___) calendar days after transmittal* **by any of the methods specified above to the** *address; fax number* **of the recipient listed in this Agreement. Either party may change its address or FAX number by giving the other party notice of the change in any manner permitted by this Agreement.**

Be sure to include a complete listing — either on the signature page, as part of the above clause, as an attachment or in some other appropriate location in the agreement — of those persons authorized to receive notices on behalf of each party and their addresses, FAX and telephone numbers and e-mail addresses. (See *Authorized Representatives*.)

Because e-mail and FAXes are sometimes subject to failure, keep hard copies of all transmittals or require that the receiving party e-mail or FAX back to you confirmation of receipt. You want a means of assuring that important notices are, in fact, received, and that a solid trail of documentation exists if someone later claims a notice was not properly given.

In addition, define what you mean by *day(s)* and be consistent in how you use it. In general, if you are silent on the issue in your contract, the courts will interpret days as calendar days. Nevertheless, to avoid misunderstandings, it doesn't hurt to decide on a definition. It makes no difference which definition you choose as long as you agree to it and are satisfied with the number of days for each purpose. Perhaps the easiest definition is "calendar days of 24 hours." You might add the following to your Notices clause, above, or to your Definitions section of your agreement:

DEFINITION OF "DAYS"

Wherever used in this Agreement, the term "days" shall mean consecutive calendar days of 24 hours each, or fraction thereof.

Clients should have no objection to either of these provisions, as they simply help to clarify how each of you will comply with the requirements called for by the contract.

SEE ALSO:

Authorized Representatives
Billing and Payment
CADD/Electronic Files
Definitions
Suspension of Services
Termination

RELEVANT STANDARD FORM AGREEMENT PROVISIONS:

AIA B141-1997:	No applicable provisions.
EJCDC 1910-1 (1996 edition):	Articles 3.01C; 6.12

VIII-44

OWNERSHIP OF INSTRUMENTS OF SERVICE

The architect, engineer and environmental consultant provide a professional service to their clients, not a product. Construction documents — drawings, specifications and reports, whether on hard copy or electronic files — are instruments of that service; that is, they are the written or graphic depiction of the intellectual process that is architecture, engineering or consulting. As such, these documents should remain the property of the professional who conceived and prepared them. It is not unusual, however, for clients to request ownership. They may want to "own" the designs for one of several reasons: to prevent the design from being repeated on other projects, to protect the privacy of the information, to facilitate operation and maintenance of the project, or to reuse the design on other projects without involving the consultant again. Some of these reasons may be acceptable, with suitable protective measures in place; others are not appropriate and are unacceptable regardless of the contractual safeguards obtained by the consultant.

THE PROBLEM

Unauthorized reuse is the most serious problem that can arise if you transfer ownership of your drawings and specifications to others. This could result in a claim being filed against you years after the fact by someone who relied on your design for another project in another location at another time. Worse still, a client who owns your documents could make unauthorized changes that could result in a claim against you. (Refer to *Unauthorized Changes to Plans*.)

Another problem may also arise. If instruments of service were legally perceived as products, defects in them (errors or omissions) could be considered "product defects," subject to strict liability rather than the professional standard of care. (The doctrine of strict liability says that a damage- or injury-causing defect in a product is enough to establish liability, whether or not the producer of that product was negligent in the design or production of the product. As a professional, you have greater protection under the law, where your professional liability is based on negligence only.) Thus far, courts have not generally deemed designs to be products, but the current trend is toward liberalizing liability.

Ownership of Instruments of Service

You are far better off not tempting the courts by appearing to have "sold" your plans as though they were a tangible product.

THE SOLUTION

Do your utmost to retain ownership of your drawings and specifications. Discuss this with your clients; find out why they think they want ownership; educate them. Explain the problems that could arise from reuse under other site conditions or other geographic or climatic situations and without your involvement during construction. Your client should understand your concern over potential liability. If you suspect your client intends to reuse your designs elsewhere without your involvement, you will have to take decisive steps to deal with that risk. Either refuse the job, get a "gold-plated" indemnity or charge such a large fee that you can afford failures.

If your client is concerned about protecting information about the project or the design concepts, you can address that by means of a Confidentiality clause without giving up ownership of the reports and plans. (See *Confidentiality* for more information and sample clause language.)

If necessary, you can provide your client with a reproducible copy of the final documents for use in maintenance and operation of the project without giving up ownership of the original documents. In any case, attempt to obtain a clarifying clause such as the following:

OWNERSHIP OF INSTRUMENTS OF SERVICE

All reports, drawings, specifications, computer files, field data, notes and other documents and instruments prepared by the Consultant as instruments of service shall remain the property of the Consultant. The Consultant shall retain all common law, statutory and other reserved rights, including the copyright thereto.

If your client insists on ownership of documents, it should be possible to strike a compromise whereby you transfer ownership of the final documents on completion of the project and upon payment in full for your services (another excellent yet subtle weapon in your collections arsenal) but *only* if the client indemnifies you against unauthorized reuse and unauthorized changes to your documents. (Refer to *Prototype Designs* for a discussion of designs intended for reuse.) Note that "final documents" means just that and does not include your drafts, notes, sketches and preliminary documents, which should always remain your property.

A transfer-of-ownership clause may read as follows:

OWNERSHIP OF INSTRUMENTS OF SERVICE

The Client acknowledges the Consultant's construction documents, including electronic files, as instruments of professional service. Nevertheless, the final construction documents prepared under this Agreement shall become the property of the Client upon completion of the services and payment in full of all monies due to the Consultant. The Client shall not reuse or make any modification to the construction documents without the prior written authorization of the Consultant. The Client agrees, to the fullest extent permitted by law, to indemnify and hold harmless the Consultant, its officers, directors, employees and subconsultants (collectively, Consultant) against any damages, liabilities or costs, including reasonable attorneys' fees and defense costs, arising from or allegedly arising from or in any way connected with the unauthorized reuse or modification of the construction documents by the Client or any person or entity that acquires or obtains the construction documents from or through the Client without the written authorization of the Consultant.

Another effective measure is to retain copyright of your materials and, if it is your intention to allow the reuse of your documents, grant your client a license to use the design for a future specific project, with appropriate indemnity protection for you. (See *Copyrights* and *Indemnities* for more information.)

If the documents you are transferring are on electronic media, be sure you have a CADD clause in your agreement. Alternatively, you could incorporate some of the appropriate CADD provisions into the above clause, especially "no sale, no warranty" language. (See *CADD/Electronic Files* for discussion and sample clauses.)

Ownership of Instruments of Service

SEE ALSO:

CADD/Electronic Files
Confidentiality
Copyrights
Indemnities
Prototype Designs
Unauthorized Changes to Plans

RELEVANT STANDARD FORM AGREEMENT PROVISIONS:

AIA B141-1997:	Article 1.3.2
EJCDC 1910-1 (1996 edition):	Article 6.04A

SEVERABILITY AND SURVIVAL

Severability and *Survival* are two simple but important concepts that are quite independent of each other but are often grouped together in a single contract clause. They both deal, in general, with how the parties wish the courts to interpret the terms of the agreement. But beyond that, they are very distinct and separate issues.

A *Severability* provision is needed in the event a contract clause is found to be invalid and is severed from the body of the contract by operation of law (that is, if a judge or a statute renders the provision invalid). It is important to retain all other provisions of the contract in full force.

A *Survival* provision is needed because even after the services and other obligations of a contract have been completed or terminated by one of the parties, some terms and conditions should survive and remain enforceable.

THE PROBLEM

If any provision of a contract is found to be illegal by the enforcing court (even a law that is enacted or changed after your contract is signed), there is a danger that the entire contract could be declared void in some jurisdictions. This would leave you in the unfortunate and untenable position of not having an enforceable contract with your client.

Further, unless your contract explicitly states otherwise, some jurisdictions may construe your contract to be terminated once your services have been fully performed and you have been paid. This might negate any indemnities, limitations of liability or other protections you want to remain enforceable after the completion of the contract. There are also some questions that arise when a contract is terminated prematurely; you still want the right to enforce the payment terms, interest, attorneys' fees, ownership of the documents and other provisions.

THE SOLUTION

First, if the issues of severability and survival are addressed in a single clause, separate them and make them two distinct contract provisions. Then, make sure each provision

Severability and Survival

clearly states your intent regarding these issues. Because these clauses benefit both of you, your client should have no objection.

To address the severability issues, you might include a provision such as this:

SEVERABILITY

Any term or provision of this Agreement found to be invalid under any applicable statute or rule of law shall be deemed omitted and the remainder of this Agreement shall remain in full force and effect.

One contractual approach to survival issues is a blanket clause that applies to all obligations of the parties. This would be helpful if, for any reason, you or the client terminates the agreement before the project is completed, as it keeps all unfulfilled rights and obligations in force. Here is an example:

SURVIVAL

Notwithstanding completion or termination of this Agreement for any reason, all rights, duties and obligations of the parties to this Agreement shall survive such completion or termination and remain in full force and effect until fulfilled.

A narrower approach might be to specify the types of provisions you want to survive. This might read:

SURVIVAL

All limitations of liability, indemnifications, warranties and representations contained in this Agreement shall survive the completion or termination of this Agreement and shall remain in full force and effect.

It should be understood that this latter language is bilateral; that is, it provides that protective clauses favoring the client (such as you indemnifying the client) will survive as well as those that benefit you (such as the client indemnifying you or limiting your liability).

Another approach is to specifically list by article number those provisions you wish to survive, such as limitation of liability or dispute resolution. Include indemnities that are in your favor, too, particularly those pertaining to hazardous materials and any other protection you might wish to rely on in the future. Your clients may likewise want to add any indemnities or protections that favor them. Here is a model clause:

SURVIVAL

It is expressly agreed that the rights, duties and obligations contained in Articles ____, ____ and ____ shall survive the completion or any termination of this Agreement and shall remain in full force and effect.

By making certain your agreement will remain in force even if some provisions are found invalid and by providing for the survival of certain clauses after termination, you and your client can ensure your contractual intentions are carried out and your hard-won protections will remain intact.

SEE ALSO:

Billing and Payment
Dispute Avoidance and Resolution
Hazardous Materials
Indemnities
Limitation of Liability
Statutes of Repose and Limitation

RELEVANT STANDARD FORM AGREEMENT PROVISIONS:

AIA B141-1997: No applicable provisions.
EJCDC 1910-1 (1996 edition): Articles 6.13; 6.14

VIII-52

TITLES

In professional services agreements, each clause or provision may be given a title or heading that generally describes the subject of the clause. Such titles make it easier to locate and refer to the various issues covered by the agreement.

THE PROBLEM

No one will argue that titling the clauses of an agreement makes it easier to use. Several issues arise, however, when selecting these titles. If a clause's title addresses a single subject but the clause actually encompasses more than one, or if both parties do not interpret the title in the same way, it could be argued that there were provisions hidden by misleading or incomplete titles. As lame as this argument may sound, it will be looked at by a court in light of the other circumstances of the contract's formation and wording. This is especially important if the contract being used was written or offered by you. Courts almost always interpret any ambiguity against the party whose contract was used.

There is something else to remember. If you negotiate changes in the text of a clause (such as changing "as-builts" to "record documents" or changing "supervision" to "observation") but fail to change these words in the title, the resulting agreement is, at best, ambiguous. (See *Record Documents* and *Construction Observation*.)

THE SOLUTION

Your professional services agreement should be an honest, straightforward document that puts forth the understandings, duties and responsibilities of each party in clear and comprehensible language. Nothing should be hidden; titles should be consistent with and descriptive of the text of each clause.

Titles should be carefully selected and clearly describe the content of each provision. It is permissible to include more than one subject in a clause, especially when they are closely related. If you do so, the heading should include both subjects (Severability and Survival, for instance, or Governing Law and Venue).

Titles

VIII-54

After negotiating changes to the wording of your agreement, double-check to be sure the titles are consistent with the new language being used.

In addition, claims of misleading titles might be avoided if you simply state in your agreement that there is no legal significance to these titles. Such a provision is usually one of the last paragraphs of the agreement, near the signature line, and is normally a non-controversial "housekeeping" item in the contract:

TITLES

The paragraph titles used in this Agreement are for general reference only and are not part of the Agreement.

Regardless of whether you include such a clause, you and your client should always read the agreement thoroughly before signing it and have it reviewed by your attorneys if you have doubts about any of the terms and how they will be enforced.

SEE ALSO:

Definitions
Limitation of Liability
Record Documents
Severability and Survival

RELEVANT STANDARD FORM AGREEMENT PROVISIONS:

AIA B141-1997:	No applicable provisions.
EJCDC 1910-1 (1996 edition):	Article 6.16

Part IX

Specific Services

CADD/Electronic Files

Condominiums

Emergency Services

International Projects

Renovation/Remodeling

Subconsultants

Supplanting Another Consultant

Testing Laboratories

Underground Improvements

Value Engineering

Year 2000 (Y2K)

IX-2

CADD/Electronic Files

The use of computers has become commonplace in architecture and engineering. Almost every design and consulting firm in North America now has some computer-aided design and drafting (CADD) capability and the typical firm uses CADD on nearly all of its projects. These firms understand that computers can reduce the risk of conflicts, errors and omissions, improve communications between members of the consulting or design team, and enhance design and analysis capabilities as well as data presentation. What many may not realize, however, is that along with these advantages comes a whole array of electronic data-related liability issues they must consider.

The Problem

Increasingly, clients, contractors and public agencies are requesting your designs, specifications, reports and data in an electronic format. This can give rise to several problems. For starters, some people have expectations about CADD or other electronic media that cannot possibly be satisfied. They may believe that this new technology will save you time and increase your productivity, which in turn will save them vast sums of money. They may also think that electronic files are an efficient long-term storage medium for design materials and data. Some may even believe that because a design or report is computer generated it has a higher degree of accuracy.

A client agreement that requires you to deliver *all* your documents on electronic media may actually add to your costs. This is especially true when you are required to follow an elaborate CADD specification, say for some public agency. This can mean increased learning time for your operators, time-consuming translation from one format to another and painstaking effort to follow complicated specs. It may also prohibit or restrict use of your existing software library. If your client doesn't understand this, it will probably balk at compensating you for the additional costs.

Even without client-imposed computer requirements, if you and your client have not agreed in advance on CADD specifications — exactly what hardware and software are to be used as detailed computer-design elements, and just which of your documents are to be delivered on electronic files — you may find yourself having to purchase new hardware,

CADD/Electronic Files

hurriedly training personnel or duplicating work already completed in order to comply with a client's requirements.

Some clients may want the electronic files for archival purposes or for space planning. Some may think documents on disk will be useful for facility maintenance of their project. A few may want to use your drawings and specifications for future remodeling or expansion. Still others may regard your plans on disk as record documents or "as-builts" and hope to rely on them, without realizing they have the same limitations as hard-copy "as-builts." (See **Record Documents** for a related discussion.)

Then there are clients who may have other ideas about reuse of your files. Unless you have protected your designs or other deliverables by contract and copyright, they could be reused without your knowledge or consent. Some clients may decide to make "a few little changes" to your files; it takes but a few keystrokes to alter your report, specification or design and increase your liability. (See **Copyrights**.)

Many architects and engineers report that increasingly, contractors want to use the designers' electronic files to prepare shop drawings. While this may save the contractors a great deal of time and money, it also heightens your risk. (See **Shop Drawing Review**.)

Critical errors can occur during the transmission of data. If a problem arises and you are unable to prove you relied on erroneous information transmitted by someone else, you may bear the financial consequences. Further, you may find the data unreadable or its format unusable, or you may have little or no technical support from the person who prepared the information. Conversely, problems can arise when you transmit design data to your client or the contractor. Again, if you cannot show the errors were not yours, you may be held responsible.

You may have heard of the expected computer problems predicted at the turn of the century. Technology watchers tell us that the Year-2000 (Y2K) dilemma will cause widespread data loss and erroneous data, resulting in a tremendous litigation boom. (See **Year 2000** for more information.)

Another source of concern is the software itself. The proliferation of available technical-application software is astonishing. It sometimes seems everyone with a laptop is generating programs. Unfortunately, defects in software packages may not be detected until your design is complete or the project is under construction and problems are discovered. What's more, unfamiliarity with these very sophisticated programs can cause very serious problems. Changes to the software by your in-house computer whiz or inadequate training of your staff also can result in errors — for which you can be held responsible. In addition, some consultants and design firms are developing their own software and selling it to the public. They may not be aware that these programs, without proper safeguards in place, subject their firms to claims of strict liability for failures resulting from defects in the software products.

THE SOLUTION

The good news is that for each of these problems there is at least a partial solution.

First, find out why your client wants your electronic data files. It is possible the client may not need the plans or deliverables in electronic format, or at least not all of them. Perhaps your client does not understand that a requirement for *all* work to be performed on CADD or electronic media will likely result in increased costs. If he or she wants the disks for facility maintenance or future repair work, explain that information magnetically stored is easily damaged and its accuracy cannot be depended upon for very long. What's more, facility maintenance rarely requires all the drawings in a construction set. Instead, you could offer to generate a set (the electrical and mechanical portion, for instance) on disk especially for maintenance. If your client wants project data for archival purposes, again you should describe the limitations of relying on computer disks. Information stored on disks requires certain operating systems and software that may be obsolete in the not-so-distant future.

Your client may have perfectly appropriate reasons for wanting copies of some of your electronic files, however. If so, you must take certain precautions in order to protect yourself against the reuse or misuse of that information. Many architects and engineers protect themselves by stating in their agreements that the printed, signed and sealed hard copy is the actual contract deliverable and that any electronic copies are for the client's convenience only.

There are several places you can address these issues in your agreement: in a Scope of Services paragraph regarding deliverables, for example, or in your Ownership of Instruments of Service provision. (Refer to these sections for more information.) We recommend instead that you add a detailed CADD/Electronic Files clause to your contract. The provision should describe your construction documents — including computer files — as instruments of your service and state that you will retain all ownership rights. It should also establish the software specifications and list in detail the requirements for compatibility of hardware, software and design elements. You'll want to say that your hard-copy drawings and specifications take precedence over electronic files in the event of a discrepancy. You should also specify an acceptance period — keep it short — of 30 to 60 days at most, after which you will not be responsible for deterioration or defects in the data. Finally, such a clause should also include a waiver and indemnity for claims resulting from unauthorized reuse of the electronic files or unauthorized changes made by the client or others. (See *Indemnities* and *Unauthorized Changes to Plans*.) Consider this example:

DELIVERY OF ELECTRONIC FILES

In accepting and utilizing any drawings, reports and data on any form of electronic media generated and furnished by the Consultant, the Client agrees that all such electronic files are instruments of service of the Consultant, who shall be deemed the author, and shall retain all common law, statutory law and other rights, including copyrights.

The Client agrees not to reuse these electronic files, in whole or in part, for any purpose other than for the Project. The Client agrees not to transfer these electronic files to others without the prior written consent of the Consultant. The Client further agrees to waive all claims against the Consultant resulting in any way from any unauthorized changes to or reuse of the electronic files for any other project by anyone other than the Consultant.

The Client and the Consultant agree that any electronic files furnished by either party shall conform to the specifications listed in Exhibit ___. Any changes to the electronic specifications by either the Client or the Consultant are subject to review and acceptance by the other party. Additional services by the Consultant made necessary by changes to the electronic file specifications shall be compensated for as Additional Services.

Electronic files furnished by either party shall be subject to an acceptance period of _____ (___) days during which the receiving party agrees to perform appropriate acceptance tests. The party furnishing the electronic file shall correct any discrepancies or errors detected and reported within the acceptance period. After the acceptance period, the electronic files shall be deemed to be accepted and neither party shall have any obligation to correct errors or maintain electronic files.

The Client is aware that differences may exist between the electronic files delivered and the printed hard-copy construction documents. In the event of a conflict between the signed

> construction documents prepared by the Consultant and electronic files, the signed or sealed hard-copy construction documents shall govern.
>
> In addition, the Client agrees, to the fullest extent permitted by law, to indemnify and hold harmless the Consultant, its officers, directors, employees and subconsultants (collectively, Consultant) against all damages, liabilities or costs, including reasonable attorneys' fees and defense costs, arising from any changes made by anyone other than the Consultant or from any reuse of the electronic files without the prior written consent of the Consultant.
>
> Under no circumstances shall delivery of electronic files for use by the Client be deemed a sale by the Consultant, and the Consultant makes no warranties, either express or implied, of merchantability and fitness for any particular purpose. In no event shall the Consultant be liable for indirect or consequential damages as a result of the Client's use or reuse of the electronic files.

There is little you can do to protect your electronic files from unauthorized modification once they are delivered to another party. Because of this, most design professionals and environmental consultants remove their electronic seals and signatures and all mention of their firm (title blocks, logos, proprietary symbols and other identifying marks) from every electronic file before transmission to the client or anyone else. More important, though, is to set up office procedures that log the transmission of data to and from your client. Keep hard copies of everything that is transmitted.

If, in spite of your best negotiating efforts, your client insists on ownership of your documents in either hard copy or electronic form, tie the transfer of ownership to receipt of final payment of your fees — just as you should for hard copy. In this case, your contract should definitely contain all of the protection discussed above; it is especially critical if you give up ownership of your documents. Refer to all deliverable materials as instruments of your service and disavow any warranty of merchantability and fitness for any particular purpose. Again, insist on a strong waiver and indemnity for unauthorized changes and reuse of the data. Consider this provision:

CADD AND ELECTRONIC FILES

The Client acknowledges the Consultant's drawings and specifications, including all documents on electronic media, as instruments of the Consultant's professional service. Nevertheless, the drawings and specifications prepared under this Agreement shall become the property of the Client upon completion of the services and payment in full of all monies due to the Consultant. The Client shall not reuse or make or permit to be made any modification to the drawings and specifications without the prior written authorization of the Consultant. The Client agrees to waive any claim against the Consultant arising from any unauthorized transfer, reuse or modification of the drawings and specifications.

The Client and the Consultant agree that any electronic files furnished by either party shall conform to the specifications listed in Exhibit ___. Any changes to these specifications by either the Client or the Consultant are subject to review and acceptance by the other party. Additional efforts by the Consultant made necessary by a change to the electronic file specifications shall be compensated for as Additional Services.

Electronic files furnished by either party shall be subject to an acceptance period of _____ (___) days during which the receiving party agrees to perform appropriate acceptance tests. The party furnishing the electronic file shall correct any discrepancies or errors detected and reported within the acceptance period. After the acceptance period the electronic files shall be deemed to be accepted and neither party shall have any obligation to correct errors or maintain electronic files.

The Client is aware that differences may exist between the electronic files delivered and the printed hard-copy construction documents. In the event of a conflict between the signed or sealed hard-copy construction documents prepared by the Consultant and electronic files, the signed or sealed hard-copy construction documents shall govern.

> In addition, the Client agrees, to the fullest extent permitted by law, to indemnify and hold harmless the Consultant, its officers, directors, employees and subconsultants (collectively, Consultant) against all damages, liabilities or costs, including reasonable attorneys' fees and defense costs, arising from any changes made by anyone other than the Consultant or from any transfer or reuse of the electronic files without the prior written consent of the Consultant.
>
> Under no circumstances shall delivery of the electronic files for use by the Client be deemed a sale by the Consultant, and the Consultant makes no warranties, either express or implied, of merchantability and fitness for any particular purpose. In no event shall the Consultant be liable for any loss of profit or any consequential damages as a result of the Client's use or reuse of the electronic files.

We also recommend you include some provision that addresses the Year-2000 (Y2K) issue. You can add it to the CADD language above or it can stand alone. (See *Year 2000* [Y2K] for a suggested clause.) In either case, you will want to mention Y2K readiness in your electronic specifications.

Consultants who are working directly for owners normally avoid any contractual relationship with the contractor. However, there may be instances when you are pressured into providing your electronic files directly to contractors for their use in preparing shop drawings. If you cannot avoid this, protect yourself with a strongly worded contract or letter agreement, and — because of the risk and direct costs — in return for an appropriate fee. If the contractor objects to the former, refuse. If the contractor objects to the latter, stick to your guns and remind the contractor that, in addition to your direct costs to provide these files, use of your electronic files not only increases your liability but also saves the contractor substantial time and money.

Exhibit 9 provides some sample language you and your attorney might adapt for your use in a letter agreement.

CADD/ELECTRONIC FILE TRANSFER TO CONTRACTOR

Dear {Contractor's name}:

At your request, we will provide electronic files for your convenience and use in the preparation of shop drawings related to {name of project}, subject to the following terms and conditions:

Our electronic files are compatible with: {software, hardware specifications}. We make no representation as to the compatibility of these files with your hardware or your software beyond the specified release of the referenced specifications.

Data contained on these electronic files are part of our instruments of service and shall not be used by you or anyone else receiving these data through or from you for any purpose other than as a convenience in the preparation of shop drawings for the referenced project. Any other use or reuse by you or by others will be at your sole risk and without liability or legal exposure to us. You agree to make no claim and hereby waive, to the fullest extent permitted by law, any claim or cause of action of any nature against us, our officers, directors, employees, agents or subconsultants that may arise out of or in connection with your use of the electronic files.

Furthermore, you shall, to the fullest extent permitted by law, indemnify and hold us harmless against all damages, liabilities or costs, including reasonable attorneys' fees and defense costs, arising out of or resulting from your use of these electronic files.

These electronic files are not construction documents. Differences may exist between these electronic files and corresponding hard-copy construction documents. We make no representation regarding the accuracy or completeness of the electronic files you receive. In the event that a conflict arises between the signed or sealed hard-copy construction documents prepared by us and the electronic files, the signed or sealed hard-copy construction documents shall govern. You are responsible for determining if any conflict exists. By your use of these electronic files, you are not relieved of your duty to fully comply with the contract documents, including, and without limitation, the need to check, confirm and coordinate all dimensions and details, take field measurements, verify field conditions and coordinate your work with that of other contractors for the project.

Because information presented on the electronic files can be modified, unintentionally or otherwise, we reserve the right to remove all indicia of ownership and/or involvement from each electronic display.

We will furnish you electronic files of the following drawing sheets: _____
_____

A service fee of $___ (___ hundred dollars) per sheet shall be remitted to us prior to delivery of the electronic files.

Under no circumstances shall delivery of the electronic files for use by you be deemed a sale by us, and we make no warranties, either express or implied, of merchantability and fitness for any particular purpose. In no event shall we be liable for any loss of profit or any consequential damages as a result of your use or reuse of these electronic files.

_____   _____
{Consultant name and firm name}   {Contractor name and firm name}

If your client is to provide information to you electronically, you will also want to be very clear about hardware and software specifications, the scope of the information on disk, who will be responsible for the content and condition of the disks, and the source of the data. These are matters to be discussed and negotiated with your client. If the client is to be responsible, you can modify your Information Provided by Others provision to include electronic files. (See that section for more information.) If you have the responsibility, you need to consider, when you are determining your fee, the time and cost required to verify the information received.

If commercial software you are using is found to have "bugs," you might still be held responsible for the accuracy of your completed designs or deliverables. To minimize your liability for software-related problems, you must be able to show that you exercised reasonable care in researching, selecting, testing and using your software and databases and training your staff. If you have documented such steps, a court may find that you performed within the standard of care even though there was a failure because of defects in the software. You need to keep informed of improvements in computer technology. Thoroughly investigate any new software package before you buy it, make sure it is applicable to the kinds of projects your firm undertakes, and negotiate with your software vendors for appropriate contractual assurance and training support. In general, rely on time-tested software you have thoroughly checked in-house against a design with known results. Insist that your staff be thoroughly trained. Make sure an experienced staff member checks any work produced on a computer before it is incorporated into the design or reports. And, as in all aspects of a sound professional practice, document and keep good records.

SEE ALSO:

Copyrights
Information Provided by Others
Ownership of Instruments of Service
Record Documents
Scope of Services
Shop Drawing Review
Unauthorized Changes to Plans
Year 2000 (Y2K)

RELEVANT STANDARD FORM AGREEMENT PROVISIONS:

AIA B141-1997:	Articles 1.3.2.1; 1.3.2.4
EJCDC 1910-1 (1996 edition):	Article 6.4

IX-12

CONDOMINIUMS

Condominiums are far and away the most liability-prone projects design and technical consultants undertake. The problem is so significant that one industry study by the University of California found a third of all condominium projects reported construction defects — and nearly 40 percent of those had major flaws. Almost 14 percent of the owners had filed lawsuits against their developers and another 12 percent had threatened suit. As too many consulting firms have learned, suits against developers have an unfortunate tendency to envelop all the consultants connected in any way with a project.

There are several reasons why condominiums have such a high claims history:

- Condominium developers are often financially highly leveraged and care more about cutting costs than about the quality of their projects.

- Frequently the design team isn't given the chance to provide construction phase services; construction observation may be "on call" at the developer's discretion or eliminated altogether to save money.

- The occupants are frequently first-time homebuyers or older people with limited resources or perhaps less sophisticated consumers. They believe the advertisements, promotional material and marketing tactics that promise much more than their dollars can realistically buy.

- Condominium homeowners' associations are reluctant to set dues high enough to cover all the necessary upkeep and maintenance required for the common areas and building exteriors. The result is poor maintenance, deferred maintenance or no maintenance at all.

- Homeowners' associations provide ready vehicles for class action suits. Condominium boards often are targets of aggressive law firms who market their legal services by directly soliciting the homeowner associations. These firms promise recovery from the developers, contractors and designers for every conceivable defect from leaky windows to cracked sidewalks to inadequate HVAC systems. Even the threat of such a suit can be enough to make some defendants throw in the towel and offer to settle, simply because the cost of defense is so high.

- When a claim is filed, the contractors and developers are often nowhere to be found. Contractors can bankrupt their organizations and disappear; developers frequently set up separate corporations for developing single projects and later dissolve them. The only (or most vulnerable) deep pockets remaining to face the lawyers and the condominium association are those of the design team.

The frequency of claims against condominium designers is so high that, for a time, almost no professional liability insurer would cover architects or engineers who designed condominiums. Even when insurance again became available, condo designers found it expensive, difficult to obtain and with no assurance of future availability.

A 1996 study, DPIC's *Focus on Claims*, showed that DPIC-insured architects generated only 1 percent of their fees from condominium projects. Yet condos have accounted for more than 7 percent of architects' total closed claims — and have consumed 14 percent of the total claims dollars expended by DPIC on behalf of architects.

1. IF YOUR DESIGN COULD BE CONVERTED INTO CONDOMINIUMS

If an apartment building you design is converted — perhaps years from now — to a condominium, you unwittingly inherit the liability and risk almost as if you had designed the project as a condominium in the first place. You might not even be aware of the conversion until a claim is presented.

THE PROBLEM

Where you once owed a duty of care to a single client, you may now owe that same duty to 500 owners if an apartment complex you designed has "gone condo." Because you did not enter into agreements with these new condominium owners, you have no contractual protection of any kind. The contractor may have disappeared, the original developer is gone, and you weren't consulted and didn't participate in the conversion of your design. What's more, your liability may be further extended because the codes and regulations governing condominiums differ from those for a rental project.

THE SOLUTION

Frankly, there is limited protection available in this situation. Nevertheless, we recommend you add a clause to any agreement for a project that could conceivably be converted to condominiums in the future. Such a clause would provide that your client (presumably the original developer) indemnifies you in the event of a conversion:

Condominium Conversion

> The Client does not now expect that this Project will be converted into condominiums. Because this Project will not be designed for condominium ownership, the Client agrees that, if the Client decides to convert the Project into condominiums in the future, the Client will, to the fullest extent permitted by law, indemnify and hold harmless the Consultant, its officers, directors, employees, and subconsultants (collectively, Consultant) against all damages, liabilities or costs, including reasonable attorneys' fees and defense costs, arising out of or in any way connected with the conversion to condominium ownership, except for the sole negligence or willful misconduct of the Consultant.

This provision may offer you limited protection if your client still owns the project when it is converted. If there has been a change of ownership, that protection probably disappears. Even if your client still owns the building, however, any indemnity is only as good as your client's financial resources. If a million-dollar judgment is beyond the client's means, you will still be at risk.

Of course, it is important to talk to your attorney about any proposed indemnity language to ensure it is consistent with applicable laws and as enforceable as you can make it. (See *Indemnities* for more information.)

2. IF YOU DESIGN CONDOMINIUMS

In some ways, knowingly designing a condominium project has advantages over a surprise conversion. At least you are aware of the risks and liability pitfalls and can structure your agreement, services and loss prevention practices accordingly.

THE PROBLEM

You know that condominium projects are liability minefields. Your problem, therefore, is to devise a strategy to maximize your loss prevention measures and contractual safeguards in order to minimize your exposure to claims. Even with the most carefully chosen preventive steps and the most protective contract terms, you must recognize that condominium projects still represent a high-risk undertaking.

On most projects, you have three good loss prevention techniques at your disposal: a good contract, a good set of documents, and the opportunity to provide full construction phase services. On condominiums, unfortunately, you probably won't have any of these to protect you. Developers are notoriously inflexible when it comes to contract negotiation. They often hire the toughest attorneys who write onerous, one-sided contracts. Then, instead of a good set of plans and specifications, developers often want just a "builder's set" of plans — with detailing held to a minimum and specifications relatively open — just enough to allow them to obtain their permits. These developers often prefer documents that give subcontractors great flexibility in the materials to be used and the equipment to be installed. Once the permit is in hand, developers often don't want to see you during construction — unless, of course, there is a problem. And you can be fairly certain that you won't get a call until the problem is a serious one and too far gone for a quick solution. The purpose of that meeting may be to find out how much you are willing to contribute to solve the problem.

THE SOLUTION

If you choose to swim in these waters, you had better have a shark-proof bathing suit and a large throwaway inheritance — you'll need both! And don't be surprised if professional liability insurers aren't lining up to write a policy for your firm.

Nevertheless, if you are still determined to work on condominiums (and want to keep that inheritance as well as insurance coverage), your first concern ought to be selectivity — deciding which projects and clients you are willing to gamble on. Try to select clients who will be around for many years after completion of the project and who care about quality. You want a client who is as concerned as you are about the high-risk nature of condominiums. In fact, your choice of client may be the single most important factor in a successful and trouble-free venture.

First, look for a client who has experience in condominium projects, is sufficiently financed and is not litigation happy. Then ask yourself, "Is the reward enough to merit the risk?" If the answer is yes, try to anticipate and minimize problems early on by employing every loss prevention technique you can. You may want to suggest a project peer review, for instance, and a constructibility review. Condominium projects may be excellent candidates for partnering agreements, too. (See *Dispute Avoidance and Resolution* for more information.) You also should stress the importance of full construction phase services. (See *Exhibit 10* for a list of specific loss prevention recommendations.)

You might want to propose that the client purchase project insurance, if it is available. Your client should understand that your professional liability rates probably will increase over the next several years if you work on condominium projects, and it is appropriate that the owner assume some of those costs directly, by paying for a project policy. Furthermore, project insurance is a good way to protect your claims record with your insurance company. In any event, suggesting a project policy may be a good way to "smoke out" a litigation-prone client. (See *Insurance* for more information.)

In addition to the must-have contract clauses listed in *Exhibit 11*, we recommend three contractual concepts that separately may be helpful and, taken together, might give you substantial protection.

First, you should have a strong indemnity in your contract that requires your client, if still in existence and financially viable, to protect you from third-party claims. Have your attorney help you draw up the broadest, most enforceable language possible, perhaps including a waiver. As a starting point, consider the following language:

INDEMNIFICATION FOR CONDOMINIUM PROJECT RISK

The Client acknowledges the risks to the Consultant inherent in condominium projects and the disparity between the Consultant's fee and the Consultant's potential liability for problems or alleged problems with such condominium projects. Therefore, the Client agrees, to the fullest extent permitted by law, to indemnify and hold harmless the Consultant, its officers, directors, employees and subconsultants (collectively, Consultant) against all damages, liabilities or costs, including reasonable attorneys' fees and defense costs, arising out of or in any way connected with the services performed under this Agreement, except for the Consultant's sole negligence or willful misconduct.

WAIVER

In consideration of the substantial risks to the Consultant in rendering professional services in connection with this Project, the Client agrees to make no claim and hereby waives, to the fullest extent permitted by law, any claim or cause of action of any nature against the Consultant, its officers, directors, employees and subconsultants (collectively, Consultant), which may arise out of or in connection with this Project or the performance, by any of the parties above named, of the services under this Agreement.

Two other creative contractual solutions have appeared in recent years. The first is the development of a *maintenance manual* as part of the scope of basic services. All professional consultants on the project would develop, as part of their scope of services, written recommendations for the required minimum maintenance of their particular component of the project, such as the decking, plumbing, lighting, HVAC, roofing, sidewalks and so on. These recommendations would then be compiled into a maintenance manual for the project. Your client would agree to write into the bylaws of the condominium homeowners' association a requirement that the recommended maintenance be the responsibility of the association. The bylaws would require periodic inspection of each component by a qualified outside inspection service, which would report its findings and maintenance recommendations to the homeowners' association. Each purchaser would receive a copy of the maintenance manual at the time of purchase and would acknowledge understanding of the responsibility of the homeowners' association to have the necessary maintenance performed. A clause to accomplish this might read:

MAINTENANCE MANUAL

The Client agrees that the bylaws of the Homeowners' Association established for this Project will require that the Association will perform, as recommended in the Maintenance Manual, all necessary routine maintenance, maintenance inspections and any other necessary repairs and maintenance called for as a result of these maintenance inspections. The bylaws shall also contain an appropriate waiver and indemnity in favor of the Client, the Consultant and his or her subconsultants and the Contractor if the maintenance recommendations contained in the Maintenance Manual are not performed.

Another clause sometimes employed in an attempt to cut off claims at their source — the homeowners' association or individual owners — is *ADR by Covenant*. This is a relatively simple idea, developed by the ASFE: Professional Firms Practicing in the Geosciences, that provides in your agreement with the developer/client that he or she prepare and record a covenant to the deed for the parcel of land being developed. This covenant would then "run with the land" in any future sales and would bind all future owners of the condominium units. The covenant would provide that any dispute between the homeowners and the original developer or the developer's design professionals or contractors must be submitted first to nonbinding mediation. Attempting mediation of a dispute before resorting to litigation can lead to the resolution of many conflicts quickly and inexpensively. (See

Dispute Avoidance and Resolution for more information. Also refer to *Additional Resources* for details on how to contact the ASFE.)

Some condominium developers follow another innovative approach to resolving disputes with disgruntled buyers. The developer can include an option in the CC&Rs (covenants, conditions and rules) to repurchase the unit for the initial price plus a certain percentage increase per year. Because such an offer demonstrates confidence in the project, some developers have made it a part of their sales program. Although this may not be an item to include in your contract, any quality developer who has made this offer should certainly be at the top of your "preferred client" list.

Whatever solution (or solutions) you and your attorney decide upon, your agreement must be carefully crafted to include several other must-have provisions. These clauses should be considered **Deal Makers**. Remember, condominium design is so risky that if you cannot obtain adequate protection in your contract, you should consider walking away from the project. (See *Exhibit 11* for a list of important contract clauses for condominium projects.)

SEE ALSO:

Construction Observation
Contingency Fund
Dispute Avoidance and Resolution
Indemnities
Insurance
Limitation of Liability
Prototype Designs
Scope of Services
Unauthorized Changes to Plans

THERE ARE NO RELEVANT PROVISIONS IN THE AIA OR EJCDC STANDARD FORM AGREEMENTS.

Exhibit 10

CONDOMINIUM LOSS PREVENTION CHECKLIST

❏ Carefully select your developer/client. Is there adequate financing? Is there commitment to quality? Has the developer done other condominium projects and were they successful? Does the developer have a long track record and is it likely to be around in the future? Will the developer build the project with its own forces or act as a "paper developer"? What are the contractor selection criteria?

❏ Develop a fair agreements that properly addresses the allocation of risks associated with the project. Be certain it contains most if not all the **Deal-Maker** clauses for condominium projects. (See *Exhibit 11*.) Is the developer fair and reasonable regarding the contractual protection you seek?

❏ Insist on a strong indemnity from the client/developer and attempt to negotiate a waiver into your agreement.

❏ Investigate the availability of project insurance and propose that the owner pay for a separate policy for the design team. Make sure your subconsultants are adequately insured.

❏ Find out how the developer plans to market the project. Will the advertising be realistic? Will your name be used?

❏ Require a project peer review and a constructibility review of the design.

❏ Make sure there are adequate contingency funds budgeted for the project that will apply to design defects as well as construction problems.

❏ Insist on providing full-service construction observation and administration. Watch carefully for any substitutions requested by the developer or contractor. Document clearly any objections you may have.

❏ Carefully document all meetings and conversations pertaining to the project. In particular, note any recommendations you make that are not followed by the developer or contractor.

❏ Develop a maintenance manual; have it incorporated into the homeowners' association bylaws and require that homeowners be educated about their responsibilities for upkeep and for following the stated recommendations. Make the provisions of the manual binding upon the homeowners' association as well as individual purchasers.

❏ Require that the developer have each purchaser inspect the unit and common areas for defects and have the purchaser sign some type of certificate of satisfaction.

❏ Require the developer to incorporate an ADR by Covenant provision into the CC&Rs.

EXHIBIT 11

DEAL-MAKER CLAUSES FOR CONDOMINIUM PROJECTS

Attorneys' Fees
Construction Observation
Contingency Fund
Corporate Protection
Defects in Service
Dispute Avoidance and Resolution
Excluded Services
Hazardous Materials
Indemnities
Interpretation
Jobsite Safety
Limitation of Liability
Opinions (Estimates) of Probable Construction Costs
Ownership of Instruments of Service
Severability and Survival
Standard of Care
Statutes of Repose and Limitation
Termination
Third-Party Beneficiaries
Unauthorized Changes to Plans

IX-22

Emergency Services

In the aftermath of disasters — earthquakes, hurricanes, floods, mudslides, fires, explosions and other calamities — people turn to architects, engineers and environmental consultants to provide much-needed assistance. Worldwide, design and environmental professionals willingly come forward to help protect the public and to speed recovery efforts. These professionals may inspect a damaged building to determine if it is safe to enter or inhabit, examine a bridge for structural integrity, monitor an embankment for stability following an earthquake or determine the safety of drinking water after a flood or toxic spill — often under difficult and sometimes dangerous conditions, and frequently for little or no fee.

The Problem

After you have done your best to help your neighbors, it seems so unfair to get your thanks in the form of a lawsuit! True, under the exigencies of the moment, you may not have had sufficient time to do your usual professional analysis and give careful consideration to all the available options. But when the aftershocks have ceased, the ashes have cooled or the winds have died down, victims sometimes forget the conditions under which you were forced to work. They only know that they are facing a huge loss, and they may cast about for any and every source of recovery — including the well-intentioned, public-spirited consultant.

The law doesn't provide much help. A few states have enacted legislation (generally referred to as Good Samaritan laws) that provides limited protection from liability for architects and engineers acting at the request of authorized public officials and usually for a limited number of days after a declared disaster. These laws are commendable but very limited in scope.

If you are retained by an insurance company to inspect the damaged properties of their policyholders, you have another concern. Once you have rendered your opinion to the insurance company, the insurer then makes a decision about the existence or nonexistence of coverage and the amount of damages the company will compensate. These decisions are based on your report, as well as many other factors out of your control, including policy language, underwriting criteria, marketing considerations, even public relations.

Emergency Services

Policyholders who feel their insurer has dealt in "bad faith" for denying coverage or mishandling their claims will probably sue. You will often be brought into these lawsuits.

THE SOLUTION

Obviously, in the midst of an earthquake or its immediate aftershocks, you won't be thinking about asking your neighbors to sign a broad-form indemnity. Caring individuals will do what they can at the moment and deal with the consequences later.

In the *aftermath* of a disaster (while it may sound a little cold-hearted), you should get some kind of written agreement for your services, even if you are not accepting a fee. Rest assured, it doesn't have to be a full-blown AIA B141. On the contrary, a very simple agreement will suffice. Some firms have developed a short-form Emergency Services Agreement. Many send their personnel into the field with a pad of these short forms and have them executed on the spot by homeowners or other distressed parties. Other firms prefer to send a simple letter agreement to the client that contains waiver and indemnity provisions. (See **Indemnities** for a related discussion.)

Remember, when you are helping individuals who have just suffered a big loss, they aren't likely to have their attorney standing by to advise them. They need your help to understand what they are facing. Take the time to sit down with them, explain the services you will and won't be providing and discuss your agreement. You will be doing both of you a favor. The client will then know just what he or she can expect, and there will be less chance of a misunderstanding later when the smoke clears or the waters recede.

If the client is unwilling to sign, then you are faced with a moral dilemma. You are under no legal obligation to provide these services. If you accept the project, however, you have the absolute duty under your license to protect the health and safety of the public and to reasonably exercise your professional skill and knowledge *under the circumstances*. Although emergency situations create unusual circumstances, the difficulty is recreating these circumstances and expectations when defending a claim months or years later.

In *Appendix I*, you will find an example of a short-form Agreement for Emergency Professional Services for you and your attorney to review and adapt to your firm's practice and philosophy.

If you choose not to use a short-form agreement and prefer to use letter agreements for post-emergency situations, you might consider including a waiver and indemnity such as the following:

EMERGENCY SERVICES

The Client understands that emergency conditions exist because of {name of disaster}. The Client further recognizes that time and circumstances do not permit the Consultant to perform his or her services with the degree of skill and care normally provided under non-emergency circumstances. The Client desires, however, to have the Consultant use reasonable efforts to perform his or her services under these emergency conditions. In consideration of the substantial risks to the Consultant in performing these emergency services for or on behalf of the Client, the Client agrees to the fullest extent permitted by law to indemnify and hold harmless the Consultant against all damages, liabilities or costs, including reasonable attorneys' fees and defense costs, arising out of or resulting from the Consultant's providing emergency services for or on behalf of the Client excepting only those damages, liabilities or costs arising directly from the negligence or willful misconduct of the Consultant.

In addition, the Client agrees, to the maximum extent permitted by law, to waive any claims against the Consultant arising out of the performance of these emergency services.

The Client acknowledges that (1) the Consultant has discussed the risks and difficulties of performing services under the existing emergency conditions; (2) the Client is aware of the legal implications of agreeing to the waiver and indemnity provisions; and (3) the Client enters into this Agreement freely and without reservation.

Initialed: _____ Client _____ Consultant

Notice that the waiver and indemnity provisions are stated in two separate paragraphs. This lessens the likelihood of having both provisions disallowed by a judge. The "Miranda-warning" third paragraph is intended to prevent a client from later claiming you buried the clause in your letter or forced him or her to sign the agreement on a "take-it-or-leave-it" basis. This may sound harsh. The pros and cons of this should be thoroughly discussed within your firm and with your attorney. You should consider both the provision's content

Emergency Services

and enforceability as well as your firm's moral and philosophical position on providing services under unfavorable conditions.

When using a letter agreement in emergency situations, you should describe and limit the scope of your services to prevent future misunderstandings. Here is a sample of rather protective wording you might adapt to your situation:

> The Consultant is a *structural* engineer (or architect, etc.) and all observations, opinions and conclusions are limited to structural review. The Consultant cannot investigate any possible electrical or mechanical damage nor can the Consultant render an opinion on the existence of asbestos or any other toxic material or contaminants on the site.
>
> The Consultant has not had the opportunity to review plans, calculations or soils data for the structure or other information normally available to consultants, nor has the Consultant been able to perform detailed analyses or structural calculations. Because of the existing emergency situation, the Consultant's opinions and conclusions are based on limited visual observations and, as such, should be considered preliminary only. The Client must have these opinions and conclusions verified by detailed analysis once the emergency period has passed. No other warranty, either express or implied, is made or intended.

If you are providing inspection services for insurance companies, you should seek protection from being drawn into suits from policyholders whose real complaint is with the insurance carrier. Under no circumstances should you provide these services without a written agreement, which should contain both an indemnity and a waiver:

> **In consideration of the substantial risks to the Consultant in performing these emergency services for or on behalf of the Insurance Company, to the maximum extent permitted by law, the Insurance Company agrees to indemnify and hold harmless the Consultant against any damages, liabilities or costs, including reasonable attorneys' fees and defense costs, arising out of or resulting from the Consultant providing emergency services for or on behalf of the Insurance Company, excepting only those damages, liabilities or costs arising from the sole negligence or willful misconduct of the Consultant.**
>
> **In addition, the Insurance Company agrees, to the maximum extent permitted by law, to waive any claims against the Consultant arising out of the performance of these emergency services.**

Before disaster strikes, educate all your key employees on the liability exposures associated with providing emergency services. Instruct them to keep careful notes (as good as the circumstances allow) on all their disaster-site visits. (Video or still cameras and tape recorders are especially helpful in these situations.) Field staff should document their observations and recommendations to your client in writing as soon as possible.

Check to see if your state has a Good Samaritan law. If it does, work with your professional society and licensing boards to broaden existing legislation to provide better protection. If your state does not have such a law on the books, you and your colleagues should urge your state legislators to enact one. Contact your national professional association for model language and guidance.

SEE ALSO:

Appendix I
Indemnities
Inspection
Limitation of Liability
Public Responsibility
Standard of Care

THERE ARE NO RELEVANT PROVISIONS IN THE AIA OR EJCDC STANDARD FORM AGREEMENTS.

INTERNATIONAL PROJECTS

Many North American design and environmental professionals are working in international markets. Although this represents a tremendous opportunity, an architect, engineer or environmental consultant providing services in another country must surmount a host of cultural differences as well as face legal, political and financial risks. Language barriers, differences in construction-industry practices, variances in social and business customs, unfamiliar legal standards and requirements, and even novel contracting, bonding, insurance, licensing, bidding and accounting procedures — all present significant challenges to the consultant who wishes to practice in other countries.

THE PROBLEM

Laws and industry customs vary so widely from country to country that it is imperative to thoroughly understand your professional obligations wherever you choose to practice. In many countries, for example, the U.S.-style standard of care is unheard of. In some jurisdictions, you are presumed liable as soon as a defect in a structure becomes evident; the burden of proof lies with you. (This is sometimes known as the "Duty of Result," which differs significantly from our own "Duty of Care." For more information, refer to *Standard of Care*.) Some countries embrace the doctrine of strict liability for design professionals — that is, you are held responsible for a defect even if you are not negligent. In some locations, there is exposure to criminal liability if injury or death occur.

Even more confusing, the definition of *defect* can range from "something unfit for the intended purpose" in some places to "a compete failure" in others. Similarly, there may be a guarantee period during which an owner can claim compensation from a contractor *or designer* for that defect, varying from six months in one country to thirty years in another — with every possible permutation in between. For example, most new road work in Europe requires a 10-year defect-liability period. The manner in which such a guarantee is applied can also vary, depending upon the particular nation, region, building function, or type of client.

Professional standards and practices may differ significantly in other countries. Just because local professionals have titles similar to your own doesn't mean, for example, that they provide a similar type of service. The division of responsibilities among professionals

International Projects

(for instance between architects and engineers or architects and builders) may also be dissimilar. In some Asian countries, architects tend to play a different role in the building process from their counterparts in the West; they are more like the "master builders" of ancient times. Their education, standards, licensing and testing procedures also differ. Some countries license professionals through professional societies while others have no registration requirements.

Not all risks are directly related to professional liability; some are economic. Not getting paid is a major financial risk. And even an iron-clad assurance of compensation is useless if you are paid in a currency that suddenly free-falls in value against the dollar, wiping out your profit. As if that isn't enough risk, there are also blocked currencies or currency restrictions on repatriating funds.

On the other side of the ledger, the figures can be equally discouraging. The expenses of competing for work and succeeding in an international market can be considerable. It can cost a great deal of money for travel, senior staff time and presentations just to get into the competition. If you are awarded the project, overhead can be high. There are office expenses to consider, as well as the costs associated with U.S. employees working abroad — housing, schools, transportation, home leave, medical care. There may also be some hidden costs in hiring locals or third-country nationals, such as those that result from local taxes, redundancy payments, termination and social welfare programs.

In many countries you may have to pay taxes both in that country and in the United States. Tax laws of different countries may not only involve income taxes but also gross business and personal taxes as well as value-added taxes and withholding taxes if your firm is not registered with tax authorities. These taxes may be imposed on your firm, the services provided, the instruments of service and the employees providing services. What's more, in computing your foreign taxes, you may have many expenses that are not deductible, such as home-office support costs.

Many lucrative international projects are in nations that are subject to government instability. Coups, political upheaval or even peaceful changes in government could mean termination of your contracts, seizure of your assets — or your employees! In developing nations, there is also the risk of political violence. There's no ignoring the fact that terrorism aimed at international corporate targets has been reported worldwide.

Failure to understand cultural subtleties can mean the difference between winning and losing a contract in many countries. For example, the aggressive marketing style so admired in the U.S. may not be well received in Europe and Asia. A patient and indirect approach may be more effective in many cultures. Westerners often have to learn that many societies take their time, that some things can't be hurried and that personal relationships have to be built before business can be done.

Similarly, business dealings may be handled differently in other countries. Although written contracts will generally be honored, many societies put more faith in personal relationships built on friendship. In these countries, when disputes arise, trust and face-to-face negotiation, rather than litigation, are relied upon for resolution of the matter.

All these difficulties are compounded by language differences. The qualifications and abilities of professional interpreters differ widely and this can pose a risk, especially in sensitive negotiations. If you are not conversant in the local language, you are at the mercy of an interpreter who might not catch (or pass on to you) the nuances — or sometimes even the essence — of what is being communicated. Much can get lost in the translation.

Governmental and bureaucratic procedures must be considered. It may be very difficult to get good information, even on simple matters. In some countries, you may need a business license to practice. There may be differing legal restrictions on development in certain regions, even within the same country. Permission may be needed from a variety of different authorities in order to undertake the simplest project. You may require work permits for expatriate staff, which can take months and yards of paperwork to obtain. Environmental issues are becoming more important in many emerging markets.

What's more, insurance requirements differ from country to country. Compulsory insurance in some countries usually includes auto, general liability and some form of workers compensation (usually called something else, such as National Health). Sometimes these coverages must be obtained from an insurance carrier licensed to do business in that country or from that country's social welfare system. A U.S. policy may be needed as well, to fill in some gaps in coverage and provide reasonable limits over a very minimal local compulsory coverage.

Unethical practices occur in every country. But practices that might be considered unethical in one's own country may be considered quite acceptable in another. For instance, you may have to pay for certain government information that, in our country, you would expect to get free of charge. Be aware, however, that the Foreign Corrupt Practices Act bars U.S. companies from engaging in certain practices when doing business overseas. Although graft may be standard business practice in some regions, including South America, the Middle East and the republics of the former Soviet Union, you must comply with our law.

THE SOLUTION

All the foregoing difficulties notwithstanding, international projects can be challenging and profitable — if you work smart. Here or abroad, the basics still apply. You have to do your homework, find the right people with whom to work and partner, have the right legal and tax advice, negotiate a reasonable contract and strive to solve problems without resorting to litigation.

The number one loss prevention rule for any project — international or domestic — is to know your client. You also need to know the country and the enterprise carefully before committing yourself. There are many resources available to you. The U.S. Department of Commerce can provide some information about a given country's business and payment

International Projects

practices. Look into the National Trade Data Bank (NTDB or STAT-USA) from Commerce, which collects the federal government's offerings of information on international trade, export promotion, trade contacts, country profiles and other international economic data. It is available singly or by subscription on CD-ROM or on the Internet, or it can be reviewed at government depository libraries. Check with the Export-Import Bank and providers such as Dun and Bradstreet to learn about a client's assets and credit rating. And contact professional societies both overseas and at home. The U.S. Department of State and the U.S. embassy's commercial attaché are good sources for help and/or referrals. The ACEC's International Committee has several subcommittees that deal with issues ranging from environmental consulting to working with federal agencies. The AIA's International Committee has several helpful publications about working abroad. (See *Additional Resources* and the last page of this section.)

You will also need local help. Find an in-country consultant or joint-venturing partner who can research the business environment, potential clients, upcoming opportunities and local practitioners. If you decide to pursue a project, you'll need local attorneys and accountants. These people can help you address special issues such as currency, repatriation of funds, tax considerations, permits and/or licensure and local employment regulations, and will guide you through other local legal and cultural minefields.

Some consulting firms enter into joint ventures or long-term strategic alliances with local firms. Other architects and engineers caution against jumping into long-term partnerships until a relationship has been developed over time. They feel it is better to work together on a project-by-project basis until they really know and trust each other. These firms believe it makes sense to start slowly or on a smaller scale by joint venturing with local firms on specific projects. Whatever your arrangement, though, have a good written agreement with anyone you work and make certain the firm is fiscally responsible and insured (which is often not the case).

Many design firms lower their risk by providing only "front-end" services on international projects. U.S. firms may contract to provide the schematic design and design development and limit their participation in the working-drawing and construction phases to reviews for quality control. Working drawings and construction phase services can perhaps be done less expensively by in-country firms, who probably also have a better grasp of the local language and codes and construction practices. (In fact, such an arrangement is required by law in some countries.) In addition to lowering your risk, an added bonus is that clients and some international funding institutions such as the World Bank like the concept, because it will save them money. Then, too, some clients prefer — or even demand — that some of the money paid for consulting services be kept at home. By contracting with local firms and paying them in their own currency, you can satisfy those requirements. Key to loss prevention here is to have a detailed contract and a precise Scope of Services, with special attention given to defining Basic, Additional and Excluded Services. (See *Scope of Services* and *Excluded Services*.) It is important that both you and the local firms have a clear understanding of your duties and responsibilities.

In order to maintain a positive cash flow and to minimize payment problems, some firms get as much of their fee paid in advance as possible. They often ask for a large retainer (sometimes called an *advance payment* or *mobilization fee*) to be credited against the initial six to 12 monthly invoices. In fact, where there is a question of political stability or of client funding, some firms ask for payment — sometimes, though rarely, the entire fee — up front for certain tasks that are approved by the client prior to beginning work. Some firms structure the payment schedule so that they can forgo the final payment, which is often difficult to get.

If your contract is not with a U.S. company, the U.S. government or an organization such as the World Bank, you need to arrange a secure method of payment. Perhaps the best solution is to be paid in U.S. dollars via a bank wire transfer. Failing that, insist on payment only in some other stable currency that is readily convertible. Some clients and international funding agencies want you to take some of your fee in the local currency. If you must, don't accept more than you expect to spend on your local joint-venture partner, rent, equipment, hiring locals, local travel and subsistence.

One of the most common payment arrangements is through a letter of credit. A letter of credit is especially important when it is difficult to get reliable credit information on an overseas client (perhaps a family-owned business or an operation in emerging areas such as Russia, Southeast Asia or Africa). If the client firm isn't able to get a letter of credit, it is an indication that it probably doesn't have a good credit record with its bank. Accept only an irrevocable letter of credit, which cannot be canceled without your knowledge, or a confirmed or advised letter of credit, in which an additional bank adds its guarantee.

Finally, you'll want to protect your business and your assets abroad through appropriate insurance coverage. Consultation with an insurance broker who is knowledgeable in international coverage is strongly advised. Together, you should review the kinds of coverage your U.S. policies provide to make sure they are written or can be endorsed for the international protection you need. You may also need parallel coverage by insurance companies who are indigenous to or licensed in the international jurisdiction. Indeed, some countries require coverage by local insurers. Or you may decide that a local policy alone is sufficient to cover claims in that country. On the other hand, some local policies may not be broad enough in coverage and your U.S. carrier may provide coverage to fill in the gaps. It might also be difficult to pursue a claim against a local or distant insurer. In other words, you may end up needing two policies — U.S. and international — for each type of coverage, including general liability, workers compensation, auto, property and, possibly, professional liability.

Several U.S. professional liability insurers (including DPIC) cover projects anywhere in the world. Other carriers may be willing to add this coverage by endorsement. The policies can vary, however, between *defense and indemnity* coverage and *indemnity-only* coverage. The difference is important. If you have an indemnity-only policy, the carrier has the right but not the duty to provide a defense for a claim brought in an international jurisdiction. If the carrier chooses not to exercise the right to defend a claim, then you must undertake your own defense — with the advice and consent of the carrier — and the insurance company

International Projects

will reimburse you for defense costs and any judgments or settlements in excess of your deductible. The reasoning behind this is simple. For example, if you have gone into business in Vietnam, you probably have obtained local counsel, local contacts and perhaps a local business partner. If your U.S. insurance carrier has no local office (and few do) and no selected lawyers to defend litigation in that country, you are probably in a better position than it is to undertake your own defense. Your insurer may ask you to do so and keep it advised on the progress of the case. In accordance with the terms and conditions of the policy, your insurer will reimburse your defense costs as well as any judgments or settlements that you are obligated to make.

There is U.S. insurance available to help protect your personnel. International workers compensation insurance for U.S.-hired employees who are sent overseas on assignment is very much like 24-hour medical coverage. If an employee becomes ill or injured while on assignment abroad, it might be claimed that he or she was in that country because of work and, therefore, the illness or injury was work connected. Repatriation insurance is another coverage available for use in emerging countries. This covers the cost to transport sick or injured U.S. employees home or to a third country to obtain necessary emergency treatment.

Bear in mind that most countries have their own social welfare laws, such as National Health and workers compensation, that apply to their citizens working for you within that country. These requirements, however, may also apply to your U.S. employees and any third-country nationals in your employ, so make sure you are familiar with the local laws and requirements.

You may wish to consider kidnap and ransom insurance policies. These policies generally cover losses incurred by paying the ransom, the hostage's salary while he or she is held captive, as well as other costs associated with a kidnapping. This should be purchased quietly; the fewer who know about the coverage, the better.

It comes as a surprise to many consultants that the U.S. government offers several ways to help manage risks overseas. The Overseas Private Investment Corporation (OPIC) supports, finances and insures projects that have a "positive effect on U.S. employment, are financially sound and promise significant benefits to the host country." OPIC currently offers insurance for three kinds of political risks. *Currency inconvertibility coverage* compensates insureds if currency restrictions in another country change to prevent the conversion and/or transfer of remittances. *Expropriation coverage* insures against the loss of an investment due to expropriation, nationalization or confiscation of assets by another government. *Political violence coverage* insures against the loss of assets or income due to war, revolution, insurrection or politically motivated civil strife, terrorism and sabotage. There are stringent reporting and application requirements, so contact OPIC very early in the project. (See **Additional Resources**.)

Another U.S. agency, the Export-Import Bank, can help consultants by providing international credit-risk protection. *Export credit insurance*, although one of the most expensive ways to protect international receivables, enables small businesses to offer competitive payment terms. Insured architects or engineers, for example, might offer more liberal payment terms — 180 days, for example — if they are assured by Ex-Im Bank of getting paid. There are two types of risks covered: *commercial risk of default* and *political risks of default*. It is worth noting that two of Ex-Im Bank's major goals are to increase the export of environmental goods and services, which are in strong demand among the developing nations, and to expand the number of small businesses using Ex-Im programs.

You will need a knowledgeable attorney who understands international construction issues and can help you draft an agreement that takes into account the many variables of working overseas. Together, you will have some important decisions to make. Will your client draft the contract or will you use your own contract language? Will your client accept standard EJCDC or AIA forms? Often clients are more familiar with the standard agreements developed by the Federation Internationale des Ingenieurs-Conseils (FIDIC). Will you need to insert additional provisions so you will have appropriate protection? Your counsel will probably need to consult with your legal counsel abroad and perhaps your tax, accounting and business consultants, both U.S. and in-country. (See **Additional Resources** and the end of this section.)

International construction agreements are often executed in more than one language and sometimes stipulate that both translations will be treated equally. This increases the risk that a dispute could arise from differing translations or interpretations of your intent. Instead, your agreement should provide that only one language (ideally English) will control the meaning of the terms and be used in all project correspondence and dispute resolution.

Should problems arise on a project, do everything you can to ensure equitable treatment if you have to defend yourself against a claim of professional negligence. This means specifying both an acceptable jurisdiction where a suit would be heard, and an acceptable choice of what law would be applied. (See **Governing Law and Jurisdiction**.)

The choice of law that will govern the agreement, for instance, involves a lot more than geography. Will you choose U.S. law or that of the project site or the country where your client has its headquarters? Is the project in a country that operates under civil or common law? Contracts under the two systems are very different. The choice of law can also impact lien rights, limitations of liability, statutes of limitation, employment relations and even modes of dispute resolution. If your client or the project is in a country where the legal system is substantially different from that of the United States, specify in your contract the jurisdiction and governing law that will be applied to any dispute. It is important to understand that a civil judgment in another country usually can be enforced against your assets in the United States, if the country has a bilateral agreement with the U.S., if notice of the dispute was given, and if an opportunity to defend was allowed. After consulting with your lawyers, you may decide that the local laws of the country where the project or client is located would be preferable. Some countries, for instance, have laws regarding jobsite safety that completely protect the design professional. In Mexico, there are caps on damages, and each party must pay for its own defense, regardless of who "wins." In the European Community and many other places, limitation of a design professional's liability is an accepted standard contract provision. (See *Attorneys' Fees*, *Jobsite Safety* and *Limitation of Liability* for related discussions.) Most often, however, you should strive to negotiate a provision requiring that all disputes be heard and resolved under the applicable laws of the principal place of your business. Here is a sample clause:

GOVERNING LAW AND JURISDICTION

The Client and the Consultant agree that this Agreement and any legal actions concerning its validity, interpretation and performance shall be governed by the laws of *{insert the principal place of business of the Consultant or other country or state, as appropriate}.*

It is further agreed that any legal action between the Client and the Consultant arising out of this Agreement or the performance of the services shall be brought in a court of competent jurisdiction in *{insert the principal place of business of the Consultant or other country, state, or international forum as appropriate}.*

Another possibility is to specify the laws of a country, forum or alternative dispute resolution arena that is neutral to both you and your client, but preferably one whose laws are based on the English Common Law. Recognize, however, that despite the jurisdiction and law you and your client decide upon for your disputes, that decision will not be binding upon third-party claims. (See *Third-Party Beneficiaries* for more information.)

Know your **Deal-Breaker** positions before going into contract negotiations. In addition to the choice of language, law and jurisdiction, you will need to address other issues. A limitation of liability, for instance, is not uncommon in international contracts. Your contract should clearly set forth provisions for payment of your fees. Stipulate the method of payment, the currency, whether the fee is net of tax, the size of a retainer or advance payment, and your right to withhold your plans, suspend or even terminate your services should payment be delayed or withheld.

Your standard of care should be understood and well-defined. If you're not providing environmental consulting services, protect yourself against the possibility of discovering unanticipated contaminants on the site (see *Hazardous Materials*). You and your attorney may choose to set your own statutes of limitation or repose by contract, depending on your choice of governing law. Also make sure you have an Attorneys' Fees provision in your contract in the event of a dispute over fees. (See *Billing and Payment*, *Standard of Care*, *Statutes of Repose and Limitation*, *Suspension of Services* and *Termination*.) And — just in case all your risk management efforts weren't enough — provide for dispute resolution in your contract. (See *Dispute Avoidance and Resolution*.)

One prominent U.S. engineering firm with a lot of experience in international projects commonly asks for the most simple form of dispute resolution procedure, similar to this:

DISPUTE RESOLUTION

In the event of any dispute arising out of or connected with this Agreement, such dispute shall be referred to and resolved in the following manner: Within ten days of the receipt of notice of a claim by either party, each side shall select an arbitrator and the two arbitrators shall promptly select a third. These three arbitrators shall meet and decide upon the appropriate language, governing law, jurisdiction, rules of discovery and procedures to be used, and shall promptly notify both parties of these decisions. The arbitration shall be conducted in accordance with these rules and procedures and a written arbitration ruling shall be rendered to both parties. Any ruling of the arbitrators so rendered shall be enforceable in the manner prescribed by the arbitrators.

This arbitration may be commenced at any time prior to or after completion of the Project, provided that if it is commenced prior to the completion of the Project, the obligations of the parties under the terms of this Agreement shall not be altered by reason of the arbitration being conducted.

Finally, consider this: many international clients are appalled by the high rate of liability claims U.S. consultants incur. This reputation may put American firms at a disadvantage when competing in the international market. Perhaps one way to counter this is to demonstrate to your client that reliance on methods of dispute avoidance and alternative dispute resolution — rather than litigation — is your firm's policy. And to prove it, ask that your contract provide for partnering and mandatory nonbinding mediation should problems arise between the two of you. (See *Partnering* in *Dispute Avoidance and Resolution*.)

International Projects

SEE ALSO:

Attorneys' Fees
Billing and Payment
Dispute Avoidance and Resolution
Excluded Services
Governing Law and Jurisdiction
Hazardous Materials
Insurance
Jobsite Safety
Limitation of Liability
Retainers
Scope of Services
Standard of Care
Statutes of Repose and Limitation
Suspension of Services
Termination
Third-Party Beneficiaries

OTHER RESOURCES:

Export-Import Bank
811 Vermont Avenue, NW, Washington DC 20571
202/565-EXIM, 800/565-EXIM. www.exim.gov

International Federation of Consulting Engineers
(Federation Internationale des Ingenieurs-Conseils) FIDIC
P.O. Box 86, 1000 Lausanne 12, Switzerland
Telephone: 41 21,653,50,03. www.fidic.org

International Chamber of Commerce
38, Cours Albert 1er, Paris, France 75008
Telephone: +33 (1) 49.53.28.28
FAX: +33 (1) 49.53.29.42. www.iccwbo.org

Overseas Private Investment Corporation
1100 New York Avenue, NW, Washington DC 20527
Infoline: 202/336-8799, Factsline: 202/336-8700. www.opic.gov

National Trade Data Bank (STAT-USA) www.stat-usa.gov/stat-usa.html

RELEVANT STANDARD FORM AGREEMENT PROVISIONS:

Engineers working internationally might wish to refer to the FIDIC standard agreements, available either directly from FIDIC or the ACEC.

RENOVATION/REMODELING

The restoration, renovation and remodeling of existing structures make up a significant portion of total architectural or engineering activity in some locations. Whether the work is preservation of historical landmarks, adaptive reuse, structural reinforcement or mechanical/electrical retrofit, these jobs are especially risk-prone.

Because alteration projects often call for special procedures and skills not normally required on new building projects, the consultant needs to tread carefully. Archival research, thorough testing, detailed cost estimates, creative approaches to code conformance, increased consultant's role during the building phase — all require a different focus from that of new construction.

THE PROBLEM

Most difficulties associated with rehabilitation projects stem from a failure — for whatever reason — to understand the existing structure. In virtually every renovation project, you must make some assumptions about the construction methods and materials originally used in the building. Record drawings of older buildings are rarely accurate (if they even exist), and complete documentation is almost never available. Each column or beam can contain an unpleasant surprise and the very real possibility of discovering asbestos or other hazardous materials. Few owners are willing to spend the money necessary for essential preliminary research and testing, yet you are still expected to work, with sketchy information supplied by a variety of outside sources — test results, samplings, property surveys, and maps showing the location of buried utilities, for example — for which you are not responsible and cannot, therefore, assume accuracy. Designing to bring older buildings up to code is difficult and time-consuming, perhaps because many codes were not written with renovation work in mind. And now there are new liability risks to consider. Failure to conform to the Americans with Disabilities Act could mean being charged with a criminal violation. (See *Americans with Disabilities Act* for more information.)

Furthermore, you take on an expanded role when rehabilitating an older building. The design and documentation phase for preservation work, for example, is more extensive than that for similarly sized new construction. Increased involvement during construction and added coordination with the contractor are also commonplace. This can expose you to more liability if you act beyond your normal scope of services and give in to the temptation to suggest means or methods of construction to solve problems arising on the jobsite.

THE SOLUTION

Talk to your client. Make sure he or she understands the uncertainties involved in alterations work and the scope of the project. Explain that hidden conditions will undoubtedly affect the work and can cause costly changes or delays. Find out, up front, how much preliminary research and destructive investigation and testing your client is willing to fund. Work with your client to develop and carefully define your scope of services, with the understanding that if circumstances change, so will your project costs, your role and your compensation. Insist on an adequate contingency in the project budget and be sure that it applies to both design and construction. (See *Changed Conditions*, *Contingency Fund* and *Scope of Services*.)

No matter how unlikely it seems that you will encounter toxic substances on the site, you must plan for that possibility. We recommend that you always insert a clause that provides for the possibility of discovering hazardous materials on the jobsite. (Refer to *Hazardous Materials* for discussion and sample language.)

As yet, there are no standard association agreements specifically for alteration projects. However, because of the risks associated with these services, pay special attention to your agreement. When working with your attorney to create the agreement best suited to the project, be sure to include a number of other important provisions. (Refer to the *See Also* list at the end of this section and those specific sections in this book.) Finally, you will want to address the uncertain nature of renovation work and your client's expectations. Consider the following as a starting point:

VERIFICATION OF EXISTING CONDITIONS

Inasmuch as the remodeling and/or rehabilitation of the existing structure requires that certain assumptions be made by the Consultant regarding existing conditions, and because some of these assumptions may not be verifiable without the Client's expending substantial sums of money or destroying otherwise adequate or serviceable portions of the structure, the Client agrees, to the fullest extent permitted by law, to indemnify and hold harmless the Consultant, its officers, directors, employees and subconsultants (collectively, Consultant) against all damages, liabilities or costs, including reasonable attorneys' fees and defense costs, arising out of or in any way connected

> with this Project, excepting only those damages, liabilities or costs attributable to the sole negligence and willful misconduct by the Consultant.

The above clause calls for a broad indemnity from your client for all your services on the project. Given the risks of most renovation projects, such protection is warranted and equitable. If your client is unwilling to agree to such a provision, though, you might offer as a fall-back position a somewhat less protective version, by modifying the clause as follows:

> ... serviceable portions of the structure, the Client agrees to bear all costs, losses and expenses, including the cost of the Consultant's Additional Services, arising from the discovery of concealed or unknown conditions in the existing structure.

This language is not as defensive as that of the first clause, but it does provide you with some protection from the costs associated with the discovery of unanticipated conditions. Alternatively, you could include a Changed Conditions clause in your contract. (See that section for suggested language.)

You will also need to protect yourself from inaccurate or inadequate plans or data on the existing structure provided to you by your client or others. If you do not have an Information Provided by Others clause elsewhere in your contract, you may want to add the following words to the end of the above clause:

> ... existing structure, or from any deficiencies or inaccuracies in any information or documentation furnished to the Consultant by the Client.

If possible, you will want to add an indemnity for such deficiencies in any information provided to you by or through your client. (See *Information Provided by Others*.)

**Renovation/
Remodeling**

SEE ALSO:

Americans with Disabilities Act
Changed Conditions
Code Compliance
Construction Observation
Contingency Fund
Excluded Services
Hazardous Materials
Information Provided by Others
Jobsite Safety
Scope of Services
Termination

**THERE ARE NO RELEVANT PROVISIONS IN
THE AIA OR EJCDC STANDARD FORM AGREEMENTS.**

SUBCONSULTANTS

If a project is very large and complex, it is not unusual to require on the design team the services of many experts in a variety of disciplines. As building technologies evolve, in addition to the subconsultants traditionally employed, other specialists may be required, coming from fields as diverse as vertical transportation, acoustical engineering, environmental analysis, soils testing, drilling, security, communications, waste handling, lighting and a host of other professions. While there are times when these specialists contract directly with the owner of a project, more often they will be employed as subconsultants by a prime consultant. (See *Multiple Prime Contracts*.)

THE PROBLEM

It's astonishing how many subconsulting assignments continue to be performed without written contracts. This is a dangerous practice regardless of whether you are the prime or the subconsultant. No matter how competent the other party and no matter how long-standing your working relationship, if you have only a verbal agreement, you are both taking an enormous risk. Should something go wrong, your rights, duties, fees and other business terms will be difficult to establish.

A second problem is the cost — in both staff time and direct legal expense — of having to defend yourself if a claim arises and you are named because of something your prime or subconsultant did wrong. As the prime, you have vicarious liability for the negligence of your subconsultants — whom you selected and for whose services you are responsible. As a subconsultant, you could be named in an action against the prime. In either event, if you have done nothing wrong, it is unfair to have to spend large sums to defend yourself because of someone else's error or omission.

Often, consulting firms "borrow" employees from one another for work on a short-term basis. But if there is a claim arising from a loaned temp employee's services on a project for the borrowing firm, the lending firm is generally brought into the suit.

Finally, there is another issue. There is a growing trend on the part of some prime consultants to treat specialty services for which they subcontract (or recommend that owners contract for), such as geotechnical consulting, testing, surveying or environmental services, as mere commodities. Although architects and engineers argue passionately that their own services should be obtained through qualification-based selection (QBS), many of these same firms hire subconsultants strictly on price. It makes little sense. Primes and owners expect the services of high-quality subconsultants while continuing to bid them out just as they would the services of a roofer or a plumber. Yet quality-conscious subconsultants find it next to impossible to compete when price is the only criteria. Perhaps primes and owners do not recognize the risks of contracting with "low bidder" consultants, who may be forced to cut corners and are not paid enough to do a thorough job, especially during the construction phase.

THE SOLUTION

Many seasoned prime consultants recommend that you develop a short list of experienced quality specialists in various fields. Your goal is to cultivate a long-term relationship with this team of subconsultants upon whom you will call again and again — or whom you can recommend to the owner to retain. Look for firms that have performed consistently and well for you, that have standards for design quality and efficiency similar to yours. You want consultants who stay on top of their disciplines and are creative in their problem-solving approaches. And you want to work with firms that share your view of client service and business ethics.

Likewise, if you are a subconsultant, it is in your best interest to develop a long-term affiliation with one prime consultant or several with whom you work well, whose work you respect and whose payment terms are acceptable. Both of you will benefit from such an association. You develop a better understanding of each other's requirements and procedures; communication is easier with someone you have worked with before.

Such a long-term relationship also helps resolve disputes more quickly and encourages better cooperation. If you both hope to work together on future projects — if the prime knows he or she can rely on the quality and productivity of the sub; if the sub knows he or she can expect a steady stream of future revenues through the prime — you both have incentive to cooperate and to work out any problems that arise.

Long-term associations also make it easier to obtain fair, written agreements for every job. If you do a lot of projects together, you could develop a single master contract with your prime or subconsultant (that is in effect for a year or longer) and then simply use individual task orders that detail the workscope for each project. It also means the basic terms of your agreement won't change; you always know what to expect contractually.

In any case, whether the same prime and subconsultant are involved in multiple projects or a one-time project, we strongly recommend that you do not undertake a project without a written agreement signed by both of you.

In these contracts, there are two important points you should address. First, if you are going to include an indemnity, use one that is both fair and insurable. We recommend you use a mutual indemnity, which gives both of you equal protection. If there is a lawsuit for negligence arising out of the project, you both will almost certainly be named as co-defendants. Even if you are exonerated, the expense of defending yourself will likely consume a large portion of your insurance deductible (if you are insured) as well as a substantial amount of your time and that of your staff. By providing for mutual indemnity based on comparative fault, you are saying that you will reimburse the other party to the extent your fault (negligence) exceeds his or her fault. As a practical matter, this will only be determined if the claim ultimately is decided by a court, admittedly a rare event. But if this does happen, it is a practical way to recoup a portion of your legal and defense costs, depending upon your degree of fault. (Please refer to *Indemnities* for a detailed discussion.) A suggested mutual-indemnity provision is repeated below:

INDEMNIFICATION

The Consultant and the Subconsultant mutually agree, to the fullest extent permitted by law, to indemnify and hold each other harmless from any and all damages, liabilities or costs, including reasonable attorneys' fees and defense costs, arising from their own negligent acts, errors or omissions in the performance of their services under this Agreement, to the extent that each party is responsible for such damages, liabilities or costs on a comparative basis of fault.

Second, require in your agreement that each of you will maintain and furnish proof of appropriate insurance to the other. (Refer to *Insurance* for a discussion, and talk with your professional liability insurance specialist about what coverages and limits to specify.) Whether on an annual or individual project basis, your agreement should require each of you to provide to the other certificates of insurance that show the coverages you carry.

There are several other provisions you will need to discuss and negotiate. For instance, who will retain ownership of the documents? (See *Copyrights* and *Ownership of Instruments of Service* for more discussion.) How will you handle payment? (Refer to *Billing and Payment* and *Pay-When-Paid*.) Will the subconsultant perform construction observation? (See *Construction Observation* and *Design Without Construction Administration*.)

Whether you are a prime or subconsultant, it is worthwhile to develop, with the help of a knowledgeable attorney — and this *Guide* — a standard subconsulting contract agreement form with which you are comfortable. You can start with one of the professional association subcontract forms (both EJCDC and the AIA have consultant agreements) or develop a form of your own. As a starting point for negotiation, it is best to offer your preferred contract. Remember that your goal — in both your business and contractual relationships — is to arrive at agreements that are reasonable and fair and allow each of you to reach your objectives.

Subconsultants

If you are a prime consultant, we recommend you pass through to your subconsultants any liability protections (such as indemnities and limitations of liability) that you are able to obtain from your client. This can be done in a variety of ways. First, in your agreement with your client, you can include your subconsultants among the parties to be indemnified or whose liability is to be limited. (Refer to *Indemnities* and *Limitation of Liability* for recommended language.) Second, you can pass down in your subconsulting agreements protective language similar to that which you obtain in your prime contract with your client. Third, you can have a general provision in your prime contract that extends all protective measures to your subconsultants. (See *Extension of Protection*.)

Finally, if you loan your employees to (or borrow employees from) another consulting firm, you should have a contract that sets forth who will take responsibility for claims that arise from the employees' services. Probably the best solution is to have the "borrowing" firm assume the responsibility and indemnify the other firm. (See *Indemnities*.)

SEE ALSO:

Billing and Payment
Construction Observation
Copyrights
Design Without Construction Administration
Extension of Protection
Indemnities
Insurance
Multiple Prime Contracts
Ownership of Instruments of Service
Pay-When-Paid
Retaining Subconsultants
Scope of Services
Unauthorized Changes to Plans

ARCHITECTS AND ENGINEERS CONTRACTING FOR SUBCONSULTING SERVICES SHOULD REFER TO THE FOLLOWING DOCUMENTS:

AIA:	B141-1997
	C141-1997
	C142-1997
	C727-1992
EJCDC:	1910-1 (1996 edition)
	1910-10 (1985 edition)
	1910-14 (1985 edition)
	1910-27A (1989 edition)
	1910-27B (1986 edition)

Supplanting Another Consultant

From time to time, a design or environmental professional will replace another on a project, either to complete work already started or to take on the next phase of services, such as observation of construction or remediation.

The Problem

The interruption of a consultant's service can cause serious difficulties and liability exposure for the architect, engineer or environmental professional who leaves a project, as well as for the supplanting consultant.

If you are replaced mid-project, you cannot complete the services you started. Instead, it is left to someone else to follow through on decisions you have made. Similarly, if you are the replacement consultant, you, too, are working at a disadvantage: the consultant who preceded you had an understanding of details that cannot be totally conveyed through drawings or specifications, whether they are complete or not. Something is bound to fall through the cracks. Certainly all of the original design will have to be reviewed and evaluated. Absent a discussion with your predecessor, you will be forced to make numerous assumptions — and that creates substantial risk. If problems arise, there will be a question of who is at fault. It is possible, too, that the very fact you are supplanting another architect or engineer could indicate that you are walking into a problem-plagued project.

Be aware, too, that if you supplant another consultant, depending upon the terms and conditions of his or her contract, you may need permission to complete unfinished designs, or you could be liable for copyright infringement — a risk that may or may not be covered by your professional liability policy. (See *Copyrights*.)

The Solution

If you are the original architect, engineer or environmental professional on a project, consider using contract language that protects you if your work is completed by another. Such language could be as follows:

Supplanting Another Consultant

Replacement of the Consultant

If the Consultant for any reason is not allowed to complete all the services called for by this Agreement, the Consultant shall not be held responsible for the accuracy, completeness or constructibility of the construction documents prepared by the Consultant if used, changed or completed by the Client or by another party. Accordingly, the Client agrees, to the fullest extent permitted by law, to indemnify and hold harmless the Consultant, its officers, directors, employees and subconsultants (collectively, Consultant) from any damages, liabilities or costs, including reasonable attorneys' fees and defense costs, arising or allegedly arising from such use, change or completion by any other party of any construction documents prepared by the Consultant.

Check with your attorney. The above clause could be a separate provision or incorporated into Suspension and/or Termination wording. (See *Suspension of Services* and *Termination*.)

On the other hand, if you are the supplanting consultant, explain to your client the critical liability issues involved. Suggest that you make an evaluation of the partially completed work on a time-and-materials basis. Seek the client's permission to discuss issues with your predecessor before you accept the project, and insist on an indemnity for claims arising from any services performed by the prior consultant. Make certain, too, that your contract has an Information Provided by Others provision that gives you the right to rely upon such information and protects you with an indemnity. (See *Indemnities*.)

Protection of Supplanting Consultant

In consideration of the risks and rewards involved in this Project, the Client agrees, to the maximum extent permitted by law, to indemnify and hold harmless the Consultant from any damages, liabilities or costs, including reasonable attorneys' fees and defense costs, arising or allegedly arising from any negligent acts, errors or omissions by any prior consultant employed by the Client on this project and from any claims of copyright or patent infringement by the Consultant arising from the use of any documents prepared or provided by the Client or any prior consultant of the Client's. The Client warrants that any documents provided to the Consultant by the Client or by the prior consultant may be relied upon as to their accuracy and completeness without independent investigation by the supplanting Consultant and that the Client has the right to provide such documents to the supplanting Consultant free of any claims of copyright or patent infringement or violation of any other party's rights in intellectual property.

If your client objects, or forbids you to consult with a previously retained consultant, chances are the other consultant knows something the client does not want you to know — or is owed money, or both. No matter what indemnification you obtain, unless there is complete candor and openness between you and the client, you should strongly consider refusing the project.

Projects on which a consultant is replaced are, at best, messy and can be downright risky; your contract should always anticipate the worst-case scenario. Through diligent loss prevention practices, though, you can strive to see the worst doesn't happen.

SEE ALSO:

Assignment
Construction Observation
Copyrights
Extension of Protection
Indemnities
Information Provided by Others
Subconsultants
Termination

THERE ARE NO RELEVANT PROVISIONS IN THE AIA OR EJCDC STANDARD FORM AGREEMENTS.

IX-50

TESTING LABORATORIES

A testing laboratory is used to perform field and laboratory tests to determine the characteristics and quality of building materials or site and soil conditions. These services may be required during any phase of a project — the planning, design or construction of a building — or in the event of a failure occurring years after a structure's completion.

There are several reasons to call for testing. Local building codes sometimes require independent testing of structural components. Certainly, many Preliminary Site Assessments (PSAs) or the discovery of potentially toxic substances may require sampling and testing to be performed. When remodeling an existing structure, an architect or engineer may specify testing to determine construction techniques and even to search for asbestos or other hazardous materials. Very often, forensic testing is employed to discover the causes for a failure.

THE PROBLEM

Unless you are an environmental or geotechnical firm, laboratory testing is a service that is normally beyond the capability and experience of most architectural and engineering firms. Normally, an independent laboratory is hired by the owner. Nevertheless, the owner may want you to retain the testing laboratory as your subconsultant. By accepting this responsibility, though, you would also be accepting vicarious liability for the services of the laboratory if those services are faulty.

Regardless of the reasons for the testing, it usually involves critical issues of quality and safety and might entail the handling of hazardous materials. If you are an environmental professional performing a PSA, for instance, and have a testing lab take samples, be aware that those samples may be toxic or contaminated. Without adequate contractual protection, you may assume some liability for the proper handling, testing and disposal of those samples. You can also assume some liability for invasive testing done by the lab that involves some damage to your client's property or the property of others. And, finally, if the testing is done improperly, and important decisions are based on the incorrect findings of the laboratory, you will almost certainly be brought into the resulting lawsuit if the lab is your subcontractor.

THE SOLUTION

The best solution is to have your client contract directly with the testing laboratory. Urge the client to select the lab based on qualification rather than price, and assist the client in choosing a competent and quality-conscious laboratory. In any event, you should advise against having the contractor select or hire the lab — there are obvious conflicts of interest in this approach.

If your client insists that you subcontract with the testing lab, proceed with caution. Because there are some liability and workscope issues to be addressed, it is best to use a standard agreement in contracting for laboratory services. (The ASFE Standard Form Agreement for Subcontract Laboratory Services is one many firms use. Please see *Additional Resources* for details on contacting ASFE.) In any case, you will want to make certain the lab is reputable, adequately insured and willing to fully indemnify you for its negligent acts, errors or omissions.

Your own agreement with your client should reflect the fact that you are subcontracting the testing services only as a convenience to the client. Architects and engineers aren't generally trained to determine the quality or adequacy of laboratory test results and may not be able to determine whether the work was done properly. Because you may be in no position to judge the accuracy of the reports furnished to you by the testing lab, you need some kind of contractual absolution from your client. Here is a sample provision:

TESTING LABORATORY SERVICES

It is acknowledged that the Consultant has been requested by the Client to subcontract certain laboratory testing services on behalf of the Client to *{name of lab}*, **an independent testing laboratory. The Consultant agrees to do so in reliance upon the Client's assurance that the Client will make no claim or bring any action at law or in equity against the Consultant as a result of this subcontracted service. The Client understands that the Consultant has not performed any independent evaluation of the testing laboratory's data and the Client shall not rely upon the Consultant to determine the quality or reliability of the testing laboratory's reports. In addition, the Client agrees, to the fullest extent permitted by law, to indemnify and hold the Consultant harmless from any damages, liabilities or costs, including reasonable attorneys' fees and defense costs, arising from the services performed by** *{name of lab}* **except only those damages, liabilities or costs caused by the sole negligence or willful misconduct of the Consultant.**

There are two additional contractual issues that may need to be addressed. First, determine in advance and specify in your agreement who is to be responsible for restoration of any property damaged by the testing activity. Second, state who is responsible for the disposal of contaminated equipment and samples. If you can, try to arrange for the return of all samples to the owner for disposal, assuming the owner is your client. It is, after all, the owner's property; you did not generate any contaminants and you should not have to be responsible for their disposal. If there are contaminants in the samples, you could be held responsible as a transporter or storer of hazardous materials. If the owner refuses to dispose of the samples, the lab should be required to use the services of a reputable hazardous-waste disposal firm. It is critical that the lab keep impeccable records of the handling of these substances, whether they are returned to the owner or transferred to a disposal firm.

As always, your contract should include a Hazardous Materials provision as well as Limitation of Liability and Dispute Avoidance and Resolution clauses. You will need to decide who will retain ownership of the reports and related data. (See *Ownership of Instruments of Service*.) You and your attorney may need to include other clauses too, such as Confidentiality, Underground Improvements, Information Provided by Others, Public Responsibility, and Subconsultants. (See those sections for further discussion and sample clauses.)

SEE ALSO:

Confidentiality
Dispute Avoidance and Resolution
Excluded Services
Hazardous Materials
Indemnities
Information Provided by Others
Limitation of Liability
Ownership of Instruments of Service
Public Responsibility
Scope of Services
Subconsultants
Termination
Underground Improvements

RELEVANT STANDARD FORM AGREEMENT PROVISIONS:

AIA B141-1997:	Articles 1.2.2.4; 1.2.2.5; 1.2.3.7
ASFE:	Standard Form Agreement for Subcontract Laboratory Services
EJCDC 1910-1 (1996 edition):	Exhibit A 1.05A.3, A.12
	Exhibit B 2.01C4, O, P

IX-54

Underground Improvements

Sometimes a client will want the prime design consultant to locate existing underground utilities and lay out boring locations or to subcontract with another firm to provide these services. The client may then ask for a contractual provision that requires the consultant to accept responsibility for any damage done to underground improvements during the boring, testing or excavation on the site.

The Problem

Determining the existence and location of underground improvements is a less than exact science (there is a very good reason backhoes are sometimes referred to as "universal pipe locators"). Often you must rely on public records or utility company plans that may show underground locations inaccurately or not at all. (See *Information Provided by Others*.) And mistakes can be very costly. Soils drilling or excavation operations that damage buried utilities or other underground improvements can result in large costs and liability claims. Just imagine the consequential damages that would be claimed if an electric cable is cut during grading and an adjacent factory's production is lost, all because the line was located incorrectly on your plans or in the field. (See *Consequential Damages*.)

Boring locations are normally laid out by an independent geotechnical engineer for his or her drilling crew or boring subcontractor. But sometimes a client will want the prime consultant to provide these locations. Such services are highly specialized and are risky if you are not fully qualified to provide them, either directly or by subcontract.

The Solution

Avoid accepting responsibility for information or services that are normally — or should be — provided by others. When geotechnical services are necessary, all parties are best served if the owner selects and contracts directly with a competent geotechnical engineer, selected through a qualifications-based selection (QBS) process. Make certain the client understands the importance of contracting with the geotech to provide services during construction, so he or she has the opportunity to determine if the subsurface conditions revealed necessitate any design changes.

Underground Improvements

If you subcontract for geotechnical engineering services or if construction based on your plans will involve grading, excavation or soils boring, you need appropriate contractual protection. Require your client to accept responsibility for furnishing information on the location of underground utilities and structures and to accept the risk of damages — except for direct damages caused by your negligent use of the information furnished. You and your attorney may want to consider the following provision:

UNDERGROUND IMPROVEMENTS

The Client will furnish to the Consultant information identifying the type and location on the site of underground improvements. The Consultant (or its subconsultant) will prepare and furnish to the Client a plan showing the location of these underground improvements as provided by the Client and indicating the locations intended for subsurface penetrations. The Client will review and approve this plan and authorize the Consultant to proceed. The Consultant is entitled to rely upon the accuracy and completeness of the information furnished to the Consultant.

The Client further agrees, to the fullest extent permitted by law, to indemnify and hold harmless the Consultant, its officers, directors, employees and subconsultants (collectively, Consultant) against any damages, liabilities or costs, including reasonable attorneys' fees and defense costs, arising or allegedly arising from subsurface penetrations in locations authorized by the Client or from the inaccuracy or incompleteness of information provided to the Consultant by the Client, except for damages caused by the sole negligence of the Consultant.

The concept of having the client approve of the boring locations and other penetrations may be unique, but many engineers have successfully used this approach. It gives the client the last look and makes it crystal clear that it is the client who should bear the risk.

An indemnity is important, particularly because consequential damages could run into the millions. However, the indemnification could be placed in other clauses, such as Information Provided by Others or Consequential Damages. You also could combine those clauses into a single general indemnity. (See *Indemnities*.)

Your client may object to authorizing the location of the subsurface penetrations when he or she has provided the original information. You could, as an alternative, offer to identify the location of underground improvements as an Additional Service for an additional fee. If you offer this service, in addition to being indemnified, be sure you are technically qualified, properly licensed and insured for such work. If you don't meet all these criteria, then subcontract to a qualified surveyor or geotechnical firm who does. (See *Subconsultants*.) Make sure the subconsultant has included in his or her proposal sufficient time to have a qualified person check out the site. Calling an underground-utility locator service is not sufficient; they often do not have all the necessary information. The provision might then read:

UNDERGROUND IMPROVEMENTS

The Consultant and/or its subconsultant will conduct the research that in its professional opinion is necessary and will prepare a plan indicating the locations for subsurface penetrations with respect to assumed locations of existing underground improvements. Such services by the Consultant or its subconsultant will be performed in a manner consistent with the ordinary standard of professional care. The Client recognizes, however, that such research may not identify all underground improvements and that the information upon which the Consultant reasonably relies may contain errors or may be incomplete. Therefore, the Client agrees, to the fullest extent permitted by law, to waive all claims and causes of action against the Consultant and anyone for whom the Consultant may be legally liable, for damages to underground improvements resulting from subsurface penetrations in locations established by the Consultant that are based on properly filed and available records of said underground improvements.

SEE ALSO:

Consequential Damages
Indemnities
Information Provided by Others
Subconsultants

Underground Improvements

Relevant standard form agreement provisions:

AIA B141-1997:	No applicable provisions.
EJCDC 1910-1 (1996 edition):	Exhibits A 1.02A.2; A 2.01A.2
	Exhibit B 2.01C.4

VALUE ENGINEERING

Value engineering (VE) refers to detailed, systematic procedures intended to seek out optimum value for both the initial and long-term investments of a project. The goal is to eliminate or modify features that add cost to a facility but do not add to its quality, durability, utility or appearance. Using a non-adversarial, problem-solving approach, value engineers (VEs) look at trade-offs between design concepts, construction techniques, materials, building types, and up-front versus life-cycle costs to arrive at the best overall value. An entire subdiscipline has evolved to provide these services.

The term *value engineering* (which is sometimes called *value management* or *value analysis*) may mean different things to different parties. In fact, the process can assume many forms.

Scheduled VE is a process that is planned and scheduled at the outset of the project as an integral part of the design process. It may occur at the end of one or more phases, though typically it takes place at the end of the schematic design phase. Scheduled VE may also include a regular review and re-evaluation, conducted throughout the design process, of the status of the design and the choices made regarding building systems, materials and means of construction. Ideally, a value engineering team, led by an experienced value engineering specialist, includes key representatives of the owner, major consultants, the contractor and the construction manager.

In *informal VE*, the owner retains an individual to act as a kind of "cost consultant." The consultant may be a cost estimator or a value engineering specialist but often is a general contractor or a construction manager. The cost consultant provides cost advice to the owner and the prime consultant during each phase of the project, submits a detailed cost estimate at the end of each design phase, and also performs a value engineering study at the end of the schematic design or design development phases. With this advice, the thinking goes, and as a result of consultation with the prime consultant and the cost consultant, the owner can make critical cost decisions for the next design phase.

Unscheduled value engineering is quite a different procedure from the first two. This term refers to a process that is neither planned nor scheduled at the outset of the project and indeed may never have been conceived or discussed by the owner and design team when negotiating their agreements. Instead, it may occur as a result of a crisis in the course of the project, perhaps in response to the most recent cost estimate or to bids that substantially exceed the owner's construction budget. Sometimes the contractor or construction manager may decide that it can significantly reduce the costs of the project by recommending substantially different buildings systems, products or methods of construction.

THE PROBLEM

Unscheduled VE is the most problematic of the value engineering approaches. Introducing value engineering late in the course of the project — particularly during or after the construction documents phase — can be risky and expensive. It disrupts the orderly flow of the design and construction document preparation process and may require changing fundamental decisions made earlier, resulting in redesign and redrawing of the documents to reflect the changes. All this will require additional time and fees.

The introduction of new players late in the design process usually introduces new agendas, sometimes undisclosed, and perhaps a different set of values. Unscheduled and late VE can sometimes deteriorate into what amounts to the second-guessing of your design concepts by someone whose sole purpose is to cut the initial costs of a project. The result can be reduced quality, increased life-cycle costs or threatened project safety. All too often, the decisions arising out of unscheduled value engineering exclude or severely limit the involvement of key design-team members: now the contractor or construction manager unilaterally makes "cost-cutting" recommendations directly to the owner.

If the value engineering process does not include all key members of the project team, suspicions may develop about motives. Certainly, in an adversarial process, there is a much greater likelihood of conflict and, perhaps, claims. There is a greater potential for error in revising the construction documents after bids have been received because of the tight time constraints under which such revisions typically need to be made. Changes made in haste may not allow for proper coordination and checking.

Even formal, scheduled value engineering doesn't always translate into net savings for the owner. There is the very real risk that the owner could spend time and money pursuing alternatives that will not increase the value or reduce the cost of the project. In any VE process, the owner should consider the cost and time impacts of revising any previously completed construction documents and the additional cost of coordinating changes that may be required to other documents.

In terms of contracts and liability, value engineering raises many questions. If you are the original designer whose work is being evaluated, what is the extent of your responsibility? Unless your contract and/or workscope state otherwise, you could be expected to perform substantial redesign work — with no compensation. What if you disagree with the VE's recommendations? It is quite possible that reasonable yet alternative design solutions will produce a similar result. If you must make changes that you don't believe are appropriate, what is your responsibility?

On the other hand, if you are the value engineer, how much liability will you incur for mistakes made by the building's original designer? If you must make assumptions based on information provided to you by the designer of record, how much protection do you have if that information is flawed? How much responsibility is yours if the owner elects not to implement your recommendations?

THE SOLUTION

Whether or not you know before going into a project that your client will call for VE or another independent evaluation process, such as a project peer review or a constructibility review, it is a good idea to anticipate the situation in your agreement. At the very least, make certain the time and effort you spend in preparing for, participating in and responding to the process will be compensated for. Any redesign you provide as a result of these reviews should be performed as an Additional Service and compensated for accordingly.

Develop a clear understanding with your client as to the extent of your obligations to redesign to accommodate any decisions based on value engineering. Your contract should include a clause to limit responsibility for redesign and to give you the ability to object to the recommendations of the value engineer. Here is a sample clause:

VALUE ENGINEERING

If the Client retains the services of a Value Engineer (VE) to review the Construction Documents prepared by the Consultant, it shall be at the Client's sole expense and shall be performed in a timely manner so as not to delay the orderly progress of the Consultant's services. The Client shall promptly notify the Consultant of the identity of the VE and shall define the VE's scope of services and responsibilities for the Consultant. All recommendations of the VE shall be given to the Consultant for review, and adequate time will be provided for the Consultant to respond to these recommendations.

If the Consultant objects to any recommendations made by the VE, it shall so state in writing to the Client, along with the reasons for objecting. If the Client requires the incorporation of changes in the Construction Documents to which the Consultant has objected, the Client agrees, to the fullest extent permitted by law, to waive all claims against the Consultant and to indemnify and hold harmless the Consultant from any

damages, liabilities or costs, including reasonable attorneys' fees and costs of defense, which arise in connection with or as a result of the incorporation of such design changes required by the Client.

In addition, the Consultant shall be compensated for services necessary to incorporate recommended value engineering changes into reports, drawings, specifications, bidding or other documents. The Consultant shall be compensated as Additional Service for all time spent to prepare for, review and respond to the recommendations of the VE. The Consultant's time for performance of its services shall be equitably adjusted.

Of course, if there is a potential threat to public health and safety if certain recommendations are implemented, you must document your concerns thoroughly and follow up with both the VE and your client to reach a resolution. In addition, you may have a duty to notify appropriate building-safety agencies in accordance with your obligations under your license. (See *Public Responsibility* for more information and sample contract wording.)

In any project where value engineering is contemplated, skilled, trained value engineering specialists should direct it. (Many government projects require the presence of a certified value engineer on the design team. See *Additional Resources* for details on how to contact the Society of American Value Engineers regarding certification requirements.) Furthermore, compensation for value engineers should never be based on the savings achieved. Such an arrangement creates a clear conflict of interest.

If your firm is performing the value engineering, you will want contractual protection for your liability arising out of the design and construction phase services provided by the original designers of record. You will want a waiver and an indemnity from your client, if permitted in your jurisdiction. In addition, we recommend that you include a Limitation of Liability provision as well as a clause to protect you from flawed information given to you by the original designer or the owner. (See *Indemnities*, *Information Provided by Others* and *Limitation of Liability* for more information.) Here is a starting point:

VALUE ENGINEERING

In consideration of the Consultant performing a Value-Engineering review of the Project, the Client agrees that the Consultant shall be entitled to rely upon the completeness and accuracy of all information provided to the Consultant. The Client further agrees that the Consultant shall not be responsible in any way for errors or omissions contained in any drawings or specifications prepared by others or for errors or omissions by others in incorporating the recommendations made by the Consultant into the reports, drawings or specifications. In addition, the Client agrees to waive all claims against the Consultant arising from the services performed by others on the Project or from the services to be provided by the Consultant under this Agreement, except for the sole negligence or willful misconduct of the Consultant.

In addition, the Client agrees, to the fullest extent permitted by law, to indemnify and hold harmless the Consultant from all damages, liabilities or costs, including reasonable attorneys' fees and defense costs, arising or allegedly arising from the services performed by others on the Project or from the services provided by the Consultant under this Agreement, except for the sole negligence or willful misconduct of the Consultant.

Remember that if you serve as the value engineer, it is not your role to make the design changes; your charter is to furnish recommendations. It is important that the original architect or engineer review those recommendations and have an opportunity to respond. All final decisions about redesign must be made by the owner and agreed to and incorporated in the documents by the original designer of record — after all alternatives have been discussed and the impact of any changes carefully considered. Talk to your attorney. Your contract must make clear that the responsibility and liability for the final design decisions and their incorporations into the documents do not belong to you, the value engineer.

SEE ALSO:

Indemnities
Information Provided by Others
Limitation of Liability
Public Responsibility

RELEVANT STANDARD FORM AGREEMENT PROVISIONS:

AIA B141-1997:	Articles 2.1.3; 2.8.3.15
EJCDC 1910-1 (1996 edition):	Exhibit A 2.01A.11
	Exhibit B 2.01J

IX-64

Year 2000 (Y2K)

If the experts are to be believed, at the stroke of midnight on December 31, 1999, computers around the world will either cease to function, malfunction or spew out faulty data. Worried techno-gurus predict all sorts of calamities: ATMs will suddenly become inoperative, mass transit and air-traffic control systems will not work, security and climate-control systems will malfunction, communications networks will fail, and huge amounts of data will become unreliable or disappear completely. Some admittedly pessimistic estimates put the likely failure rate of IBM-compatible equipment at 80 to 90 percent.

All this deleted, erroneous or inaccessible data may result in many thousands of liability claims. In fact, law firms across the country are gearing up for what they expect to be a litigation bonanza.

How has this situation come about? The culprits are a couple of little numbers. The data fields of most computer programs and microprocessors are limited to two digits that designate the decade and the year (98, for example). The century designation, which has held steady at "19" since computers were developed, has been merely assumed. What this means is that most computers — from a teenager's desktop to the mainframes at the IRS — will be unable to recognize dates beyond the millennium.

Without corrective action, serious problems may occur, especially in the public sector. Local, state and federal governments are working frantically to become Year-2000 (or Y2K, as it is popularly known) compliant; that is, to program or reprogram and test computer hardware or software to handle the transition from 1999 to 2000.

But in many instances, it may be too late. Some problems have already begun to surface. Mastercard and Visa, for example, report that some of the credit cards they have issued are already being rejected at the point of sale because the computers read an expiration date of "00" as 1900.

The Problem

In addition to the global failures predicted, you are likely to have problems within your own firm. Some experts say you can count on it if you have hardware that is more than two or three years old. What if your computers lock up on January 1, 2000, and it takes three months to fix the problem — thus delaying a client's project? And if your firm uses date-sensitive programs — including estimating software, financial and accounting programs, spreadsheets, design programs and surveying programs — they will produce errors unless they are current or upgraded. Increased errors put you at greater risk for claims.

True, if your firm has newer hardware and software, you may have fewer internal problems. But there are external factors to consider. What happens when you try to read the specifications of a subconsultant who is not Y2K ready? Or when you send valid data to a client who has noncompliant systems that compute inaccurate results? Or if a public agency client won't pay your invoices because its computer system has erased any record of your agreement?

Many public and private clients are already aware of the Year-2000 situation and are understandably looking for ways to protect themselves. What if you specify equipment such as automated climate control, security or automated elevator systems that are not Y2K ready? You may be seeing clauses in agreements that require you to certify or guarantee Y2K compliance. But certifying such compliance (like any certification or warranty) is unwise — you would be promising something that you have no way of knowing to be true. You would also be leaving yourself open to other causes of action, for breach of warranty and breach of contract. (See *Certifications, Guarantees and Warranties* for more information.)

THE SOLUTION

If you have not done so already, take a good look at your own firm's status. Fixing the Y2K problem won't be easy and it won't be cheap. To date, there is no universal software solution. Many firms are hiring computer consultants (if they can find them) for compliance assessment and reprogramming. Because the fixes are limited in their applicability and require extensive time-consuming testing and debugging, some experts believe it may actually be too late to fix all systems in time. That is why it is so important to move quickly.

Besides preventing a possible disaster, there is another good reason to act at once. In the event of a lawsuit, it is important that you be able to demonstrate that your firm acted reasonably in anticipating and mitigating the problems associated with Y2K.

You must act now. Inventory and assess all software you have purchased and any software developed in-house, for Y2K compliance. Assess your hardware, especially older systems, to be sure they comply. Evaluate, too, your non-computer equipment, such as telephones, building HVAC controls and security systems. Develop an internal remediation plan, using formal project-management procedures. You may want to make hard copies of all critical information. Test all your "fixes," whether developed by your own information systems people, a consultant or your subconsultants. Finally, make certain you document and store evidence of your efforts to achieve Y2K readiness.

You should also assess your external risk. Identify all clients, subconsultants, contractors, vendors and business partners — anyone with whom you exchange data — and determine their level of commitment to addressing the Year-2000 problem. If you do business with local, state or federal government agencies, find out if their systems are compliant. Consider putting all these parties on formal notice that you expect them to achieve Y2K compliance, with a letter that requires an affirmative response.

You should be conversant with the Year-2000 situation and address it in your designs. Determine the Y2K readiness of materials, systems and equipment you include in your drawings and specifications. You may need to obtain specification sheets, warranties and documentation from manufacturers stating that their products are Year-2000 ready. You'll want to document your research efforts carefully. Your goal is be able to demonstrate that you have performed in a reasonably professional manner. (See *Specification of Materials*.)

If a client presents you with an onerous contract clause requiring you to certify Year-2000 compliance, delete it. As an alternative, offer to work with your client to test Y2K readiness on both your parts, as well as that of the contractors, consultants and vendors. Your clients should welcome this; it is in their best interest as well as yours. If you cannot delete the clause, make it mutual and modify the language by adding terms such as *endeavor to* or *attempt to*. One example follows:

YEAR-2000 READINESS

The Client and the Consultant agree that any electronic files prepared for use on the Project by either party shall conform to the specifications listed in Exhibit ___, and each party shall endeavor to make such files Year-2000 compatible, as defined in the Electronic File specifications.

In addition, the Consultant shall endeavor to include in its design such materials, products and equipment that are Year-2000 compatible.

This clause can stand alone or be added to the provision that deals with delivery of electronic files. (See *CADD/Electronic Files* for that provision.) A caution, however: when you and your client develop your computer specifications, do not inadvertently word them so that they contain guarantee language.

If your client later presents you with a contract addendum that requires you to certify compliance, you have a few options. Explain to your client that while you are just as

Year 2000 (Y2K)

interested as he or she is in Y2K issues, you are unwilling to open yourself up to additional (and uninsurable) liability by guaranteeing complete compliance. If, as we suggest, you have a provision in your Certifications, Guarantees and Warranties clause that prohibits the client from forcing you to certify or guarantee anything you cannot know with certainty, you are under no obligation to certify compliance.

Interestingly, some firms are approaching the Year-2000 problem as a marketing opportunity. They are offering to provide Y2K readiness assessments of buildings and facilities as an additional service to their clients.

SEE ALSO:

CADD/Electronic Files
Certification, Guarantees and Warranties
Specification of Materials

THERE ARE NO RELEVANT PROVISIONS IN THE AIA OR EJCDC STANDARD FORM AGREEMENTS.

PART X

PROJECT DELIVERY

Construction Management

Design-Build

Fast Track Projects

Multiple Prime Contracts

X-2

CONSTRUCTION MANAGEMENT

Construction management (CM) can be different things to different people. The scope of CM services can be tailored to respond to a variety of owner and project needs. It may be used on traditional project-delivery jobs or on design-build, fast track or multiple-prime projects — or on any combination of these. Thus, a construction manager's responsibilities may vary radically from project to project. Although there are many variations, and although the variations may have different names, there are only two primary roles for a design or environmental professional in the CM process.

A *CM-advisor* generally has only an arm's-length advisory role, representing the owner in overseeing the progress of the project. He or she administers — but does not hold — the contracts with the contractors and keeps track of the work and the payments. This construction manager does not perform (directly or indirectly) any actual labor or construction work; neither does he or she furnish materials or labor. The cash does not flow through the CM-advisor and he or she offers no guarantees about the time, cost or quality of the construction.

On the other hand, a *CM-constructor* (or *CM-at-risk*, as it is sometimes called) may be actively and solely responsible for everything from the design to jobsite safety, from bids to permits, and from ordering materials to bringing the project in for a guaranteed maximum price (GMP).

There is a third type of construction manager: a *CM-agent*. Although some people use the terms CM-agent and CM-advisor interchangeably, as defined by some associations, a CM-agent is an infrequently used project-delivery option in which the construction manager assumes many of the powers of the owner, with decision-making and financial authority delegated under an agency agreement. Since the law prohibits many public agencies from delegating fiscal responsibilities, a CM-agent is used almost exclusively on private-sector projects.

Construction management has evolved for several reasons. Some public owners are drawn to CM because it allows them to select the construction team based on qualifications rather than price. Some owners don't have project-management capabilities available in-house. Today's projects are more complex, and clients want them delivered faster. They are worried about delays, budget overruns, poor cost/quality return and time-consuming disputes. They may also believe that a construction manager can better represent and protect their interests on the project and relieve them of the responsibility of resolving problems and conflicts during design and construction. Many owners feel that accelerated project delivery, achieved through fast tracking, is best achieved with a construction manager. Finally, some owners who are unfamiliar with the construction process and its exposures to risk prefer simply to hand over the responsibility to someone more knowledgeable and experienced.

THE PROBLEM

Because CM is fairly new, determining your liability as a construction manager may be difficult. Thus far, there is little case law on which to rely. And since construction managers' roles vary so widely, their liability can change substantially from project to project. In general, you can think of your liability as a CM-advisor as comparable to your liability as an architect or engineer. A CM-at-risk's liability could thus be likened to that of a contractor. And there are all shades of gray in between, depending on the scope of services.

Nevertheless, there are some specific risks you need to consider — and address in your contracts. For instance, if you, as a construction manager, review the design as it develops and provide constructibility reviews, you may join the architect or engineer of record in being subject to claims involving design error.

Likewise, you may have exposure arising from recommending construction materials and subsystems. There are risks involving failure to identify long-lead procurement items. There is also a higher expectation of the accuracy of a construction manager's construction-cost estimates, so if bids exceed your estimates, there is substantial risk of a claim. Scheduling and coordination of project activities are common CM responsibilities, which could bring you into claims arising from delays.

Jobsite safety is a major issue for construction managers. They have substantially greater risk than design or technical consultants of being cited by Occupational Safety and Health Administration (OSHA) or state safety agencies for jobsite safety violations. Construction managers often assume responsibility for developing or reviewing jobsite safety programs or procedures of contractors, monitoring safety plans, training, or being involved in other aspects of safety. Recent rulings by the OSHA Review Commission concerning responsibilities of architects, engineers and construction managers have generally concluded that a construction manager's responsibilities for jobsite safety are akin to those of a general contractor. For starters, the title says it all: a "construction manager" obviously *manages* (i.e., directs, controls, supervises) *construction*. As far as OSHA is concerned, there may be no distinction between a CM-advisor and a CM-constructor. In OSHA's eyes, design professionals providing CM services are "in charge of the construction" and, therefore, responsible for jobsite safety. In fact, the OSHA Review Commission has held in a number of recent cases that construction managers who have the power to control schedules, allocate resources, or control or direct work are "engaged in construction" and therefore subject to OSHA health and safety standards, just as contractors are.

Hazardous or toxic site conditions open up two other important risk management issues. First, as a construction manager, you could assume liability for the existing hazardous site conditions. Second, if toxic materials on the site must be disposed of or transported, there is the possibility that you, as a construction manager, could be deemed an "operator" of the site or an "arranger" of the disposal, and thus be subject to severe (and sometimes criminal) sanctions in the event of an accidental spill or toxic release.

Under the language of most standard form CM agreements, CM-advisors assume no more liability regarding inspection and supervision of the contractor's work than traditional design and environmental professionals normally have. However, there is the danger that you will increase your risk if you change this agreement and expand your scope. This could create exposure to claims for failure to detect defective work and may even increase responsibility for jobsite safety.

Except for CMs-at-risk, professional liability insurance is probably not a problem for construction mangers. Most (but not all) policies available today will cover claims arising from the *professional* services the consultant renders as a construction manager. However, most policies don't cover any aspect of the *construction* risk: estimating errors, faulty fabrication, erection, installation assembly, or delays in the completion of construction. Claims arising out of these construction activities are commonly excluded by most design professional liability policies. In addition, there is no coverage available for the economic risk of providing a guaranteed maximum price, as is often done by CMs-at-risk and by contractors.

Caution: a few professional liability insurance policies specifically exclude claims arising out of professional services relating to safety. Some policies contain a general exclusion for claims arising out of services not "usual and customary" to the practice of architecture or engineering, or they may only cover those professional disciplines specified in the policy. Unless these exclusions can be modified or CM is specifically listed as an insured service, there may not be professional liability coverage for your CM activities.

If you are not providing the CM services but your client elects to employ a construction manager on your job, this raises new issues. You'll want to know if your client will use a construction manager, before you and your client agree to the scope of duties, authority and limitations. These need to be coordinated with those of the construction manager and carefully described in your agreement. If the decision to employ a construction manager is made after your agreement has been negotiated and signed, you are entitled to additional fees and time to coordinate with and respond to the client's construction manager.

THE SOLUTION

There are several important steps you can take to mitigate some of the risks of CM. First — as always — choose your projects and clients prudently. This becomes doubly important when you are acting as a construction manager, since you will doubtless be brought into any major litigation that arises on the project. Steer clear of those situations that are more likely to give rise to disputes — litigation-prone contractors or clients, one-sided construction contracts, performance guarantees, inadequate funding or too-tight schedules.

Choose your CM role with care. Offer only those services you are qualified to provide. You may prefer to get started in construction management in the role of CM-advisor. This is not vastly different from the role you are accustomed to when you provide an expanded level of construction phase services or full-time resident project representatives.

Make certain you have qualified people to do the job. Does your staff have the requisite knowledge, experience and ability to provide CM services? Many design professionals have the expertise to provide normal cost estimating, bidder qualification and construction administration. But when providing CM as a separate service, those responsibilities will require greater expertise and may involve more extensive services in such areas as project scheduling and procurement strategies.

Develop a detailed and precise scope of services. This may be more critical in providing construction management than in providing any other services. There are so many variations of CM that clear contractual lines of authority and responsibility are crucial. Together with the owner, develop a workscope that describes the specific responsibilities of each party to the project, including the owner. Make sure your contract accurately reflects your agreed-upon workscope.

Although many consultants prefer to draft their own agreements, until CM is more generally understood and there is more and better case law available, it is probably wisest to use standard form contracts for all project participants. The AIA, the Associated General Contractors (AGC) and the Construction Management Association of America (CMAA) have published standard form agreements for construction management. These model agreements are excellent starting points that can be tailored by you and your attorney to fit your specific project needs. Because these documents are integrated with other documents from the same family, there is less chance of ambiguity and gaps, especially in allocating risk and defining the scope of services.

Watch the terminology in your contracts. Pay particular attention to the old chestnuts: *inspect*, *supervise*, *certify* and *guarantee*. If you use these terms, be sure to define them in your agreement. (See **Definitions**, **Inspection** and **Certifications, Guarantees and Warrantees** for more discussion.)

Limit your exposure to claims involving jobsite safety. Be certain you include appropriate "means and methods" disclaimers in your contract and allocate health and safety risks through indemnities and insurance. If your duties include some aspect of safety, such as recommending, reviewing or coordinating the contractor's safety program, make sure your responsibilities (and those of the contractor) are carefully defined. Equally important: train your field people so their actions don't undermine these contractual protections.

Make sure you do not assume any of the owner's liability for existing site conditions. Insist on a contractual clause that provides for the possibility of discovering hazardous materials on the jobsite. Or, if you know or suspect you will encounter pollutants, you will need the strongest possible indemnity protection from your client. (See *Hazardous Materials*.)

Check your insurance. Before offering your services as a construction manager, talk with your insurance broker to be sure you have appropriate coverage. Pay particular attention to your professional liability policy; make sure it covers the services you intend to provide. As always, ask to be added as a named insured on the contractor's general liability policy. Finally, if you perform as a CM-constructor, you will need to address bonding, workers compensation and general liability issues you probably have not faced before. Get professional advice on these issues before you go too far.

If you are not providing CM services but your client decides to hire a construction manager after you have executed your agreement, you'll need some contractual protection for the resulting cost and risk involved.

CONSTRUCTION MANAGEMENT

If the Client elects to employ a construction manager, the Client will promptly notify the Consultant of the duties, responsibilities and authority of the construction manager and their relationship to the duties, responsibilities and authority of the Consultant.

If the employment of such construction manager by the Client results in additional time or expense to the Consultant to prepare for, coordinate with or respond to the construction manager, the Consultant shall be entitled to an equitable adjustment in fees and time for performance of these services.

SEE ALSO:

Certifications, Guarantees and Warranties
Definitions
Hazardous Materials
Inspection
Insurance
Jobsite Safety
Scope of Services

Relevant standard form agreement provisions:

AIA B141-1997:	Articles 1.1.2.7; 2.8.3.18
EJCDC 1910-1 (1996 edition):	Exhibit A 2.01A.11
	Exhibit B 2.01L

Architects and engineers providing construction management services may wish to refer to the AIA, CMAA and AGC standard form CM agreements.

Design-Build

Design-build is a general term for a series of project-delivery systems that provide the owner with a single point of responsibility for both design and construction. The concept seems quite simple. Instead of the traditional method of design-bid-build — in which the owner obtains completed plans from the designer and furnishes them to the contractor — design-build allows the owner to contract with a single entity for the design and construction of the project. Depending upon the contract terms, the design-builder may become responsible to the owner for a guaranteed cost of a project.

Some owners like design-build because they think it relieves them of their normal risks and responsibilities and puts the risks and responsibilities for the entire project squarely on the shoulders of one entity. The owner is no longer responsible for warranting to the contractor the adequacy of the plans and specifications. If there are errors or omissions in the design, the design-builder bears the consequences. The owner can also expect that the completed construction work will be warranted to be of good quality, free of defects and in strict accordance with the contract documents. If there is a problem, the owner won't have to worry about who was at fault and will look to the design-builder to make it right.

Although the idea behind design-build is simple, the parties' roles and responsibilities may vary greatly. Look at **Exhibit 12**. As you can see, there are many different relationships that are referred to as *design-build*. Each of these relationships, or scenarios, is defined by a series of contracts between the owner and the design-builder and between the design-builder and the designer and contractor (both of whom in turn may have subconsultants and subcontractors). Although there are scores of variations, the most common scenarios are Scenario One: contractor-led design-build, Scenario Two: consultant-led design-build, Scenario Three: consultant and contractor jointly acting as a design-build entity, Scenario Four: design-build organization with in-house design and contractor staff, and Scenario Five: bridging or owner's consultant.

Design-Build

X-10

EXHIBIT 12

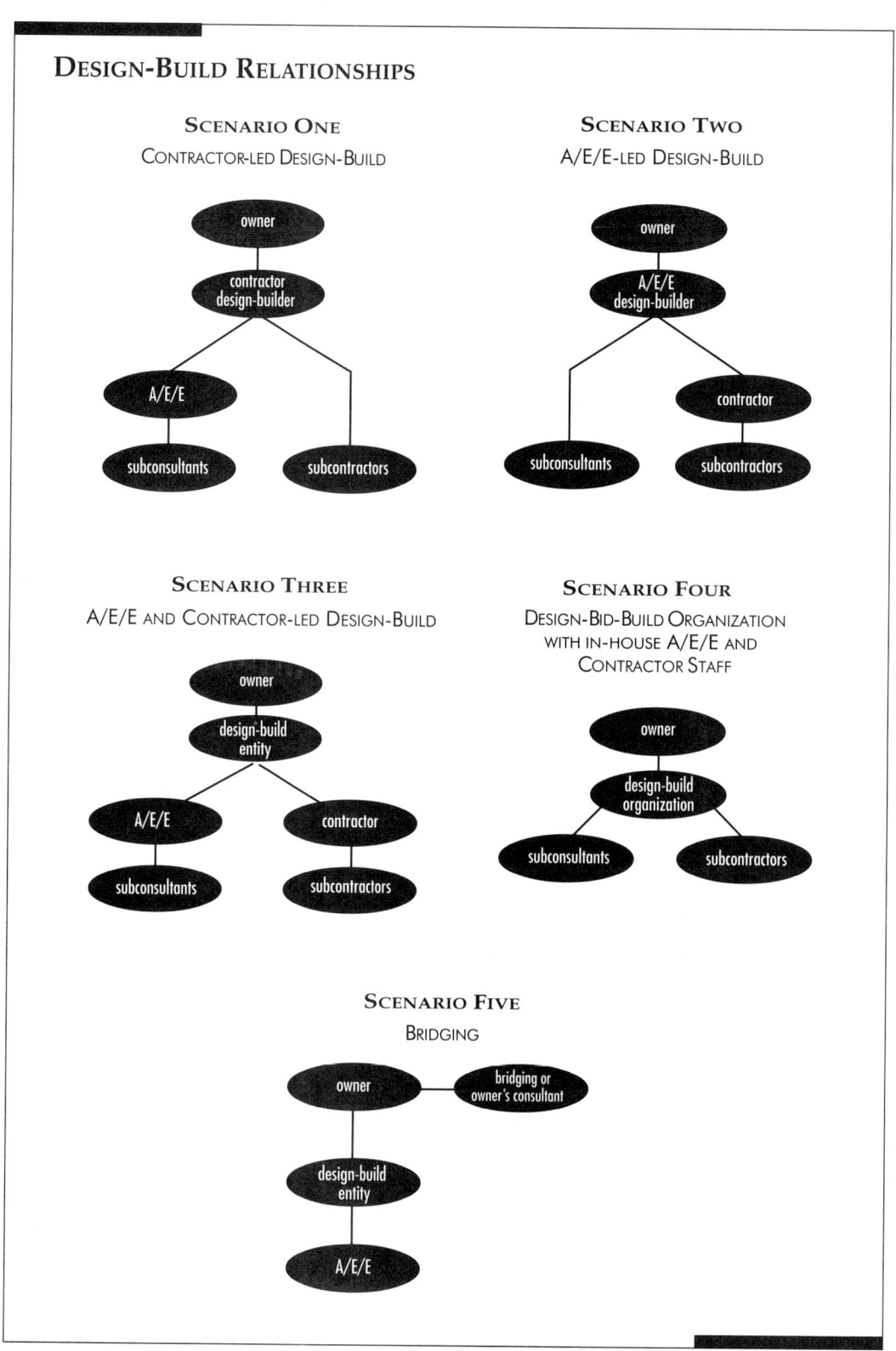

The Problem

Because they assume greater responsibility, design-builders also face expanded liability. Under the traditional project-delivery method, if you are the licensed professional consultant, you are held to a professional standard of care in the performance of your services, including the preparation of drawings and specifications. Claims brought against you are usually based on negligence. The contractor is required to construct the project in conformance with your drawings and specifications. Failure to do so can result in claims against the contractor based on a variety of legal theories — breach of contract, breach of warranty and strict liability. The design-builder, however, has the total responsibility for managing, directing and coordinating the design and construction, including responsibility for the adequacy of the plans and for the construction means, methods, techniques, sequences and procedures, as well as for jobsite safety. The design-builder's liability, therefore, encompasses that of both the consultant and the contractor; in addition, the design-builder assumes some of the duties and risks that traditionally fall to the project owner.

Your risk on a design-build project varies depending on what role and contractual responsibilities you undertake. If you lead a design-build, project, or if you and the contractor jointly form a design-build entity, you may be assuming most or all of the project risk. Under other scenarios, such as contractor-led design-build, or if you are serving as an owner's consultant, your risk may be little different from that in the design-bid-build project-delivery method.

Design-build presents some real challenges, each of which must be addressed. For instance, public procurement laws in some states may not permit you or a contractor to provide design-build services; other states may require special licenses. Furthermore, many architects and engineers find the costs of participating in a design-build competition to be prohibitive. Some worry that if they contract with a contractor or a design-build organization, they will not have direct access to or communication with the owner and will have to rely on the design-builder to interpret the program requirements. That also means they are dependent on the contractor or the design-builder to explain design choices and obtain owner decisions in a timely manner.

The insurance for design-build is both intricate and critical. Your coverage needs will vary depending on who leads the project. If you are the lead or are part of a design-build entity, your insurance requirements will be very much like those of a contractor. You'll need to investigate the availability and cost of appropriate general liability coverage for contractor operations. You may be required to provide surety or may have to rely on the contractor's bonding capability. Many consultants — and owners — are astonished to learn that there is no insurance available to cover the contractor's risk of faulty workmanship (i.e., to fix construction errors and omissions) or failure to complete the work on time.

The Solution

If you are considering participating in a design-build project, you need to do your homework; the issues can be extremely complex. Find out first if design-build is, in fact, legal in the state where the project is situated. In a few states, it is illegal for architects and engineers to offer contracting services (Scenario Two) without a contractor's license. Conversely, in other states it is illegal for contractors to offer design services (Scenario One) without an architect's or engineer's license, as appropriate. Both the Design-Build Institute of America (DBIA) and the American Bar Association have published surveys of state procurement and licensing laws with regard to design-build. (See *Additional Resources*.)

You also need to carefully evaluate the project and the client to determine whether the budget and schedule are realistic. Find out, too, whether the client has secured adequate financing. It is equally important to look at the other participants on the design-build team and see how they will be selected. Determine if they have a history of disputes and litigation. Check references and investigate the project experience, financial condition and claims condition of the other consultants and contractors.

You may want to consider forming a separate entity to isolate the risks of design-build or facilitate obtaining insurance or surety. There are many states that permit limited-liability partnerships or limited-liability companies, structures some lawyers feel may provide additional protection. Consult with your attorney and accountant on the protections, costs, advantages and disadvantages of each approach.

Make certain that all members of the design-build team carry appropriate insurance with adequate limits. Given the potential liability on a design-build project, it is critical that there be no gaps in your coverage or that of the other team members. Understand that even if you have professional liability design-build coverage, it will apply only to claims arising from your *professional* activities. Appropriate general liability insurance for both you and the contractor is critical. If you form a joint venture with a contractor, as in Scenario Three, you may need a special coverage endorsement to your professional liability policy. Also remember that surety bonds are very difficult for most consultants to obtain, so a contractor's "bondability" is important. Clearly, the insurance and surety requirements are complicated; still other coverages may be necessary. You should seek the help of a knowledgeable agent or broker who specializes in insuring construction and design professionals. (See *Insurance*.)

Good contracts are especially important on design-build. The unique aspects of every project mean that you, the owner and the contractor must carefully think through and define the responsibilities and expectations of each party. The AIA, EJCDC and FIDIC have all published sets of standard form agreements for professionals providing design-build services. The AGC has also developed documents for its members, and the Design-Build Institute of America (DBIA) has published one document. These model agreements are good starting points, but they must be tailored by you and your attorney to fit your specific project. Understand, too, that these standard documents differ in several aspects — in defining the standard of care, addressing different site conditions, specifying the responsibilities of owner's consultants, establishing the beginning of design-builder involvement, describing the treatment of changes in the Work and outlining the procedures for dispute resolution and termination. The standard agreements are generally silent on limitation of liability and liquidated damages. (See *Limitation of Liability* and *Liquidated Damages*.)

Responsibilities of the parties may vary from project to project, depending on the owner's requirements and contractual terms. You should define and draft a specific, comprehensive scope of services that carefully describes the exact responsibilities of each party to the project and the allocation of risks to each party — including the owner. (See also *Scope of Services*.)

Under the standard owner/design-builder contracts, the design-builder is responsible for supervising the Work and for the means, methods, techniques, sequences and procedures of construction, as well as for safety on the jobsite. In the design-builder/contractor agreements, these responsibilities are allocated to the contractor, along traditional lines. If you are leading the design-build team (Scenario Two) or are part of a joint venture (Scenario Three), you may have vicarious liability for jobsite safety, however, and this needs to be addressed. For instance, you can be named on the contractor's general-liability policy and have the contractor contractually indemnify you from claims involving jobsite safety. You also have the responsibility for complying with OSHA requirements, which is not generally an insurable exposure and may not be something you can be indemnified for contractually. (See also *Construction Observation*, *Indemnities* and *Jobsite Safety*.)

Owners often choose design-build in an attempt to get a fixed price before all the risks of a project are identified and resolved. However, you, the owner and the contractor must plan for changes and extra costs; they will occur. The design-build team should include in its budget an appropriate contingency, including a provision for the cost to correct minor design defects. You and other team members should agree how design errors and faulty workmanship will be paid for and how schedule slippage will be handled. The owner/design-builder contract should be explicit about what constitutes a change and how claims for adjustments in the contract price will be treated. You should also provide for lender changes, acts of God, changes to codes or regulations and subsurface or concealed conditions. (See *Changed Conditions*, *Delays*, *Hazardous Materials*, *Lenders' Requirements* and *Underground Improvements*.)

Finally, have a plan to promptly resolve disputes as they arise — and make sure it is incorporated into the contracts between all parties. Partnering and dispute resolution boards (DRBs) are two excellent techniques to consider as dispute avoidance mechanisms. As in all your professional service agreements, provide for mediation of any disputes that do arise as the first step in reaching resolution. (See *Dispute Avoidance and Resolution*.)

On larger or more complex design-build projects, consider a project-specific insurance policy. It may be possible to include the contractor's vicarious and direct exposure for professional liability under such a policy, a step that would facilitate and expedite dispute resolution among project participants. (See *Insurance* for more information.)

Design-Build

SEE ALSO:

Construction Observation
Delays
Dispute Avoidance and Resolution
Hazardous Materials
Insurance
Jobsite Safety
Lenders' Requirements
Limitation of Liability
Liquidated Damages
Scope of Services
Underground Improvements

DESIGN-BUILD CONTRACT DOCUMENTS:

	AIA	DBIA	EJCDC
Owner/Design-Builder	A191		1910-40
Owner/Owner's Consultant		DBIA-1	1910-43
Design-Builder/Contractor	A491		1910-48
Design-Builder/Consultant	B901		1910-41

FAST TRACK PROJECTS

Fast track projects — those in which construction begins before all of the drawings and specifications are complete — have a single purpose: to benefit the client's pocketbook. Also known as phased construction, the method is intended to save time by bypassing the traditional sequence of completing plans, bidding or negotiating, and then starting construction.

If everything goes just right, fast tracking can perhaps expedite certain projects and may result in savings to the client. Materials might be purchased early, for instance, thus locking in lower prices. Rising labor costs may be anticipated, too, and averted. Perhaps construction can be completed more quickly and the client can move in, or lease the property sooner. As with any shortcut, however, there are risks — especially to the architect and engineers involved.

THE PROBLEM

Fast track projects have *high risk* written all over them. Consider, for example, the following:

- On fast track projects, you often need to make major design decisions out of sequence or earlier than you would on a traditionally sequenced project, and before you can fully appreciate their consequences.

- You will need more design time to "spin off" separate construction documents for each of the early bid packages; this also means duplication of effort.

- Your preliminary design assumptions may prove to be untrue after you have designed and prepared documentation for the earlier construction documents bid packages.

- Downstream design decisions will require you to redesign earlier designed portions of the project and to prepare redocumentation — all at additional time and cost.

- You may find it harder to maintain consistency in design and detailing when you have to do it piecemeal or out of sequence.

- You will need more time to administer the bidding and construction administration phases, while the remainder of your project team completes the construction documents. In smaller firms, this means you may have to suspend your design efforts while focusing on the bidding and early construction.

- Fast track projects usually mean more change orders to handle coordination issues not addressed in the early bid packages. An increase in change orders also means you must spend more time in coordination and construction administration activities.

- You may not have the time to work closely with municipal building officials to anticipate and design around code problems. An adverse code interpretation could mean costly modifications.

- Design changes may mean some of the construction work itself will also need to be modified.

- Fast track projects are inherently more expensive for design professionals.

Perhaps the biggest challenge you may face, however, is the inexperienced or unrealistic client. Many believe the fast track construction documents for each bid package will be at least as complete as those prepared for traditionally phased projects. Unless convinced otherwise, the client will not appreciate the design changes and change orders usually associated with fast track. He or she may think those additional costs were your fault.

Unless your client clearly understands the process and pitfalls of fast tracking and acknowledges the likelihood of design changes and change orders — with their resulting delays and costs — your client's expectations may be much too high. And unrealistic expectations often are the harbingers of claims.

THE SOLUTION

The only way to avoid fast track problems is to avoid fast track projects altogether. There are, however, several steps you can take that will lessen the risk. The first is education — bringing the client's expectations in line with reality. Find out why the client has opted for a fast track process and what he or she expects to achieve. Then make sure the client understands and acknowledges the risks and potential liabilities he or she must bear by choosing fast track. Your client must appreciate that certain modifications to the early construction documents will not be due to your errors or omissions but will be rather part and parcel of the fast track process. The client must also understand that previously constructed portions of the project may have to be removed or reconstructed. Explain that there will be changes, delays and resulting extra costs.

On any project, clients tend to expect your plans and specifications to be perfect. This is a bigger problem than usual on fast track projects, where there is a greater likelihood that the various packages of construction documents will require design changes and modifications. You can confront this difficulty head-on, by establishing realistic expectations in your contract. Recommend that these costs be anticipated in the project budget and that a larger than usual contingency be established to include both design and construction changes. (Refer to *Contingency Fund* for more information.)

Furthermore, your risk and potential liability must also be acknowledged and addressed. You need enough time to provide the Additional Services that are necessary on a fast track project and you need to be adequately compensated. Many firms negotiate a significant fee for this type of project, depending on the client and amount of fast tracking or phasing involved.

Address all of these issues in your contract. Your agreement should describe the potential risks in a fast track process to both you and the client, allocate these risks and provide for some of the additional costs in a design contingency. Consider the following sample clause:

FAST TRACK DESIGN AND CONSTRUCTION

In consideration of the benefits to the Client of employing the fast track process (in which some of the Consultant's design services overlap the construction work and are out of sequence with the traditional project delivery method), and in recognition of the inherent risks of fast tracking to the Consultant, the Client agrees to waive all claims against the Consultant for design changes and modification of portions of the Work already constructed due to the Client's decision to employ the fast track process.

In addition, the Client agrees, to the fullest extent permitted by law, to indemnify and hold harmless the Consultant, its officers, directors, employees and subconsultants (collectively, Consultant) against all damages, liabilities or costs, including reasonable attorneys' fees and defense costs, arising out of or in any way connected with this Project, excepting only those damages, liabilities or costs attributable to the sole negligence or willful misconduct by the Consultant.

The Client further agrees to compensate the Consultant for all Additional Services required to modify, correct or adjust the Construction Documents and coordinate them in order to meet the Client's program requirements because of the Client's decision to construct the Project in a fast track manner.

You will also want to establish the client's responsibility when authorizing deviations from your plans and specifications. On fast track projects, the client is likely to become very involved with potential change orders and their impact on the budget. He or she may be tempted to directly authorize changes in the construction documents without your approval and, sometimes, even without your knowledge. (See *Unauthorized Changes to Plans* for more information.)

No matter how strongly your agreement is worded, you should go to extraordinary lengths to document every step of your involvement in a fast track project. Keep detailed notes on why decisions were made, why some tasks were done out of sequence, who made the decisions and under what set of assumptions. On risky work of this nature, you must make every reasonable effort to document and protect yourself.

The decision to participate in a fast track project should start with careful client selection and you should proceed only if you have a quality project, a strong contract, an adequate fee, experienced contractors and good working relationships all around. To encourage teamwork and cooperation, consider suggesting a partnering arrangement between the owner, contractors and all major consultants on the project. (See the *Partnering* discussion in the *Dispute Avoidance and Resolution* section for more information.)

SEE ALSO:

Code Compliance
Contingency Fund
Delays
Dispute Avoidance and Resolution
Indemnities
Limitation of Liability
Standard of Care
Timeliness of Performance
Unauthorized Changes to Plans

RELEVANT STANDARD FORM AGREEMENT PROVISIONS:

AIA B141-1997: Article 1.1.2.6
EJCDC 1910-1 (1996 edition): Exhibit A 1.03B

MULTIPLE PRIME CONTRACTS

Multiple prime design projects are those in which a client contracts with all or most of the consultants directly, rather than using the more traditional hierarchical method of contracting — owner to prime consultant to subconsultants. Although owners sometimes contract directly with multiple construction contractors as well, the focus here is on multiple prime design or consulting-services contracts.

As projects become more complex and engineering and architectural systems increasingly critical, more responsibility rests with the consultants who design them. Owners may wish to retain the best specialists in a given field or ones with whom they have worked before. One way to accomplish this is for clients to contract with them directly, bypassing the traditional prime consultant.

Some consulting engineers, whose role is typically that of a subconsultant, believe that the "multi-prime" system makes sense. They may feel a more prominent role in the design process will improve communication among all consultants. If they are brought into the project earlier and get input directly from the owner — rather than filtered through the prime — they reason they can better understand and meet the owner's needs. Some also feel that, because they do not have to transmit their invoices through the prime designer, they may be paid more promptly and might even enhance their profitability by negotiating their fees directly with the owner. (See *Pay-When-Paid*.)

In some ways, the multiple prime — also termed *separate contracts* — system offers advantages for the consultant who usually acts as the prime. By changing the traditional contracting arrangement, the prime's liability is reduced somewhat, and his or her professional liability insurance premium may also be reduced by not having subconsultant fees included in his or her revenue. There is the further inducement of avoiding the added administrative duties that are part of acting as the prime consultant. (Refer to *Subconsultants*.)

There is a down side, though. Some owners choose multiple prime contracting not because of better communications or enhanced quality but in an attempt to save money by squeezing down the fees for subconsultants or by eliminating the administrative fees paid to the prime for coordinating the work. These owners are deceiving themselves, however, and may actually be setting the stage for a project plagued by problems.

Multiple Prime Contracts

THE PROBLEM

If your clients elect to use separate design contracts because they think this will save them money, they will be disappointed. Multiple prime contracting rarely results in lower project costs to the owner. Whether there are separate contracts or not, the work of the various consultants still must be coordinated by someone. And proper coordination of all the consultants requires time and expertise to integrate documents and resolve technical issues. The effort and corresponding fees required for such coordination remain fairly constant, whatever contracting approach your clients choose.

If there is no designated project coordinator, the workscope of each multiple contract consultant must be exceptionally detailed and coordinated with that of every other consultant. Even so, your client may find that the resulting confusion over who is responsible for what and the inevitable inconsistencies can be very costly indeed. It could prove to be expensive for you, too. If something goes wrong, chances are all the consultants will be named in a lawsuit, and you might spend a great deal of time and money extricating yourself from a situation in which you had no culpability.

If it is not provided for by contract, no one will be required to take the lead in coordinating the design. Nor will other consultants be required to cooperate with anyone who attempts to act as coordinator. With many disciplines working on the same project without a single focal point, details are bound to "fall through the cracks." For example, everyone is aware that two or more objects (like beams and ducts) cannot occupy the same space. Who's going to sort this out, make the decisions and require the cooperation of the other consultants?

THE SOLUTION

There are several alternative approaches. One would put responsibility on each consultant to coordinate his or her designs with the primary consultant. Another school of thought, however, holds that it might be better to designate someone — probably whoever would traditionally be the prime consultant — as project coordinator. If you are to be that coordinator, that designation should be spelled out in your workscope and included in your fee calculations. You and your attorney might want to discuss this with your client. If you follow this approach, your client should also agree that all the client/consultant contracts he or she enters into should likewise identify the coordinator.

If you are the consulting firm who would otherwise be prime but you are not responsible for coordination, you should obtain an indemnity from your client against claims arising from lack of coordination by others. Consider the following suggested contract clause:

Owner's Consultants

It is understood and agreed that the Client shall contract directly with other consultants for the following services:

Consulting Firm   Professional Services

_____   _____

_____   _____

_____   _____

The Client agrees that the Consultant shall have no responsibility for any portion of the Project designed by other consultants engaged by the Client. The Consultant shall not be required to check or verify other consultants' construction documents or reports and shall be entitled to rely on the accuracy and completeness thereof, as well as the compliance of such documents or reports with applicable laws, codes, statutes, ordinances and regulations.

The Client agrees, to the fullest extent permitted by law, to indemnify and hold harmless the Consultant from any damages, liabilities or costs, including reasonable attorneys' fees and defense costs, arising out of or connected in any way with the services performed by other consultants engaged by the Client.

If your client requires the other consultants to coordinate their designs with yours, you may want to add the following to the above language:

The Client further agrees to require all other consultants engaged by the Client to coordinate their construction documents or reports with those of the Consultant, to promptly report any conflicts or inconsistencies to the Consultant and to cooperate fully with the Consultant in the resolution of those conflicts or inconsistencies.

On the other hand, if your client wants you to take responsibility for coordinating the work of the other consultants, consider this addition:

> **It is further agreed that the Consultant shall coordinate the construction documents or reports of the professional consultants listed above but only for conformance with the design concepts and information as expressed in the construction documents prepared by the Consultant. The Client agrees to require all other consultants engaged by the Client to cooperate fully with the Consultant in the resolution of any conflicts or inconsistencies discovered.**

If your client decides against naming a project coordinator, it is important that both your work and your contract reflect this fact. Do not assume responsibility for coordinating anyone's work but your own. Make sure your contract also has provisions that protect you from delays by others and faulty information provided to you. (Refer to *Delays, Information Provided by Others* and *Requests for Information* for discussions and possible contract language.) Ask your client to review the agreements with his or her other consultants; it is critical that all these contracts reflect the same understandings and responsibilities.

SEE ALSO:

Delays
Indemnities
Information Provided by Others
Pay-When-Paid
Requests for Information
Subconsultants

RELEVANT STANDARD FORM AGREEMENT PROVISIONS:

AIA B141-1997:	Articles 2.1.1; 2.8.3.9; 2.8.3.18
EJCDC 1910-1 (1996 edition):	Exhibit A 1.03B&C
	Exhibit B 2.01M

Appendix I

XI-1

AGREEMENT FOR EMERGENCY PROFESSIONAL SERVICES

Consultant _____ Client _____

Address _____ Address _____

_____ _____

Date _____ Project No. _____

Project Name and Location _____

_____

Description of the services to be provided (or listed on the attached Exhibits numbered____):

_____

_____

Professional fee $ _____ or basis of compensation _____

Payment terms _____

Retainer (payable upon execution of this Agreement) $ _____

Special Conditions _____

_____

_____

The Terms and Conditions on the reverse of this form, when initialed by both parties, are incorporated and made a part of this Agreement.

Offered by: **Accepted by:**

_____ _____
signature *date* *signature* *date*

_____ _____
printed name/title *printed name/title*

_____ _____
name of consulting firm *name of client*

_____
license #

Appendix I

XI-2

Terms and Conditions

Performance of Services: The Consultant shall perform the services outlined on the reverse side of this Agreement and on the attached **Exhibit** _____ in consideration of the stated fee and payment terms.

Additional Services: For additional services not included above, the Consultant shall be compensated as follows:
_____

Access to Site: Unless otherwise stated, the Consultant will have access to the site for activities necessary for the performance of the services. The Consultant will take reasonable precautions to minimize damage due to these activities, but has not included in the fee the cost of restoration of any resulting damage and will not be responsible for such costs.

Retainer/Billing/Payment: The Client agrees to pay the Consultant for all services performed and all costs incurred. Prior to the provision of services, the Client shall deposit a retainer of $_____ with the Consultant. Invoices for the Consultant's services shall be submitted, at the Consultant's option, either upon completion of such services or on a monthly basis. Invoices shall be due and payable upon receipt. If any invoice is not paid within 15 days, the Consultant may, without waiving any claim or right against the Client, and without liability whatsoever to the Client, suspend or terminate the performance of services. The retainer shall be credited on the final invoice. Accounts unpaid 30 days after the invoice date may be subject to a monthly service charge of 1.5% (or the maximum legal rate) on the unpaid balance. In the event any portion of an account remains unpaid 60 days after the billing, the Consultant may institute collection action and the Client shall pay all costs of collection, including reasonable attorneys' fees.

Indemnification: The Client shall, to the fullest extent permitted by law, indemnify and hold harmless the Consultant, his or her officers, directors, employees, agents and subconsultants from and against all damage, liability and cost, including reasonable attorneys' fees and defense costs, arising out of or in any way connected with the performance of the services under this Agreement, excepting only those damages, liabilities or costs attributable to the sole negligence or willful misconduct of the Consultant.

Waiver: In addition, the Client agrees, to the maximum extent permitted by law, to waive any claims against the Consultant arising out of the performance of these emergency services, except for the sole negligence or willful misconduct of the Consultant.

Information for the Sole Use and Benefit of the Client: All opinions and conclusions of the Consultant, whether written or oral, and any plans, specifications or other documents and services provided by the Consultant are for the sole use and benefit of the Client and are not to be provided to any other person or entity without the prior written consent of the Consultant. Nothing contained in this Agreement shall create a contractual relationship with or a cause of action in favor of any third party against either the Consultant or the Client.

Certifications, Guarantees and Warranties: The Consultant shall not be required to execute any document that would result in the Consultant certifying, guaranteeing or warranting the existence of any conditions.

Limitation of Liability: In recognition of the relative risks, rewards and benefits of the project to both the Client and the Consultant, the risks have been allocated such that the Client agrees that, to the fullest extent permitted by law, the Consultant's total liability to the Client for any and all injuries, damages, claims, losses, expenses or claim expenses arising out of this Agreement from any cause or causes, shall not exceed $_____ . Such causes include, but are not limited to, the Consultant's negligence, errors, omissions, strict liability, breach of contract or breach of warranty. Initialed: _____ *Consultant* _____ *Client*

Ownership of Documents: All documents produced by the Consultant under this Agreement are instruments of the Consultant's professional service and shall remain the property of the Consultant and may not be used by the Client for any other purpose without the prior written consent of the Consultant.

Dispute Resolution: Any claims or disputes between the Client and the Consultant arising out of the services to be provided by the Consultant or out of this Agreement shall be submitted to nonbinding mediation. The Client and the Consultant agree to include a similar mediation agreement with all contractors, subconsultants, subcontractors, suppliers and fabricators, providing for mediation as the primary method for dispute resolution among all parties.

Termination of Services: This Agreement may be terminated at any time by either party should the other party fail to perform its obligations hereunder. In the event of termination for any reason whatsoever, the Client shall pay the Consultant for all services rendered to the date of termination, and all reimbursable expenses incurred prior to termination and reasonable termination expenses incurred as the result of termination.

It is agreed the above terms and conditions are incorporated into and made a part of the Agreement on the reverse side of this sheet. Initialed:_____ *Consultant* _____ *Client*

Caution: The clauses that appear on this form are examples only and do not reflect variations in law among the fifty states. Consult your attorney for legal advice on specific wording applicable in your jurisdiction.

APPENDIX II

THE TEAMWORK ETHIC

In times past, owners, contractors, subcontractors and consultants cooperated to solve problems as they arose on a construction project. Over the years, however, the industry has changed. Almost gone is the approach of working together to get the job done — on time and within budget. Extras, delays, problems, disputes, claims and lawyers are now the rule rather than the exception. Unfortunately, we've all heard of at least one contractor who fails to report problems promptly, withholding information with the intent of magnifying the cost of extras and thereby enlarging his or her profit. This certainly violates the spirit, and in many instances the letter, of the construction contract and increases the risk for the consultant. If the underlying defects are in the plans or specifications, the client will no doubt look to the consultant to pay to correct any problems — problems that might have been eliminated or at least mitigated if the contractor had reported them early.

Many in the construction process deplore the waste and frustration caused by the current system and are looking for a better way — a return to the teamwork ethic. Dispute resolution methods other than litigation are taking root, alternative project-delivery systems are being employed, and processes that foster a team spirit — such as *partnering* — are being introduced.

This kind of teamwork means that the owner and contractors need to acknowledge their own responsibilities for the success of the project. For example, they have an obligation to report promptly to the consultant any defects they observe in the contract documents. To foster the spirit of partnership — the idea that "we're all in this together" — and to set up realistic expectations for both the client and the contractor, some consultants ask their clients to insert language similar to the following into the General Conditions:

Appendix II

XI-4

> The Contractor acknowledges and understands that the Contract Documents may represent imperfect data and may contain errors, omissions, conflicts, inconsistencies, code violations and improper use of materials. Such deficiencies will be corrected when identified. The Contractor agrees to carefully study and compare the individual Contract Documents and report at once in writing to the Owner any deficiencies the Contractor may discover. The Contractor further agrees to require each subcontractor to likewise study the documents and report at once any deficiencies discovered.
>
> The Contractor shall resolve all reported deficiencies with the Consultant prior to awarding any subcontracts or starting any work with the Contractor's own employees. If any deficiencies cannot be resolved by the Contractor without additional time or additional expense, the Contractor shall so inform the Owner in writing. Any work performed prior to receipt of instructions from the Owner will be done at the Contractor's risk.

Such a clause acknowledges the obvious but sometimes unspoken truth that the plans will not be perfect. Some architects and engineers may be reluctant to admit this lack of perfection, but such a realistic statement may help diffuse a later claim from an owner or contractor that he or she expected perfection from the consultant. This provision — coupled with a reasonable Standard of Care clause in the consultant's agreement — should go far in establishing proper expectations for all parties.

FURTHER READING

Architect's Handbook of Professional Practice. 12th ed. Washington, DC: The American Institute of Architects, 1994. Annual updates.

Beard, Jeffrey L. and Daniel W. Duncan. *Design Build: The Project Delivery System for Design and Construction.* New York: McGraw-Hill Text, 1998. ISBN: 0070063117 (available through AIAONLINE).

Capezio, Peter and Debra Morehouse. *Taking the Mystery Out of TQM.* Hawthorne, NJ: Career Press, 1995. ISBN: 1564141977 (available through the ACEC, order #2224).

Construction Management. Monterey, CA: DPIC Companies, Inc., 1997.

Cooper, Mary. *Records and Information Management: Order Out of Chaos.* Washington, DC: American Consulting Engineers Council, 1996 (ACEC order #308).

Diamond, Susan Z. *Records Management: A Practical Guide to Policies, Practices, Resources, Technologies.* 3rd ed. New York: AMACON. ISBN: 081440295X (available through the ACEC, order #1661-95).

Dyer, Sue. *Partner Your Project: Working together to bring your project in on time and on budget . . . A step-by-step guide to partnering your project.* Livermore, CA: Pendulum Publishing, 1997. ISBN: 0965224309.

Expert Witness: A Guide to Service as a Forensic Professional and Expert Witness. Professional Liability Agents Network. Monterey, CA: DPIC Companies, Inc., 1995.

Fisher, Robert, William Ury and Bruce Patton. *Getting to Yes: Negotiating Agreement Without Giving In.* 2nd ed. Massachusetts: Penguin USA, 1991. ISBN: 0140157352.

Focus on Claims. Monterey, CA: DPIC Companies, Inc., 1996.

Guide to Professional Liability Insurance. The ACEC Professional Risk Management Committee. Washington, DC: American Consulting Engineers Council, 1996. ISBN: 0910090033 (ACEC Order #313-96).

Further Reading

Handbook on Project Delivery. Sacramento, CA: The American Institute of Architects California Council, 1996.

Hatem, David J., ed. *Subsurface Conditions: Risk Management for Design and Construction Management Professionals.* New York: John Wiley & Sons, 1997. ISBN: 0471156078.

Kaplan, L. G. *Emergency and Disaster Planning Manual.* New York: McGraw-Hill Text, 1996. ISBN: 0070340838.

Lessons in Professional Liability: DPIC's Loss Prevention Handbook for Design Professionals. Revised ed. Monterey, CA: DPIC Companies, Inc., 1998.

Lessons in Professional Liability: DPIC's Loss Prevention Handbook for Environmental Consultants. Monterey, CA: DPIC Companies, Inc., 1996.

The LoL Handbook: A Guide to the Use of Limitation of Liability for Design Professionals. Professional Liability Agents Network. Monterey, CA: DPIC Companies, Inc., 1996.

Marcus, Phillip A., ed., et al. *Moving Ahead With ISO 14000: Improving Environmental Management and Advancing Sustainable Development.* New York: John Wiley & Sons, Wiley Series in Environmental Quality Management, 1997. ISBN: 0471168777.

Matyas, Robert M., et al. *Construction Dispute Review Board Manual.* ASCE Task Committee on Dispute Review Boards. New York: McGraw-Hill Text, 1996. ISBN: 0070410607.

McIntyre, Marla, ed. *Partnering: Changing Attitudes in Construction.* Washington, DC: Associated General Contractors of America, 1995. (AGC order #1225).

Moore, C. W. *The Mediation Process: Practical Strategies for Resolving Conflict.* 2nd ed. San Francisco, CA: Jossey-Bass Publishers, 1996. ISBN: 0787902489.

Negotiating for Design Professional Services: Estimating, Negotiating, Contracting. ACEC Procurement Committee. Washington, DC: American Consulting Engineers Council, 1997 (ACEC order #235-97).

Nunnally, Stephens W. *Construction Methods and Management.* New York: Prentice Hall Press, 1997. ISBN: 0135703670.

Phillips, Barbara Ashley. *Finding Common Ground: A Field Guide to Mediation.* Austin TX: Hells Canyon Publishing, 1994. ISBN: 0963391976.

The Practice of Engineering as a Business Corporation. Virginia: National Society of Professional Engineers, 1998 (NSPE order #1940).

Project Delivery Systems for Building Construction. Washington, DC: Associated General Contractors of America, 1997 (AGC order #2903).

Project Representatives Manual. Silver Springs, MD: Professional Liability Agents Network, 1996.

Safford, Dan. *Proposals: On Target, On Time.* Washington, DC: American Consulting Engineers Council (ACEC order #415). ISBN: 0910090068.

Schwartz, Arthur E. and Mary Ann Diggs, eds. *A State-by-State Summary of Liability Laws Affecting the Practice of Engineering.* Professional Liability Committee of the Professional Engineers in Private Practice. Alexandria, VA: National Society of Professional Engineers, 1997 (NSPE order #1918).

Sweet, Justin. *Legal Aspects of Architecture, Engineering and the Construction Process.* 5th ed. Elgin, MN: West/Wadsworth, 1994. ISBN: 0314027068.

Tort Liability Today: A Guide for State and Local Governments. Arlington, VA: Public Risk Management Association, 1998.

Twomey, Timothy R. *Understanding the Legal Aspects of Design/Build.* Kingston, MA: R. S. Means Company, Inc., 1989. ISBN: 087629137X.

Ury, William. *Getting Past No: Negotiating Your Way from Confrontation to Cooperation.* New York: Bantam Doubleday Dell Publishing, 1993. ISBN: 0553371312.

Vance, Thomas L. and Jack Doran. *Professional Liability in the Construction Process: A Guide for Risk Managers.* Monterey, CA: DPIC Companies, Inc., 1997.

What Every Owner Needs to Know About Value Engineering. Monterey, CA: DPIC Companies, Inc., 1996.

What Every Owner Needs to Know About Fast Track Projects. Monterey, CA: DPIC Companies, Inc., 1996.

What Every Owner Needs to Know About RFIs. Monterey, CA: DPIC Companies, Inc., 1996.

Wilkoff, W. M. L., James S. Brady and Laura W Abed. *Practicing Universal Design: An Interpretation of the ADA.* New York: John Wiley & Sons, 1997. ISBN: 0471285455.

Wilson, L. *The Copyright Guide: A Friendly Guide to Protecting and Profiting from Copyrights.* New York: Allworth Press, 1996. ISBN: 1880559439.

Working with CADD and Electronic Media. Monterey, CA: DPIC Companies, Inc., 1998.

Y2K: Are You Ready for the Year 2000? Monterey, CA: DPIC Companies, Inc., 1998.

Further Reading

XII-4

ADDITIONAL RESOURCES

The American Academy of Environmental Engineers (AAEE)
130 Holiday Court, Suite 100
Annapolis, MD 21401
Voice 410.266.3311, Fax 410.266.7653
www.enviro-engrs.org

American Arbitration Association (AAA)
140 West 51st Street
New York, NY 10020-1203
Voice 212.484.4000, Fax 212.307.4387
www.adr.org

American Bar Association (ABA)
750 North Lake Shore Drive
Chicago, IL 60611
Voice 312.988.5000
www.abanet.org

American Consulting Engineers Council (ACEC)
1015 15th Street NW, Suite 802
Washington, DC 20005
Voice 202.347.7474, Fax 202.898.0068
www.acec.org

American Council of Independent Laboratories (ACIL)
1629 K Street NW, Suite 400
Washington, DC 20006
Voice 202.887.5872, Fax 202.887.0021
www.acil.org

American Institute of Professional Geologists (AIPG)
7828 Vance Drive, Suite 103
Arvada, CO 80003-2124
Voice 303.431.0831, Fax 303.431.1332
www.nbmg.unr.edu/aipg

Additional Resources

Americans with Disabilities Act Information Office
U.S. Department of Justice
Civil Rights Division
P.O. Box 66738
Washington, DC 20035
Voice 800.514.0301 or 202.514.0301
www.usdoj.gov/crt/ada/adahom1.htm

The American Institute of Architects (AIA)
1735 New York Avenue NW
Washington, DC 20006
Voice 202.626.7300, Fax 202.626.7587
www.aiaonline.org

American Institute of Architects California Council (AIACC)
1303 J Street, Suite 200
Sacramento, CA 95814
Voice 916.448.9082, Fax 916.442.5346
www.aiacc.org

American Society of Civil Engineers (ASCE)
1801 Alexander Bell Drive
Reston, VA 20191-4400
Voice 703.295.6300, Fax 703.295.6444
www.asce.org

American Society of Heating, Refrigerating and Air Conditioning Engineers, Inc. (ASHRAE)
1791 Tullie Circle NE
Atlanta, GA 30329
Voice 404.636.8400, Fax 404.321.5478
www.ashrae.org

American Society of Interior Designers (ASID)
608 Massachusetts Avenue NE
Washington, DC 20002-6006
Voice 202.546.3480, Fax 202.546.3240
www.asid.org

American Society of Landscape Architects (ASLA)
636 I Street NW
Washington, DC 20001-3736
Voice 202.898.2444, Fax 202.898.1185
www.asla.org

American Society of Mechanical Engineers (ASME)
345 East 47th Street
New York, NY 10017-2392
Voice 800.THE.ASME
www.asme.org

American Society of Professional Estimators (ASPE)
11141 Georgia Avenue, Suite 412
Wheaton, MD 20902
Voice 301.929.8848, Fax 301.929.0231
www.cmpi.com/aspe

American Society for Testing and Materials (ASTM)
100 Barr Harbor Drive
West Conshohocken, PA 19428-2959
Voice 610.832.9585, Fax 610.832.9555
www.astm.org

ASFE: Professional Firms Practicing in the Geosciences
8811 Colesville Road, Suite G106
Silver Spring, MD 20910
Voice 301.565.2733, Fax 301.589.2017
www.asfe.org

American Tort Reform Association (ATRA)
1850 M Street NW
Washington, DC 20036
Voice 202.682.1163, Fax 202.682.1022
www.atra.org

Associated General Contractors of America (AGC)
1957 E Street NW
Washington, DC 20006
Voice 202.393.2040, Fax 202.347.4004
www.agc.org

Coalition of American Structural Engineers (CASE)
1015 15th Street NW, Suite 802
Washington, DC 20005
Voice 202.347.7474, Fax 202.898.0068
www.acec.org

Additional Resources

XIII-4

Construction Industry Institute (CII)
3208 Red River Street, Suite 300
Austin TX 78705-2697
Voice 512.471.4319, Fax 512.499.8108
http://construction-institute.org

Construction Management Association of America (CMAA)
7918 Jones Branch Drive, Suite 540
McLean, VA 22102
Voice 703.356.2622, Fax 703.356.6388
www.access.digex.net/~cmaa/index.html

The Construction Specifications Institute (CSI)
601 Madison Street
Alexandria, VA 22314-1791
Voice 800.689.2900, Fax 703.684.0463
www.csinet.org

Consulting Engineers and Land Surveyors of California (CELSOC)
1303 J Street, Suite 370
Sacramento, CA 95814
Voice 916.441.7991, Fax 916.441.6312
www.celsoc.org

CPR Institute for Dispute Resolution
366 Madison Avenue
New York, NY 10017
Voice 212.949.6490, Fax 212.949.8859
www.cpradr.org

Design-Build Institute of America (DBIA)
1010 Massachusetts Avenue NW, Suite 350
Washington, DC 20001
Voice 202.682.0110, Fax 202.682.5877
www.dbia.org

DPIC Companies, Inc.
2959 Monterey-Salinas Highway
Monterey, CA 93940
Voice 800.227.4284, Fax 408.649.3240
www.dpic.com

Additional Resources

XIII-5

Environmental Protection Agency (EPA)
401 M Street SW
Washington, DC 20460
Voice 202.260.2090
www.epa.gov

Export-Import Bank
811 Vermont Avenue NW
Washington DC 20571
Voice 202.565.EXIM or 800.565.EXIM
www.exim.gov

Hazardous Waste Action Coalition (HWAC)
1015 Fifteenth Street NW, Suite 802
Washington, DC 20005
Voice 202.347.7474, Fax 202.898.0076
www.hwac.org

International Chamber of Commerce (ICC)
38 Cours Albert 1er
Paris, France 75008
33.1.49.53.28.28
www.iccwbo.org

International Federation of Consulting Engineers
(Federation Internationale des Ingenieurs-Conseils) FIDIC
P.O. Box 86
1000 Lausanne 12, Switzerland
41.21.653.50.03
www.fidic.org

National Ground Water Association (NGWA)
601 Dempsey Road
Westerville, OH 43081
Voice 800.551.7379, Fax 614.898.7786
www.ngwa.org

National Society of Professional Engineers (NSPE)
1420 King Street
Alexandria, VA 22314-2715
Voice 703.684.2800, Fax 703.836.4875
www.nspe.org

National Trade Data Bank (STAT-USA)
www.stat-usa.gov/stat-usa.html

Additional Resources

Occupational Safety and Health Administration (OSHA)
820 1st Street NE, Suite 440
Washington, DC 20002-1627
Voice 202.523.1452, Fax 202.523.3573
www.osha.gov

Overseas Private Investment Corporation (OPIC)
1100 New York Avenue NW
Washington, DC 20527
Infoline: 202.336.8799, Factsline: 202.336.8700
www.opic.gov

Professional Liability Agents Network (PLAN)
P.O. Box 1632
Monterey, CA 93942
Voice 877.960.PLAN, Fax 408.644.0437
www.plan.org

Public Risk Managers Association (PRMA)
1815 North Fort Myer Drive, Suite 1020
Arlington, VA 22209
Voice 703.528.7701, Fax 703.528.7966
www.primacentral.org

Risk and Insurance Management Society, Inc. (RIMS)
655 Third Avenue
New York, NY 10017
Voice 212.286.9292
www.rims.org

Society of American Value Engineers (SAVE)
60 Revere Drive, Suite 500
Northbrook, IL 60062
Voice 847.480.1730, Fax 847.480.9282
www.value-eng.com

United Nations Commission on International Trade Law (UNCITRAL)
UNCITRAL Secretariat
P.O. Box 500
Vienna International Centre
A-1400 Vienna, Austria
Voice 43 1 26060.4060 or 4061, Fax 43 1 26060.5813
www.un.or.at/uncitral

United States Copyright Office
Information Section, Library of Congress
Washington, DC 20559
Voice 202.707.3000
http://lcweb.loc.gov/copyright

United States Department of Commerce
14th and Constitution Avenue NW
Washington, DC 20230
Voice 202.482.2000
www.doc.gov

United States Department of Energy
Forrestal Building
1000 Independence Avenue SW
Washington, DC 20585
Voice 202.586.5575
www.doe.gov

United States Department of State
2201 C Street NW
Washington, DC 20520
Voice 202.647.4000
www.state.gov

XIII-8

INDEX

A

Accessibility guidelines (ADAAG) VII-3–VII-7

Acts of God IV-31

Adaptive reuse IX-39

Additional insureds III-21, V-34, V-41, V-43, V-44

Additional Service II-3, II-29, II-30, II-31, III-3, III-4, III-10, III-23, III-30, III-31, IV-3, IV-9, IV-27, V-22, VII-10, VII-11, VII-24, VIII-3, IX-6, IX-8, IX-41, IX-62, X-17

ADR by Covenant IX-18, IX-20

Advisory arbitration VI-15, VI-26, VI-32

Aggregate limits V-40

Agreement (*see* Contracts)

All V-3, VII-9, VII-23

Allocation of Risk **V-1–V-77**

Alteration projects IX-39, IX-40

American Arbitration Association VI-29

American Bar Association X-12

American Consulting Engineers Council (ACEC) I-19, VI-18, VI-40, IX-32

American Institute of Architects (AIA) I-15, I-19, I-20, VI-18, IX-32

American Society of Civil Engineers I-19

Americans with Disabilities Act (ADA) I-9, V-3, **VII-3–VII-8**, IX-39
   in remodeling projects VII-6
   on new construction VII-7

Application and certificate for payment (AIA Form G702) V-6

Arbitration VI-15, VI-26, VI-28, VI-30
   advisory VI-32
   binding VI-28
   expedited VI-28
   mandatory VI-28
   non-binding VI-28

specialized VI-28
voluntary VI-28
voluntary nonbinding VI-31, VI-32

Architectural Works Copyright Protection Act VII-13

Army Corps of Engineers VI-18

Asbestos IV-9, VII-17, VII-18, VII-31

As-builts III-23, VIII-23, IX-4

ASFE Standard Form Agreement for Subcontract Laboratory Services IX-52

ASFE: Professional Firms Practicing in the Geosciences I-21, VI-26, IX-18

Assignment I-38, IV-27, IV-28, VII-13, **VIII-3–VIII-5**, VIII-37

Associated General Contractors of America VI-18

Assure V-4

Attorneys' Fees I-15, I-37, IV-20, IV-21, **VI-3–VI-6**, VII-14, VIII-49, IX-36

Authorized Representatives **VIII-7–VIII-9**, VIII-42

Automobile liability insurance V-44

B

Backcharges IV-5

Bargaining power V-31

Basic services II-7, II-8, II-29, II-30, III-9, III-30, IV-3, V-22, VII-10, VII-23, VII-24

Beneficiaries VI-18

Betterment **VI-7–VI-9**

Bid bonds V-68

Bidder qualification X-6

Bidding documents II-34

Billing and Payment I-18, I-24, **IV-3–IV-7**, IV-14, IV-19, IV-20, IV-24, IV-26, IV-27, V-18, V-22, VI-5, VIII-41, IX-33, IX-36, IX-45

Bonds V-68, X-12
bid V-68
payment V-68
performance V-68

Boring locations IX-55, IX-56

Breach of contract I-7, V-4, V-49, V-61, V-65, VII-9, VIII-15, VIII-41, X-11

Breach of express warranty V-49

Breach of warranty V-4, V-49, V-65, V-71, X-11

Bridging X-9

Building codes VII-4, VII-5, VII-28, IX-51

Building Inspection Services III-14, III-15

Building materials VII-31

Buried utilities IX-55

C

CADD/Electronic Files III-23, V-37, V-75, V-76, VIII-47, **IX-3–IX-11**, IX-67
   acceptance period IX-5
   archiving IX-4, IX-5
   copyrights IX-4
   delivery of files IX-3, IX-4, IX-7, IX-8
   facility maintenance IX-4, IX-5
   file translation IX-3
   hardware specifications IX-11
   liability issues IX-3
   ownership IX-4, IX-5, IX-7
   software IX-4
   software specifications IX-3, IX-11
   storage IX-3
   transmission of data IX-4, IX-7
   unauthorized changes to IX-5, IX-7, IX-8

Calendar day VIII-41, VIII-42

Carvalho v. Toll Brothers & Developers III-19

Causes of action V-49

Certificate of merit VI-4, VI-38, VI-39, VI-40, VIII-29

Certificates of insurance IX-45

Certification VIII-24

Certifications, Guarantees and Warranties I-16, I-24, I-38, III-8, III-11, **V-3–V-7**, V-71, VII-5, VIII-24, VIII-37, IX-66, IX-68

Certify V-6, VIII-24, X-6

Certify, definition of V-6, VIII-24

Change in service II-3, II-29, III-31

Change orders V-13, V-14, X-18

Changed Conditions **IV-9–IV-11**, IV-26, IV-27, V-22, VII-9, VII-20, IX-40, IX-41, X-13

Civil law IX-35

Civil rights legislation VII-3, VII-4

Civil rights prosecution VII-4

Claims Arbiter Service **III-3–III-5**

Index

Claims handling I-31

Class action suits IX-13

Client selection I-4, IV-20, VII-27, IX-16, IX-31, X-5, X-12, X-18

Client-generated agreements I-15, I-23

Close-out services IV-33

CM-advisor X-3

CM-agent X-3

CM-at-risk X-3

CM-constructor X-3

Coalition of American Structural Engineers (CASE) I-21, III-14, VI-26

Code Compliance I-9, V-4, V-22, VII-4, VII-5, **VII-9–VII-12**, VII-33, VIII-37

Codes, changes to IV-9

Codes, conflict between VII-9, VII-11

Collection costs IV-3, IV-4, IV-20, VI-5

Commercial general liability insurance (CGL) V-34, V-42

Common law V-69, VIII-38, IX-35, IX-36

Comparative fault IX-45

Compensation I-10, I-11

Competent parties I-8, I-9

Completion date IV-24

Computer-aided design (*see* CADD/Electronic Files)

Computers IX-65
   Year 2000 IX-65

Conciliation VI-34

Condominium Loss Prevention Checklist IX-20

Condominiums I-37, V-32, V-57, **IX-13–IX-21**
   conversion IX-14
   Deal-Maker clauses IX-21
   design IX-15
   risks of IX-13

Confidential Communications **VIII-11–VIII-13**

Confidentiality VII-20, **VIII-15–VIII-17**, VIII-46

Consequential Damages I-4, I-6, **V-9–V-11**, V-50, VII-18, IX-55, IX-56

Consideration I-8

Constructibility reviews IX-61, X-4

Construction Administration **III-1–III-40**, X-6

Construction administration, limited II-5

Construction defects IX-13

Construction documents V-75, VIII-45, IX-60
    ownership of V-75, V-76, VIII-45, VIII-46, IX-4, IX-5
    unauthorized changes to V-75, V-76, IX-5, IX-6, IX-7, IX-8

Construction Industry Institute (CII) VI-18, VI-22

Construction Management III-20, V-35, V-40, **X-3–X-8**

Construction manager IX-59

Construction means and methods X-13

Construction Observation I-5, II-3, II-4, **III-7–III-12**, III-13, III-14, III-20, V-75, VI-17, VIII-53, IX-13, IX-16, IX-20

Construction phase services II-3, VI-18

Consultant-Drafted Agreements I-17

Consulting Engineers and Land Surveyors of California (CELSOC) I-18

Contingency Fund III-30, **V-13–V-15**, V-71, VI-8, IX-20, IX-40, X-17

Contract
    subconsultant IV-14
    subconsulting IV-14

Contract Basics **I-7–I-12**

Contract of adhesion V-31

Contract renegotiation IV-10

Contractor insurance and indemnity requirements V-34

Contractor selection III-31, V-62

Contracts
    acceptance of I-8
    agreement I-8
    basic rules of I-9
    binding I-8
    client-generated I-15, I-23
    consultant-drafted I-16
    continuing services agreements I-18
    emergency services XI-1
    enforceable I-7
    express I-7
    four corners rule I-10
    headings VIII-53
    implied I-7
    international IX-35
    letter agreements I-17

Index

    master IX-44
    multiple prime IX-43
    negotiation I-33
    oral I-7, I-17
    professional association standard agreements I-15, I-19, I-21
    review I-23, I-29, VIII-54
    separate IX-43
    short form I-18
    steps to I-10
    subconsulting IV-14, IX-43, IX-44, IX-45
    titles of clauses VIII-53
    unenforceable I-8
    verbal IX-43
    void, voidable I-8
    written I-3, I-7, IX-43, IX-44

Contractual Reference to the Consultant I-15, **VIII-19–VIII-21**

Controlling law VIII-30

Copyrights V-77, **VII-13–VII-16**, VIII-37, VIII-47, IX-4, IX-45, IX-47

Corporate Protection V-26, **VI-11–VI-13**

Corrected specifications III-23

Correspondence V-70

Cost estimate, definition of VIII-24

Cost estimates VIII-23, VIII-24, X-4 (*see* Opinions (Estimates) of Probable Construction Costs)

Cost estimating X-6

Cost estimator II-12, IX-59

Council of American Structural Engineers (CASE) I-15

Court costs VI-3

Cross liability V-43

Currency inconvertibility coverage IX-34

D

Day, definition of VIII-25, VIII-43

Days IV-25, VIII-41, VIII-42
    calendar IV-25
    definition VIII-43

Deal Breaker provisions I-35, I-38

Deal Maker provisions I-35, I-37

Deal Makers and Deal Breakers **I-35–I-38**

Dealing with Risk **I-5–I-6**

Declare V-4, V-6

Defects III-8, III-9, V-17, IX-29, X-13, XI-3
    obligating client and contractor to report V-17, V-18, XI-3

Defects in Service IV-5, V-14, **V-17–V-19**

Defending the client V-29

Definition of hazardous materials VII-18

Definitions II-13, III-10, III-14, III-25, V-6, VII-18, VIII-20, **VIII-23–VIII-26**, VIII-43

Delay claims III-27, III-31, III-33, III-39

Delays I-24, IV-31, IV-33, V-9, **V-21–V-23**, V-61, VI-17, X-4, X-13

Delivery of electronic files IX-6

Depositions VI-25, VI-28

Design Build Institute of America (DBIA) I-21, X-12

Design Without Construction Administration **II-3–II-6**, II-15, III-8, III-11, V-75, V-77, VI-17, IX-16

Design-Build III-20, V-35, V-40, V-68, X-3, **X-9–X-14**
    dispute resolution X-13
    insurance X-11, X-12, X-13
    licenses X-11, X-12, X-13
    project selection X-12
    risk X-9, X-11
    roles and responsibilities X-9, X-11, X-13
    scope of services X-13
    standard form agreements X-12

Differing site conditions IV-9

Discounts IV-5

Discovery VI-25, VI-28, VIII-30

Disparate bargaining power V-31

Disposal of samples IX-53

Dispute Avoidance and Resolution I-6, I-24, I-37, II-5, **VI-1–VI-40**, VII-29, VIII-51, IX-37, IX-53, X-13

Dispute resolution IV-3, IV-6, V-14, VI-17, IX-35

Dispute resolution boards X-13

Dispute review board (DRB) VI-21, VI-22, VI-23, VI-34

Disputed invoices IV-6

Documentation VIII-42

Documents, ownership of VII-13

Dun and Bradstreet IX-32

Duty of care V-69, V-73, VI-11, IX-14, IX-24

Duty of result IX-29

E

Economic loss doctrine VIII-3

Electronic files VIII-45

Electronic mail VIII-42

Electronic media IX-3

Emergency inspection services III-15

Emergency Services III-15, **IX-23–IX-27**

Emergency services agreement XI-1

Employees IX-43
   loaned IX-43, IX-46
   temporary IX-43, IX-46

Engineers Joint Contract Documents Committee (EJCDC) I-15, I-19, I-21

"English Rule" VI-3

Ensure V-4

Entire Agreement **VIII-27–VIII-28**

Environmental Protection Agency (EPA) V-6

Errors and omissions insurance (*see* Professional liability insurance)

Errors or omissions V-13, V-67

Estey v. Mackenzie Engineering Inc. V-55

Estimates (*see* Opinions (Estimates) of Probable Construction Costs)

Evaluations of the work III-10

Every V-3

Excavation IX-55

Excluded Services I-6, I-11, II-4, **II-7–II-9**, II-29, II-30, IX-32, IX-33 (*see* Scope of Services)

Excluded Services, Permits and Approvals I-11

Execution of documents V-6

Existing conditions IX-40

Existing site conditions X-7

Expense within the limits V-41

Expert witness fees VI-3

Export-Import Bank IX-32, IX-34

Expropriation coverage IX-34

Extended discovery period VII-37

Extension of Protection **V-25–V-26**, IX-46

F

Facility maintenance VIII-46, IX-4, IX-5

Facsimile VIII-42

Fast track X-3, X-15–X-18

Fast track arbitration IV-6

Fast Track Projects I-37, X-4, **X-15–X-18**
 change orders X-16, X-18
 client selection X-18
 contingency fund X-17
 indemnitiy X-17
 risks X-15, X-16

Federation Internationale des Ingenieurs-Conseils (FIDIC) I-21, IX-35

Fee disputes VI-29

Fee proposal IV-3

Fees IV-9

Field manual III-11, III-22

Field personnel III-11, III-29

Final documents VIII-46

Focus on claims IX-14

Foreign Corrupt Practices Act IX-31

Forensic testing IX-51

Frivolous Lawsuits VI-4, **VI-37–VI-40**

Funding, project IV-20

G

General Conditions II-5, III-10, III-21, III-24, III-35, V-14, V-19, V-34, V-62, V-64, V-71, V-76, VI-20, VI-21, VI-23, VI-26, VII-15, VII-37, VIII-33
 use of standard forms V-63

General liability (*see* Commercial General Liability)

General liability insurance V-41

General Terms and Conditions I-10, I-11, **VIII-1–VIII-54**

Geotechnical services IX-55, IX-56, IX-57

Index

Gibbes Incorporated v. Law Engineering V-71

Glossary VIII-25

Good Samaritan law IX-23, IX-27

Governing Law and Jurisdiction **VIII-29–VIII-31**, IX-35, IX-36

Guarantee X-6

Guaranteed maximum price (GMP) X-3

Guarantees V-3, X-6

H

Hardware IX-65, IX-66

Hardware, specifcations for IX-3

Hazardous Materials I-6, I-18, I-24, I-37, II-28, III-14, V-3, V-32, V-57, **VII-17–VII-22**, VII-27, VII-33, VIII-37, IX-36, IX-40, IX-51, IX-53, X-5, X-7, X-13

Hazardous Materials — Suspension of Services VII-19

Hazardous Materials Indemnity VII-19

Hold harmless (*see* Indemnities)

Holdbacks IV-17, IV-19

Homeowners' associations IX-13, IX-18

How to Review Client-Generated Agreements **I-23–I-28**

I

Incorporation by Reference VIII-25, **VIII-33–VIII-35**

Indemnitees V-29

Indemnities I-6, I-24, I-38, II-4, III-4, III-22, V-25, V-26, **V-27–V-36**, V-49, V-50, V-51, VI-13, VII-5, VII-20, VIII-4, VIII-49, VIII-51, IX-5, X-17
    ADA VII-5
    building inspection services III-15
    by the client V-32, V-33
    by the consultant V-28–V-31
    by the contractor V-34, V-35
    by the subconsultant V-35, V-36
    choice of jurisdiction VIII-29
    claims arbiter service III-4
    condominium conversion IX-15
    condominium design IX-17
    confidential communications VIII-12
    design-build X-13
    design without construction administration II-4

    emergency services IX-24
    excluded services II-8
    existing conditions IX-40
    fast track projects X-17
    hazardous materials II-28, VII-19
    including subconsultants IX-46
    information provided by others IX-48
    inspection III-14
    insurance inspections IX-26
    mutual V-30
    package plans II-18
    protection of supplanting consultant IX-48
    prototype designs II-16
    public responsibility VII-29
    rejection of work III-40
    renovation/remodeling IX-40
    replacement of the consultant IX-48
    site adaptation II-17
    specification of materials VII-33
    subconsulting IX-44, IX-45
    temporary employees IX-46
    testing II-28
    testing laboratory services IX-52
    unauthorized changes to plans V-76, VIII-47
    unauthorized reuse of plans VIII-46, VIII-47, IX-5, IX-8
    underground improvements IX-56
    value engineering IX-61, IX-62

Independent testing IX-51

Information Provided by Others III-14, III-24, **V-37–V-38**, IX-11, IX-41, IX-48, IX-55, IX-62

Inspect III-7, III-10, III-13, III-14, VIII-23, VIII-25, X-6

Inspect, definition of VIII-25

Inspection III-7, III-10, **III-13–III-17**, VIII-25, IX-26
    building III-14
    emergency III-15
    for insurance companies IX-26
    municipal III-15

Inspector III-13, III-14

Instruments of service VIII-45, VIII-46, IX-45

Insurance I-24, I-38, II-12, V-34, **V-39–V-47**, VII-37, IX-31, IX-33, IX-45, X-5–X-7, X-12–X-14
    automobile liabilty V-43
    certificates V-44
    construction management X-5

Index

credit risk IX-35
currency inconvertibility IX-34
design-build X-12
endorsements V-43
expropriation IX-34
international projects V-44, IX-31, IX-33
non-owned automobile liability V-44
political violence IX-34
workers compensation V-43

Insurance broker I-29

Insurance carrier I-30, I-31

Insure V-4

Integration VIII-27

Interest IV-3, IV-4, IV-15, IV-20, VIII-49

International Chamber of Commerce (ICC) VI-34, VI-35

International commercial arbitration VI-34

International disputes VI-29, VI-34

International Projects IV-21, V-44, VI-29, VIII-29, **IX-29–IX-38**

International projects insurance V-44

Interpretation V-28, **V-49–V-51**, VII-20, VIII-29, VIII-30

ISO 9000 II-20

J

Jobsite dispute resolution VI-15, VI-22, VI-23

Jobsite Safety I-24, I-37, I-38, III-8, III-9, III-10, III-13, **III-19–III-22**, III-34, III-39, V-34, V-35, VI-18, VII-27, VIII-19, VIII-29, IX-36, X-3, X-4, X-5, X-6, X-11, X-13

Joint venture IX-32, X-12

Judicial relief I-7

Jurisdiction, choice of (*see* Governing Law and Jurisdiction)

Jurisdiction, international IX-33, IX-35

L

Laws, changes to IV-9

Laws, compliance with VII-9

Lawsuits, frivolous VI-37

Lead-based paint VII-31

Legal counsel I-29

Legal form I-8

Legal purpose I-8, I-9

Lenders' Requirements V-5, VII-13, VIII-4, **VIII-37–VIII-39**, X-13

Letter agreements I-17

Letter of credit IX-33

Liability V-54, VI-11, VIII-33, IX-30
    personal V-54, VI-11

Libel VIII-11, VIII-12

Lien rights IV-3, IV-7, IX-35

Liens VIII-29

Limitation of Liability I-6, I-15, I-18, I-37, II-5, V-10, V-25, V-26, V-33, V-49, V-51, **V-53–V-59**, VI-13, VII-21, VIII-29, VIII-49, VIII-51, IX-35, IX-46, IX-53, IX-62, X-13
    Contractor and Subcontractor Claims V-58

Limited liability companies X-12

Limited liability partnerships X-12

Limited services agreements III-8

Liquidated Damages I-11, I-16, I-38, IV-33, **V-61–V-64**, X-13
    in general conditions V-63

Litigation IV-3, IV-9, V-54, VI-4, VI-8, VI-15, VI-22, VI-25, VI-26, VI-28, VII-31, VIII-29, IX-4, IX-65, X-5
    international IX-34

M

Maintenance manual IX-18, IX-20

Mandatory binding arbitration VI-28, VI-29

Markborough v. Superior Court V-55

Materials II-33
    specifying II-33, VII-31
    substitution of II-33

Materials, specifying VII-31

Mediation V-14, VI-15, VI-20, VI-25, VI-27, VI-29, VI-32, VI-34, IX-18

Mediation/arbitration VI-15, VI-31

Mediation-then-arbitration VI-31

Minitrials VI-26, VI-31, VI-34

Mobilization fee IX-33

Motion for summary judgment VI-39

Motions VIII-30

Multiple Prime Contracts I-37, IX-43, **X-19–X-22**

Multiple-prime projects X-3

Municipal inspection services III-15, III-16

N

National Society of Professional Engineers I-19

National Trade Data Bank (NTDB or STAT-USA) IX-32

Negligence IV-3, IV-17, V-4, V-29, V-30, V-35, V-49, V-50, V-65, V-73, VI-3, VI-4, VI-8, VI-11, VII-9, VIII-45, IX-45, X-11

Negligence per se VII-9

Negotiating a Contract **I-33–I-34**

Negotiation I-33

No warranty II-13, V-66, V-71, VIII-24, VIII-47, IX-7, IX-8

Nonmeritorious lawsuits VI-4, VI-37

Non-negligent Services V-4, **V-65–V-66**, V-70

Non-owned automobile liability V-44

Nonpayment of fees IV-3, IV-24, IV-25, IV-27, IV-29

No-responsibility-for-delays IV-33

Notice of delay IV-33

Notices IV-25, VIII-9, **VIII-41–VIII-43**

O

Observation III-14

Occupational Safety and Health Administration (OSHA) III-19, X-4

Office package policy V-43

Opinion of probable cost VIII-23

Opinions (Estimates) of Probable Construction Costs I-24, **II-11–II-14**, VIII-24

"or equal" II-34

Oral Agreements I-17

OSHA Review Commission X-4

Overseas Private Investment Corporation (OPIC) IX-34

Owner's consultant X-9

Ownership of Instruments of Service I-24, I-37, II-5, II-15, IV-7, IV-27, V-76, V-77, VII-13–VII-15, VIII-4, VIII-37, **VIII-45–VIII-48**, IX-5, IX-45, IX-53

P

Package plans II-15, II-16, II-18

Paralyzed Veterans of America v. Ellerbe Beckett Architects and Engineers, PC VII-4

Parties to the contract VIII-19

Partnering V-17, V-64, VI-15, VI-17, VI-18, VI-20, VI-22, VI-34, IX-16, IX-37, X-13, X-18

Partnership VI-12

Patent ambiguity I-9

Payment bonds V-68

Payment due IV-4

Payment to consultant IV-3, IV-19, IV-24, IV-25, V-19, IX-33, IX-45

Payment to subconsultant IV-13

Pay-When-Paid **IV-13–IV-15**, IX-45

PCB IV-9, VII-18

Peer review IX-16, IX-20, IX-61

Peer review programs II-20

Performance Bonds I-16, IV-17, V-39, **V-67–V-68**

Periodic III-11

Permit approval IV-7

Permits and Approvals I-11, II-27, II-28, **VII-23–VII-25**

Plain meaning I-9

Plans, ownership of VII-13

Political violence coverage IX-34

Preamble VI-19, VIII-20, VIII-23

Pre-construction Services **II-1–II-36**

Pre-design activities IV-32

Pre-engineered buildings II-15, II-16, II-17

Preliminary site assessments (PSAs) V-3, IX-51

Prime consultant-subconsultant agreement IV-14

Private litigation VI-31, VI-32

Privity of contract V-73

Procedural law VIII-30

Product liabiliy VIII-45

Professional Association Standard Agreements I-15, **I-19–I-21**
   modifying I-20

Professional Liability Agents Network (PLAN) I-30

Index

Professional Liability in the Construction Process: A Guide for Risk Managers (1997) I-23

Professional liability insurance I-5, I-16, I-30, I-31, IV-31, V-4, V-5, V-29, V-30, V-36, V-40, V-41, V-54, V-55, V-61, V-65, V-69, VI-11, VI-12, VIII-33, VIII-37, VIII-38, IX-14, IX-45, X-5
- aggregate limits V-40
- claims handling I-31
- claims made policy V-40
- defense and indemnity IX-33
- expense within limits V-40
- indemnity only IX-33
- international projects IX-33
- retroactive date V-40

Professional liability insurance agent V-39

Professional liability insurance specialist VII-37

Professional Services Agreements **I-1–I-38**

Project Delivery **X-1–X-22**

Project insurance V-41, V-42, V-55, IX-16, IX-20

Project partnering (*see* Partnering)

Project policy VII-37, X-13

Project proposals V-70

Project representatives III-9, III-10, III-22, VIII-7, X-6

Project schedule IV-32

Project selection X-5, X-12

Promotional literature V-70

Property insurance V-43

Proprietary information VIII-16

Proprietorship VI-12

Prototype Designs I-37, **II-15–II-18**, V-75, V-77, VII-15, VIII-46

Public health and safety IX-24, IX-62

Public procurement laws X-11

Public records IX-55

Public Responsibility II-8, VII-20, **VII-27–VII-29**, VII-32, VIII-15, IX-62

Punitive damages VIII-12

Purchase orders I-16

Q

Qualifications-Based Selection **I-13**

Quality control manual II-19, II-20

Quality Control Standards **II-19–II-21**

R

Record Documents **III-23–III-25**, V-38, VIII-25, VIII-53, IX-4
 stamp III-24

Record documents, definition of VIII-25

Referee system VI-34

Regulation, compliance with VII-9

Rejection of work III-40

Remodeling IX-39

Renovation project IV-9

Renovation/Remodeling I-37, V-32, V-37, VII-11, VII-15, VII-18, **IX-39–IX-42**

Rent-a-judge VI-32

Repatriation of funds IX-32

Replacement of the Consultant IX-48

Request for Proposal (RFP) I-10

Requests for clarification or interpretation III-29, III-30

Requests for Information II-15, II-34, **III-27–III-32**, V-22

Resolving international disputes VI-29

Resources for Contract Review **I-29–I-31**

Restoration IX-39

Retainage I-16, **IV-17–IV-18**, IV-19

Retainers IV-3, IV-4, IV-17, **IV-19–IV-21**, IV-24, IV-25, IV-26, IX-33

Retaining Subconsultants **II-23–II-25**

Retroactive date V-40

Right of Entry **II-27–II-28**

Risk I-4, V-32

Risk allocation I-4, I-5, IV-9, V-27, V-54, V-56, VI-13

Rules of evidence VI-28, VIII-30

Index

S

Satisfaction with services IV-6

Schedule I-10, I-11, IV-9, IV-24, IV-31, V-22, V-62, VII-20

Schedule for rendering services IV-32

Schedule, Payment and Termination **IV-1–IV-33**

Scope of Services I-5, I-10, I-11, II-7, II-8, II-9, **II-29–II-31**, III-11, III-14, III-22, IV-27, VII-9, VII-10, IX-32, IX-40, X-4, X-6

Seal, electronic IX-7

Secretary of Labor III-19

Secretary of Labor v. Simpson Gumpertz III-19

Separate contracts X-19

Services, excluded (*see* Excluded Services)

Set-offs IV-5

Severability VIII-49, VIII-50

Severability and Survival I-9, V-33, VII-20, **VIII-49–VIII-51**

Severability of interest V-43

Shop Drawing Review II-4, **III-33–III-37**, V-23

Shop drawing stamp III-35, III-37

Shop drawings IX-4, IX-10

Sick building syndrome VII-17

Site adaptation II-15–II-17

Slander VIII-11, VIII-12

Society of American Value Engineers IX-62

Software, computer IX-65, IX-66
    defects in IX-4, IX-11

Software, specifications for IX-3

Soils drilling IX-55

Special inspectors III-16

Specific Services **IX-1–IX-68**

Specification of Materials VII-20, **VII-31–VII-34**, IX-67

Specifying materials II-33, II-34

Standard of Care I-15, II-19, III-33, IV-17, V-4, V-13, V-30, V-53, V-62, V-65, V-66, **V-69–V-72**, VI-8, VI-11, VI-39, VII-9, VII-31, VII-32, VIII-38, VIII-45, IX-11, IX-29, IX-36, X-11

Standard of practice V-69

Standing arbitrator VI-23

Standing mediator VI-23

Standing neutral VI-22

State V-4, V-6

Statutes of limitation V-4, V-49, V-65, V-71, VII-35, IX-35

Statutes of repose VII-35

Statutes of Repose and Limitation I-4, I-6, VI-11, VI-39, **VII-35–VII-38**, VIII-29, IX-36

Statutes, Codes and Regulations **VII-1–VII-38**

Step negotiations VI-22, VI-23

Stepped dispute resolution VI-32

Stop Work Authority I-38, III-21, **III-39–III-40**

Strategic alliances IX-32

Strict liability V-49, VIII-45, IX-4, IX-29, X-11

Subconsultants II-12, IV-13, V-25, **IX-43–IX-46**
    billing and payment IX-45
    construction observation IX-45
    fees IV-14
    negligence IX-43
    ownership of documents IX-45
    payment terms IV-13, IV-14
    right to retain II-23, II-24, II-25
    selection IX-44
    vicarious liability IX-43

Submittals III-33, III-34, III-35

Substantial completion VII-36

Substantive law VIII-30

Substitution approval request form II-35, II-36

Substitutions **II-33–II-36**, V-22

Subsurface penetration IX-56, IX-57

Summary jury trial VI-31, VI-32

Supervise III-7, III-10, X-6

Supervision VIII-53

Supplanting Another Consultant II-5, V-75, V-77, VII-14, **IX-47–IX-49**

Surety company V-67

Survival VIII-49, VIII-50

Suspension IV-3, IX-48

Suspension costs IV-23–IV-25

Suspension of Services I-24, IV-5, IV-20, IV-21, **IV-23–IV-26**, IV-29, VII-18, VIII-41, IX-36

Index

T

Termination I-24, I-37, II-31, IV-3, IV-10, IV-21, IV-23, IV-24, IV-26, **IV-27–IV-30**, V-77, VII-19, VII-28, VII-32, VIII-41, IX-36, IX-48

Termination costs IV-28, IV-29

Termination of services IV-5

Testing Laboratories **IX-51–IX-53**
  disposal of samples IX-53
  property damage IX-53
  selection IX-52
  standard agreement IX-52

Third-Party Beneficiaries I-5, **V-73–V-74**

Third-party claims V-32, V-54, V-73, VII-36

Third-party suits VI-13

Time bar to legal action VII-35, VII-36

"Time is of the essence" IV-31

Timeliness of Performance I-11, IV-24, **IV-31–IV-33**, V-61, V-62

Title block, electronic IX-7

Titles **VIII-53–VIII-54**

Total agreement VIII-27

Total quality management (TQM) II-20

Trier of fact I-7

Types of Agreements You'll Encounter **I-15–I-18**

U

Unauthorized Changes to Plans II-4, II-5, II-15, II-17, **V-75–V-77**, VII-15, VIII-45, IX-5, X-18

Underground improvements V-37, **IX-55–IX-58**, X-13

Uniform building code III-15

United Nations Commission on International Trade Law VI-35

United States Copyright Office VII-14, VII-15

United States Department of Commerce IX-32

United States Department of Justice VII-3, VII-5

United States Department of State IX-32

Unjust enrichment VI-7, VI-8

V

Value Engineering II-33, III-28, III-30, V-22, **IX-59–IX-63**
   informal IX-59
   scheduled IX-59
   unscheduled IX-59

Vicarious liability IX-43

Visual Artists Rights Act of 1990 VII-15

Voluntary nonbinding arbitration VI-31, VI-32

W

Waiver II-4, II-16, II-17, II-18, III-4, V-32, V-50, V-51, VII-5, VII-20, IX-17, IX-24
   ADA VII-5
   by the client V-33
   CADD/Electronic Files IX-8
   claims arbiter service III-4
   condominium design IX-17
   hazardous materials VII-20
   insurance inspections IX-26
   package plans II-18
   pre-engineered buildings II-17, IX-17
   prototype designs II-16
   specification of materials VII-33
   unauthorized changes to plans V-76
   unauthorized reuse of electronic files IX-6
   underground improvements IX-57
   value engineering IX-61, IX-62

Waiver of claims for hazardous materials VII-20

Waiver of subrogation V-43

Walk-through inspection III-14

Warranties V-3

Why Have A Written Agreement? **I-3–I-4**

Workers compensation III-20, V-34, V-43, IX-33

Workscope IV-9 (*see* Scope of Services)

World Bank IX-32, IX-33

Y

Year 2000 (Y2K) IX-4, IX-9, **IX-65–IX-68**